A Spiritual Bloomsbury

Dear Martin —

all good wishes a years to

can marking 46 years of

our friendship

as ever

Tony

Other Books by Antony Copley

The Political Career of C. Rajagopalachari 1937–1954: A Moralist in Politics

C. Rajagopalachari: Gandhi's Southern Commander

Gandhi: Against the Tide

Sexual Moralities in France: 1780–1980

Religions in Conflict

Indian Diary 1995–1996

Editions

Indians in Britain: Past and Present (together with Rozina Visram)

Gandhi and the Contemporary World (together with George Paxton)

Gurus and Their Followers

Hinduism in Public and Private

A Spiritual Bloomsbury

Hinduism and Homosexuality in the
Lives and Writings of Edward Carpenter,
E. M. Forster, and Christopher Isherwood

Antony Copley

LEXINGTON BOOKS

A division of
ROWMAN & LITTLEFIELD PUBLISHERS, INC.
Lanham • Boulder • New York • Toronto • Oxford

LEXINGTON BOOKS

A division of Rowman & Littlefield Publishers, Inc.
A wholly owned subsidary of The Rowman & Littlefield Publishing Group, Inc.
4501 Forbes Boulevard, Suite 200
Lanham, MD 20706

PO Box 317
Oxford
OX2 9RU, UK

British Library Cataloguing in Publication Information Available

Library of Congress Cataloging-in-Publication Data

Copley, A. R. H. (Antony R. H.), 1937–
   A spiritual Bloomsbury : Hinduism and homosexuality in the lives and writings of
Edward Carpenter, E. M. Forster, and Christopher Isherwood / Antony Copley.
     p. cm.
   Includes bibliographical references and index.
   ISBN-13: 978-0-7391-1464-3 (cloth : alk. paper)
   ISBN-10: 0-7391-1464-6 (cloth : alk. paper)
   ISBN-13: 978-0-7391-1465-0 (pbk. : alk. paper)
   ISBN-10: 0-7391-1465-4 (pbk. : alk. paper)
   1. Carpenter, Edward, 1844–1929—Religion. 2. Forster, E. M. (Edward Morgan),
1879–1970—Religion. 3. Isherwood, Christopher, 1904–1986—Religion. 4. Gay
authors—England—Religious life. 5. Homosexuality—Religious aspects—Hinduism.
6. Hinduism—Influence. I. Title.
PR4451.Z5C67 2006
823'.91209382945—dc22   2006009981

Printed in the United States of America

⊗™ The paper used in this publication meets the minimum requirements of
American National Standard for Information Sciences—Permanence of Paper for
Printed Library Materials, ANSI/NISO Z39.48-1992.

In memory of
Brian Kember 1930–2004
Best of Mates
And in gratitude for the generosity of my late uncles
Robert Copley and Edgar Pohlman

Contents

~

Preface

This study in the Indo-British encounter began as a chapter in a projected book provisionally entitled *Indian Spirituality: Insiders and Outsiders*. Carpenter, Forster, and Isherwood all seemed appropriate choices as outsiders who had tried to make sense of Hindu mysticism. But on further reflection I realized that my interest in all three was strong enough to convert the chapter into a book. I had already undertaken some research on Carpenter back in the 1970s when he featured prominently in a course I helped to teach at the University of Kent titled *Literature, Sex and Morality*. Forster was equally prominent in our teaching, his leitmotif "only connect" the mantra of our interdisciplinary part I. We all had to read *Howard's End* and I was also closely involved in a course titled *Colonialism and the Emergent Nations* with Forster's *A Passage to India*, a key text in reading imperial relationships. As a starry-eyed poet myself in the 1950s I'd become aware of Isherwood as one of the 1930s generation of writers, although my hero then was Stephen Spender. It was only during a walking holiday in Austria in the early 1980s that I began to rethink Isherwood on reading and being deeply moved by his *My Guru and His Disciple*. Here is the real origin of this book. At that point in time I had planned a comparative study of attitudes toward sexuality in Britain and France but ended up by just looking at France in my *Sexual Moralities in France 1780–1980* (Routledge: 1989). To that extent this present text is a sister volume. But there has had to be a paradigm shift in how I thought about all three writers, seeing Carpenter as more the mystic than the sexologist, Forster more the explorer of Indian religions than

Anglo-Indian relationships, Isherwood the would-be mystic rather than the documentarist of interwar Europe.

I am indebted to a generous grant from the British Academy which covered the costs of a research trip to India in 1999 and subsequent visits to the Forster archives in King's College, Cambridge, and the Carpenter papers in the Sheffield Archives. I owe a great debt of gratitude to all those who facilitated this research. Within India I thank the library staff of the Ramakrishna Mission Institute of Culture, Kolkata and of the Theosophical Society, Adyar. I have always put great faith in conversations and this was a journey endlessly graced by fascinating meetings, and elsewhere I list all those I interviewed. My most dramatic was with Swami Chidananda and I am indebted to Swami Ranganathananda for a letter of introduction. I very much enjoyed my conversations with Professor Das Gupta in Kolkata and Major Pawer (Bhoj Maharaj) in Dewas. I thank the travel agents Soul of India and Nazir Bhatt and his team from Magic India, Tours and Travel, New Delhi, for their impeccable arrangements. I was very much in the hands of my excellent guides and I especially thank Swastik Kotnala for so knowledgeably helping me to explore Rishikesh, Mathuresh Chandra Bharadvaj for opening up Krishna country around Mathura, and Wahib Qureshi for brilliantly navigating me through Forster country in Madya Pradesh. One is equally dependent on one's drivers and I thank, amongst others, Vikram Chaudhuri, Rakat, Israr Khan—the last to undertake huge journeys within Madya Pradesh. At home I am especially indebted to King's College for permission to consult and cite the Forster papers and thank the archivist, Jacqueline Cox, for her help. I also thank the Society of Authors in their role as agent for the Provost and Scholars of King's College in granting this permission. I am also grateful to the Humanities Research Center, The University of Texas at Austin, for sending me copies of Edward Carpenter's letters to Havelock Ellis. I thank Margaret Turner and her staff for making my reading of the Carpenter collection in the Sheffield Archives so rewarding an experience. This was a research project where I made especial use of the interlibrary loan system and I particularly thank Angela Faunch in the Library of the University of Kent for all her assistance. The secretariat of the History Office in Rutherford College were as ever unfailingly helpful. This manuscript would never have seen the light of day but for the brilliant secretarial assistance of Trish Hatton. I also thank Pravrajika Anandaprana for generously sending me her personal memoir of Swami Prabhavananda. Dr. Tony Brown kindly let me consult and use his unpublished thesis on Carpenter's influence on Forster.

A number of chapters were first aired at conferences, Chapter 6 at the European Conference of Modern South Asian Studies, Edinburgh, 2000 and

Chapters 7 and 5 at the Sanskrit Tradition in the Modern World Seminar (STIMW), University of Newcastle, 2001 and 2002. I am grateful for the commentary of David Hart and William Radice on Isherwood and Forster, respectively. I thank the Theosophical Society for an invitation to lecture on Isherwood. An invitation from the Department of Theology and Religious Studies, University of Lampeter, allowed me to try out my conclusion. My former colleague, Leon Schlamm, by my sitting in on his course *Gurus and Their Disciples*, introduced me at a late stage to many new ideas. Readers are alerted that chapter 6 is top-heavy and they can always skip the Appendix.

As this was a project largely written in retirement it was necessarily a more lonely occupation than in the past. I have to say I found an audience for the content of this book more readily in India than here though some of my friends, Rashid Maxwell in particular, were on its wavelength. But both in India and here the hospitality of friends was as strong as ever. It is a great sadness to me that Professor Ranjit Roy, who always looked after me so well in Kolkata, is no longer here to see the appearance of this book. He had much to offer and his premature death is a great loss. I already miss his home visits graced by his excellent cooking. My heart goes out to his wife, Papiya, and their young son, Krishna. I also thank Muzaffur Alam, Kaku Bose, Binoy and Tripti Chaudhuri, Sujon Chandra, Professor S. Gopalakrishnan, Godwin Joseph, Professor Akit Neogy, K. N. Panikkar, Gowher Rizvi, Uma and Tapan Roy, Harbans Singh, Dr G. J. Sudhakar, George and Meera Verghese, Susan Walters, and many others for their friendship and generous hospitality. Some of my closest friends in India were out of station in 1999. At home for the same I have to thank Elizabeth Deighton, Christine and Malcolm Andrews, Bill and Sheila Bell, John and Jean Buss, Richard and Celia Crampton, William and Clare Fortescue, Peter Gibson, Martin and Esther Gilbert, David and Hilary Harkness, Juanita Homan, Rod and Carol Kedward, Hugh and Vicki Maddox, Roy and Rose Oxlade, Lewis and Mildred Ryder, Robert and Lorraine Tollemache, Martin and Lyn Scofield, Edward Towne, Michael Williams, and others. I had to endure ill health whilst writing the book and I am very grateful to my stepmother, Elizabeth Copley, for her care during the recovery period, as I am to William and Clare Fortescue. Elizabeth Taylor proved a very sympathetic listener at this juncture and indeed was the first to learn of much of the content of the book. My friend, Brian Kember, and his wife, Ivy, have been as supportive as ever. Sadly he is not well at this time.

Antony Copley, Adisham, Canterbury. June 2003.

~

Prologue

Given two such powerful drives as the sexual and the religious, often in conflict, it is deeply intriguing to see just how any one individual manages their rivalry and seeks their reconciliation. This is the story of three individuals from successive generations, Edward Carpenter (1844–1929), E. M. Forster (1879–1970), and Christopher Isherwood (1904–1986), all of whom shared a similar sexuality and sought in Hindu spirituality one way of achieving personal autonomy and fulfillment. They form a natural trinity. And, indeed, so strong was the influence of each one on the following that there is the feel of an apostolic succession. In Carpenter's openness as a homosexual Forster found an example that could help him to come to terms with his own sexuality. In so far as his skeptical temperament allowed he adopted Carpenter as his mentor. Isherwood greatly admired Forster as a novelist and to a considerable degree adopted him as his literary model. At a more personal level Isherwood saw in Forster an example of one who had come through the Test, Forster with his unflappable nature, a reflection of Isherwood's obsessive concern at working out how to live one's life, without neurosis and with calm acceptance. It is tempting to write their story backwards, seeing the origins of Isherwood's and Forster's attitudes in Carpenter's, Carpenter the only one of the three with any pretensions to guru status.

Friendship, the leitmotif of Bloomsbury, was central to all three. Not that they were members of that self-conscious brotherhood. Only Forster was on its fringes. But all three shared its moral code of the centrality of personal relationships. To make sense of their values one has to explore the varying kinds of personal friendships they enjoyed. There were the most highly personalized, the sexual. The text will only select those which inform on the time of spiritual quest or *sadhana*, Carpenter's love for George Hukin and George Merrill, Forster's would-be sexual with Masood and sexually fulfilled with Mohammed el Adl, and Isherwood's, with his German boyfriend, Heinz, and a number of American lovers until he settled down into a householder relationship with Don Bachardy. For all three there were powerfully influential platonic friendships which led them toward Indian spirituality, Carpenter with the Sri Lankan, Arunachalam Ponnanbalam, Forster with Masood and the Maharajahs of Chhatarpur and Dewas, and Isherwood with Gerald Heard and Swami Prabhavananda.

Were these relationships exploitative? Could one accuse all three of "slumming," seeking but sexual gratification in their relationship with working-class men, and, in their journeys abroad, of sexual tourism? Libidinal desire often, if not always, needs difference for its stimulus. Heterosexuality has the difference of gender. Often differences of class, race or age are the stimulus of sexual desire for homosexuals. All three writers were attracted to the working class and this was to be a lasting passion for both Carpenter and Forster though Isherwood was to turn away from working class boys in Berlin to a more classless all American youth. Forster was the most strongly drawn to men of color, Carpenter, if to a lesser degree and one suspects through less opportunity, anticipated him, but Isherwood seems not to have shared this preference, though in his travels to India in the 1960s did belatedly feel attracted to Bengali young men. Age is the most problematic of these differences, and though homosexuals adamantly and rightly differentiate between homosexuality and pedophilia, it does appear from a recent biography[1] that Isherwood in his adolescence was still in the grip of public schoolboy crushes and was attracted quite alarmingly to young boys. But would we want to accuse these three writers of exploitation of class and race? Carpenter was driven by a passionate form of humanist socialism and he reached out to the working class in a spirit of comradeship, an ideal close to that most neglected of the three revolutionary ideals, fraternity. It can be no accident that a Marxism that ridiculed class fraternization was in twentieth-century communism often to despite homosexuality. Forster in a more muted way was also a social progressive and was clearly appalled by the racism inherent in imperialism. Isherwood shared the socialist beliefs of the 1930s generation although does not seem to have been drawn into the anti-colonial movement in the same way as Carpenter and Forster. There is everything here to suggest their relationships with the working class and men of color was shaped by a profound and generous humanity.

But there is another way of interpreting these relationships, a psychological one. If in terms of class and race the writers were in a superior economic and, given the imperial context, dominant racial position, in terms of the psychological balance it often went the other way. The text will try where there is evidence to explore the psychological input of their working class lovers to these relationships and in some cases this could be intense. But the evidence certainly points to a greater investment of anguish by all three and here they were the ones making the running and undergoing the mental torture of the uncertainty of love.

Another leitmotif of the text, and one crucial to the way tradition is passed on in Indian spirituality, is the *guru-sisya*, teacher–disciple relationship. It played an especially prominent role in the spiritual development of both Carpenter and Isherwood. Carpenter's *sadhana* or spiritual quest was to be profoundly shaped by two gurus, Walt Whitman and Ilakkanam the Grammarian. Subsequently he assumed guru status. Isherwood had a strong predisposition toward gurus. His life makes no sense without addressing this aspect of his makeup. He was, indeed, in danger of collecting too many. In the end, though, he settled for the Ramakrishna monk, Swami Prabhavananda, typically, though, with his Forsterian cult of the primacy of personal relationships, seeing him as both friend and guru. If any one book can be said to have inspired this project it is My *Guru and His Disciple*. I tried to gain more critical insight into this relationship through conversations with religious men mainly in Rishikesh during my research trip to India in 1999.

All three were homosexual and this probably constitutes their strongest connection. It was absolutely at the heart of who they saw themselves to be. In the aftermath of the Labouchere amendment, a carelessly added measure to a piece of legislation designed to expose the hypocrisy of the white slave traffic of prostitution at the time, all three were to experience a sense of social isolation and outlawry. From 1885 until its abolition in 1967 all homosexuals in the U.K. were to live in fear of legal prosecution or blackmail.[2] Not that it is easy to disentangle internalized feelings of self-oppression or guilt from actual fears of persecution. But here was a quite appalling psychological burden each had to bear. It drove them into various forms of rebellion or exile. Carpenter grew up before the full weight of this oppressive legislation became operative, although capital punishment for sodomy was only abolished in 1861 and homosexuality was essentially an underground form of behavior, and if his was still to be a prolonged struggle with his sexuality this may account for his being the best adjusted, together with his most open and honest acceptance. Nevertheless, this southerner, cleric, academic was still to rebel against all three and to be driven into a form of internal exile and into the arms of the northern working class. It led Isherwood to exile abroad, to Berlin by 1928, then elsewhere in Europe, until departure for America in 1939. Not that flight in itself dealt with the sense of guilt and anger. The struggle persisted. If Forster dealt with the problematic in a more moderate fashion, his privileging of the private over the public, his cult of personal relationships, together with limited foreign travel, was yet another version of rebellion and internal exile.

Another strategy open to all three was flight into another religion and culture. Here was the psychological preconditioning for their attraction to Hinduism. All three were to be characters in search of the divine. For Carpenter it was an interest from an early age, certainly by his time at Cambridge and to prove long-lasting. Probably no other English person at the time, with the possible exception of Annie Besant, was to be so prolongedly engaged with Hindu spirituality. Forster needed the catalyst of Masood's friendship and it remains uncertain just how long term the impact proved to be and yet quite probably, despite himself, he was to reach out, possibly at the deepest level of all three, to Indian mysticism. For Isherwood it seemed the only way out from a sense of spiritual bankruptcy and it was to be the making of the second stage of his life.

Their quest was not to be mystical in a western and Christian sense. Whereas a western approach would only see the mystical experience as a consequence of the infusion of God's grace,[3] a Hindu would lay a far greater emphasis on the role of human effort. After all, the divine is not in some impossible elsewhere but lies within. Both Carpenter and Isherwood were to be strongly drawn to this Vedantist approach. It presupposed the possibility of absorption of the ego with the divine. Forster was too much the humanist ever wholly to surrender to this concept of transcendence, too much the dualist, although he did try to understand its appeal. His access into Hindu mysticism was to be by another route, the Krishna cult. Here, however intense the search for the divine, there was no absorption, there was always to be a gap between the seeker and the divine, crucially opening up the prospect of a personal relationship and the possibility of love. This is closer to western mysticism.

Interconnected with this battle over sexuality and the pursuit of the divine lies a conflict, maybe of special intensity for homosexuals, over the maternal and the feminine. Ironically, by turning toward Hinduism they exacerbated the problem for Hinduism is a belief system exceptional in its reverence for the feminine. All three were closely involved with their mothers. In Carpenter's case, whilst having to come to terms with the emotional coldness of his mother, he was to be at ease with the maternal. But both Forster and Isherwood were to be locked into life-long struggles with their mothers—Forster the more compliant, Isherwood the more rebellious. The question has to be posed, just how great a barrier toward the mystical experience did this conflict with the mother constitute? Put another way, to what degree is access to the mystical a question of coming to terms with the feminine? There is Freud's highly suggestive concept of *anaclisis*: the child's initial self-preservative dependence on the mother's breast, only latterly sexualized.[4] Does indeed the mystical experience lie on the other side of the maternal incest taboo?

Another problematic for the literary biographer is the extent to which the fiction of the writer can be drawn on for their biography. For the postmodernist the fiction is a law unto itself. But traditionally the fiction could and often was all too literally plundered for this purpose. It is not a problem that particularly besets this text. Carpenter wrote but little fiction. In Forster's case, though *A Passage to India* is a seminal text for reading his response to Hinduism, it is paralleled by an autobiographical one, *The Hill of Devi*, and there is a wealth of additional autobiographical material. The novel does not have to bear the burden of interpretation although it is, of course, highly suggestive. And little use is made of Isherwood's fiction. The commentary of his engagement with Hindu mysticism rests largely on his diaries and letters. His postwar novels are rightly seen as Vedantist and could be used to trace his spiritual quest, especially *A Single Man* and *A Meeting by the River*. It is interesting, for example, to learn that the latter is written around the ceremony of his friend John Yale taking *sannyas* at Belur. However, the account given here relies only marginally on the fiction.

The text will only be loosely rather than rigorously comparativist in its interpretation, for all three lead wholly fascinating lives in their own right. But it will be broadly analogous. In all three cases we have to explore their family and social backgrounds, their education, the differing ways in which all three dealt with their loss of Christian belief. The problematic of relating their sexuality to their pursuit of mysticism lies at the heart of the text. Carpenter went to great lengths to make the connection. Forster is far more gnomic and we have to treat his writings as gnostic texts in which we search for clues. With Isherwood the sense of conflict is most in evidence and in his initial Vedantist quest in the 1940s, the hub of this inquiry, he comes across as a divided self. Only later could he bring the sexual and the spiritual together and achieve personal happiness.

Notes

1. Peter Parker's "official" biography, *Isherwood* (Basingstoke and Oxford: Picador, 2004), came out too late for me to attempt to include some of his findings in my own

text. In fact we approach the subject in different ways. Quite apart from mine being a selective thematic study on the connection between Isherwood's sexuality and Hindu mysticism compared to a full-scale biography, Parker prioritizes personal relationships whereas I concentrate on Isherwood's ideas on pacifism and Vedantism.

2. The whole subject of homosexual law reform in Britain has spawned a considerable literature. See Jeffrey Weeks, *Sex, Politics and Society: The Regulation of Sexuality since 1800* (London: Longmans, 1981); Jeffrey Weeks, *Coming Out: Homosexual Politics in Britain from the Nineteenth Century to the Present* (London: Quartet Books, 1977); Stephen Jeffrey-Poulter, *Peers, Queers and Commons: The Struggle for Gay Law Reform from 1950 to the Present* (London: Routledge, 1991).

3. David Knowles's, *What is Mysticism?: Prayer and Practice* (London: Sheed and Ward, 1966) is a good summary of this position.

4. For a brief definition of the instinct, see J. Laplanche and J. B. Pontalis, *The Language of Psychoanalysis* (London: Hogarth, 1983), 29–32.

PART ONE

MANAGING THE TRANSGRESSIVE

CHAPTER ONE

~

Between Two Gurus:
Edward Carpenter and
Walt Whitman

In no other English writer was an engagement with Indian spirituality to be so prolonged and so influential.[1] Quite probably it was the sheer difficulty he experienced in bringing his liberal ideas into an ongoing dialogue with Hindu metaphysics and mysticism that makes him so awkward a writer to comprehend: as one commentator has put it: "locating Carpenter, without editing away the contradictions and difficulties inherent in his life and work is an exceedingly difficult task."[2] His has been an erratic reputation.[3] Initially almost ignored, his 1894 text *Love's Coming of Age* went on to sell 100,000 copies. But by the 1920s neglect set in. It took the so-called sexual revolution of the 1960s to revive an interest in Carpenter and he became an icon of the gay liberation movement.[4] But a subsequent post-colonialist and feminist critique found him wanting and he was branded both a sexual colonialist and as lacking in any insight into the sexual needs of women, both straight and lesbian. But this is a moral censoriousness almost as distasteful as that of the imperialism and patriarchy it rightly criticizes. Surely it only makes sense to assess Carpenter in terms of the man he tried to be, his often brave attempt to be a homosexual with a deep attraction to the working class at a time of homophobia and chronic class prejudice?

Two facts stand out about Edward Carpenter: he was deeply driven by his homosexuality, he was obsessed by the idea of the evolution of consciousness. We lack any good modern biography and his autobiography, *My Days and Dreams*, remains the most helpful biographical source.[5] One novel way into making sense of his life and thought is to deploy one of the themes of this text, the *guru-sisya* relationship and see Carpenter as both disciple and would-be guru, a role-playing the better to resolve that constant tension in his life between his deviant sexuality and his religious and mystical quest. Far too little attention has been paid to the strength of the religious impulse in Carpenter. After all he began his life as a priest and as George Bernard Shaw waspishly observed, he never ceased to be one. He sought out gurus to come to terms with both his sexual and religio-mystical needs, above all to Walt Whitman as a guru who could liberate his sexual love for the working class and to Ramaswamy, a *gnani* in India, to structure some more coherent account of his mystical quest. It is in the nature of this relationship for the disciple to turn guru and if possible as much through the needs of those who sought his advice as through any spiritual ambitions of his own he was to become one himself for a more enlightened approach to sexuality and for a quasi-mystical social philosophy which in many ways anticipates Aurobindos's vision of the descent of the supermind and a divinized humanity.

Carpenter's key concept was democracy. Here was a reaching out to the working class that turned him into an ethical socialist. However spiritualized a utopian vision, this was to be an earthly paradise. Carpenter continually challenged taboos, both sexual and religious, and seeking guru status was one way of achieving the spiritual authority to sanction this transgression. Such was the embattled but vulnerable man who sought in the Indian mystical tradition one means of legitimizing his sexuality and utopian vision of a spiritualized quasi-socialist society.

Background

If Carpenter's was to be a radical rejection of his early perfectly comfortable middle class life in Brighton it was not to be a rejection of his family. His father, Charles, born 1797, came from a naval family, whose own father rose to be an Admiral and it was his house and wealth he was in time to inherit in Brighton. He had likewise served in the navy, 1810–1820, interestingly enough invalided out through an illness contracted whilst serving in Trincomalee—it was to be in Sri Lanka that Edward was in time to meet the second of his gurus—subsequently trained as a barrister and briefly practiced until moving to Brighton, where be became a respected city magistrate. Father and son could communicate. Charles was of a strongly religious disposition if unorthodox in his Christian beliefs—he believed in intelligence in animals and insects—was attached to a broad church mysticism and even explored Indian mysticism. His grasp of the nature of Nirvana, acquired from his reading of Schopenhauer, was arguably sounder in the early 1870s than that of his son. In a letter to Edward,

30 January 1876, he wrote of man's becoming "conscious of the indwelling and inworking of deity," in time to become absorbed into the Absolute.[6] But the young son always had to listen to his father's anxious concerns over his financial affairs and Tony Brown speculates that here was to be the beginning of his distaste for investment capitalism.

If much in the path of mysticism hinges on accessibility to the maternal and feminine then Carpenter's relationship with his mother is clearly crucial. His father married Sophia Wilson in 1833. She likewise came from a naval background, her father, Thomas, later turning to shipbuilding. Her background was Scottish and she brought a strongly inhibiting Puritanism to the family. Carpenter was clearly devoted to his mother but his feelings were not to be reciprocated. He wrote of a "tragedy as of dumbness itself." She could never express the love within, "all expression of tender feeling little short of sin." She had "an inflexible sense of truth and justice" together with a rigid obedience to social convention. Her death, 25 January 1881, affected Carpenter profoundly: "For months, even years after, I seemed to feel her, even see her close to me—always figuring as a semi-luminous presence, very real, but faint in outline, larger than mortal . . . more as it were an actual part of myself."[7] But, significantly, her death—though reading the *Gita* at the time was also a factor—released his creativity: "all at once I found myself in touch with a mood of exaltation and inspiration—a kind of superconsciousness—which passed all I had experienced before." When his friend, Havelock Ellis, lost his mother Carpenter tried to console him: "But indeed a mother's death must alter all one's life, as it changes too the whole household—perhaps you will still however feel her very near you."[8]

His father, belatedly aware of how dependent he had been on his wife and anguished at her death, died quite soon afterwards, April 1882.

Born 29 August 1844 Carpenter was the seventh of ten children—three brothers, six sisters. Again he never rejected this family. He admired his eldest brother, Charles Wilson, although their correspondence does not suggest they were on the same wavelength. But his two elder brothers left home early to make their careers, both with an Indian content, Charles in the ICS, Alfred in the navy, fighting in the Burma war of 1885. Being surrounded by six sisters quite probably affected his sexual orientation. He was fondest of his invalid sister, Lizzie. She was probably the nearest that any member of the family came to being a confidante.

It was a childhood in which he turned in on himself, a time, as he put it, of "silent concealment and loneliness." Being a dayboy at Brighton College compounded this isolation. He made no schoolboy friends. But the loneliness was greatly increased by awareness from the age of eight or nine of his attraction to his own sex. In his contribution to Havelock Ellis's research into sexual inversion he confessed: "My own sexual nature was a mystery to me. I found myself cut off from the understanding of others, felt myself an outcast and with a highly loving nature and clinging temperament, was intensely miserable." Seeing himself "as a hopeless monstrosity" he could not summon up the nerve to make any advances to those who attracted him, mainly older boys at school. "I was once or twice on the brink of despair and madness with repressed passion and torment."[9] Carpenter was always heading toward some kind of breakdown. One way out was nature and he found relief walking on the Downs above Brighton. Another was religion. Even at the age of fourteen, he wrote, this was seen as a likely route: "no doubt from the first there was a fatal bias towards religion."[10] He went up to Trinity Hall, Cambridge, 1864. At least there he made important friendships, above all with Charles George Oates, a lifetime friend and confidante and probable lover, and Edward Anthony Beck, later Master of the College, though here there was flirtation at best.

If it were not for his homosexuality one supposes Carpenter was heading for a steady, unexciting, academic career. He read mathematics and on the strength of early promise was offered in 1867 the clerical fellowship that Lesley Stephens had given up to marry. In 1868 he graduated tenth wrangler in the tripos and became a university lecturer and clerical fellow. In May 1869 he became a deacon and in June 1870 was ordained. He became curate of St. Edwards. And here Frederick Maurice, with his attractive broad church Christianity and his interest in Indian religions came in 1870 to be the incumbent. His death April 1872 released Carpenter from any sense of obligation to the church. There was even the extraordinary possibility in 1871 of his becoming tutor to Prince Albert Victor, eldest son of the Prince of Wales, and second in line to the throne although Carpenter sensed this was not for him, even if a personal friend, the Reverend John Neale Dalton was to accept.[11]

Already he was the poet. Walking along the banks at Cambridge he experienced "I don't know what kind of longing it was—something partly sexual, partly religious and both, owing to my strangely slow-growing temperament, still very obscure and undefined."[12] But by 1873 these subterranean forces had brought him to near breakdown. Jane Olive Daubeny, related to him through his sister Emily's marriage, told him he had to get away. A lifetime pattern began to emerge of foreign travel as a means of managing acute psychological stress. Rome it was on this occasion, with Carpenter eased by the sight of classical sculpture of the male nude. If he moved cautiously the break had to come. On 27 June 1874 he relinquished holy orders. He took advantage of the recent 1870 Clerical Disabilities Act which permitted voluntary surrender of priesthood: previously, once a priest, always a priest. In Burua's account sincerity rather than veracity was the issue. He had not ceased to believe. He just no longer felt right in the clergy. In fact, Carpenter's loss of Christian faith posed an intellectual challenge all his life. There had seemingly been the possibility of exchanging his clerical fellowship for a lay but this fell through. Instead, he became, in 1874, one of the first lecturers in the University Extension Scheme, initiated only the year before. So began his search for the northern working class and an entirely new way of life.

But the origin of this dramatic turnaround lay in his discovery of the poetry of Walt Whitman.

Walt Whitman

In the summer of 1868 or 1869 a fellow of Trinity Hall, W. D. Warr, lended him W. M. Rossetti's expurgated edition of *Leaves of Grass* (only three to four years later did he read the full version). It was a revelation; as Tony Brown puts it: "at the age of twenty-five he had finally found someone who not only felt as he did but did so with no sense of guilt."[13] Barua sees it as the most important event in his time at Cambridge. In 1871 he read *Democratic Vistas*, possibly an even more powerful influence: "from that time a profound change set in within me . . . a current of sympathy carrying my life westward across the Atlantic."[14] But only in his last days at Cambridge did he write to Whitman, prompted by a young workman coming to mend his college door, "with the old divine light in his eyes:" "you have made men not to be ashamed of the noblest instinct of their nature. Women are beautiful; but, to some, there is that which passes the love of women . . . the cramps and crazes of the old superstitions are relaxing, the idiotic ignorance of class contempt is dissipating."[15] He did not write again till 3 January 1876: "You have made the earth sacred to me I believe . . . that you have been the first to enunciate the law of purity and health which sooner or later must assert itself."[16] In April 1877 he went on his first visit to Whitman.

The Whitman (1819–1892) Carpenter met was at a low point in his life and career.[17] He lived in Camden, a dormitory town of Philadelphia, deemed a "proto-typical rising industrial city," living at the time with his brother George and wife Louise at 431 Stevens Street. 19 January 1873 he had suffered a stroke and Carpenter described his continuing physical impairment, his "dragging somewhat his paralyzed leg."[18] Then came a psychological blow of equal ferocity, the death of his mother, Louisa, 23 May 1873: "the only staggering, staying blow and trouble I have had—but *unspeakable*—my physical sickness, bad as it is, is nothing to it."[19] To address his laggard sales and reputation in America, never strong in his lifetime, and as a plug for the centennial edition of *Leaves of Grass*, he sent one of those anonymous pieces, in fact written by himself, entitled *Walt Whitman's Actual American Position*, printed in the *West Jersey* press, January 1876, and to be "the most widely circulated and commented on of all Whitman's anonymous works."[20] In his personal life he had by then distanced himself from his first great love, Peter Doyle, replacing him with the young Harry Stafford who lived nearby with his family, farmers at Timber Creek. But there was the added complication of the presence in Philadelphia of Anne Gilchrist, widow of Blake's biographer, herself smitten by that same Rossetti edition of his poetry, and in America with her family on a forlorn quest to win Whitman's love. Whitman rose to the challenge, virtually setting up home in her house, his room set aside as the prophet's. And if his reputation flagged in America it had taken off in Britain, Gilchrist's presence in America visible proof and when Carpenter came as representative figure of this response Whitman was to be uncharacteristically receptive to such a social visionary. He later told his biographer: "Edward was beautiful then—is so now, one of the torch bearers as they say: an exemplar of a loftier England."[21]

At the time of his second visit, June 1884, Whitman then lived under his own roof for the first time in his life, 328 Mickle Street, Camden, cared for by a housekeeper, Mary Davis. Nelly, the widow of his close friend William O' Connor had sought this role for herself but Whitman, sensing and fearing her ulterior purpose of marriage, had politely turned her down. His bedroom, littered with papers, reminded visitors of a newspaper office. But Whitman was now more at ease with himself and the subject of a selective but intense American cult. He gave "an overall impression of sunniness, equanimity and contemplative leisure."[22] "In the self-absorption of old age Whitman became his own iconographer."[23] stage-managing his portraits. Kaplan comments: "sometimes Whitman was hardly conscious of reshaping his past to make it conform to the ample, serene and masterful identity he achieved long after."[24] And Carpenter had himself moved on. In 1876 he was still an extension lecturer unfulfilled in his sexual needs. By 1884 he had set up home with a scythe maker, Albert Fearnehough and his wife, Albert his lover, in rural Derbyshire, outside Sheffield, and was far more self-fulfilled.

Whitman's Disciple

Had Carpenter approached Whitman as Master? He wrote up his account of visiting Whitman after his visit to Sri Lanka and India and quite probably intruded an Indian religio-cultural perspective. But he claimed his was an objective account and in many ways it was shrewd and critical. His initial and lasting reaction was to Whitman's physical appearance and to his personality. Within ten minutes of their first meeting he became aware "of immense vista or background in his personality." "I never met anyone who gave me more the impression of *knowing what he was doing* than he did." His eyes "were essentially not contemplative but perceptive." But he kept his distance. If "he gave you that sense of *nowness*" he would only enter into conversation on "a basis of personal affection" and could all too readily withdraw: "I have seldom known any one who, though so cordial and near to others, detached and withdrew himself at times more decisively than he did, or who on the whole spent more time in solitude." He picked up on that "strange omnivorous egotism, controlled and restrained by that wonderful genius of his for human affection and love." This was the aspect he picked up on again on his second visit: "I am impressed more than ever with W's contradictory, self-willed, tenacious, obstinate character." There was that "queer brusque way of parting, just coldly saying ta-ta and going off as if he didn't care if he ever saw us again." But there remained "his extraordinarily voluminous hold on life, his strong implication in the life of the body and the senses." There was also a cussedness, a contradictoriness that Carpenter believed warred against the chances of his successfully being in love. Still, this same "waywardness became refined into something majestic." (Of course, such contrariness is invariably the trademark of the guru; having to cope with such contradiction would be the making of the disciples.) Comparing later two photographs of his two gurus, both taken in 1890, he took the more to Whitman's, for here was a face marked by human experience, "his voluminous enfoldment in the earth life—the Nessus—shirt of Hercules."

If attempting a critical portrait in the round of Whitman the person, Carpenter was to abandon any such restraint in his account of Whitman the philosopher. Here he became the guru figure. Extraordinary claims are made for Whitman as prophet and seer. He stood alone against modern society. He reached "a stage of human evolution not yet reached and hardly suspected by humanity at large." "His utterance and its daemonic reach and sweep is somewhat staggering." Carpenter always emphasized the intuitive, the mystic, the illumined in Whitman: "it is probable indeed that never in historical times has the cosmic intuition found a fuller and more complete utterance." And this was inherently transgressive: "subversive, inconvenient, contrary; annunciative of a new order."

However, here there was divergence, for if both Whitman and Carpenter sought a resolution of a personal tension between sexuality and religion, Whitman did so by turning sex into a religion whereas Carpenter always sought a degree of transcendence. In the end, however, Carpenter always came back to recognizing the claims of Whitman's this-worldly vision: "his unrivalled knowledge of the actual world and of actual life and his absolute acceptance of the same, give him so high a distinction among the Prophets."[25] This was to prove the vital difference when it came to choosing between Whitman and his Indian guru.

Other Disciples

Carpenter was not alone in adopting Whitman as guru. A coterie in America was in the process of developing a Whitman myth. His John the Baptist, to use Kaplan's language, was poet turned short story writer, William O'Connor. They first met in 1860, O'Connor was twenty-eight at the time. Whitman later described him as "a gallant, handsome, gay-hearted, fine-voiced, glowing-eyed man."[26] In his pamphlet *The Good Gray Poet* published at the end of the Civil War, O'Connor pronounced Whitman the prophet both of humanity and America. But they were to fall out over black civil rights, O'Connor always a strong abolitionist and champion of the black vote, Whitman less enthusiastic. He died 1889. His St. Peter was Horace Traubel, proxy, editorial assistant, messenger, companion and "elective son"; his St. Luke and St. Paul was Richard Maurice Bucke, a frontier man in ways Whitman himself had never been, who lost a foot and the toes on the other in a winter in Sierra Nevada, later becoming superintendent of an insane asylum. He had discovered Whitman through Rossetti's edition at much the same time as Carpenter, in 1872 was to experience moments of transcendence and ever afterwards, in much the same way as Carpenter, became obsessed by the theme of spiritual evolution. He met Whitman for the first time in 1877. Both Traubel and Bucke were to be his biographers. John Burroughs, a Treasury clerk who met Whitman in his Washington days, was his most level-headed admirer. Harvard Divinity student, William Sloane Kennedy, to the contrary, extravagantly saw Whitman as the equal of Christ. John Townsend Trowbridge was one of his earliest and most prolonged admirers.

Another Harvard divinity student, Moncure Conway, the initial bridge between Emerson and Whitman in 1855, also took on the role of propagandist in England in 1867, linking up with Rossetti, and then staying on as pastor of an ultra-liberal Congregational Church in Islington.

But it was William Rossetti's article in *The Chronicle* 6 July 1867 that put Whitman on the English map: "in transatlantic perspective the bard became colossal and fascinating, an Adamic figure with a thrilling message from a young country."[27] It was a younger and radical generation who responded to Whitman, above all to the homoerotic ideal of brotherhood. If Carpenter in fact only began to champion Whitman's name after 1892 "he is of unique importance as the one young reader of Whitman in all nineteenth century

England who felt himself dedicated heart and soul to the life work of interpreting and expanding Whitman's dream of democratic brotherhood."[28]

Leaves of Grass

This was of course the bible of the cult. It went through nine editions. Just possibly Whitman's monstrous egotism was as much in aid of his book as himself. In Reynold's account Whitman took time to find the voice of *Leaves of Grass*. His earlier poetry was filled with a kind of metaphysical angst, trying to purge his own inner demons. But then he turned from authority figures to the common people, with an intense pride in artisan values. Only at the age of thirty-five did he begin to write out his poems. Was he addressing a crisis in 1850s America, with its corruption and threatening political conflict, or compensating for his own inner self-doubt and guilt? For so flamboyant a self-publicist it had a surprisingly quiet beginning, registered 15 May 1855 with the New York authorities, with only 795 copies being printed. Whitman had dreamt of its becoming widely popular, hence its appearing in pocket book size. But it was not to be. For the second edition he added the Calamus and Children of Adam poems and steadily it grew in sheer bulk, the twelve untitled poems of 1855 and its 95 pages to be 293 poems and 382 pages by the 6th edition of 1881. The 7th edition was to be in 1882—though the charge was withdrawn—the subject of a trial for indecency. As Kaplan puts it this new Bible became for nearly forty years "the center of his life, the instrument of health and survival itself."[29] In England his publisher, John Camden Hotten, "an enterprising but shady operator,"[30] insisted on cuts to meet a squeamish English public—Whitman wrote of "the horrible dismemberment of my book"[31]—but it did the trick and anyway Whitman was becoming recognized much more widely, with Turgenev, for example translating some of his poems into Russian and his being taken up by the French symbolists. Carpenter was to pay the work its greatest complement by using it as a model for his own epic cycle *Towards Democracy*.

Whitman's Gurus?

It suited Carpenter's own mysticism both to ascribe a transcendentalist influence on Whitman and even more dubiously a Vedantist. There was a strong transcendentalist movement in America at the time, centered on Ralph Waldo Emerson (1803–1882) and Henry David Thoreau (1817–1862). Emerson's concept of the Over-Soul owed as much to neo-Platonism as to Hinduism, but he was strongly influenced by his reading of Wilkins' translation of the *Bhagavad Gita* and the writings of Rammohan Roy and his concept of World Soul merged with that of *brahman*. Thoreau was likewise moved by the

Gita and possibly his retreat to Walden Pond was inspired by an Indian ascetic ideal.[32] Quite probably reading Emerson had been a catalyst for Whitman's
poetry, and certainly Emerson was an early enthusiast for *Leaves of Grass* but
became cross at the way Whitman exploited his private letter of support and
here was a real temperamental divide. During his visit in 1877 Carpenter met
an Emerson already in decline with serious memory loss though he "greatly
enjoyed his talk" and discussed his feelings toward Whitman. If recognizing
Whitman's real inspiration came out of personal experience Carpenter still
cannot resist annexing Whitman to Emerson:

> At the same time it seems to me quite likely that at some moment the mag-
> nificent intuitive outlook of Emerson, as of an eagle in high-soaring vision of
> seas and continents, sweeping the whole world into the compass of his thought
> did give Whitman just what he might have been waiting for (though probably
> in any case it would have come to him sometime) the magic touch and inspi-
> ration which set his kosmos in order.[33]

If Thoreau was undoubtedly one inspiration for Carpenter's own experiment in simple living no such claim can be made for any influence on Whitman. They met in New York after the publication of the poetry, Thoreau
silent during the interview, for here were two highly egocentric men. But
Thoreau was always later to recognize Whitman's genius.

But Carpenter was even more contrived in his trying to graft Whitman
onto a Vedantist tradition. In their first encounter Whitman spoke of his
reading *Sakuntala* and the *Ramayana* but it was during their final meeting in
the second visit, following Whitman's strange account of himself "as furtive
like an old hen" in writing *Leaves of Grass* that the Indian influence came up.
He went on to remark "there are truths which it is necessary to envelop or
wrap up." Carpenter replied that "the old mysteries" had been held back and
then added, "we had something yet to learn from India in these matters." But
Whitman was dismissive: "I do not myself think there is anything more to
come from that source; we must rather look to modern science to open the
way."[34] Reynolds suggests that India for Whitman meant "rhapsody, passive-
ness, meditation"[35] and such knowledge as he had of its religions came
through reading Emerson.

But Carpenter will not take "no" for an answer. Whilst acknowledging
that Whitman's knowledge of the vedic texts is "doubtful" he goes on: "but
that he had read here and there among them, quite enough to gain insight
into the heart of them and to know that his message was contiguous with
theirs is quite certain."[36] And whilst half conceding that Whitman was essentially a champion of individualism and hostile to any concept of *nirvana*,

he still ascribes to Whitman an entirely Vedantist definition of the Self: "the Self, individual and separate, yet conjoined and continuous throughout Creation's mass"—that is the theme which undoubtedly runs through the whole of his poems and prophetic utterances. And it is the theme of the eldest Upanishads of the Vedic ages."[37] Unconvincingly, he places alongside extracts of *Leaves of Grass* quotations from Vedantist, Taoist and Buddhist texts to demonstrate Whitman's belonging to the perennial philosophy.

Yet Carpenter was correct to emphasize the religious component in Whitman. Reynolds sees Whitman as the founder of a new religion: "a poetic religion based on progressive science and idealist philosophy that preached the miracle of the commonplace and the possibilities of the soul."[38] Hegel was a major ingredient. Here was a heady brew taking in Swedenborgianism, mesmerism, and spiritualism. From Swedenborg came the possibilities of erotic mysticism. Whereas Carpenter loftily linked Whitman to Buddha, Jesus, and St Francis as an inclusivist, an accepter rather than a denier, one who tried to incorporate all of humanity into his religious outlook, Whitman makes more sense in terms of some dialectic between his attitudes to sexuality and religion.

It was over his refusal to collude with his English disciples that his concept of comradeship was essentially an endorsement of homosexuality that Whitman most signally failed to live up their expectations of him as guru. John Addington Symonds pressed him the hardest and in the end out of exasperation Whitman replied dismissively: "such gratuitous and quite at the time entirely undream'd and unreck'd possibility of morbid inferences—wh' are disavow'd by me and seem damnable."[39] Yet Whitman was homosexual.[40] Even if sodomy was not criminalized till 1882 it seems he was publicly humiliated for some sexual relationship with one of his pupils whilst a primary schoolteacher in Smithson, Long Island, between November 1840 and March 1841. Quite possibly his first fully realized love affair was with Peter Doyle, though it was one that disturbed him and he saw the need to practice restraint, to rein in its "perturbation." The Calamus poems—and one might well suppose this was a reference to some Greek Ganymede but in fact it refers to some rush or reed common to the eastern and southern states, one with markedly phallic appearance—is unashamedly homoerotic. But as Reynolds explains, Whitman grew up in a culture which was at ease with homoerotic friendship—the term friend and lover was interchangeable—and the whole notion of gender was still highly fluid. Both Emerson and Thoreau believed friendship to be a higher ideal than sexual passion. Whitman absorbed much of Fourier's ideas of the passions. From phrenology he took the vital distinction between adhesiveness and amativeness, the one endorsing friendship and the vital force drawing society together, the other essentially sexual in nature. Here was the source of Whitman's most influential concept, comradeship, the way male bonding would underpin the idealized democracy of the future.

Carpenter was a good deal less resistant to this sanitized version of his sexuality than Symonds. He would have liked to fit Whitman into his concept, one that he had taken from the German psychologist, Karl Ulrichs (1825–1895) of the invert possessing a female soul in a male body. And clearly there was a curious transgender feel to Whitman, his capacity to relate erotically to both sexes, his androgynous personality.[41] But Whitman contrasted the manly male with the effeminate and there was always a Hemingwayesque tendency to assert the ultra-masculine and to deny a feminine side. Possibly he saw his relationships with young men as increasingly paternal or avuncular. Did Carpenter grasp how much more radical an agenda Whitman's concept of comradeship be, for it extended homosexuality far beyond some self-conscious gay minority to society at large? It will be argued below that he probably did not. But here really was a basis for a utopian society, one Carpenter was to take in a far more socialist direction than Whitman ever conceived, with his idealizing at most a large democratic class of small-owners, an essentially artisan ideal.

Havelock Ellis, a close friend of Carpenter's, got closer to aspects of Whitman's personality. He made much of the impact of his hospital visits during the Civil War, 1862–1865, his acquiring "a divine tenderness, a divine compassion for all things human." Here was the explanation for "his large emotional nature," for his becoming "one of the very greatest emotional forces of modern times." And Ellis will have none of Whitman as Vedantist: "he has few or no marks upon him of that mysticism—that eastern spirit of glad renunciation of the self in a larger self—which is the essence of religion." Whitman did not write on behalf of an abstract Man or Humanity: "there is nothing anywhere in the universe for him but individuals, undying, everlastingly aggrandizing individuals."[42]

Toward Democracy

In a small hut in the garden of the farm at Bradway outside Sheffield, "far far away from anything polite or respectable or any sign or symbol of my hated old life,"[43] between April 1881 and early 1882 Carpenter wrote his equivalent poem to *Leaves of Grass*. Indeed Havelock Ellis, on first glance, notoriously branded it "Whitman and water" but came to see it as "a genuine and original book full of inspiring and beautiful and consoling things and to become for some people a kind of bible."[44] Later he wrote to Carpenter: "I think that TD compared with L of G is (in no bad sense) feminine. W(hitman) is so strenuously masculine."[45] It largely anticipates Carpenter's subsequent prose critique of his own society, "civilization" as he called it, his writings on socialism, his Vedantism, and his radical sexual agenda and love of the working class. Here were the ingredients for his cult of democracy and comradeship.

But it is a baffling text. One of its problems is decoding the authorial voice, the "I" of the poem. There is inter alia "the One moving unseen hither and thither; the Son of man; the Word I have spoken; I AM, know me—I am the master, showing myself from time to time as occasion serves;" "I am the lover and the loved, I have lost and found an identity;" "the dedication of Humanity, the wider embrace that passes all barriers of class and race."[46]Tony Brown sees him in the role of the stranger "who wanders Tiresias-like through the wasteland Victorian capitalism has created."[47] In one of his guises the poet is Wagner's the Wanderer, in another a pre-Mahler "spirit of the Earth." Alternatively, there is the ring of a Nietzschean prophet: "I am a voice singing the song of deliverance." He anticipates Eliot's vision of a dystopic London:

I beheld a vision of Earth with innumerable paths
And I saw, going up and down the world—old faces of humanity

But Tony Brown also registers a Krishna-like voice speaking to a civilization caught within an illusory world of selfishness and materialism. And Barua, more persuaded of Carpenter's grasp of Vedantism at the time, sees the "I" as the universal or the Great Self.

Clearly a large part of the answer lies in his discipleship of Whitman. And if Tony Brown is surely right to see the poem as "Carpenter's deeply felt response to the ecstatic vision of Whitman's poetry," a more direct influence on its message is Whitman's prose work, *Democratic Vistas* (1871), the nearest he came to drawing up a political agenda. Whitman saw in writers, "national expressers," as he described them, the best prospect of overcoming American decadence and revitalizing its democracy. Carpenter was surely responding to his clarion call: "the poet of the modern is wanted." The writers would inspire "the fervid and tremendous IDEA melting everything else with resistless heat." But Carpenter and Whitman were not entirely of one mind. Whitman drew heavily on his experience of the Civil War, the soldiers of both sides, for his sense of the people with "their measureless wealth of latent power and capacity, the vast artistic contrasts of light and shades," and here Carpenter was wholly at one. But Whitman was also driven by individualism, by his ideal of a "rich, luxuriant, varied personalism;" the only reason for immersing oneself in the people was to fashion such individualism "for it is mainly or altogether to serve independent separatism that we favor a strong generalization, consolidation." Here Carpenter differed, more strongly drawn to the working class as a collective movement.[48] But both shared in a cult of Nature and the outdoors.

But it was in reading the *Bhagavad gita*, pressed on him by his Sri Lankan friend, Arunachalam, that he found a far more personal voice. As he put it: "all at once I found myself in touch with a mood of exaltation and inspiration—a kind of super-consciousness—which passed all I had experienced before."[49] The poem is studded with references to India and Hinduism, e.g., "Gentle and venerable India well pleased now at last to hear fulfilled the words of her ancient sages."[50] "I am Arjuna reasoning on the battlefield with Krishna—learning the lessons of divine knowledge."[51] There are frequent Vedantist passages:

> I am come to be the interpreter of yourself to yourself
> But beyond Maya I now descend into materials[52]
> I know that you shall never rest till you have found your self[53]
> Say not thou "I desire this or that"
> For the "I" neither desires nor fears anything but is free and in everlasting
> glory, dwelling in heaven and pouring out joy like the sun on all sides.[54]

In his Vedantist belief in the overlapping identity of atman and brahman, in his concept of a higher self, Carpenter moves well beyond Whitman's cult of individualism.

Not that Whitman rejected a religious dimension to his idealized democracy. "Moral conscientiousness" was at a high premium. But whilst recognizing the faith of the past, including the sacred texts of the Hindus "with hymns and apothegms and endless epics," for Whitman his writers were to go beyond, "to become orbic bards with unconditional uncompromising sway . . . social democratic despots of the west." And, interestingly, in a poem written at the same time as *Democratic Vistas*, *Passage to India*, whilst again recognizing that journey of the soul in the Indian tradition, there was still the need to reach out to new frontiers. Whitman's passage to India was in fact as much an expression of triumphalism in the engineering feats of American capitalism as any deference to Indian spirituality. Carpenter was a long way from sharing in any sense America's manifest destiny.

The tension in the poem lies in its trying to reconcile this Vedantism with a progressive sexual code, above all Carpenter's cult of the working class male. Here he was unusually courageous in his openness. He was unashamedly writing for "the confessed passionate lovers of your own sex . . . heroes of the en-franchisement of the body."[55] There were visions of the stoker, "grimy and oil-besmeared," "the quiet look, the straight untroubled unseeking eyes resting upon me—giving me without any ado the thing I needed."[56] There were sim-ilar encounters with firemen and railway porters. Here was a profound rejec-tion of all the Victorian proprieties: "men and women . . . frozen up, starched, starved, coffined, each in their own little cells of propriety, respectability, dirty property, and dismal poverty."[57]

And this permits a quite different reading of the "I" of the poem. Scott Mckracken suggests here is the personal voice in place of that impersonal he used when providing Havelock Ellis with an account of his sexuality: "this 'I' is inclusive when the third person 'independent' observer is exclusive, dis-tancing and defining through classification." Here the "I" is universalized: "Carpenter is aiming at a utopian universality, the inclusiveness of which will dissolve division and difference."[58] Carpenter believed such sexual transgres-sion was compatible with Vedantism. In the poetry of another mystical tra-dition, the fourteenth-century Iranian sufi poet, Hafiz, he found an unashamed homoerotic mysticism.[59] As Mckracken concludes: "Carpenter managed to preserve his identity as a Uranian through mysticism."

In much the same way as Whitman cherished and continually added to *Leaves of Grass* so Carpenter with *Towards Democracy*. He later wrote to Havelock Ellis that he believed it to be "much superior to my prose work. When I occasionally read the former again I feel comfortable-like about it. And its want of success does not bother me."[60] He wrote of additions to an-other new edition: "As a matter of fact the new material is about on a par with the old—neither better nor worse, nor more nor less conventional than I know of."[61] In his lifetime it ran into nine editions.

Socialism: the God that Failed

Between his discipleship of Whitman in the 1870s and of the *gnani* in the 1890s Carpenter became an influential figure in the socialist movement. Al-ready he showed signs of himself becoming a guru in his own right. He car-ried forward all the concerns of *Towards Democracy* and it is only a matter of preponderance that his socialism took precedence over his mysticism and sexology. It was a unique phase in the history of socialism, in both Britain and Europe, a time when concerns of the private sphere overlapped with those of the public, when personal relationships counted as much as struc-tural and collective change, when a religious approach more than matched a materialistic. Until the time when a realistic prospect of coming to power fashioned a more ruthless and disciplined party politics the socialist movement was inherently more pluralistic and open-ended. Carpenter was instinctively drawn toward the anarchist wing of the movement—he joined the Labor Emancipation League, an anarchist group, in 1885—rather than to its Marxist. Through his cult of comradeship, though, he remained wedded to an ideal of a sexualized democracy. His was an ethical socialism at best. Constitutionally incapable of sinking himself in the tough administrative demands of a labor movement—but he was to make a stab at it—almost inevitably his interests by the 1890s were to shift from socialism to a deeper engagement with Indian spirituality and an ever bolder exploration of sexuality. During the 1880s, however, the governing idea of his philosophy, the evolution of consciousness, took shape.

Between 1882 and 1883 some two hundred men and women, E. P. Thompson suggests, were to reject their middle-class privileged background and commit themselves to socialism: "they represented a small eddy of ideas, part old, part new, rather than the movement of the masses; and this fact goes far to explain the doctrinal and sectarian outlook of several of the pioneers."[62] Carpenter did not find his socialism in Whitman. It took reading Hyndman's marxisant *England for All* to convert Carpenter to the movement. As one might predict of one as anarchist-minded as Carpenter, he was always most active and effective at a local rather than a national level. In 1884 a separate Sheffield Working Men's Radical Association was set up and Carpenter was a regular participant and speaker in its café meetings. "We are busy opening our Socialist Club and Coffee House," he informed Havelock Ellis: "I have a large attic here in the midst of the slums in an air laden with smoke and the sound of dogs." [63] He bicycled out to meetings in the vicinity. He played the harmonium on these occasions and also collected socialist songs, to be published in his *Chants of Labor* (1888). At long last he was mixing with manual workers.

In the factionalism of the time Carpenter's natural instinct was to act as reconciler and try to keep in touch with all sides. Although he did not join Hyndman's Social Democratic Federation he made a sizeable contribution of £300 to its journal *Justice* and always kept in touch with him; he did join the breakaway Socialist League, engineered by Edward Aveling and Eleanor Marx but with William Morris its most charismatic leader, and Carpenter was strongly drawn to the tough, squat, corpulent Morris, another middle-class rebel. Later he was to say to Havelock Ellis of Morris: "I think he will stand out to future generations as quite the finest figure in England today—notwithstanding his sectarianism as you call it—which is simply the cap—

'capo rosso'—wh. any man who lives and works today must put on—tho' it is not part of him."[64] Another way into the plural politics of socialism was through the Fellowship of the New Life, the parent body of the Fabians, and Carpenter got to know Shaw, but the modernizing Fabians were little sympathetic to Carpenter's essentially arcadian, rural vision of socialism. A little oddly, Carpenter never identified with Unionism and Tsuzuki concludes that Carpenter "by and large remained disillusioned with national Socialist politics."[65] He attended the 1889 Paris meeting of the Second International, admired Morris's speech, sympathized more with the anarchists than the Marxist Social Democrats, and was to make contributions to Kropotkin's vision of the industrial village. If never drawn to anarchist plots he found himself acting as character witness for Fred Charles in the anarchist Walsall trial of 1893. Alone among prominent British socialists of the time he saw a role for violence, though not for such individual acts. Maybe, though, as Barua suggests, Carpenter came to believe that social change would come about through the influence of a committed few.

As both speaker and writer Carpenter could prove transformative. Here is the response of a railway worker to hearing Carpenter talk on the theme of the simplification of life:

> As one listened to the man one mentally sloughed off the conventional husks which seemed to encase one's spirits . . . in a curious way he seemed to take one both forward and backward; forward to a freer and less care-worn world yet backward to something which all of us had lost.[66]

A leading socialist activist in Bristol where Carpenter had strong links, Katherine St. John Conway, after reading Carpenter's *England's Ideal* was to undergo a conversion experience:

> I vaguely realized that every value life had previously held for me had been changed as by some mysterious spiritual alchemy.[67]

It is instructive, to have a better grasp of the degree of his socialist commitment, to compare William Morris with Carpenter. Here a whole series of revolts against the values of his society, its utilitarianism, the shoddiness of its capitalist products, the Gothic revival, coping with an unhappy marriage, 'a vast accumulation of half-conscious anxieties and guilts,"[68] all these led him to socialism: "the transformation of the eccentric artist and romantic literary man into the socialist agitator may be counted among the great conversions of the world."[69] In Thompson's account Morris is seen as recognizing the need for a total commitment to the cause, a readiness to sink himself in matters organizational and strategic. If he shared Carpenter's anarchism and was something of a "purist"—Thompson makes the intriguing observation that Morris feared the penetration of the movement by the outlook of the middle class—at the end he became reconciled to a pragmatic parliamentary approach. Yet, to give Carpenter his due in this comparison, Morris recognized that at Millthorpe Carpenter had got closer to a simplified life than he had done through his artisan products. And Thompson is ready to concede, "because Carpenter's revolt was individualistic, undisciplined and (backed by a legacy of £6000) not especially arduous, it is easy to underestimate him today."[70]

Yet Carpenter's socialism with its cult of the simple and rural life can feel almost whimsical. No doubt recalling his father's endless anxieties over his investments Carpenter gave a sharply mordant account on middle-class dependence on stocks and shares. Familiar with Marx's writings he shared in his labor theory of value. But it was Thoreau's *Walden*—and Thoreau he saw as "a thorough economist" and "a thoroughly educated man in the true sense of he word"[71]—that inspired his ideal of the rural small holding. It was a not impractical agenda, his recognizing the need for capital if rural cooperatives were to be set up. In a letter to Havelock Ellis he rather downplayed his cult of the simple life: would people see it, he feared, "as a statement of an ideal way of living, instead of (as I rather intend it) as a dry suggestion of how to get thro' life with less work or bother than at present."[72] But more dynamically this was a revolt against Victorian polite society. He was preaching a change in lifestyle: "by all the gods I would rather with pick and shovel dig a year long drain beneath the open sky, breathing freely than I would live in this jungle of idiotic duties and thin-lipped responsibilities that money breeds."[73] And aware that he could sound too much the moralist, the charge of pharisaism, he proposed in this rural idyll the occasional orgy. Yet quite obviously Carpenter was going against the grain of an urban, collectivist, socialist movement.

He was, however, wholly attuned to the religiosity of socialism in this decade. Stephen Yeo has made a persuasive case of a coming to socialism at the time as akin to a religious conversion. Nevertheless, Yeo discourages categorizing these socialists as "fuzzy, peculiarly British, soft, nonrevolutionary, socialists who could not quite moult religious feathers," or, in E. P. Thompson's phrase, prone to "cosmic mooning."[74] Barua sees in a cluster of religious outlooks, immanentism, pantheism, mysticism in the early 1880s an expectation of "some great change in the spiritual basis of society." The ideas of Edward Maitland and Dr. Anna Kingsford of the Hermetic Society were incorporated into *Towards Democracy*.[75] The strongest expression of this tie between religion and socialism came with the Labor Church movement, set up in Manchester in 1892, Carpenter to prove one of its most popular lecturers. Yeo characterizes Carpenter's writings as "mystical, nature based, eclectic appropriations of Christian and other religions"; *Towards Democracy* "gulped thirstily into the consciousness of groups of workers." Carpenter is rated an exceptional advocate of socialism: "men like Morris, Carpenter and Blatchford do not appear in every generation."[76] Carpenter himself saw belonging to the movement in religious terms, those "cold" on the outside could not imagine the "hot" on its inside. And this compounds the sense of Carpenter still the priest. Stanley Pierson accentuates another aspect of this make-up and portrays Carpenter as a millenarian.[77] This leads into his sense of time and history and his critical response to the dominant Victorian paradigm of evolution.

Carpenter here owed much to his reading of the American anthropologist, Lewis H. Morgan's study of human evolution, his *Ancient Society or Researches in the line of Human Progress from Savagery through Barbarism to Civilisation.*[78] Morgan did his fieldwork among the Iroquois Indians. Carpenter collapsed his distinction between savagery and barbarism and tended to refer to precivilization as Nature. In *Savagery* Morgan discovered a strongly democratic society, rooted in the *gens*: "liberty, equality and fraternity, though never formulated were cardinal principles of the *gens*."[79] Mankind owed, he believed, a huge debt "to the struggle, the suffering, the heroic exertions and the patient toil of our barbarous and more remotely of our savage ancestors."[80]With the alphabet, the emergence of the nuclear family and of private property came the transition to Civilization, though Morgan was skeptical of its achievements and saw the need for a further stage, the need to move onto democracy: "it will be a revival in a higher form of the liberty, equality and fraternity of the ancient gentes."[81]

Carpenter's twist was to see Civilization in far more negative terms. He saw it as "a disease." So-called civilized man had lost that feeling of unity, that sense of spontaneity, and a sense of sin had blighted a sacramental enjoyment of sex. And in branding private property as the source of the disease he found the point of departure for his socialism. These ideas expressed in *Civilization: Its Cause and Cure*[82] were to be, of course, one major influence on Gandhi's own quarrel with western civilization.

Spiritualizing the concept of evolution was a characteristic of late nineteenth-century mysticism, from Madame Blavatsky, to Henri Bergson, to Aurobindo, to Teilhard de Chardin. Carpenter was in strong company. And here he was yet further indebted to Whitman, from whom he appropriated the term "exfoliation," a redeployment of Lamarck's (1744–1829) belief that acquired characteristics are inherited.[83] He named this inner force "desire." Exfoliation he saw as a true evolution, one from within, as opposed to an accretive Darwinian account of evolution from without: in his view "the dismal insufficiency of the Darwin theory of the survival of the fittest."[84] This became the basis for a full-scale critique by Carpenter of a nineteenth century science, seen as based on an inductive process, with its wholly misguided belief that the intellect rather than feeling can explain the universe. There was a need for "an inner illumination."

Much of this was informed by Carpenter's Vedantism. In this account man had to come into contact with "his more universal and incorruptible part;" 'the condition of health in the mind is loyalty to the divine Man within it."[85]And here Carpenter more exactly describes the nature of the disease of Civilization. But the manner of its cure equally reveals a rather Victorian belief in a kind of progress. Mankind in Civilization is afflicted with self-consciousness. There can be no going back to savagery to recover its experience of unity. There had to be "the disentanglement of the true self from the fleeting and perishable self" and a moving on to some higher, transcendent form of consciousness: "where the cosmic self is there is no more self-consciousness."[86] Yet he still saw this in physical terms, as "the desire and longing for the perfect human form," and quite clearly the demands of his sexuality still lay behind this mystical quest.

Was Carpenter indeed projecting his own self-consciousness onto Victorian society, or Civilization as he defined it, as a whole? Was he not painfully aware of himself, as Tariq Rahman has forcibly argued,[87] as a kind of "monstrosity," experiencing "self-alienation" and a crisis of identity, trapped within a morality which saw his sexuality as unnatural and sinful? Carpenter's was a profound revolt against a Victorian cult of masculinity that denied man's feminine side. His was a quest once again for wholeness, with an emphasis on feeling rather than intellect, and in Vedantism, especially with Hinduism, as he was later to argue, endorsing a sacramental attitude to sex, he found the means for both his self-acceptance and self-transcendence. Or as Tariq Rahman puts: "the idea of the soul seeking union with the universal spirit-Brahman" appealed to him because it portrayed, in symbolic terms, "the lover's desire to attain union with the beloved." Stanley Pierson has a rather cruel account of this crisis of identity at the age of thirty: "he displayed such characteristic symptoms as narcissism, an indiscriminate condemnation of all social and cultural forms, the sense of being controlled by hidden forms, extreme self-idealization and homosexuality" He continues: "the effort to escape from the torment of self-consciousness, from the 'mirror prison of the self' was a recurrent theme in Carpenter's later writings."[88]

Clearly the way out lay in a fulfilled sex life. The street life of Paris had provided no answer. In the new way of life at Bradway and then Millthorpe, where Carpenter moved in October 1883, there was progress; Carpenter became sexually intimate with both of those who successively managed his market garden—Albert Fearnehough and George Adams.

But his greatest passion was for razor maker George Hukin, twenty-six years old when they met, "with a Dutch-featured face and Dutch build." He was secretary of the Sheffield Socialist Society and maybe that is where they became friends. The story of this unhappy affair can be traced through his correspondence with Oates. It all began so promisingly. "My friend George." Carpenter reported to Oates, "has turned out too good almost to be true."[89] In the next bulletin he informed Oates: "George is as good as ever and we are great chums. He does me good, being very easy going, yet deep feeling underneath—and I trust to help him too. He generally stays the night with me on Saturdays—either at Millthorpe or at my quarters in Sheffield."[90] By April he reported "his love is so disinterested and so tender—I hardly dare think it is true."[91] In a letter 21 May Hukin, however, told Carpenter of his intention to marry his girlfriend Fannie. Probably Hukin was always heterosexual and there was always some awkwardness in his returning Carpenter's affection. As ever, Carpenter dealt with an emotional crisis by going abroad. On holiday in Italy he was struck by the handsomeness of a fellow passenger on the train, possibly an artist: "I could have kissed his hands—and would have I think if we had been alone . . . a man nearly forty with black short beard and large perceptive eyes—so tender and warm-hearted a face, yet not too refined—but wonderfully well balanced. How I wished to see him again!" But this prompted the thought; "I keep wondering whether I shall ever settle down in England if anything were to go wrong with me and George." Sleeplessness reflected his anguish: "I think the long strain and suffering have pulled me down. Maybe it would be for the best" he reflected, "if he kept his distance from George and Fannie." It was then he struck up a new friendship with George Adams, to be Fearnehough's successor as caretaker at Millthorpe. They went on holiday together to Whitby. Over the summer Hukin married Fannie. By 27 August he agonized to Oates: "tho' they are very affectionate it caused most terrible spasms of jealousy to see them . . . Really these things are . . . *overpossessing*—the fierce and frightful waging for a male—and then mockery of *women* always thrust in the way. I fear it will be a life-long struggle—with defeat certain—yet one *must* go on."[92] Misguidedly, Carpenter sent them a double bed as a wedding present, prompting Hukin shyly but embarrassedly to express a wish that one day they might enjoy a threesome. In time the pain eased: "I cannot say that I love him as passionately as once I did but my love is very sincere—and jealousy troubles our mutual relations less."[93]

But the friendship had been every bit as troubling for Hukin. Initially he felt overwhelmed by his friendship. "I would rather withdraw from than approach any nearer to you. I feel so mean and little beside you, altogether unworthy of your friendship. It is not your fault that I feel so now. You have always tried to put me at my ease, to make me feel at home with you—sorry I cannot come any nearer to you. How I should like to yet I feel I can't."[94] But then he relaxed: "It is so good of you to love me. I don' t think I ever felt so happy in my life. And I' m sure that I love you more than any other friend I have in the world. You don't know how tempted I am to come and join you in Brighton and I would come but we have so much to do."[95] At the time Carpenter was sorting out his father's estate in Brighton: "just now" he told Havelock Ellis, "I am in the center of a cyclone—the ancestral mansion was sold yesterday."[96] But then came the engagement. He could still write: "I should so like to be with you for just one hour. It seems so very quiet and lonely in the room without you here. I miss you much more than I thought I should and I don't find it so nice, sleeping alone as I used to think it was." But he was meeting Fannie every evening: "but don't think that we have forgotten you, dear Ted, for if we didn't both of us love you so much I don't think we should love each other as much as we do. I am sure we both love you more than ever, Ted. And you really must come and live with us when we do marry."[97] But, of course, Carpenter was not keen on sharing Hukin with Fannie. Later, in the same vein, Hukin wrote: "I think more about you and love you more than ever. But I can't bear to think that you are unhappy and know that I am the cause of it all. I sometimes think that I can never bring anything but unhappiness to either you or Fannie and I feel so miserable that I would like to die . . . I don't care what becomes of me so long as you and Fannie are happy."[98] It was a letter Carpenter laid to rest with a telegram: "I am so glad" Hukin responded, "that you feel better dear Ted, you may feel quite at rest about me now, we shan't be unhappy any more. You are so good to forgive me all the pain I've caused you Ted, you have always been so good and loving to me."[99] There was that rather embarrassed reply to the wedding gift of the bed: "I do wish you could sleep with us sometimes Ted, but I don't know whether Fannie would quite like it yet and I doubt I could press it on her anyway. Still I often think how nice it would be if we three could only love each other so that we might sleep together sometimes without feeling there was anything wrong in doing so. Dearest Ted, I often think about you whole days when I'm at work and there are so many things I think of too that I should like to tell you and I never can."[100]

In fact Hukin proved Carpenter's most reliable working class friend, holding the socialist fort in Sheffield when Carpenter was away and most crucially protecting Carpenter's reputation when a mad Irishman, M. D. O'Brien, spread slanderous rumors in the autumn of 1908. They never ceased to correspond when they were apart. He went on working with his brother in the razor trade till retirement in 1910, only to die prematurely, at the age of fifty-seven from asthmatic troubles, no doubt work related, March 1917. Hukin was bisexual at best, possibly not even that, and Carpenter was always at risk of impossible love objects.

In the end he had to settle for the less attractive but more compliant George Merrill They met in the winter of 1889 but he was not to move in as housekeeper at Millthorpe till George Adams and his wife had moved out, in 1898. The late 1880s, seen by Tsuzuki as a rather mysterious period in Carpenter's life, was clearly one of considerable anguish.

Did Carpenter deceive himself about the tolerance and generosity of the working class, often notoriously prejudiced against homosexuality? Not all socialist leaders were ready to go along Carpenter's route. When he pressed on Robert Blatchford along with *Civilization* some radical literature on sexual reform, Blatchford demurred: "I am radical but the whole subject is 'nasty' to me. Be charitable. I can't help it."[101]

Hiatus

So there remained a personal crisis. Socialism had proved to be a god that failed. Carpenter was increasingly ill at ease in a movement shaping up for a power struggle. In many ways he was a rural romantic, a back to nature advocate, both living and thinking against the grain of a unionizing, urban socialist movement. He had yet to work out any long-term solution to his homosexuality. Did Vedantism have the answer? "I sometimes think," he confessed to Oates, "that I shall go off to India or some distant region before long—not for good—but to renovate my faith and unfold the frozen buds wh. civilization and fog have nipped."[102] The time had come to accept the long extended invitation to join his Sri Lankan friend, Arunachalam, and to visit the East.

Notes

1. Only Annie Besant is his rival but she took up Hinduism much later in life.
2. Keith Nield, ed., Tony Brown, *Edward Carpenter and Late Victorian Radicalism* (London: Cass, 1990), 17.

3. The point of departure for research on Carpenter has to be two bibliographical essays by Tony Brown, "Figuring in History: The Reputation of Edward Carpenter, 1883–1987." Annotated Secondary Bibliography 1 and 11 *English Literature in Transition* 32, no. 1 (1989); 32 no. 2 (1989).

4. e.g., Noel Greig, ed. *Edward Carpenter Selected Writings Vol 1 Sex* (London: Gay Modern Classics, 1984).

5. Sheila Rowbotham's account in Sheila Rowbotham and Jeffrey Weeks, *Socialism and the New Life: the Personal and Sexual Politics of Edward Carpenter and Havelock Ellis* (London: Pluto Press, 1997) is the most sympathetic account but is more of an interpretative essay than a biography. Chushichi Tsuzuki's *Edward Carpenter 1844–1929: Prophet of Human Fellowship* (Cambridge: Cambridge University Press, 1980) concentrates rather too narrowly on his involvement in the socialist movement. The fullest account of his response to Hinduism comes in Dilip Kumar Barua, *Edward Carpenter 1844–1929. An Apostle of Freedom* (Burdwan: University of Burdwan, 1991). First submitted as a doctorate, Shefffield, 1966.

6. Quoted in A. D. Brown, *The Personal and Social Ideals of E. M. Forster and Edward Carpenter* (Unpublished PhD, University of Bangor, 1982). I am indebted to the author for permission to consult and make use of the thesis.

7. Edward Carpenter, *My Days and Dreams* (London: Allen and Unwin, 1916), 42–44, 106.

8. Carpenter to Havelock Ellis, 2 May 1888. Carpenter Correspondence, Austin, Texas.

9. Case study VII in Havelock Ellis, *Sexual Inversion Vol II Studies in the Psychology of Sex 3rd edn Philadelphia: 1922*, 107–8.

10. Carpenter, *My Days and Dreams*, 14.

11. This is explored in a suggestive way by Theo Aronson, *Prince Eddy and the Homosexual Underworld* (London: John Murray, 1994). Not only was Dalton clearly very attracted to Carpenter personally, there is considerable circumstantial evidence that the prince was himself homosexual. And Dalton's son, Hugh Dalton, a future Labour Chancellor, 1945 onwards, shared Carpenter's ideal of comradeship.

12. Carpenter, *My Days and Dreams*, 49.

13. Tony Brown, Thesis, 30.

14. Carpenter, *My Days and Dreams*, 64.

15. Dated 12 July 1873 Quoted Tsuzuki, 29–31.

16. Tsuzuki, 32.

17. For biographical information and commentary on Walt Whitman I have relied on Justin Kaplan, *Walt Whitman: A Life* (New York: Simon Schuster, 1980) and David S. Reynolds, *Walt Whitman's America: A Cultural Biography* (New York: Knopf, 1995).

18. Edward Carpenter, *Days with Walt Whitman* (London: George Allen, 1906), 4.

19. In a letter to his mother's friend, Abby Price, quoted Kaplan, 347.

22. Kaplan, 355.

21. Traubel. Quoted Harold Blodgett, *Walt Whitman in England* (New York: Russell and Russell, 1934, reissued 1973), 202.

22. How one admirer. John Burroughs saw him, in Kaplan's paraphrase, 15.

23. Kaplan, 39.

24. Kaplan, 19.

25. These are all quotations from Carpenter, *Days with Walt Whitman*.

26. Kaplan, 255.

27. Harold Blodgett, *Walt Whitman in England*.

28. Harold Blodgett, *Walt Whitman in England*, 201

29. Kaplan, 198.

30. Kaplan, 323.

31. Quoted Kaplan, 325.

32. For a concise account of American transcendentalism see J. J. Clarke, *Oriental Enlightenment: the Encounter between Asian and Western Thought* (London: Routledge, 1997), 84–7. Oddly there is no reference in this text to Carpenter.

33. Carpenter, *Days with Walt Whitman*, 163.

34. Carpenter, *Days with Walt Whitman*, 43–4.

35. Reynolds, *Walt Whitman's America*, 258.

36. Carpenter, *Days with Walt Whitman*, 76–7.

37. Carpenter, *Days with Walt Whitman*, 85.

38. Reynolds, *Walt Whitman's America*, 257.

39. In a letter 19 August 1890, quoted Kaplan, 47.

40. And here I am largely following Reynolds's account.

41. Carpenter dealt with the rumour of Whitman's six children—so he claimed to Symonds—by accepting that the poet did have female liaisons, one in particular—"both sexes seem to come equally within the scope of his love"—but after aged forty-five or so his affections were all male-directed. See Carpenter, "Walt Whitman's Children." *The Reformer* VI, no. 38, 87–93 MSS Carpenter C Per 106.

42. See his essay on Whitman in *The New Spirit* (London: 1890).

43. Carpenter, *My Days and Dreams*, 107.

44. In a letter to Olive Schreiner. Quoted Tsuzuki, 61.

45. Havelock Ellis to Carpenter 29 October 1885, MSS 357/2.

46. All these are references from Carpenter, *Towards Democracy*. First published 1883 but to undergo several further editions and expansion. All references here and hereafter to the London: 1912 edition.

47. Brown, *Edward Carpenter*, 55.

48. See Walt Whitman, *Complete Poetry and Collected Prose* (New York: Literary Classics of the United States, 1982) for his *Democratic Vistas*, 930–92.

49. Carpenter, *My Days and Dreams*, 106.

50. Carpenter, *Towards Democracy*, 13.

51. Carpenter, *Towards Democracy*, 87.

52. Carpenter, *Towards Democracy*, 66.

53. Carpenter, *Towards Democracy*, 108.

54. Carpenter, *Towards Democracy*, 346.

55. Carpenter, *Towards Democracy*, 29.

56. Carpenter, *Towards Democracy*, 141.

57. Carpenter, *Towards Democracy*, 394.

58. See Scott McKracken, "Writing the Body," in Tony Brown ed., *Edward Carpenter and Late Victorian Radicalism*, 184–89.

59. The poem in *Towards Democracy* "Hafiz to the Cup-Bearer," 416–17, is addressed to his new lover, George Merrill.

60. Carpenter to Havelock Ellis, 20 March 1889, Carpenter Correspondence, Humanities Research Centre, University of Texas. Austin.

61. Carpenter to Havelock Ellis, 4 October 1891, Carpenter Correspondence.

62. E. P. Thompson, *William Morris: Romantic to Revolutionary* (first published 1955, Whitstable: Merlin Press, 1977), 297.

63. Carpenter to Havelock Ellis, 1887 nd, Carpenter Correspondence.

64. Carpenter to Havelock Ellis, 7 March 1890, Carpenter Correspondence.

65. Tsuzuki, *Edward Carpenter*, 62.

66. Quoted in Stehen Yeo, "A New Life: The Religion of Socialism in Britain 1883–1890," *History Workshop* 4, (Autumn 1977), 29.

67. Stephen Yeo, "A New Life," 12.

68. Thompson, *William Morris*, 143.

69. Thompson, *William Morris*, 243.

70. Thompson, *William Morris*, 290.

71. Edward Carpenter, *England's Ideal* (1st published 1884, London: Swan Sonnenschein and Co., 1895), 17.

72. Carpenter to Havelock Ellis, 16 January 1886.

73. Carpenter to Havelock Ellis, 16 January 1886, 89.

74. Stephen Yeo, "A New Life," 14.

75. Barua, *Edward Carpenter*, 72. Edward Maitland had been a friend of Carpenter's father. Carpenter writes at some length about Maitland and Anna Kingsford in his autobiography and clearly held them in some regard but in the end was alienated by Anna Kingsford's absurd claims as a prophetess. In this regard he compared her to Madame Blavatsky. Carpenter often kept uncomfortable company. See Carpenter, *Days and Dreams*, 240–45.

76. Carpenter, *Days and Dreams*, 14, 29, 32.

77. Stanley Pierson. "Edward Carpenter, Prophet of a Socialist Millennium," *Victorian Studies* 13, (1969–1970).

78. Lewis Morgan, *Ancient Society or Researches in the Line of Human Progress from Savagery through Barbarism to Civilisation* (first published New York: 1877. A reprint, New York: Gordon Press, 1976).

79. Lewis Morgan, *Ancient Society*, 85.

80. Lewis Morgan, *Ancient Society*, 554.

81. Lewis Morgan, *Ancient Society*, 552.

82. First published London: 1889.

83. Harry Gerschenowitz, "Two Lamarckians: Walt Whitman and Edward Carpenter," *Walt Whitman Quarterly Review* 2(1) (Summer 1984), 35–39.

84. Carpenter, *Civilisation: Its Cause and Cure* (London: Swan Sonnenschein, 1891), 60.

85. Carpenter, *Civilisation*, 14.

86. Carpenter, *Civilisation*, 44.

87. Tariq Rahman, "The Alienated Prophet: The Relationship between Edward Carpenter's Psyche and the Development of his Metaphysic," *Forum for Modern Language Studies* XXIII, no. (3 July 1987).

88. Pierson, 303.

89. Carpenter to Oates, 28 October 1886, Edward Carpenter papers, Sheffield Archives. MSS 351/36.

90. Carpenter to Oates, 20 December 1886, MSS 351/37.

91. Carpenter to Oates, 10 April 1887, MSS 351/38.

92. Carpenter to Oates, 27 August 1887, MSS 351/42.

93. Carpenter to Oates, 17 February 1888, MSS 351/45.

94. Hukin to Carpenter, 8 July 1886, MSS 362/1.

95. Hukin to Carpenter, 28 October 1886, MSS 362?5.

96. Carpenter to Havelock Ellis, 27 October 1986, MSS Austin, Texas.

97. Hukin to Carpenter, 21 May 187, MSS 362/10,

98. Hukin to Carpenter, 24 May 1887, MSS 362/11.

99. Hukin to Carpenter, 1 June 1887, MSS 362/13.

100. Hukin to Carpenter, 21 November 1887, MSS 361/16.

101. Quoted Pierson, 313.

102. Carpenter to Oates, 23 February 1890, MSS 351/53.

CHAPTER TWO

~

Between Two Gurus:
Edward Carpenter and
Ilakkanam the Grammarian

He set out from Genoa on his journey east for Colombo in October 1890 on the Norddeutcher Lloyd steamer *Kaiser Wilhelm*, arriving on the 31st. He was to spend some three months in Sri Lanka, almost two in India. His longest stay in any one place was with his friend Arunachalam in Kurunegela—he was its District Judge—some fifty miles north of Colombo. Here was his meeting, and the reason for his visit to Sri Lanka, with his *gnani* or guru, Ramaswamy or Ilakkanam the Grammarian. On 1 January he climbed the sacred mountain, Adam's Peak and then undertook the usual cultural circuit of the north, Dambulla and Anuradhapura, though not Polonnarawu and Sigirija. In late January, by steamer from Colombo, he crossed to Tuticorin and embarked on a quite ambitious tour of India, taking in the great temples at Madurai, Tanjore and Chidambaram en route to Madras. On 6 February 1891 he reached Calcutta by boat and then proceeded to Benares, thence to Allahabad—where he met friends of his late brother,—to Delhi, to Aligarh—where he met up with Theodore Beck—to Agra and so, on his way out, to Bombay. He left early March in the SS Siam. All this is described in a not inconsiderable piece of travel writing, *From Adam's Peak to Elephanta*, in its turn to exercise a major influence over Forster's personal and literary response to India.

Quite clearly his preference was for Sri Lanka over India. This was partly just a question of time. As he put it to his friend Kate Salt:

Nations, races, languages, creeds, customs and manners are whirling in my brain. I just realize what an immense place India is. I also realize how difficult it is for the mere current(?) traveler to see into the real life of the people. I saw much more of that in Ceylon in staying in one place.

And the landscape was also in Sri Lanka's favor:

> The country (as far as I have seen it) is not half so beautiful as Ceylon—parched and brown, and even the trees look dwindled for want of water. No doubt it is different in the hills but I have only seen the plains.[1]

But it went deeper, with a preference for the more open, spontaneous Sinhalese,[2] their freedom from the constraints of caste, in contrast to the "severity" of India, both of its climate and its people: "but here such barriers, such a *noli-me-tangere* atmosphere," between Muslim and Hindu, between both and the English.[3]

Apart from a visit to Morocco in 1903[4] this brief exploration of the subcontinent was Carpenter's only encounter with non-European cultures. Inevitably the post-colonialist question has been raised, did he respond as an Orientalist?[5]

Carpenter journeyed as a seeker. He sought answers both to his mystical quest and to his sexuality. One could emphasize one over the other: Barua does so for the mystical, Bakshi for the sexual. Yet they were clearly inextricably linked. In some ways Carpenter seemingly denigrated South Asian culture in describing it as "primitive" and this would suggest Carpenter the orientalist. But as Tariq Rahman notes[6] this is to miss the point that Carpenter used the concept "civilized" almost as a term of abuse and when he describes his Indian guru as a "pre-civilization man of a very high type"[7] he was in fact paying him a compliment. In the tension between tradition and modernity, be it east and west, India and empire, and probably Carpenter did not grasp those modernizing tendencies imbedded within Indian tradition, Carpenter came down, though there was ambivalence, on the side of tradition. He did so through discovering in the Vedantism he learnt from Ilakkanam the Grammarian confirmation of his sense of some cosmic expression of consciousness and because in Hinduism he found, or so he believed, a sacramental regard for sex. Does this make him an orientalist?

During his visit Carpenter both sought out new intimate friends and continuously assessed the erotic appeal of those he saw. Does this also make him as Bakshi suggests a sexual colonialist? Surely it would have been far more racially discriminatory had Carpenter *not* looked for friendship with Sri Lankan and Indian males in just the way he did amongst the northern working-class. Rather more worryingly, Carpenter seemingly subscribed to a colonialist view of the effeminacy of the Sinhalese and Indian male—most notoriously, the charge that the raj brought against the Bengali *babus*—but this again would be to miss the point, for Carpenter here was trying to see in South Asians examples of the urning or uranian, of that feminine sensibility within a male body, seen as the future of the human race (besides being one himself), and here was another hidden form of flattery. Indeed, increasingly Carpenter came to see uranians or the third sex as a kind of elite. Bakshi's conclusion is worth quoting: "While many homosexual writers in nineteenth-century English literature counterposed the Orient against the Occident, and paganism and classicism against Christianity, Carpenter ultimately tries to bridge the individualism of the West with the emotional and sexual energies of the East."[8] But this is to anticipate.

Connections with India

His Brother Charles

Carpenter's only family connection with India was through his seven years older brother, Charles Wilson. He joined the Bengal Civil Service in 1857. He was to die young, but thirty-six, 3 March 1876, as a result of a riding accident. It had been a career of considerable promise. And clearly he had been ambitious: letters home to his mother indicate the store he set on a personal meeting with the Governor-General, John Lawrence, even to the extent of considering changing his name to Lawrence and posing as his fourteenth cousin. Service was initially in the North Western Provinces, dispatched to Roorkee to acquire engineering skills: he asked his father to send him a simple book on road building. He was then appointed settlement officer in Bijnor (replacing Auckland Colvin, interestingly Lieutenant-Governor of the province at the time of Carpenter's visit and they met); in April 1873 appointed Magistrate in Allahabad, in a rare combination jointly its District and Settlement officer. He sat on the Poona Ryots Commission. In 1874 he was promoted to Acting Commissioner of the Central Provinces, based at Jubbulpore, "sound, cool and deliberate" according to his obituarist and with a reputation as "one of the first men of the first flight of the service;" "a typical English gentleman" "none more absolutely reliable in the conduct of public business." There was every prospect of his being confirmed as Chief Commissioner.[9]

Did any of this rub off on the young Edward? Clearly at Brighton College he had looked up to his brother as something of a schoolboy hero. But their correspondence suggests that Charles had little insight into his younger brother's real feelings. He wrote from India of the importance of playing games and physical fitness. He worried that a choice of Mathematics at Cambridge over Classics was a mistake, for Mathematics was too abstract a discipline and of little practical use whereas Classics set one up better to become a man of society. Maybe, he conceded, the Church would suit Edward as a career but he still held out the possibility of his entering business. However, he came to recognize that he was probably on a quite different wavelength to his clever academic brother.[10] Charles's premature death did not greatly disturb Carpenter: "it will be a terrible shock to my people at home," he wrote to Oates, "it is less sad for me, for of late years his absence has made him a comparative stranger and before he went I was too young to be his companion."[11] Even so, Barua feels Charles might have had some influence over his response to India. Unusually, Charles had seen 1857 as promise of some positive new beginning in India's history: "the elder brother must have communicated to Edward Carpenter some of his warmth of interest in the future of India."[12]

Cambridge Friends

Two Cambridge friends, Harold Cox and Theodore Beck, were in India in the 1880s, both at the Anglo-Oriental College, Aligarh, Cox as its Professor of Mathematics, 1885–1887, Beck as its Principal, 1883–1899. It was Cox who sent him those Kashmiri sandals, Carpenter to become somewhat notorious as promoter of this footwear. George Adams made them, some hundred a year at Millthorpe. Whereas Cox had started out the progressive, participating, together with Lowes Dickinson, in another of those experimental utopian agrarian communities at Tilford in Surrey, but then turned illiberal on his return from India, Beck opened up the prospect in his *Essays on Indian Topics* (1888) of greater friendship between European and Indian. And, indeed, Carpenter found Aligarh during his visit "a striking example of a *rapprochement* between the rulers and the ruled." Both Cox and Beck had, he claimed, brought those attached to the College, the boys and their parents, into friendly relations with the Civilians. Carpenter did, however, fall back on the conventional colonial belief that their was some natural kinship between the Muslim Indian and the Europeans: "there is something in the Mohammedan, with his love of action and dogmatic sense of duty which makes him more akin to the Englishman than is the philosophical and supple-minded Hindu."[13] But a Cambridge friendship of far greater consequence was with Arunachalan, whom Carpenter met when he was a student at Christ's College in the 1870s.

Ponnanbalam Arunachalam

To an extent Arunachalam played the same role in Carpenter's life that Masood was to do in Forster's (see below). They were both to be crucial catalysts in arousing an interest in South Asia. There was no sexual element in Carpenter's friendship with Arunachalam, however and his role lay in leading Carpenter into a deeper interest in Hindu culture. But there was always affection. To his lesbian companion, Kate Salt from Kurenegala he wrote: "Arunachalam is a most bright and sympathetic creature, has a very gentle darkee wife who talks ever so pretty and three lively children," all speaking detestable Tamil.[14] In his memorial volume on Arunachalam he wrote of "a surprising rapidity of thought," "a certain almost elfish spirit of chaff and opposition." He went on to speculate that such independence of mind characterized the Tamils as a whole. "For the Tamils, indeed as a people, I have always felt a strange sympathy and admiration. Their perception of the occult and the Magical is quite remarkable."[15]

It is all too easy and misleading to characterize Arunachalam as representative of Sri Lanka's westernized elite that was to dominate the island's national politics till independence. Its Tamil constituent at the time prevailed over its Sinhalese. Jeyaratnam Wilson writes of the years 1879–1948 as "the halcyon days of the Tamil middle and upper classes."[16] Certainly in terms of a style of politics Arunachalam comes across as a politician in the Gokhale rather than the Tilak mould, more the Moderate than the Extremist. But he shared Tilak's hostility to the 1892 Age of Consent Act: if it was no doubt better, he reasoned with Carpenter, for Tamil Vellalas to postpone marriage, "it is impolitic to force social reform on the people unless grave abuse exists, which has not been proved."[17] Behind this constitutional political facade lay a tormented quest to rediscover his cultural roots, both Tamil and Hindu, and it was this largely religious pursuit that was to have so profound an influence on Carpenter.

Born 14 September 1853, youngest of three sons of Ponnanbulam Modaliyar, he and his brother Ramanathan were to tower over the politics of the Legislative Council in the first two decades of the twentieth century.[18] Here was a constitutional politics set in motion by the Bentinck-style reforms of William Colebroke and Charles Cameron in the 1830s, introducing a common system of law, the spread of English education and the setting up of the Executive and Legislative Councils.[19] In taking up a place at Christ's College, Cambridge in 1870 to study Classics and Mathematics he was but following a pattern set by two sons of Mudaliyar de Saram going to Trinity College in 1811; he was to be awarded its Foundation scholarship. Subsequently he qualified as a Barrister at Lincoln's Inn. In 1875 he was to be the first Sri Lankan to enter the island's Civil Service by competitive examination. Quickly he was to reveal his progressive views, influencing his English friend William Digby into writing an article, An Oriental Colony Ripe for Self-Government, for *The Calcutta Review* January 1871. (This was the same

William Digby who wrote one of the most favorable reviews of *Towards De-mocracy*).[20] Arunachalam joined the Judicial branch, but it was those same liberal views that got him into trouble, this time his advocating the intro-duction of Ripon's local self-government reforms to the island, and as pun-ishment he was dispatched as District Judge from Colombo to Kurunegala. His highest post was to be Registrar-General though at one stage he was re-ferred to as the Unofficial Police Magistrate for the whole island: in Jeyarat-nam Wilson's assessment, here was "by any standard a civil servant of the first rank."[21] He had also become involved in educational reform. In January 1906 he initiated the University Association, in time to lead to the University of Ceylon. He resigned from the Civil Service in 1913.

In the meanwhile his career had become more overtly political. Here the Gokhale in him and the anglicized does seem to predominate. As one com-mentator puts it of the politics of the Legislative Council, here was "a search for a greater share in the administration rather than any wish to govern themselves;" "the native counterpart of the oligarchical class rule of the Eu-ropean."[22] In 1906 he was nominated to the Legislative Council, in 1912 ap-pointed to the Executive Council, and in 1913 knighted.

But there were alternative currents, possibly influenced by Carpenter, cer-tainly by way of reaction to the government's high-handed response to labor unrest in 1915 with its imposition of martial law. He became increasingly ac-tive in labor organizations: 29 January 1915, for example, he inaugurated the Ceylon Social Service League. This had a Carpenterish concern with village cottage industries and cooperative credit. In June 1919 in association with the Gandhian C. F. Andrews he set up the Ceylon Worker's Welfare League, actively concerned with the conditions of Tamil workers on the plantations. Clearly his was an active retirement. After quite a long break in their corre-spondence, he wrote in a letter on 29 August 1917 to Carpenter: "I have got entangled in various social and political activities and have not had the rest I had looked forward to when I retired from the Civil Service. What with the general mismanagement by Government, resulting in frightful oppression and misery during the years 1915 and 1916 and innocent people shot down like game and with the hopeful spirit of liberty brought by the war, politics looms much in view."[3]

And politics were uppermost. This was all a part of the fall-out from Sec-retary of State Montagu's visit in 1917. There was Arunachalam's keynote speech, Our Political Needs, 2 April 1917 to the Ceylon Reform League. Whilst recognizing the benefits of colonial rule, both economic and educa-tional, he insisted on a greater Sri Lankan representation in both the admin-istration and government. But his appeal was also interestingly Vedantist: "I look to youth to spiritualize public life. They will each seek his own well-being in the well-being of all, will identify his own life with the life of all, and his own interest with the interest of all."[24] Here were overtones of Carpenter's own faith in some kind of spiritualized democracy. Arunachalam was to be unanimously elected the first President of the Ceylon National Congress, inaugurated 11 December 1919.

But then it all fell apart. In the new territorial arrangements of the 1920s the elite failed in its promise to select Arunachalam for the seat for the western provinces: the Jaffna Tamils, where he sought alternative support, were to laugh him out of court. He was to die—on a pilgrimage to Madurai, 9 January 1924—a disappointed man, convinced, as Wilson puts it "that he had been let down by the Sinhalese political elite." His brother, Ramanathan, died in 1930. The Tamils are seen as entering 1924–1934 "a slough of despond," the Arunachalam/Ramanathan family "in many ways irreplaceable."[25] But behind this political history lay a cultural, both in terms of Arunachalam's search for his own cultural identity and, more disturbingly, a growing cultural divide between Tamil and Sinhalese.

The prospect of returning to Sri Lanka after Cambridge had filled him with disquiet. "I shall find absolutely no sympathy or friendship" he worried "Not that," he continued in his letter to Carpenter, "I have had much real sympathy or friendship in England except from you. I shall miss your friendly interest in me most of anything I have experienced in England." Would that he could stay in England to let this mature.[26] Carpenter sketched how they had first met at some discussion society in Cambridge, the young Arunachalam quick to assimilate English ways and clearly popular with his fellow undergraduates. "Altogether he was a very taking, all-round sort of fellow," Carpenter recalled, "capable of taking on most subjects, and full of interesting inquiry about all."[27] In fact, quite quickly on his return he began to reject his western conditioning and rediscover his Sri Lankan roots, to a degree Buddhist, but mainly Hindu and Tamil.

The Tamil bit came last and in part reflects that fissure opening up by the 1920s within the island's elite. Arunacahalam had always been concerned with the island's past: he was to be the first Sri Lankan President of its Royal Asiatic Society. Initially questions of language and religion had not concerned the elite. And it's hard to say at what point anyone foresaw the communal nightmare which lay ahead after independence. Arunachalan himself became increasingly caught up with Tamil literature. He translated the Tamil classics. But when he commented to Carpenter on the need to protect this tradition it was still in terms of a colonial conflict, out of a fear of its being neglected "in the rage for English," of a need to safeguard "some of the spiritual atmosphere of the East from the material western civilization:" "the asuras (Titans) of our legends must have been of the same type of civilization and after long periods of splendor came to utter grief like these modern nations."[28] When Arunachalam set up the Ceylon Tamil league in 1923 he did so still in the hope of a rapprochement with the Sinhalese.

Did Carpenter have any foresight here? He was certainly aware of communal antagonism. The Tamils seemed to have it over the Sinhalese, the Tamils seen as "more enterprising, pushing and industrious people than the Cinghalese." His instinctive preference was for the Tamil over the Sinhalese.[29] But he did not foresee the fratricide to come.

Arunachalam's interest in Buddhism seems to have been a passing phase. In a letter to Carpenter of 1880 he wrote of "a going out of his way to understand Buddhism." In part he was inspired to do so by the leaders of the Theosophical Society, Colonel Olcott and Madame Blavatsky, who had taken up Buddhism and he delighted in their spat with Christian mission, a conflict that would bring home to Sri Lankans, he felt, that not all Europeans were Christian and persuade a few that Indian religions "are worth studying and even embracing."[30]

Carpenter likewise tended to marginalize Buddhism in his greater involvement with Hinduism. Visits to the sacred sites in the north were to prompt somewhat negative observations, mainly by way of contrasting the greatness of Buddha himself with the decadence of his present day followers. Even so, he concluded: "we must forgive, after all, the dirty, yellow robed priests, with their greedy claws and stinking shrines. It was Buddha's fault, not theirs, when he explored poor human nature so deeply as to invest even its lowest manifestations with sanctity."[31]

But a rediscovery of Hinduism was always the most potent element in Arunachalam's cultural revivalism. He wrote of re-entering his grandfather's little domestic chapel, commenting on its lack of idols: "you must remember," he told Carpenter, "Hinduism is the most complex religion in the world: it is mainly pantheistic." He recalled his grandmother instructing him in prayers to Parvati and Siva.[32] Unfortunately, Arunachalam mislaid his letters from Carpenter during the 1880s and we do not know how he responded to Arunachalam's ever strengthening Hinduism during this decade. It was all to be profoundly enhanced by his meeting with Ramasawamy or Ilakkanam the Grammarian (where or when is not made clear but one must suppose it was during a pilgrimage in 1888 to Tanjore and it was then that he had invited Carpenter to Sri Lanka) and from that point on Arunachalam did everything possible to draw Carpenter more deeply into his spiritual life. By 18 November 1888 he could write to Carpenter: "I believe it is possible for man, if ripe

enough, to see God and be one with him while yet imprisoned in the body."
Now he would undo twenty years of English conditioning: "in my folly be-
gotten of the arrogance of the material west, and my impatience of forms and
ceremonies that I did not understand, (which) I made light of . . . it is a great
grief to me that I begin to see the light so late in life. Will the body last or
this new-born zeal till I reach the goal?"[33] Here was a spiritual teacher Carpenter had to meet and he continued: "your life seems to have been a prepa-
ration for the high stages from which the ordinary run of mankind must qual-
ify by the observation of rites, forms, injunctions of the esoteric religion of
the Hindus. You of all friends are most ripe. So come out to the East and seek
the truth. You must work out your evolution with the zeal of a hero and you
will see the truth when you are ripe for it." (Clearly Arunachalam has shifted
his loyalties from a ritualized Hinduism to Vedantism.)

All this was playing havoc with his judicial duties though in the end he
got leave to follow his guru back to Tanjore. From there he wrote to Carpenter again: "You are steadily working your way to Saivism, the essence of
the ancient religion of India, in comparison with which other religions are
mere child's play and trifling" (a rather worrying sign of incipient Hindu triumphalism). And here he had to sort out some of Carpenter's misconcep-
tions: "I have no doubt whatsoever in my mind from your last work *Civilization* that Saivism—which by the way is not Buddhism as you think, nor any
other ism but is above and beyond all isms and is your destined goal and that
it alone harmonizes your now conflicting theories and your ideals with your
practice." Here was the means to overcome Civilization's disease and recover
health: "you pine for health but will not seek the healer." But he fell back on
that essential claim of Vedantism, that it can only be won "by actual self-
experience": "that true equality which is far and away and beyond that thing
westerners like children at play dignify by the name of equality."

But the intervention of the guru was crucial. "I never realized till I met the
Master what difference there is between reading books and having them explained to you by one who knows." Without a teacher Carpenter could not
hope to understand the Upanishads and the Tamil texts; even so, "confirmation of the teacher's experience by your own experience 'was' essential to a
true understanding of them. Till then talking is mere beating the air, as I am
now doing." Arunachalam, however, retained a degree of skepticism, accepting, with a reference to his guru's guru, "for one such genuine seer there are of
course hundreds of characters in India living on the credulity of the people."[34]

Carpenter was won over, even if sexual imperatives underlay the spiritual.
But who was the guru that had so profoundly affected Arunachalam and was
to exercise so considerable a spell on Carpenter?

Illakanam the Grammarian

It was in many ways an encounter long in the making. As Carpenter put it: "during the years '80 to '90 there was a great deal of Theosophy and Oriental philosophy of various sorts current in England and much talk and speculation, sometimes very ill-founded, about 'adepts,' 'mahatmas' and 'gurus.' I too felt a great desire to see for myself one of these representatives of the ancient wisdom."[35] His encounter was to be with a practitioner of *jnana* (what he implied by his term *gnani*) rather than a *karma* yogi, a contemplative rather than an activist.

Again Carpenter's encounter with Vedantism had been long in the making. As early as 1873 in a letter to Oates he had been circling round Vedantist concepts, however inaccurately, writing of "a crack down all creation," but one which Indian philosophy could only answer by Nirvana or retirement.[36] Here was an early example of his search for a unitive experience. Barua makes serious claims for his having already grasped Vedantism by the time of writing *Towards Democracy*, its incorporating whole chapters of the *Gita*, the poem a searching exploration of mysticism, not so much, as Barua puts it, "the vision of social revolution but of self-revelation."[37] Carpenter was indeed "ripe" as Arunachalam suggested for the encounter.

We should begin with the guru's own guru, Tilleinathan Swami (Tillinathan Swami), an altogether more histrionic figure than his disciple. It was a not unfamiliar story of a man of wealth—in this case a wealthy ship owner and a parallel might be drawn with Vivekananda's wealthy lawyer father—who kicks over the traces and after a period of reflection—in Tilleneithan's case between 1850 and 1855—abandons a privileged life and becomes a man of God—Tilleneithan "went off stark naked into the woods." Carpenter listed his reappearances in Tanjore, 1857, 1859, 1864 and 1872, then his disappearance: "he is supposed to be living somewhere in the Western Ghauts."[38]

But his spiritual rebellion coincided with a political. Not only was there the far-fetched possibility that here might be Nana Sahib, on the run since 1858 and allegedly in disguise as a holy man, it coincided with a quite serious Hindu protest movement in the south, significantly led by merchants. They were outraged at the betrayal, as they saw it, of the Company's guarantee of religious neutrality, its failure any longer to offer protection to Hindu religious institutions, together with its sanctioning of the intolerable presence of an aggressively proselytizing Christian Mission. So Tilleinathan was in 1859 to be investigated by the sub-magistrate at Kumbakonam and subsequently arraigned before the courts, with the Collector outraged at his nudity, only for Tilleneithan to brief him on the four asrams or stages of the

Hindu life and to threaten that, were he to fail to deliver justice, he would burn him. And maybe all along, as Arunacahalam suggested, a Victorian shock at nudity lay behind the arrest: "the English authorities of Kumbakonam true to national character worried the great man because he went about naked in the streets, but failing to make him give up his ways they let him alone."[39] But not before he was subject to a further threat of arrest in Tanjore. Once again Tilleneithan talked his way out of difficulty. In fact Hindu resistance was on the wane by 1859 and probably the colonial authorities had the sense to see that Tilleinathan was politically harmless.[40]

But here for Carpenter was a personality of positively Whitmanesque proportions. He was a hugely charismatic spiritual teacher, combining characteristically eccentric saintly behavior with real knowledge. Arunachalam described him as "a vigorous ascetic," "a magnificent specimen, physically of the Genus *homo*; a true king among men." If "to outward appearance a madman . . . it was not the man speaking but the God within directly."[41] Here was social behavior in the Ramakrishna mold, his sharing his meals with pariah dogs and socializing with outcastes.

Ramaswamy was of an altogether more sober nature. Little is known of his background. In the past he had been friend and adviser to the Maharajah of Tanjore, and "was well up in traditional statecraft and politics." His expertise stretched to medicine and cookery. As Carpenter put it, he was "a man of good practical ability and acquaintance with the world;" "in fact it is one of the remarkable points of the Hindu philosophy that practical knowledge of life is expressly inculcated at a preliminary stage."[42] Arunachalam confirmed this description, "a vigorous practical intellect which finds no subject too great or too small, which handles thoroughly and masters everything it takes up—whether an abstruse problem of philosophy, an intricate law-suit or the cooking of some appetizing dish."[43] Somasundaram, Ramaswamy's younger son, describes the various moments of truth that led to his father's becoming a Master. First came a vision at the age of sixteen in the Chapel of God Maruga (the God of War and Wisdom, and one and the same as Subramania, and a part of the temple Carpenter was to visit) in the great temple in Tanjore. He dreamt that Maruga "placed his foot on my father's head, stroked it with his hand and rubbed ashes on it, and wrote letters on his tongue and graciously saying, 'we will come hereafter to initiate you' he disappeared." It would appear that out of this vision came Ramaswamy's expertise in Tamil grammar (and hence his name, the Grammarian, *Elukanham* a word for grammar) and knowledge of philosophy. And the actual initiation came from a chance encounter with Tilleinathan in the streets of Kambakonam, to be one of instant mutual recognition: as the son put it, "it is said in our peerless

Saiva Agamas that as soon as the teacher is *seen* or his voice is *heard* by those souls that are ripe they are drawn to him as iron to the magnet."[44]

Ramaswamy was a householder and married with two sons. Tilleinathan assured him that being a householder was compatible with the new lifestyle he was about to adopt. (Hinduism does not insist on celibacy for these spiritual vocations.) His guru stayed with him in his Tanjore home during the period of instruction in yogi. Half of this three-year period was to be spent in silence. And it became a family affair, even Ramaswamy's mother becoming in time her son's pupil. But the elder son, Samanathan, despite receiving Tilleinathan's blessing, was to rebel against his father's values. The younger, Somasundaram, however, submitted and was in time to become the guardian of his father's shrine; in Arunachalam's estimate, "very practical and sensible and helpful."[45]

Here was the man Carpenter was to spend more than a month with, in almost daily conversation, initially in the temple, later in Ramasawamy's bungalow, as well as on country roads or above the town of Kurenegala, walking Elephant Hill. Arunachalam recalled those conversations: "How shall I forget the gracious master and his walks along the country roads and discourses there: and in the house whose ceiling was such a battleground for rats and snakes; and that walk up the Rock with him and you—and we so outdistanced by him and so fatigued, and he so fresh and pouring forth living words."[46] But this was a walk too far for it was on Elephant Hill that the gnani caught the chill which was later to kill him.

As with his earlier guru, Walt Whitman, Ramasawamy's appearance was very important to Carpenter. In the asceticism of his face he saw joy, an access "to some interior source of strength and nourishment." Later, looking at a photograph of him taken in 1890 when he was seventy years old, Carpenter saw a man who looked scarcely forty: "'a brow absolutely calm and unruffled, gracious, expressive lips, well-formed features and eyes—the dominant characteristic of his countenance—dark and intense and illuminated by the vision of the seer." Then there was "his perfect simplicity of manner. Nothing could be more unembarrassed, unselfconscious, direct to the point in hand, free from kinks of any kind": "the same ease and grace and absence of self-consciousness that only the animals and a few human beings show."[47]

Would this man, so seemingly "detached from human and earthly entanglement," have a more attractive philosophy to teach him than the far more this-worldly and life-affirming of Whitman?

Ramaswamy belonged to a South Indian as opposed to Himalayan sect of adepts or gurus, seen in Carpenter's account as less democratic, more caste-minded, more brahminical. Here was a brotherhood of adepts who had retreated into the forests and hills around Tinnevelly, the agastya kutam, in

part to escape the deforestation of the raj. Their role was to popularize esoteric truths. From this milieu was to come one of the greatest of Indian spiritual teachers, Ramana Maharshi. Philosophically, Illakanam belonged to the
saiva-siddhanta system, the south's answer to the challenge of Buddhism and
Jainism, taken up by the Saivite saints, the *nayanars*, culminating in Sankara
(788–820). Subsequently in the early thirteenth century the Tamil saiva-
siddhanta philosophy, in one of its branches and the one Ramswamy adhered
to, was formally set out by Meykanda Deva. Here there was one of those hair-
splitting distinctions from Sankara's monism: "advaita is not oneness but inseparability."[48] And this was Saivism as opposed to Vaishnavism; as Sivanath
Sastri summarizes: "much more than the urbane cult of Vishnu it has exhib-
ited a close alliance with yoga and thaumaturgy, and a constant tendency to
run into the extreme of ascetic fervor."[49]

Carpenter had little patience with such philosophy: "all such systems are
hopelessly dull and may be said to carry their own death warrants on their
faces."[50] Ramaswamy's son, Somasundaram, was shocked by such a dismissive
comment. Carpenter had failed, he averred, to grasp Siddhantisim. He pointed
out that *siddhantam* translates as "determination" and so the Siddhantist philosophy, if followed correctly, "will make the student determinedly to be mixed
with the Universal being." But all this was part of his claim that a study of the
sacred texts would of itself, without the practice of yoga, lead to *gnaman* or enlightenment.[51] Carpenter would not have been persuaded by such textual
claims.

In fact Carpenter was to go to considerable lengths to get his mind round
this philosophy, however remote he felt the exercise to be: "I found it difficult to believe that I was in the end of the nineteenth century and not three
or four thousand years back among the sages of the Vedic race." He was as-
tonished to find "a man of so subtle intelligence and varied capacity calmly
asserting that the earth was the center of the physical universe and the sun
revolved around it."[52] And it bothered him that in the nature of the guru-
disciple relationship, in its balance of power, such ideas would be passed on:
"I can imagine it is difficult in some cases for the pupil to disentangle what
is authentically his own vision from that which he has merely heard." "The
whole system of teaching tends," he feared, "to paralyze activity on the
thought plane to such a degree that the spirit of healthy criticism has been
lost."[53]

Siddhantism parallels Vedantism and here was an opportunity for Carpenter to test out and strengthen his insights into the concept of consciousness. Barua writes of "the extreme lucidity" of his chapters on Ramaswamy's
thought in *From Adam's Peak*.[54] But Carpenter insisted on the problematic of

conveying such "old world knowledge" with any clarity: "it is probable nay certain that it is evolving and will evolve but slowly and many a slip and hesitant pause by the way."[55] Still, he felt himself in touch with some emergent higher consciousness: "it is more than probable that in the hidden birth of time there lurks a consciousness which is not the consciousness of sensation and which is not the consciousness of self—or, at least which includes and entirely surpasses these—a consciousness in which the contrast between the ego and the external world, and the distinction between subject and object, fall away."[56] Carpenter experienced just that same sense of discovery as Freud did when he stumbled on the unconscious. It is a consciousness open to all, even to those with "decidedly deficient or warped moral values" but by dint of a long training the teacher will lead the disciple to a cosmic consciousness, to sat-chit-ananda-Brahm. Carpenter contrasted the individual consciousness arrived at by thought in the west with this cosmic consciousness: "to attain the latter one must have the power of knowing oneself separate from the body, of passing into the state of ecstasy in fact."[57] He gave this the name of nirvana; more properly it should be samadhi. He struggled for a description: "a state of no consciousness or a state of vastly enhanced consciousness;" "the thing does not admit of definition in terms of ordinary language." But it exists: "people do not sacrifice their lives for empty words nor do mere philosophical abstractions rule the destinies of continents. No the word represents a reality, something very basic and inevitable in human nature."[58] In other words, the likes of Ramaswamy and generations of Indian mystics have not been wasting their time. Carpenter then proceeds tangentially to link this account of nirvana to the discovery of a secondary consciousness in western experiments in hypnotism and, less persuasively, to ideas of a fourth dimension.

Carpenter also picked up on what he saw to be a democratic content to Ramasawamy's outlook, however much Ramasamy deferred to caste conventions in his personal life. In the future, all such distinctions would fall away and there would be equality and democracy. Carpenter made more of this in a letter to Kate Salt: "the most intimate and esoteric teaching here is thoroughly democratic." If caste is retained for lower levels of consciousness, "it ultimately lays it aside completely—and such words as Freedom, Equality, Joy become the watchwords."[59] But this has the feel of special pleading. In rather the same way as Carpenter claimed guru Whitman as a socialist, so guru Ramaswamy was recruited as a democrat.

How to attain this higher consciousness? Carpenter warns against its abuse, the acquiring of powers over nature, the siddhi or miraculous powers: such were the ways of the inferior yogis. There were two alternative strategies, the mental and the moral. The mental was the tried and tested way of the jnana yogis. Here was an exceptional battle of the mind, initially with the suppression of thought, then the transcendence of oblivion (mindlessness) and so to *samadhi*: "it is incontestable that for centuries and centuries it has been an object of the most strenuous endeavor to vast numbers even of the very acutest and most capable intellects of India."[60] It can, and here Carpenter echoes all those who point to its dangers, go horribly wrong and simply end up "mutilating" the power of thought. But Carpenter was strongly attracted by such powers of concentration, with western man, as he saw him, "a mere slave and prey to the bat-winged phantoms that flit through the corridors of his brain."[61] (Language uncannily akin to those that Isherwood was to use.) And such concentrated thought brings one to the threshold of the mystical: "in the systemic or secondary or cosmic consciousness of man (I daresay these ought to be distinguished but I lump them together for the present) lurk the most minute and varied and far-reaching intuitions and perceptions."[62]

Carpenter's quarrel was with the "moral" approach, that alternative strategy for acquiring awareness of the Divine. The battle here was not with modes of Thought, but the role of Desire. Carpenter, of course, sought a philosophy which would legitimize his sexuality: to quote Tariq Rahman, "this quest for a metaphysic which would be spiritually satisfying, psychologically integrative and ethically exonerating took him to Hindu philosophy as well as other sources."[63] The unitive experience was also to affirm homosexual unions. Grudgingly, Carpenter conceded that diminution of sexual desire could enhance the quest for spiritual enlightenment. But there was a twist. Indian esoteric teachers, he argued, took the debate a stage further. "Any account of their methods would be defective," he added, "which passed over or blinked the fact that they go *beyond* the moral—because this fact is in some sense of the essence of the Oriental inner teaching."[64] Does Vedantism at this point, as Tariq Rahman suggests, veer towards nihilism? Is it beginning to question one basic foundation of morality, the concept of a sense of personal responsibility? Ramaswamy himself strongly insisted on a concept of non-differentiation: "you are not even to differentiate yourself in thought from others, you are not to begin to regard yourself as separate from them."[65] But where did that leave western concepts of altruism and philanthropy?

Here was an extreme solution for Carpenter's legitimizing his sexuality. Moral codes are transcended. And out of this moral nihilism came access to cosmic consciousness, and the beginnings of a whole new set of experiences. If individual self-consciousness was the source of so much experience, how much the more so would be the cosmic?

If all this constituted an attractive rejection of a stifling Victorian moral code it failed to address Carpenter's immediate personal needs. He found himself alienated from a Hindu value system which put so little emphasis on social compassion: "there is a certain quiescence and self-inclusion and absorbedness in the Hindu ideal, which amounts almost to coldness."[66] If he was ready to differentiate social compassion from "the specially individual and sexual and amatory love," such sexual love nevertheless remained at the heart of his concern. In the end he came to contrast an East with its prioritizing of the Will with a West with its emphasis on Love. But the end result would be the same. Through love there would be such an expansion of the self that it would burst out of its confines: "the life is poured out, and ceasing to be local, becomes universal."[67] One way or another Carpenter still sought the Divine.

In fact Carpenter had encountered Ramaswamy only just in time. He was to die from that fatal chill in early 1893. Arunachalam believed their encounter was but a beginning: "you are bound to come back here, if not now, hereafter, to go through the three years of discipline presented to you."[68] Ramasawamy had experienced some initial doubts at Carpenter publicizing his philosophy but thought twice. "You will be glad to know," Arunachalam informed him, "that the Master does not take the view I stated in my last letter as to the inexpediency of your publishing esoteric teaching. I was only repeating what he has often told me and I think you also at Kurenegala. But he evidently thinks the time has come for publication. Your book may, he thinks, help some ripe soul in sore need of such hints to reach the goal."[69] Somasundaram described the funeral arrangements. According to the rules of Tiruvaluvar's *Kural* the bodies of yogis and *gnanis* should not be cremated but laid in a cave, with the body in a *samadhi* posture. This was done in a garden near the family home. A lingam was placed above the ground where his head lay buried. In time a samadhi temple was built in his memory, Carpenter contributing to the costs, some 200 rupees for the tending of the garden alone. Arunachalam described it, "a simple brick building thatched with coco-nut leaf," though there were plans for a more substantial stone-roofed building. Somasundaram added fruit, flowers, and water to the garden.[70]

Hinduism

If prior to his journey Carpenter's interests had been narrowly Vedantist the visit opened up the prospect of a wider exposure to Hinduism and Carpenter proved to be an assiduous sightseer of temples and festivals. It was his way of commenting on Hinduism as a religion.

Temples in the north caught his imagination more than those in the south. The great gopurams of the southern temples, he felt, overshadowed their shrines. But Rajaraja 1's great temple in Tanjore impressed: "it is a very dignified and reposeful piece of work." But he grew very impatient with his guide and the patently untrue claim that it never threw a shadow.[71] Likewise the Minakshi temple at Madurai proved imposing: "a strange piece of work but having an impressive total effect."[72] But predatory brahmin priests demanding tips spoilt his enjoyment of the great Saivite temple at Chidambaram. He took to Benares: "the most characteristic and interesting town of India that I have hitherto seen." Here he encountered a yogi, admiring the simplicity of his life—he had even less furniture he noted than Thoreau at Walden Pond—but doubted his knowledge: "of any conscious religion and philosophy I don't think there was a spark in him." Nevertheless, he envied his way of life: 'I feel in looking at him the rare pleasure which one experiences in looking at a face without anxiety and without cunning." Cremation he deplored—"every sense is violated and sickened"—but liked the bathing, seeing here custom more than religion at work.[73] Muslim buildings came out the worse from any comparison. He was disappointed by the Jami Masjid mosque in Delhi: "there is no mysterious gloom anywhere . . . no suggestion of companionship human or divine . . . How different from Hinduism with its lingams and sexual symbols deified in the profound gloom of the temple's innermost recess."[74]

But the temple that prompted his most positive response—and here he anticipates Paul Scott's equally profound response in The Raj Quartet—was that of Elephanta outside Bombay: "this gave me a greater sense of artistic power and splendid purpose than anything in the way of religious architecture—be it mosque or Hindu temple—that I have seen in India." Those monumental three conjoined heads; Brahm, "the unrealizable and infinite God, the substratum of all;" Vishnu, the idea of Evolution, the unfolding of the inner spirit; Siva, involution, "by which thought and the sensible universe are indrawn again into quiescence;" together, "full of reserved power and dignity."[75] Intriguingly, despite the bisexual implications of his Uranian ideal, he was repelled by the explicitly bisexual statue of Siva.

One of the most vivid chapters of From Adam's Peak is Carpenter's description of the Saivite Taypusam (Tai Pacam) festival, celebrated during the full moon in January.[76] This he witnessed not in any of the great temples but a quite ordinary one, possibly in Kurenegala. The detailed account of the way the temple gods, Siva and Sakti, were floated out onto the temple tank and later paraded around its precincts undoubtedly did much to shape Forster's account of the Krishna festival in his Indian novel. But whereas Forster struggled to rise to the occasion Carpenter, rare among foreign observers, saw that this was superfluous and a false rhetoric, grasping the way it was all but a kind of social entertainment. "There was no piety in our sense of the word—or very little observable," he recognized, "they were just thoroughly enjoying themselves." The mood of the worshippers was "thoroughly whole-hearted." Here was "the pleasure of the theatre, the art-gallery, the music hall and the concert room in one." If he conceded that behind the ceremonies lay "inner and mystic meaning," over time much of this had been blurred, leading to "a total concrete result which no one theory can account for or coordinate." What, indeed, did the movements of the raft on the tank symbolize?

In the distance of the sanctum sanctorum Carpenter espied the lingam, together with the yoni, and he became ever more convinced that the worship of sex lay at the root of Hinduism, "as it does at the root of nearly all the primitive religions of the world." For Carpenter the whole experience was erotically charged, the oil from the flaming torches, for example, dropping onto naked backs: "the smell of hot coconut oil mingling with that of humanity made the air sultry." Admittedly, he was put off by the sad, inanimate faces of the temple dancers or *devadasis*. Nor was he enamored of the appalling sounds of the conch shells. If Tariq Rahman seems to stretch the evidence in suggesting that Ramaswamy himself became "a priest of love," here, quite clearly, sexual rapture and spiritual ecstasy did come together. "Sex itself, the most important of earthly functions," in Carpenter's words, "came to derive an even greater importance from its relation to the one supreme and heavenly fact, that of the soul's union with God."

And Carpenter had a very clear grasp of the significance of the camphor flame: "this burning of camphor is, like other things in the service, emblematic. The five lights represent the five senses. As camphor consumes itself and leaves no residue behind, so should the five senses, being offered to God, consume themselves and disappear." Here was an occasion when sexuality and religion converged.[77]

Sexuality and the Subcontinent

One can only guess at how sexually active Carpenter was in Sri Lanka and India.

On the way out he befriended a member of the lascar crew, the twenty-eight-year-old Sinhalese peasant, Kaludesaya (Kalua). As Carpenter reported to a friend, on board ship Kalua "came and sat with me last night in the bows of the ship."[78] He "was remarkably well made and active and powerful."[79] In his childhood, at the age of twelve or thirteen, he had been a devil dancer in the temple. No doubt through working for a German shipping line Kalua had picked up some of the German language and one could speculate that what drew him to Carpenter was a wish to keep in touch with this European part of himself. Together with a friend Carpenter set out from Kandy—it was but a mile away—to visit Kalua and his family, his elder brother Kirrah, likewise still single, and his father, "a regular jolly old savage, with broad face and broad belly." They scraped a living as rice farmers, housed together as an extended family in one hut, but twelve feet by eight. It all reminded Carpenter, as he described it in a letter to Oates, of their times in Italy, in particular of a visit to one Guido at Acqui: "we spent a delightful afternoon among the coconut groves and rice fields, talking broken English and Tamil, and a little German which Kalua had picked up when in Europe."[80] There was much that reminded him of Italy, he was to record, in the temperament of the people, "but the dark skins and the innumerable palm trees prevents any mistake." He worried that western influence would "soon destroy their naked beauty and naiveté."[81] Kalua was to be his travel companion, escorting him up and down the sacred mountain, Adam's Peak, and along the Kaluganga river. Carpenter commented on his "savage strength and insouciance."

Making friends proved more problematic in India. If there was an equivalent figure to Kalua in Calcutta it was Panna Lall, "a bright-mannered youth of about twenty, of a modest affectionate disposition and with a certain grace and dignity of bearing." He was the brother of a schoolmaster whose school for some thirty to forty boys Carpenter had visited. Panna Lal did not share his elder brother's bookish tastes, was musical, lived with his father but with a room of his own and here Carpenter would visit him and his friends. He was quite an athlete. Working out with his friends Carpenter observed, "their golden-brown skins and muscular bodies looked well when stripped." This was a time of course when Bengali youth had taken to sport and gymnastics. Vivekananda was a great wrestler in his youth.

Carpenter was an acute observer of physical appearance. When Panna Lal took off his ill-fitting patent leather shoes, a foolish gesture in Carpenter's book to western style, this allowed Carpenter to rhapsodize on the Indian male foot: "it is so broad and free and full and muscular, with a good concave curve in the inner line, and the toes standing well apart from each other, so different from the ill-nourished, unsightly thing we are accustomed to."[82] One wonders if Carpenter was aware of the Indian practice of *pranam*, touching feet as a mark of respect?

Panna Lall was to accompany him to Benares: as Carpenter put it to Kate Salt "he had nothing particular to do and he and I paid our respects to the Ganges. He bathed in the river and I sat on the steps watching the great crowd which continually goes to and from them."[83] But bystanders, after Panna Lall had taken his dip, "wanted to know whether I had come with him all this way on this pilgrimage out of friendship."[84] Indian curiosity often hits the mark.

In Bombay he finally made contact with an Indian working class, enjoying the company of some post-office, railway, and tram workers. Socializing led to political discussion and a frank exchange: "it struck me indeed," Carpenter reflected, "how much a few unpretending and friendly Englishmen might do to endear our country to the people."[85] Here was his ideal of comradeship in action, one Forster was likewise to act on during his visits to India.

But elsewhere there was frustration. In Agra, for example, he ruminated how easy it was to visit the Taj but impossible 'to explore what lies behind some of the faces that I see on the road—beautiful as they are; something even more wonderful than even the Taj itself. All this is very trying to people of democratic tendencies but perhaps it will be said that such people ought not to visit India, at any rate under such present circumstances."[86] Not only was Carpenter up against the barriers of a self-enclosed colonialism, with the British as much puzzled as shocked by Carpenter's endeavor to reach out to ordinary Indians, he was faced by a subject people conditioned to cringe before and keep their distance from a white ruling class. He put it all somewhat differently to Kate Salt, with his having to submit to the "ignominy of guides and baksheesh and all the rest of it." On Indian self-effacement he continued: "if you look straight at a man he covers his face and his hands and bows low to the ground as if in irony and the native police as you pass salute and shoulder arms. Isn't it too bad?"[87] Clearly Carpenter felt all the usual irritation of the conventional tourist. But here was a social challenge even greater than that of breaking through English class barriers.

Throughout the visit Carpenter kept up his commentary on the physical appearance of the Sri Lankan and Indian male. Bakshi uses this material to label Carpenter as a sexual predator: "ultimately Carpenter himself is guilty of sexual colonialism in his treatment of Ceylon and India."[88] There was the near nudity of Sinhalese and Indians; as Bakshi puts it accusingly, "at ease with their bodies, graceful and natural. Free of physical restrictions, they are portrayed as free of emotional constraints too, and potentially available for sexual liaisons."[89] And possibly Carpenter did have a bad conscience about it. To Kate Salt he warned: "Don't say much to friends about what I am doing here—unless one or two. You have been so good about TD (*Towards Democracy*) but so many people do talk."[90] But in post-Labouchere Amendment England, with the threat of blackmail, one had to be careful even with so sympathetic a confidante.

Not all Carpenter's responses were flattering. He shared a colonialist prejudice against the Bengalis: "by nature a versatile, flexile creature, sadly wanting in backbone." And not just the Bengalis were seen as effeminate: "the natives here" (his reference was to the Sri Lankans), he confided to Kate Salt, "are such gentle and submissive creatures."[91] He was repelled by the lustful stares of Bengalis at European female artistes of a visiting circus: "the smile which curled the lips of some of these rather Mephistophelean spectators was something which I shall not easily forget."[92]

But there was much to admire. In Aligarh a sixty-year-old local wrestling champion caught his eye: "remarkably powerful—burly—with small nose, battered ears and huge frontal prominence like some African chief or western prize-fighter."[93] In Delhi he perked up all the more: "a finer looking race than southwards—more of the Mohammedam influence." The Hindus displayed "more fling and romance, verging a little towards Greek or Italians types—but looking fine with their dark skins."[94] He supposed the Punjabis were even finer and taller. In Nagpur and Agra he found the men he passed in the street "very handsome, many of them with large eyes and well-formed noses, neither snubbed nor hooked, and short upper lips." But whatever the attractiveness of the foot, legs let Indians down: "I have come to the conclusion that their legs are too thin for them ever to do much in the world."[95] Forster was to share this verdict on the Indian male's legs. Overall the response was in part caste-conditioned, for his preference was for the lower castes, with an aversion toward the Chettiars in the south and merchant castes in Bengal. Would one want to agree with Bakshi that "the orient is diminished in order to manage the theme of homoerotic love,"[96] or alternatively, assert that Carpenter was exceptional in his wish to break down social and racial barriers and put his ideal of comradeship to the test?

Empire and Beyond

If Carpenter's anti-imperialism, of a piece with his socialism, is not the focus of this text, Empire was the context for his exploration of sexuality and mysticism and it needs to be addressed here, if in passing. Possibly out of loyalty to his brother, Charles, he was not unsympathetic to officialdom. He wrote of the ICS as "very able, disinterested, hard-working men."[97] It was their social exclusivism that appalled him. In Sri Lanka he found English officials "remarkably good-hearted, painstaking men; but one feels the gulf between them and the people—a gulf that can never be bridged." Rather oddly he attributed this to the religious feeling of the Sinhalese.[98] In Allahabad he saw race, instead, as the explanation for "a deep-set ineradicable incompatibility." But he also wondered if an explanation lay in fear: so cut off are they that they "magnify the perils of their own position and entrenching themselves in further isolation and exclusiveness, by so doing create the very danger they would avoid." Such social withdrawal had, of course, done much to bring about the rebellion of 1857. He anticipated Forster in commenting on their school boyishness, the unformed heart as Carpenter put it. The furthest Carpenter would go in his brother's memory was to write of "the broad and liberal spirit of administration with less of rapine than perhaps ever known in such a case (of Empire) before."[99]

But he was uncompromising in his hostility to the system itself. At the time of the Boer War he was to write a famous poem against Empire and a devastating indictment of imperialism, with a highly effective deployment of the Drain theory of British rule in India. Empire embraced all that was wrong with Civilization as he defined it, class-conscious, materialistic, emotionally unsympathetic. But even here he could not resist returning to his theme of friendship. Were the raj to open up the administration to Indians, "I feel sure the people would respond with an immense gratitude and frankness fully equivalent to that with which the offer was made." Why not send out some *mission* to India, he proposed, drawn from such an organization as the Humanitarian League?[100]

Probably loyalty to so traditional a figure as Ramaswamy explains Carpenter's assessment of the consequences of India's encounter with the west. Admittedly, his analysis was somewhat ambiguous. Might exposure to so-called western civilization not be after all a necessary phase for India? Could its impact be the answer to caste? This was of a piece with Carpenter's Hegelian attempts to see some positive aspects even in negative phenomenon such as Civilization and Empire. But in his short story *Narayan* his verdict was against modernization. He wrote both of the attractions and of the ultimate destructiveness of western-style industrialization on two villagers, Narayan and Ganesh. They had decided to seek a job in Bombay, en route consulting a holy man who queried their intent but who in the end sent them on their way: "therefore what is necessary for you, that fulfill: but when you are tired of the world, my children, come back to me, and it may be that what you need you will find." Young Ganesh is smashed to pieces in an accident in a spinning mill. On returning to the village Narayan recalled the words of the hermit: "what if by any chance there should be a new life there, in that old wisdom of which he with the wonderful eyes had spoken."[101]

Carpenter's position was a neo-traditionalist. Commercialism, and by this he intended western capitalism, he saw as wholly at odds with Indian traditional values: "anything more antagonistic to the genius of ancient India—the Wisdom-land—than the cheap-and-nasty puffing profit-mongering, enterprising energetic individualistic 'business' can hardly be imagined." But out of this clash, especially with western science, that Hegelianism again, would emerge a revitalized Hindu culture, a purified caste system and the freedom of women. Western science, he concluded, "will strongly and usefully criticize the prevalent religious systems and practices and give that definition and *materialism* to the popular thought which is sadly wanting in the India of today."[102] So there was a limit to his deference to Ramaswamy. At its best, this brings him into line with the new religious movements, the likes of Vivekananda; at its worst, it constitutes a grave sentimentalism and pandering to mere tradition.

Contemporary Response

Adam's Peak enjoyed a mixed response at the time. Within India *The Times of India* liked his account of the modern representatives of the gymnosophists: "he displays neither the undisciplined enthusiasm of such subjects of an Edward Arnold nor of course the smug prepossessions of the average missionary." But *The Madras Mail* felt all this was based on too little time and research. The English press was even less sympathetic. The *Morning Post*, taking up his commentary on British rule in India, damned him as typical of those "fly-by-night tourists who propound his pet theories for putting the fermenting wine of radical nostrums into some of the oldest bottles in the world." The *Tribune* was non-plussed by his account of Ramasamy's philosophy, written off as medieval mysticism: "in fact the whole Indian scheme of psychology involves so complete a rupture with western ideas and modes of thought that it is scarcely possible to find common standing ground." Rather ungenerously the *Star* found the book wanting in descriptive power, "distinctly emotionless": "the sumptuous beauty of eastern life which has obscured the vision and enfevered the judgment of so many writers upon Asia has evidently possessed little charm for the present author. Even through the wonders of the eastern temple ceremonial Mr. Carpenter bewails the intellectual stagnation which accompanies it, apparently blind to its putrid anesthetic fascination." Was Carpenter here being accused of being too little the orientalist?[103]

Conclusion

Carpenter's visit to the subcontinent had in large part been driven by a need to find in Indian spirituality some sanction for his sexuality. In this regard he drew a number of conclusions. This came less at the time, more when he had worked through his experience. Reflecting on the way a lingam had been placed on the tomb of his guru he saw here a symbol, not just of primal man, but one additionally "prophetic of a new type of Man (or Woman) already appearing in our midst—a type which is destined to unite the qualities of both sexes (the tenderness and adaptability of the female with the strength and reliability of the male) and to be the herald of the reunion of Eros and Psyche."[104] A perfected consciousness would emerge from this mixing of male and female. *Samadhi* he translated as sameness and hence he saw here the possibility of a homoerotic interpretation: "the worshipper enters into sameness with the god whom he worships." But admittedly he then veered into a more orthodox Vedantism: "the man passes into identity with the whole universe."[105]

Carpenter had to make a choice between Walt Whitman and Ilakkanam the Grammarian. Later, peering at those two photos of them, both taken in 1890, one of "the deeply-lined" face of Whitman, a man who had experienced life so passionately, the other, of an unlined face, "the most childlike, single-hearted, uncensorious, fearless character imaginable," he made his choice. It was never a simple one between the sexual and the spiritual, for Whitman certainly contained elements of both and Ramasawamy, at the least, came out of a religion which Carpenter believed sacramentalized sex. But Carpenter was always too deeply wedded to the merely human to be wholly converted to the ascetic ideal underlying Vedantism. Barua writes of Carpenter keeping "his roots firmly in the western tradition," and "unhesitatingly" choosing Whitman.[106] Yet it is not that simple. Carpenter had a career ahead of him in which he outgrew his two gurus and became one in his own right. He did so as both sexologist and mystic. If tension remained between his sexuality and his would-be mysticism, here was evidence of a lasting impact of the world-view of his Indian guru.

Notes

1. Carpenter to Kate Salt, Agra, 22 February 1891 MSS 354/12.

2. It is not always clear from Carpenter's usage of the word "Cinghalese" if he includes all the communities of Sri Lanka or just the Sinhalese without the Tamils. Possibly the best generalization today will be Sri Lankans.

3. Carpenter, *From Adam's Peak to Elephanta: Sketches in Ceylon and India* (First published London: S. Sonnenschein, 1892. References to London: George Allen and Unwin, 1910 edition).

4. Morocco raised the same question mark in Carpenter's mind as India, just how restricting were the ties of tradition? He wondered if "here in the basis of society that the real difference between the modern world and the world of Islam is to be found. In Islam the basis is fixed, nor can any great change in its world be imagined without a complete alteration of the base." He anticipates much of the Islamic intelligentsia's

hostile response to the challenge of western commercialism and science. Hence their being "so fanatical against the introduction of modern ideas." Edward Carpenter, *The New Age* (February 1907).

5. Most searchingly so by Parminder Bakshi, "Homosexuality and Orientalism: Edward Carpenter's Journey to the East," in Tony Brown, ed. *Edward Carpenter and late Victorian Radicalism* (London: Cass), 1990.

6. Tariq Rahman, "The Literary Treatment of Indian Themes in the Works of Edward Carpenter," *Durham University Journal* 80 (December 1987), 77–81.

7. Edward Carpenter, *My Days and Dreams* (London: Allen and Unwin, 1916), 142.

8. Bakshi, "Homosexuality and Orientalism," 173.

9. See his obituary, in the *Pioneer*, 11 March 1876, MSS349/80.

10. All this can be gleaned from their correspondence MSS 349/66–69.

11. Carpenter to Oates, 28 March 1876, MSS 351/22.

12. D. K. Barua, *Edward Carpenter 1844–1929: An Apostle of Freedom* (Burdwan: University of Burdwin, 1991), 131.

13. See his account in *From Adam's Peak*, 271–74.

14. Carpenter to Kate Salt, 5 November 1891, MSS 354/10.

15. Edward Carpenter, *Light from the East; Being Letters on Gnanam, the Divine Knowledge by P. Arunachalam* (London: Allen and Unwin, 1927) 27–28.

16. A. Jeyaratnam Wilson, *Sri Lankan Tamil Nationalism: Its Origins and Development in the 19th and 20th Centuries* (London: Hurst and Company, 2000), 35.

17. Arunachalam to Carpenter, 15 February 1891, MSS 271/43. Although these letters are incorporated in *Light from the East*, where I have consulted the letters in the original I will quote the manuscript reference.

18. For a biographical sketch of Arunachalam see J. T. Rutnam, *Ponambulam Arunachalam 1853–1924: Scholar and Statesman: A Brief Account of His Life and Career* (Colombo: Ponnanbalam Arunachalam Centenary, 14 September 1953).

19. To contextualise Arunachalam's story in a wider national setting I put my faith in the highly readable account of the island's history, E. F. C. Ludowyk, *The Story of Ceylon* (London: Faber and Faber, 1962. Revised edn. 1967).

20. In the *Indian Review* (May 1885). See Carpenter, *Days and Dreams* (London, Allen and Unwin), 193.

21. Jeyaratnam Wilson, *Sri Lankan Tamil Nationalism*, 49.

22. Ludowyk, *The Story of Ceylon*, 235.

23. Arunachalam to Carpenter, 29 August 1917, MSS 378/5.

24. Quoted Rutnam, *Ponambulam Arunachalam 1853–1924*, 14.

25. Jeyaratnam Wilson's appraisal, *Sri Lankan Tamil Nationalism*, 52–55.

26. Arunachalam to Carpenter, 17 May 1874, MSS 378/2(?). Arunachalam had also enjoyed the friendship of Tennyson's son and Professor Maitland.

27. Carpenter, *My Days and Dreams*, 251.

28. Arunachalam to Carpenter, 29 August 1917, MSS 378/5.

29. Carpenter, *From Adam's Peak*, 12–18.
30. Arunachalam to Carpenter, 1880 nd, MSS 271/28.
31. Carpenter, *From Adam's Peak*, 107.
32. Arunachalam to Carpenter, nd, MSS 378/3(?).
33. Arunachalam to Carpenter, 18 November 1888, MSS 271/37.
34. Arunachalam to Carpenter, Tanjore, 27 December 1889, MSS 271/39.
35. Carpenter, *My Days and Dreams*, 143.
36. Carpenter to Oates, Rome, 2 April 1873, MSS 351/10.
37. Barua, *Edward Carpenter 1844–1929*, 137.
38. Carpenter, *From Adam's Peak*, 140.
39. Arunachalam to Carpenter, 16 May 1890, MSS 371/39.
40. There is a considerable literature on this Hindu unrest, the south's equivalent to rebellion in the north, 1857–1858. I summarize the story in my *Religions in Conflict* (New Delhi: Oxford University Press, 1997), 183–84.
41. Carpenter, *Light from the East: Being Letters on Gnaman, the Divine Knowledge by P. Arunachalam* (London: Allen and Unwin, 1927), 44–45.
42. Carpenter, *From Adam's Peak*, 146.
43. Carpenter, *Light from the East*, 43.
44. Quoted in Carpenter, *Light from the East*, 59–60.
45. Carpenter, *Light from the East*, 64.
46. Arunachalam to Carpenter, 13 March 1898. Quoted Carpenter, *Light from the East*, 73.
47. A physical description taken from Carpenter, *Days with Walt Whitman* (London: George Allen, 1906), 50–51, and *From Adam's Peak*, 183–84.
48. Here I have largely put my faith in Sivanath Sastri's summary in his *History of South India, Chapters XIV and XV* (London: 1955).
49. Sastri, *History of South India*, 63.
50. Carpenter, *From Adam's Peak*, 186.
51. Somasundaram to Carpenter, July 1894, MSS 270/198.
52. Carpenter, *From Adam's Peak*, 197. It would be rebarbative to repeat Carpenter's account of Ramasawamy's medieval ideas on alchemy. astrology, physiology, etc., in Chapter XII.
53. Carpenter, *From Adam's Peak*, 193.
54. Barua, *Edward Carpenter 1844–1929*, 143.
55. Carpenter, *From Adam's Peak*, 152.
56. Carpenter, *From Adam's Peak*, 153.
57. Carpenter, *From Adam's Peak*, 155.
58. Carpenter, *From Adam's Peak*, 156.
59. Carpenter to Kate Salt, 24 November 1890, MSS 354/11.
60. Carpenter *From Adam's Peak*, 168.
61. Carpenter, *From Adam's Peak*, 170.
62. Carpenter, *From Adam's Peak*, 173.

63. Tariq Rahman, "Edward Carpenter's *From Adam's Peak to Elephanta* as a Source for E. M. Forster's *"A Passage to India,"* *Forum of Modern Language Studies* XXII, no. 1 (January 1986): 12.

64. Carpenter, *From Adam's Peak*, 175.

65. Carpenter, *From Adam's Peak*, 176.

66. Carpenter, *From Adam's Peak*, p 177.

67. Carpenter, *From Adam's Peak*, 179–80.

68. Arunachalan to Carpenter, 15 February 1891, MSS 271/43.

69. Arunachalan to Carpenter, 28 February 1893, MSS 271/46.

70. Arunachalan to Carpenter, 27 July 1898, *Light from the East*, 64–65.

71. Carpenter, *From Adam's Peak*, 211.

72. Carpenter, *From Adam's Peak*, 216.

73. Carpenter, *From Adam's Peak*, Chapter XIV.

74. Carpenter, *From Adam's Peak*, 279.

75. Carpenter, *From Adam's Peak*, 304–11.

76. This is the Tai Pacam festival, part of the worship of Murukam, celebrating the god's conquest of the passions and malevolence. It honors the god's youthfulness, virility and creativity. See Guy R. Welbon and Glenn E. Yocum, *Religious Festivals in South India and Sri Lanka* (New Delhi: Manohar, 1982), 175.

77. Carpenter, *From Adam's Peak*, Chapter VII.

78. Quoted Bakshi, "Homosexuality and Orientalism," 161.

79. Carpenter, *From Adam's Peak*, 27.

80. Carpenter to Oates, 7 December 1890, MSS 351/56.

81. Carpenter, *From Adam's Peak*, 28.

82. Carpenter, *From Adam's Peak*, 236–40.

83. Carpenter to Kate Salt, 22 February 1891, MSS 354/12.

84. Carpenter, *From Adam's Peak*, 262.

85. Carpenter, *From Adam's Peak*, 317.

86. Carpenter, *From Adam's Peak*, 284.

87. Carpenter to Kate Salt, 22 February 1891, MSS 354/12.

88. Bakshi, "Homosexuality and Orientalism," 174.

89. Bakshi, "Homosexuality and Orientalism," 163.

90. Carpenter to Kate Salt, Agra, 22 February 1891, MSS 354/12.

91. Carpenter to Kate Salt, 5 November, MSS 354/10.

92. Carpenter, *From Adam's Peak*, 231–33.

93. Carpenter, *From Adam's Peak*, 275.

94. Carpenter, *From Adam's Peak*, 277–78.

95. Carpenter, *From Adam's Peak*, 290.

96. Bakshi, "Homosexuality and Orientalism," 174.

97. Carpenter, From Adam's Peak, 265.

98. Carpenter, From Adam's Peak, 87.

99. Carpenter, "The Anglo-Indian and The Native," in *From Adam's Peak*, Chapter XV.

100. Carpenter, "Empire: in India and Elsewhere," The Humane Review (October 1900), MSS Carpenter Pamphlets Vol 5.

101. Carpenter, "Narayan: A Tale of Indian Life," *Sketches from Life in Town and Country* (London: G. Allen, 1908).

102. Carpenter, *From Adam's Peak*, 355–57.

103. See MSS Reel 35 for these press clippings.

104. Carpenter, *Light from the East*, 97n1.

105. Carpenter, *Light from the East*, 104.

106. Barua, Edward Carpenter 1844–1929, 151–52.

CHAPTER THREE

~

The Disciple Turned Guru: Edward Carpenter, Sexologist and Mystic

If the 1880s had been for Carpenter an experimental decade, in the aftermath of his visit to Sri Lanka and India he emerged far more fully formed, better able to take on the mantle of reformer, prophet, and guru. Socialism gave way to sexology and mysticism. His was to be a constant search for a link between the two. But this was a specially fraught time to be struggling for sexual enlightenment and Carpenter needed a toughness barely within his reach to confront Victorian and Edwardian moral codes. These placed an increasing emphasis on keeping up appearances, mere pharisaical convention. Whereas the early and mid Victorian decades had at least encompassed an almost grotesque sexual license together with a profound moral disquiet, by the late century the debate had hardened into hypocrisy and sanctimoniousness. Norms of behavior in public diverged ever more widely from those in private, with ever greater risk of social ostracism should there be any exposure of non-conformity.[1] It was not a good time to be openly homosexual.

Carpenter was too much a man of his time to be wholly free of Victorian attitudes. There was always to be a certain prudishness in his response to female sexuality and in the way he addressed the physical aspects of homosexuality. But he took his place in key movements of revolt, in a feminist against intolerable restraints on the freedom of women, one in aid of the so-called "new woman," together with a campaign for sexual reformism, driven by a deep personal need to legitimize homosexuality. Here he was up against almost impossible odds, following the outlawing of any expression of homosexual love by the Labouchere amendment of 1885 and the taboo status of homosexuality following the trials of Oscar Wilde in 1895, an English equivalent to France's Dreyfus affair.[2]

And the mysticism? It is tempting to speculate that Carpenter hoped to promote his rather sanitized version of homosexuality by framing it within an ambience of mysticism. But this would be wrong. His mysticism was far too engrained, far too much a part of who he was. As he looked back at his life in 1915, he saw Nature and Love as the two great ideals. But his emphasis was on the life within. "Beneath the surface waves and storms of youth, beneath the backward and forward fluctuations, there has been added," he reflected, "the calm of inner realization and union. I know that these two primordial and foundational things (or perhaps they are one) *are* there." It all hinged on fashioning the self: "constructive expression of one's self is one of the greatest joys and one of the greatest needs of life."[3] But by the self Carpenter intended the *atman*. Carpenter from 1891 onwards was to write at considerable length about both religion and spirituality and if not without criticism he kept coming back to a Vedantist approach. Here was the making of Carpenter the mystic.

Already as a socialist, even more so as a sexologist, Carpenter took on guru status. An aura of the spiritual does much to explain his appeal. The line between friendship and discipleship is not always easy to draw. Within his own generation, clearly Havelock Ellis was a friend rather than disciple. Theirs was to be an equal contribution to sexual enlightenment. Lowes Dickinson, initially a disciple, in time became a friend. Henry Salt, pioneer of vegetarianism, fell under and out of Carpenter's spell. Amongst his female followers Olive Schreiner, his intellectual equal, was more the friend, whereas lesbian Kate Salt and Edith Lees, wife to Havelock Ellis, were certainly disciples. Jealousy over George Merrill does much to explain Kate Salt's disillusionment with Carpenter. Looking ahead to a later generation, Carpenter's cult of the simple life and his progressive views on sexuality influenced the outlook of the so-called neo-pagans, centered on Rupert Brooke. If not always frank in acknowledging his influence, reluctant as he was to be associated with such a frank apologist of homosexuality, D. H. Lawrence was to be profoundly influenced by Carpenter's writings. And E. M. Forster, in so far as his skeptical temperament would allow him to adopt a mentor, was Carpenter's disciple for a while, though, as with the Salts, there was a falling away at the end. If not wholly at ease with these expectations that he become the guru, this was a role Carpenter was willing to play.

Sexologist

George Merrill

If George Hukin was the greatest love of his life, it was George Merrill who became his lifetime companion. They met shortly after Carpenter's return from India. Merrill had already become aware of Carpenter in Sheffield but took time to summon up the courage to make contact with him and only did so one winter's evening 1891 during the return rail journey Carpenter was making from Sheffield to Totley. In much the same way as Whitman and Peter Doyle had met on a tram, they "exchanged a few words together and a look of recognition." Carpenter above all was struck "by a pathetic look of wistfulness in his face." Merrill followed behind Carpenter and his friends on the road to Millthorpe and Carpenter dropped back to discover his address: "that was the beginning of our acquaintance, which became almost immediately close and intimate." As the relationship is the background to Carpenter's life and writings post-India and lies behind so much of his rhetoric on male friendship it is necessary to attempt a portrait of Merrill and explain how he came to play so central a part in Carpenter's life. Does he justify the rhetoric?[4]

In contrast to Hukin, Merrill was hardly Carpenter's idealized worker. He came from a large family of eight boys and one girl. His father, Samuel Merrill, a goods engine driver, had suffered an industrial injury, took to drink, and scraped a living in the cutlery trade. His mother, "big, racy-tongued . . . leg-of-mutton arms," to whom George was devoted, was the rock of the family. Prior to their meeting Merrill had got by with a variety of part-time jobs, at the slipper baths, in a small casting-shop, in a file-grinding shop, as a barman. At one point, picked up by a priest at Derby railway station, he had become his domestic in his seminary at Aberystwyth. Immediately before Carpenter and Merrill met he had been an assistant to an encyclopedia salesman. Merrill had also enjoyed a quite lively sex life, including a brief affair with an equerry of Edward, Prince of Wales, encountered at Sheffield railway station. Here in Carpenter's belief was a strong sexuality but one that had not coarsened him.

Post their meeting, inter alia, Merrill was a cleaner in the offices of Sheffield's *Daily Telegraph* (there he was to enjoy a lively conversation with one of its visitors, Arthur Balfour), a waiter at the Hydropathic Establishment at Baslow, conveniently close to Millthorpe, but then back into a tough industrial environment in the Vickers and Maxim ironwork in Sheffield. Clearly it was a mercy when the Adams's gave up on their role as housekeeper at Millthorpe in 1898, seeking to better themselves as sandal-makers and running a café—unlike Hukin who had befriended Merrill, George

Adams had always been resentful of him—and 2 February Merrill became housekeeper in their stead. Carpenter was to be fiercely criticized for this arrangement—how would his health and well-being fare without female attention, etc.?—but he always felt, along with giving up religious orders and turning to market gardening, it was one of the best decisions of his life.

So how to evaluate the nature of the friendship? Merrill likewise valued friendship above all. Both shared a feminine nature—Carpenter wrote of his clinging temperament—and this could have worked against the friendship. Whereas Hukin could share Carpenter's intellectual interests, not only socialist but also spiritual—Carpenter and he exchanged letters about Illakanam—Merrill here was out of his depth. His own correspondence with Carpenter is lightweight and chatty at best. But there was a saltiness and non-intellectualism very much to Carpenter's taste. Here was a child of the Sheffield slums, "quite beyond civilization. Utterly untouched by the prevailing conventions and priorities of the upper world." Carpenter fell in love with this background. Merrill had many appealing features, quite well made and muscular, a strong sense of humor, a good musical air, a capacity to entertain. But if adaptable to all comers he was not to everyone's liking. Edith Lees shared his earthy tastes and took to him: she told Carpenter to "tell him not to forget me and say that he has my sincere admiration for his super womanly gifts and good housekeeping."[5] But Kate Salt became jealous, may have said something unforgivable about Merrill and she and Carpenter drifted apart. And George could be sexually indiscreet. Admittedly the conservative villagers of Millthorpe were rather shocked but in time were won over by his spontaneous, cheerful good will. But the anti-socialist Irishman, O'Brien, was in 1909 able to exploit those indiscretions against Carpenter himself and it took a public display of support, a walking around the village by his friends, Hukin and the Salts and Lowes Dickinson to the fore, to cope with the threat. Homosexuals were at permanent risk of blackmail. Much later, after they had left Millthorpe for Guildford, Merrill, a fish out of water, took to drink and became a worry to Carpenter in his old age. It could not have helped that Carpenter was seemingly transferring his affections, certainly his dependency, onto another live-in friend, Edward Inigan. But quite probably Merrill's death in January 1928 hastened Carpenter's own, 29 June 1929.

Havelock Ellis

Havelock Ellis and Carpenter were to work closely together in the cause of sexual reform. It was a natural partnership, both being introspective and prone to mysticism, though Ellis, more the humanist, was never to follow

Carpenter all the way into Vedantism. Born 3 February 1859 and fifteen years his younger, in many ways it was to be Carpenter who deferred to Ellis and sought his advice and assistance. From an early stage in his career Ellis was taken up by such prestigious journals as the *Westminster Review* and much of Carpenter's correspondence with Ellis was given over to requesting Ellis's help in finding outlets for his own publications and over his dealings with publishers. But more importantly Carpenter turned to Ellis out of faith that as a respected medical voice his would be the more likely to break down prejudice on homosexuality. But it was never to become a wholly intimate friendship—Ellis was, for example, much closer to a fellow medical student, John Barker Smith—but they were united by common interests.

There were similar factors at work in their background.[6] Ellis's father had likewise been a naval captain. By strange chance a namesake, Dr Alfred Carpenter, delivered him and was later to facilitate his entry into St. Thomas's hospital. His unusual Christian name gave Ellis a rare connection with India; Henry Havelock of "Mutiny" fame was a distant relative. The turning point in Ellis's life had overtones of mysticism. During a four-year spell in Australia, from the age of sixteen to twenty, whilst in the outback at Sparkes Creek in the summer of 1878, rereading James Hinton's *Life in Nature* he had a "revelation": "an immense inner transformation had been effected, as it seemed, in a moment."[7] As Calder Marshall generalized about Ellis's writings; "he was a visionary, a mystic who bought to the human beings he loved the sort of reverence that most mystics give to God."[8] By this time Ellis had lost the evangelical outlook instilled in him by his lower middle class mother—at one stage he was destined for the church—and James Hinton, the catalyst for this vision, was not to last the pace as a guru[9]—he had died anyway in 1875—but here was a belief that was to survive, a faith in man's evolution and, more specifically, a belief that through sexual enlightenment man would achieve happiness. He also resolved to follow Hinton's example and train as a doctor. Intriguingly, it was to be Ellis's future wife, Edith Lees, who resurrected Hinton's name in her *Three Modern Seers* (1910).

In the politics of the 1880s Ellis, a Fabian at heart but never a political activist, shared Carpenter's disillusionment with the labor movement. For both the inter-personal took precedence. As Jeffrey Weeks summarizes Ellis's position: "he became convinced that the meaning of life was a matter of individual perception; each person constructed for himself a pattern of meaning, in effect a myth."[10] Faith in the personal led Ellis to become a founder member in October 1883 of the Fellowship of the New Life, one of those utopian groups in the 1880s sustained by a quasi-religious belief in the enhancement of the inter-personal. Its declared ambition was "the cultivation of a perfect character for each and all," its principle, "the subordination of material things to spiritual," the means, fellowship.[11] It also emphasized the worth of manual labor.

Suitably it was at a meeting of the Fellowship that Carpenter and Ellis met for the first time: "I was sitting with my back to the door and hearing someone gently open it," recalled Ellis, "I turned round for a moment and saw two brightly gleaming eyes out of the background of a quietly humorous face. In that swift glance as sometimes happens I gained a more vivid picture of Edward Carpenter's face than in all the long years I knew him afterwards."[12]

This is Carpenter's considered appraisal of Ellis:

> The personality of Havelock Ellis is that of a student, thoughtful, preoccupied, bookish, deliberate, yet unlike most students, he has a sort of grand air of Nature about him—a fine free head and figure as some great god Pan, with distant relations among the Satyrs.[13]

But the deeper connection between the two lay in the problematic they experienced in their sexuality. Carpenter's homosexuality was matched by Ellis's urolagnia, the delight he took in watching women urinate, and what he experienced as his impotence. In 1892 he married Edith Lees, a lesbian. In many ways Carpenter was to be far closer to and more spontaneous with Edith Lees than Ellis himself. In fact Ellis was mistaken about his impotence as he was to discover with his second wife, Françoise Delisle. But here was a friendship between Ellis and Carpenter that was to last. As Grosskurth explains: "while he was never easily sociable, Ellis's capacity for steadfast friendship was one of the major aspects of his character."[14]

Their mutual concerns were never narrowly sexual. They ranged across broader interests, mutual friends and the turmoils of their personal lives. There was always a process of give and take. After their meeting Carpenter sent Ellis his pamphlets on vegetarianism and on the theme of evolution and exfoliation. On Carpenter's paper on vegetarianism Ellis responded: "Most people find it difficult to advocate these things without making fads of them but you quite succeed."[15] Nervously he anticipated Ellis's judgment on *Towards Democracy*. Ellis wrote back: "it is a source of strength to know even one man is fighting so well on the right side."[16] It is not clear how much emotional support Carpenter received from Ellis during the torment of the Hukin affair but by 7 July 1887 he could inform him: "I am feeling much better and stronger than I did—things are opening out kindly on the whole—with promise of rest."[17]

By way of exchange Carpenter read Ellis's writings. He responded to essays on Thoreau, Tolstoy, and others with genuine warmth: "'Your 'New Spirit,'" he wrote, "is splendid—all is carefully worked, weighed, wrought over and over—such a great outlook all round. One feels when you speak that it must be true. It is like the Lord on his throne surveying the generations of men—all very good."[18] Carpenter encouraged Ellis in his medical career: "I think it must be interesting work—tho I dare say a lot of the suffering and disease appears very needless."[19] He reached out to Ellis over his failed love affair with Olive Schreiner, doomed by his supposed impotence. Once again Carpenter got on the better with one of Ellis's women. Schreiner visited Millthorpe, though did not take to its northern climate and failed to respond with the same gusto as Edith Lees to its homosexual milieu.

Rather less clear is whether Carpenter and Ellis were on the same religious or spiritual wavelength. Carpenter expressed surprise that Ellis had read *Towards Democracy* as "so specially religious in quality— tho I fear I have a mighty bump that way."[20] He became intrigued by Ellis's physiological account of religion and plied him with questions about the great sympathetic nervous system, to become a particular obsession of his. As he explained, he lacked the expertise to trace a connection between the vaso-motoral and the religious sentiment. But then, rather oddly, considering that all of his thought went in a contrary direction, he added, "But expansion of individual life is not especially correlated with religion." But here he was but agreeing with Ellis himself.[21]

They were to be far more drawn together when Ellis decided that sexual inversion should be the point of departure for his monumental study of sexuality. If John Addington Symonds[22] was to be his preferred initial source he also approached Carpenter and theirs was to be a lively correspondence.

The New Woman
Both Carpenter and Ellis addressed the issue of female sexual emancipation as imperfectly liberated Victorians. The Victorian sexual code with its monogamous marriage and widespread prostitution served the sexual needs of heterosexual men. Possibly Carpenter as a homosexual was predisposed to tolerate masculine sexual demands. At his worst he failed to accept gender equality. In a letter to Ellis he wrote of some inbuilt inequality in women: "I think however there is a good deal in the general position that Woman always represents a part (she is enclitic to the man) whereas Man may well represent the whole."[23] This was to endorse *Genesis* on the creation of Eve. He had no quarrel with Ellis's account of female sexuality as rooted in modesty. In a search for some links between sexuality and mysticism Carpenter invariably veered away from physicality toward a spiritualized sexuality. He was never a likely apologist of female sexual emancipation. Yet both he and

Ellis saw themselves, after the manner of Ibsen, as protagonists of "the New Woman.".

Maybe predictably, given his own sexuality, Carpenter's emphasis was on the maternal. Again, at its worst, this could be seen as a kind of compensation. As he put it to Ellis, "women at present and except as a mother (where she is divine) is a very unsatisfactory creature."[24] Of course, this privileging of the maternal role is wholly unacceptable to today's feminists. Carpenter is seen as subject to mere biological determinism.[25] By separating out sexuality from reproduction Carpenter had indeed opened up the possibility of a far more emancipated female sexuality but chose not to do so. He was in large part in rebellion against just that carnality of the Victorian age. But this feminist critique overlooks the real compassion Carpenter felt for women trapped within the conventions of his day. Much of this was shaped by his sense of the emotional starvation of his mother and the sad and pointless lives on offer to his sisters. In society at large he was appalled by the roles available to women; at the character of middle class marriage, women as mere chattels in emotionally starved relationships; at the drudgery in the lives of working class women; at the way prostitution was often the only answer to women caught in adultery and the only escape from the trap of poverty. When he argued for a greater emotional freedom within marriage he was really arguing for a relaxation of the tyranny of an imprisoning jealousy, opening up the opportunity for wives to expand their circle of friends. Of course, much of this ideal for marriage was based on his ideal for long-term homosexual relationships, though here he was somewhat disingenuous for these he certainly conceived as accommodating not only new affairs of the heart but also of the flesh. Here the comparison with heterosexual marriage seemingly broke down. However, to advocate adultery at that time would have been reckless. The vehicle for these ideas, *Love's Coming of Age* (1894), was to be his best-selling book.

If speaking from within his limited experience as a homosexual Carpenter clearly believed himself to be on the wavelength of women and he saw uranians as natural friends of married women. Indeed, such was to be the case with Edith Lees and Kate Salt though the claim may be weakened by their both being lesbian. Maybe a better test is his friendship with Olive Schreiner.[26] Carpenter's greatest weakness was his remaining far too subject to gender stereotypes and his account of the masculinity of the lesbian was inexcusably blinkered.

Carpenter's was always a vision of a more spiritualized love. Today this can seem whimsical and largely irrelevant. But he was only being true to his historical sense of a new age to come and to his Vedantism. In some quasi-socialist utopia women would be free of all economic dependence on the male, from all economic shackles of "commercialism." There was his familiar arcadian image of sex outdoors, "a kind of saturation with the free air," together with "a Nature-festival now and then," that occasional bacchanalian orgy. All this was a nature-sex-mysticism greatly to influence both the neo-pagans around Rupert Brooke and D. H. Lawrence.[27] He resorted to that tactic for moral reform of cultural relativism, characteristic of the eighteenth century *philosophes*. Above all he wanted to throw off those pharisaical conventions that inhibited spontaneity in human relationships.

But he also appropriated Ramswamy's concept of "differentiation" to legitimize a greater variety in expression of love. He drew on a Vedantist view of soul-relationship not only in terms of the love relationships of the here and now but in anticipation of a cosmic world of souls: "our terrestrial relations are merely the working out and expression of far antecedent and unmodifiable facts." He ended *Love's Coming of Age* with a positively Dantesque vision of a Rose of souls in paradise, each individual in some way harmoniously linked to all, "an eternal Fellowship in heaven and on earth—the prototype of all the communities that exist on this or any planet."[28] Here was indeed a Spiritual Bloomsbury.

All this was too much for one radical journal of the day, despite its sympathy for female sexual emancipation. "The whole atmosphere of Carpenter's book is too rarefied for ordinary human beings," its reviewer commented. Instead he advocated the sexual over the spiritual, "procreation" over Carpenter's "union": sex cell hunger, as he put it, is "the dominant factor in the majority of human relationships." "We know no 'celestial city.' His theory of immortality is outside the real scope of the book and I think weakens it."[29]

No doubt the reviewer would have been surprised to come across Carpenter's later assertion; "I think every woman in her heart of hearts wishes to be ravaged."[30]

Homogenic Love

On his return from the subcontinent Carpenter had become altogether more focused on questions of sexuality and, most courageously so, as an apologist of his own. But the interest of this text lies largely in the inner connection with his mysticism.

Carpenter and Ellis were engaged in parallel exercises and their writings were to appear the same year, 1896, Carpenter's short essay *Homogenic Love*, Ellis's far more substantial investigative project, *Sexual Inversion*, but in German. Carpenter wrote from an embattled personal position, Ellis as the dispassionate scientist. Ellis had first raised the possibility of his beginning his life's work on sexuality with a study of inversion in a letter to Carpenter 17

December 1892, both on grounds of its being so widespread and its outrageous treatment in law: "We want to obtain a sympathetic recognition for sexual inversion as a psychic abnormality which may be regarded as the highest ideal and to clear away many vulgar errors—preparing the way if possible for a change in the law." He went on: "I feel sure that we shall have your sympathy in this work; if you are able to supply any notes or suggestions that may help to throw light it will be doing a good deal."[31] And the case studies were indeed to become the kernel of Ellis's book, several provided by Carpenter as well as his own.

All this was grist to Carpenter's mill and he responded: "I think your proposed treatment of the subject sounds good and I don't feel that any objection ought to be made to the use of the word 'abnormal' as you explain it."[32] He critically assessed Ellis's source materials, felt Moll was too conditioned by the police evidence and in consequence overplayed effeminacy, Krafft-Ebing too narrowly medical and too pathological in his approach, hence his giving too much weight to "functional degeneration and (hereditary) nerve ailment." What of the Dorian Greeks, Carpenter rhetorically enquired? Are they to be classified as "nervous weaklings"? "Neither writer," Carpenter reflected, "quite envisages the phenomenon of a thoroughly healthy manifestation of inverted sexuality—tho' this is abundantly indicated in many of the 'cases' quoted." Carpenter cited Walt Whitman as example. He ended this long letter by expressing the problematic of arriving at any satisfactory generalization: "the conjunction of some mental characteristics of one sex with the generative organs of the other seems to mark homosexuality—but it is hard to define the thing any closer."[33]

And then he began to fear if Ellis himself was up to the task. Whilst he believed it would be a great book, he added: "tho' I wonder whether you quite appreciate the 'true inwardness' of this kind of love wh(ich) appears to me to want no mark of authenticity wh(ich) the other love can show, except that question of race propagation—and which yet has a quality all its own."[34]

Carpenter's own apologetics appeared in a short essay *Homogenic Love* (1896) and a fuller one *The Intermediate Sex* (1908). In the first he wrote of the love of comrades, of how Walt Whitman had sensed how pervasive this passion be, contrasting its idealism with "the comparatively materialistic basis of matrimonial sex—intercourse and child-breeding."[35] It was innate and in no way the concern of the law. Here was the affect between classes and the emotional underpinning of the feminist movement. Such comment was to be elaborated in his second book, setting out a spectrum of sexuality from the ultra-masculine to the hyper-feminine, with the homosexual or the Urning or Uranian (he made much use of Karl Ulrichs' taxonomy) constituting "an intermediate sex." Here was a precious instinct but one open to abuse as was the case in single sex boy's schools—Forster was later to make much use of Carpenter's description of the British middle-class male and his "undeveloped affective nature." He expanded on the role of the uranian as mediator between the classes—he had Charles Ashbee in mind—and as natural counselors in unhappy marriages: "I believe it is true that Uranian men are superior to normal men in this respect through their feminine element."[36]

Ellis and Carpenter always exchanged copies of one another's books. Somewhat self-effacedly Carpenter sent a copy of The Intermediate Sex: "there is not much in the book of course—but it is an attempt to make the inner side of the subject intelligible to a people 'walking in darkness.'"[37] Ellis responded: "It seems most excellent, more needed in England than in Germany, it is quite true however that England is scarcely yet ripe for it."[38] He promised a review of it in The Journal of Mental Sciences though he warned it might have to be in a "somewhat critical form."[39]

But Carpenter had made a number of observations, conditioned by his gender stereotyping, which have alienated future commentators. He was anxious to differentiate his version of the uranian, a feminine soul within a masculine body, from the physically effeminate. Radical gay movements encompass all gays within the same community. Carpenter also insisted on that distinction between the innate and the acquired or perverse, the latter seen as a homosexuality taken up by those within institutions such as single sex schools, prisons, or the armed forces where no heterosexual outlets were available. He did not anticipate Foucault's emphasis on there just being homosexual acts.[40] And by insisting on a biological or innate etiology of homosexuality Carpenter ruled out the very much more radical implications of a Freudian understanding of sexuality as determined by social and cultural forces, its opening up in consequence a far wider potentiality for its adoption, as indeed Carpenter had demonstrated in his example of the Spartans.

But Carpenter was up against enormous resistance to any apologetics for inversion, that pathological fear of the Victorians that masturbation led to homosexuality, deemed the ultimate vice, together with their violent rejection of any insight that behind the Victorian cult of male friendship lay the homoerotic. He had to tread carefully.

Criticism was predictably crude. The British Medical Journal had this to say of The Intermediate Sex: 'these articles reiterate ad nauseam praise and laudation for creatures and custom which are generally regarded as odious.' Since the publication of Psychopathic Sexualis and Sexual Inversion, it continued, there had been many works of this nature and they were recognizable at a glance. If homosexuals were so unhappy with the state of the law then they should migrate to Tahiti. It branded Carpenter's text "a low priced book of no scientific or literary merit," encouraging "unnatural and criminal practices," "pernicious tendencies chiefly but not wholly ridiculous."[41] In his reply to the Journal Carpenter disputed that he was in any way a proselytizer: "I am certain that there is not a single passage in the book where I advocate sexual intercourse between those of the same sex—I advocate sincere attachment and warm friendship and allow that this may have fitting expression in 'caresses and embraces' but I suppose to some minds this is sufficient and it is immediately interpreted as an advocacy of lust."[42] But here he was clearly being disingenuous.

The review in The Medical Times (was this by Ellis?) was far more charitable. "There was nothing nasty here and we entreat our readers to pause before they hastily set their faces against a subject which has attracted the attention of foreign governments although as yet it has been ignored by our too conservative and at times utterly foolish profession who think it too undignified to inquire into matters of such grave importance."[43]

The Wilde Affair and Its Aftermath

Both Carpenter and Ellis became ever more embattled in their quest for sexual reform. The moral panic that homosexuality bred in late nineteenth century Britain climaxed with the trials in 1895 of Oscar Wilde. Carpenter at the time suggested to Ellis that the prosecuting counsel, Sir Edward Clarke, be sent some scientific literature on the subject. Later he proposed that a fund be set up to finance sending appropriate literature to judges and other officials, as was apparently being done in Germany: "but then there is the difficulty of making the horse drink when you have taken him to the water."[44] In a letter in The Star, undated and signed by a Helvellyn, but probably a pseudonym for Carpenter himself, the correspondent reacted angrily to the withdrawal of all of Wilde's plays from the London stage. How was his homosexual behavior anyway any worse than heterosexual? "Certainly it is strange," he commented, "that a society which is continually and habitually sacrificing women to the pleasure of men should be so eager to cast the first stone—except that it seems to be assumed that women are always men's lawful prey and any appropriation or sacrifice of them for sex purposes quite pardonable and 'natural.'" In fact, Wilde posed problems for Carpenter. As a married man his sexuality did not square with Carpenter's apologetics for an innate as opposed to an acquired homosexuality and by temperament he was averse to its flamboyant expression. Elsewhere he addressed the issue of blackmail, "a huge and organized profession," honored in the Wilde trial, giving, he observed, "a considerable impetus to this odious kind of professional." Homosexuals, one in fifty, Carpenter suggested, lead secretive lives, unable to express their feelings: "silence reigns; he feels an outcast among his fellows. He doubts himself, he doubts the truths of his affections and of his best feelings. Not infrequently his life is blighted, or taking a wrong turn, runs down into more desperation and excesses." The answer lay in "social reconstruction," the "encouragement of real affection and the teaching of clean habits and ideas especially to children and young things." But none of this was the concern of the law: "it is obvious that there can be no truly moral relations between people unless they are free."[45] One wonders how differently homosexuality would have been regarded had Carpenter with his rather pious observations been identified with the issue rather than Wilde with his "immoralism" and provocation.

From now on both Carpenter and Ellis ran up against censorship and prosecution. Carpenter ran into immediate difficulties with his essay on *Homogenic Love*. Fisher Unwin, his publisher turned it down and also withdrew *Towards Democracy* from its list: "I daresay," Carpenter suggested to Ellis "he has heard talk going on at the clubs which alarmed him."[46] In the end Carpenter settled for the Free Labor Press, Manchester. This was the first-ever commercial publication in England on the subject.[47] Ellis ran into far greater trouble in his attempt at an English edition of *Sexual Inversion*, with the police prosecution of the press in question, if arguably as much for the anarchist sympathies of its owner as for the book's subject matter. Both later discovered that these books were all but off-limits in the British museum. Only their German but not their English versions had been catalogued. Carpenter was appalled: "to absolutely ignore a vast mass of serious literature," he protested, "is an impossible policy for a great Public library and a suicidal policy." The Library filibustered and said the books were available by special application but side-stepped the question of just how, with their not being catalogued, they could be known about anyway. E. P. S. Haynes entered the fray, commenting ironically on "the superhuman anxiety" of the library for the welfare of its readers, and tartly observing its concern was only for the childlike British but not for German readers and those of other nationalities. Surely, he added, here was a subject of major scientific importance?[48] Carpenter wanted to petition, but finding that it was only works by himself and Ellis that were "being buried" abandoned the idea: "I don't want to make it too personal an affair—and yet something ought to be said."[49] Altogether more alarmingly, during the war the police threatened the publisher George Allen with prosecution for its publishing *The Intermediate Sex*, deemed "indecent and unfit for publication." Both Carpenter and the publishers stood their ground and in the end the police withdrew their threat.[50] Throughout, Carpenter himself was always at risk of blackmail or prosecution, the O'Brien affair of 1909 a scary reminder.

Homosexuality and Spirituality

And under such pressure, unsurprisingly, Carpenter began to fight back and did indeed turn propagandist. One recent commentator has gone so far as to see Carpenter as sponsoring a "uranian revolution": "the hermaphrodites would legislate."[51] But what is more indicative is the nature of his apologetics. It lay in drawing a connection between sexuality and spirituality. Carpenter had already implicitly hinted at a higher spiritual content in homosexuality over heterosexuality and he was to take this a stage further in his *Intermediate Types among Primitive Folk* (1914). Not that in fact he subscribed to any physiological description of the homosexual as hermaphrodite. He had been intrigued but repelled by the image of Siva at Elephanta as bisexual: "a tentative and confused idealization of a double-type," or, in other words, of the intermediate sex.[52] Increasingly he parried any suggestion of effeminacy by reference to homosexual warrior castes, such as the Spartans and the Samurai. Here was also a means of differentiating pederasty or boy-love from homosexuality. The love of a warrior for his military comrade or stand-by was between adult men and of roughly similar age, the same holding true for that between the medieval knight and his squire. He argued the case for a far franker approach to sex, citing the Indian example of the Upanishads; "the perfectly naïve, direct and open way in which the physical facts of human love are brought into direct touch with the supreme inspiration of religious consciousness."[53]

The thrust of the new book was to demonstrate how a whole range of specialist skills within primitive societies, e.g., inventors, teachers, medicine-men, had emerged from within the intermediate sex: inverts were the first "thinkers, dreamers, discoverers." He commented particularly on "the fitness and adaptation of the invert for the priestly or divinatory functions."[54] Here homosexuality and spirituality converged. Maybe, he speculated, this was out of a defensive move by the intermediate sex at a time when matriarchal societies came under threat from patriarchal. He turned anthropologist to prove this connection between both shamanism and divination with homosexuality. He had rather to eat his words over effeminacy when recognizing the links between shamanism and transvestism. He tried to show how this connection between homosexuality and priesthood worked:

> This interaction in fact between the masculine and the feminine, this mutual illumination of logic and meditation, may not only raise and increase the

power of each of these faculties, but it may give the mind a new quality, and a new power of perception corresponding to the blending of subject and object in consciousness. It may possibly lead to the development of that third order of perception which has been called the cosmic consciousness and which may also be termed divination.[55]

This leads naturally into a discussion of Carpenter as mystic.

Mystic

Illumined?

Was indeed Carpenter a mystic? Another Whitmanite, Richard Bucke—and this makes his advocacy somewhat incestuous, their both being so indebted to the same guru—unhesitatingly included Carpenter amongst the highly select number of the illumined. "The better known members of this group could be accommodated," Bucke observed, "all at one time in a modern drawing-room."[56] His was rather a strange list. One would expect to find on it Buddha, Jesus, Plotinus, Mohammed, St. John of the Cross, Jacob Boehme, even Dante and William Blake, not so obviously St. Paul, and surprisingly Bartolomé de Las Casas, Francis Bacon (but then Bucke was one of those who believed he wrote Shakespeare), and Balzac. Predictably Whitman himself was seen as the supreme contemporary example. On a list of also-rans were Emerson and Thoreau, neither seen as reaching enlightenment.

Carpenter did not fit all the characteristics of Bucke's taxonomy. His parents hardly matched his stipulations, "a great mother—a woman strong, athletic, spiritual, of good physique, of superior mental and especially moral powers," a father similarly physically and spiritually but, rather oddly, not intellectually endowed, together with "diverse temperaments" and a conception "under perfect conditions."[57] But Carpenter's writing of *Towards Democracy* had occurred at the auspicious age of thirty-seven, at full maturity, and if compiled from writings at an earlier age it had come together through a burst of creative energy. Here was seen to be Carpenter's experience of nirvana, of immortality. Carpenter himself always saw the poem as "given" to him. It was also written at the appropriate time of the year, a time of new birth, in its first nine months.

Bucke also claimed illumination for himself, but whilst struggling to define this experience of consciousness of the cosmos, an illumination that took one onto a new plane of existence, he had consulted Carpenter himself. This questions any indebtedness of Carpenter to Bucke's text and leaves open the question as to who influenced whom the more. In Bucke's language, in this state of "Brahmic Splendor," the cosmos no longer consisted "of dead matter governed by unconscious, rigid, and unintending law, it shows it on the contrary as entirely immaterial, entirely spiritual and entirely alive, it shows that death is an absurdity, that everyone and everything has eternal life." He adds: "a great deal of this is, of course, from the viewpoint of self consciousness, absurd."[58]

Yoga

How is this awareness of cosmic consciousness obtained? Bucke saw its source in intuition and had no faith in its being acquired by "artificial means," and by this he intended the yoga of the yogis of India. Did Carpenter himself practice yoga? He was clearly familiar with Vivekananda's Raja yoga lectures (1899).[59] Rabindranath Tagore pointed him in this direction when they met sometime in 1913. There is no other evidence that he subscribed to any particular school of yoga. However, he always insisted on the need for meditation, for "the stilling of Thought." How else, he asked, could one escape "the whirligig of the world, the attachment of the Mind which binds us to outer things . . . that ability to pass unharmed and undismayed through the grinning legions of the lower mind into the very heart of Paradise . . . the penalty of failure is and must be widespread madness." Evidently for Carpenter meditation was indispensable for a sane world. "The condition of the exercise of power and energy," he asserted, "is that it should proceed from a center of rest within one." All this was backed up by quotations from the Upanishads and the Gita. This taken from the Katha Upanishad: "As pure water poured into pure water remains the same, thus, O Gautama, is the Self of a thinker who knows." This from the Gita: "he who discovers inaction in action and action in inaction is wise amongst mortals." The secret lay in practice. He cited two exercises, concentration and effacement, e.g., of thought and mind. It takes years to achieve. Some circumstances would help, such as living in the open air, being in love. But success was bound to come with effort. There is just a suggestion that Carpenter was misled by *siddhic* expectations: "if we can get into right touch with the immense, the incalculable powers of Nature, is there anything which we may not be able to do?" But all this clearly shows that Carpenter did practice his own version of yogic meditation.[60]

The Art of Creation

On his return from India Carpenter applied himself all the more to exploring and defining his notion of mysticism. His first major attempt at a definition of cosmic consciousness came with his *The Art of Creation* (1904), as much, however, a work of phenomenology as mysticism. Here was a Berkleyan perspective on knowledge, the inseparability of the knower, the knowledge, the known. Added to this a Vedantist perspective, that through consciousness we enter into contact with all other egos, and hence, though this seems a leap, we are all part of the one ego. The framework for his thought remained evolutionary and historical, with recourse to that familiar triadic structure from the simple, to the self-conscious, to the cosmic. He added a number of new names to those he felt had attained *samadhi*, including Tennyson. He now denigrated "Civilization" in terms of the limitations of self-consciousness: all it can do is "*gnaw* off tiny particles which we call *thoughts* from the great Reality."[61]

Here Carpenter branched off into his specialist subject whilst an Extension lecturer, physiology. He had always sought some quasi-scientific account of the mystical experience. The ego itself, he saw, as made up of millions of cells, each of these a self in its own right, but all adding up to some kind of false identity, something perishable, whereas the true self really lay in oneness with the Universal self, "a Celestial city of equals and lovers." Indeed, we are back to a spiritual Bloomsbury.

But there was a hidden agenda here: this was his way of asserting the importance of the body and its delights.

Carpenter also got lost in vague theories of race consciousness, his way of linking the personal and the historical, or, in an alternative language, phylogeny and ontogeny, and here there was a worrying nod in the direction of eugenics. Tony Brown may be too charitable when he states: "writing in 1904 Carpenter could have no conception of the dangerous implications such simplistic notions of racial identity and purity might have."[62] Out of particular racial physiologies Carpenter believed came different racial myths. But in the end this again was a back-handed way of paying reverence to the body. From particular physiological centers came different emotions, love, pugnacity, sympathy, etc. "The body is not vile," affirmed Carpenter. "It is not only a temple of God, but is a collection of temples . . . Every organ and center of the body is the seat of some great emotion which in its proper activity and due proportion is truly divine."[63]

Where did the mystical come from? In some ways Carpenter was struggling toward not dissimilar insights into consciousness of Freud and Jung. If the brain was the center of consciousness, then, he argued, the sub-conscious was the great sympathetic nervous system. But he drew no analogy with the *chakras*, yoga's way of describing some kind of parallel nervous system. And he was only on the edge of Freud's discovery of the unconscious.

So could cosmic consciousness be explained? Out of this distinctive physiology and out of this race-consciousness came, Carpenter claimed, the Gods.

The variance in physiology and race bred a variety of divine pantheons. An emaciated Indian peasantry, for example, spawned India's emaciated saints. Here Carpenter inhabited the world of Frazer's *The Golden Bough*. Memories over time of some hero or warrior evolved into the Divine. A continuing experience of some emotion, such as fear, could equally lead to the emergence of a divinity. Should these emotions be flawed—"there are such things as Lust without love, Desire of food and drink without reverence for health, love of Power without Pity, love of gain without Charity"—then such "endless repeated experience" turns into the diabolical.[64] But Carpenter then turned the optimist: "the Angels overcome and eject the Devils."[65] It is out of just this process of spiritual transmutation that the cosmic consciousness will emerge. In language that echoes Nietzsche—and one of Nietzsche's overmen was the saint—will also come "the superman": the brain and self-consciousness have been midwives to the birth of the soul. The brain has ceased from "its terrified and insatiate quest." "The Man at last lets Thought go." We are back to Nirvana and *samadhi*: "this is the Divine yoga or union from which all creation flows."[66]

But consistently Carpenter fell short of a Vedantist concept of absorption. If here was "the great deliverance from the prison-life of the separate self" we do not lose all sense of our individuality: love, sympathy, faith, courage, confidence, all remain. And he saw the ultimate transformation in physical terms; we will acquire another body, "expression of our more universal nature—a body built of far-extending ethereal elements, subtle and penetrating, yet powerfully massive and material."[67] Whitman was still prevailing over Ramaswamy.

Carpenter could never quite decide whether consciousness welled up from below, from within humanity itself, or flowed from an external Absolute Self. Increasingly, Carpenter seems the transitional figure, one straddling an ancient Vedic culture, yet deferring to new evolutionary and psychological insights into the possibilities of transcendental consciousness.

Deconstructing Christianity

One personal battle Carpenter continued to fight was with Christianity. That seemingly facile surrender of his priesthood in the 1870s had in fact left a strong need to justify and explain his reaching beyond Christianity. This came in the most carefully researched of all his late writings *Pagan and Christian Creeds: Their Origin and Meaning* (1920). In his deconstruction of Christianity one strategy was to draw on all his armory of anthropology and comparative religion. Christianity he situated between pre-civilization man, a pagan world of magic, and his vision of superconsciousness; Christianity was indeed ineluctably linked to self-consciousness. He demonstrated that central aspects of Christian belief, the role of a savior figure, a virgin birth, a transfiguration, all featured in numerous other belief systems. Amongst examples cited were the Khonds of Bengal who sacrificed their *meriahs*, specially selected human sacrificial victims, and Krishna's self-sacrifice in the Gita: "I am the sacrifice, the ancestral offering;" there was the way Indra, Soma, Hari were all transformed into animals so that they could be ritually sacrificed. Out of the sacrifice of Purusha, the Universal Being, came the birds and the animals. He found a parallel for the virgin birth in the story of Devaki, the radiant virgin of Hindu mythology, wife to Vishnu, mother of Krishna. Carpenter was also able to draw on a nineteenth-century biblical scholarship which had come to doubt the historicity of Christ in favor of a legendary or mythic figure. How, he also asked, could all the multifarious events of the Passion story have possibly occurred in so short a time?

But there was a deeper quarrel with Christianity, a feeling, indeed, of moral outrage at its emphasis on a merely personal salvation. Through its self-consciousness Christianity had betrayed that mutuality which had united the pagan tribe. In pre-civilization there had been an organic tie between man and animal, man and nature. Man had worshipped nature. As an example Carpenter cited the cult of trees. In India the peepul or Bo-tree was held sacred. Women had married trees; Krishna a Basil plant. Carpenter wrote of "this conviction of our essential unity with the whole of creation, which lay from the first at the base of all Religion."[68] It was fear that had destroyed that harmony. Out of fear came a sense of man's separateness and sinfulness. To adapt another Christian myth, that of exile from the Garden of Eden, there was "a fall" into self-consciousness. Until the Council of Nicaea 325 AD early Christianity had retained some sense of mutuality. Thereafter it had become obsessed with the idea of personal salvation; "a rather sordid huckstering bargain by which Man gets the better of God by persuading the latter to sacrifice his own Son for the Redemption of the world . . . a romantic and aspiring Christianity gave place to a worldly and vulgar Churchianity."[69] This was a fear still rampant in the violence of the Great War, "a carnival of human slaughter."[70]

Carpenter went to great lengths to clear the decks of his Christian background, the better to explore the ways toward some alternative mystical experience.

Vedantism

In his search for that experience Carpenter could be narrowly Vedantist. His later writings reveal a very careful reading of the Upanishads and the Gita. But he did so with some critical detachment. He wrote of "their flashes of intuition and experience . . . those extraordinary flashes embedded in the midst of what we should call a rather rubbishy kind of argument, and a great deal of merely Brahminical talk of those days."[71] Elsewhere he wrote of them as "indeed the manuals of human entrance into the cosmic state" but with the caveat, "a vast deal of rubbish has accreted around their essential teachings. And has to be cleared away."[72] Point of departure for his awareness of a larger Self lay in just those moments of inspiration, when one sees "into the heart of creation," a union "with the rest of mankind," "a glimpse of a strange immortality." He quoted the famous, "that thou art" of the Khandogya Upanishad and the Gita's, "him whose soul is purified, whose self is the Self of all creatures." Purification lay in "stripping the veil that blind us from one another." And, as always, he claimed this Vedantism was "thoroughly scientific."

But what did this all really mean? What is "a being perceiving all but itself remaining unperceived?" He gave it a fuller definition: "in everything that has consciousness it is the Self: it watches over all operations, it overshadows all creatures; it moves in the depths of our hearts, the perceiver, the only being that is cognizant and yet free from all."[73] But then he corrected himself: "the great universal being residing there in the depths can be perceived. It is truly beyond the power of words to describe: it can only be *perceived*—and that by an inner faculty."[74] Carpenter entertained a view of the relationship with the divine as a two-way process, both inwards and outwards, both introspective and social. He always came back to the theme of the interrelatedness of all. The great sin, and this echoes a Vedantist concept of sin, was separation. He absolutely loathed the ideal of "self-goodness," "one of the most disgusting ideas which has ever infested the human brain."[75] Here we are back with his corrective of a spiritualized democracy. But how in evolutionary terms was a cosmic consciousness to be reached?

Obsessively Carpenter sought to describe how one could move from the second stage of self-consciousness to the third stage of cosmic consciousness. The second was deemed "an aberration, a divorce, a parenthesis": its modes of thought constituted an inherent barrier to the transition to the cosmic. The third would oddly be a return to something of the nature of the first, pre-civilization, with its simple state of union with the whole. Yet Carpenter was too much the Victorian, too much a believer in progress, not to see some positive benefits in the second phase: listed as "all sorts of mental and technical knowledge and skill, emotional developments, finesse and adaptability of mind"— and all of these would be incorporated into "a vastly extended harmony."[76] And his millenarianism was still in evidence. Even the catastrophe of the Great War, "the scum and dregs created by the past order" (he was writing in 1919), might yet register as "the end of a dispensation." There is a

Hegelian feel to his view that "the world as it is carries the doom of its own transformation in its bosom"; the ignorance and non-perception, those great failings of the second phase "destroy themselves." But, perceptively as it happens, he had his doubts and feared the second phase had yet to play itself out, "still more and more terrible struggles may be necessary."[77]

In many ways Carpenter's was an inverted Marxism: superstructure would determine infrastructure; self-consciousness bred commercialism; cosmic consciousness would put an end to the material crisis of existence and usher in the Golden City. Some new universalist faith would replace all the world's religions. If acknowledging here a debt to Comte and positivism he disparagingly commented that its Holy Human Church had been made "so profoundly dull that it never flourished."[78] This was a world religion long in the making. As one of its key concepts he cited the Vedantist of non-differentiation, or rather, not-two-ness. Self-consciousness, however, would not be wholly abandoned, and here his Hegelian synthesis is back in the reckoning, and indeed it would only really come into its own "when it recognized its affiliation with the whole."[79] And then he fell back on a whimsical forecast, rather Forsterian in tone, that the transition would come about "as by a growth and expansion of the human heart and a change in its psychology and powers of perception."[80]

Mysticism and Sexuality

How did Carpenter's mystical quest connect with his apologetics for sexual emancipation? The initial connection was expressed negatively, his anger against Christian attitudes to sex. Christianity had narrowed sexual relationships down to mere procreation: "a violent effort was made to wrench apart the spiritual and corporeal aspects of it."[81] All he could see in the Christian approach was a wishy-washy altruism, entirely lacking in the drive of the true romantics: "to regard love as a kind of refined and delicate altruism is driveling nonsense."[82] Explanations for this alienation of the early Church from sex and the body could lie in its reaction against the sexual excess of the late Roman world. But his bête-noire of self-consciousness was inevitably part of the explanation. That quest for personal salvation became mingled with a sense of sin and indecency. Self-consciousness "grew powerful enough to penetrate to the center of human vitality, the *sanctum* of man's inner life, his sexual instinct, and to deal it a terrific blow."[83] And Civilization bred a shameless commercialization of sex. By 1919 Carpenter could refer to Freud's warning on the psychological damage that such sexual repression could do.

But once again resorting to the dialectic he saw in Civilization a prospect for change: "the negative, Christian dispensation is rapidly approaching its close."[84] Out of civilization's very contempt for sex would emerge a greater awareness of love. Turning cultural relativist, he saw alternative attitudes prevailing in pagan and non-European cultures. In India, for example, the omnipresence of lingams pointed to a franker acceptance of sex. In his ideal of union, sex and love would be united. Union with the divine is, of course, the underlying concept in yoga. Even Nietzche's pagan blond beast was preferable to the Christian rhetoric of altruism and self-sacrifice. But how compatible was this neo-paganism with spirituality?

Patently there was a tension between Carpenter's neo-Vedantism with its quest for transcendence and his belief in the physical delights of the body. He addressed this issue in his final work *Light from the East* (1928). At his most brutal he compared *samadhi* and orgasm:

> In all this there is much that reminds one of the manifestation of sex in the body—its burning withering intensity—the fixed almost rigid condition which precedes its culmination, the threads like lightning, streaming from all parts of the organism to their fulfillment, and the ecstatic deliverance. The man becomes God. No wonder that this condition has from the farthest back times been glorified as holy![85]

This was to echo his earlier assertion in *Adam's Peak* of "the deep-lying truth that the whole universe conspires in the sexual act, and that the orgasm itself is a flash of the universal consciousness."[86]

But some critics simply see Carpenter here in denial of the self-abnegation of Vedantism. With reference to Carpenter's attitudes to the teachings of his guru, Ramaswamy, Bakshi writes: "he is attracted to the tranquility and the casting off of material trappings but the consecutive renunciation of love and individual fulfillment does not appeal to him."[87]

Yet Carpenter was never to abandon a search for synthesis between sexuality and spirituality. He pointed to the homoerotic implications of Arjuna's attraction toward Krishna. In *Light from the East* he returned to his theme of a specialist homosexual or bi-sexual spiritual elite. The future lay in a reconnection of the body and the spirit. In many ways Carpenter's closest parallel lay with Aurobindo and his concept of a divinized body. Both pursued, though independently, a vision of a this-worldly Kingdom of God.

Death

Coping with death is the ultimate test of mysticism. What answer did Carpenter have to the question of immortality? It lay in the least satisfactory of his late writings *The Drama of Love and Death*. He had some faith in it at the time; he wrote to Ellis of his "dealing with both this side and that of the veil.

It is pretty bold and original I think."[88] A certain "suspension of disbelief" is called for to come to terms with some of Carpenter's late writings. Carpenter here showed himself open to much that properly belongs to the territory of the paranormal, with his readiness to pay attention to mediums and to near-death experiences. Here was the material to answer the question, just what aspects of consciousness survive death?

Once again his theme was man's relationship with the All-Self. In terms of consciousness and death he had no doubts about the "survival of the deep-est most universal portions of our nature."[89] He looked on death as another form of birth: "the human self is expelled inwardly through the debris and lit-ter of the mind into another less material and more subtle world than ours."[90] Memory would survive: "each stream would flow into the central self and there be stored." It might survive "for an indefinite time in the crystal mirror of the deeper consciousness."[91]

Carpenter also subscribed to an eastern belief in reincarnation, both phy-logenetic or racial—and here the individual would only share "in a streaky fashion"—and ontogenetic or individual, "reincarnated or re-embodied com-plete through successive materializations and condensations."[92] Admittedly there might be a period of purgatory in some intermediate astral region and, given all the muddle of our lives, "if there is to be any sanity or sequence in the conclusion it must mean a long period of brooding and reconciliation of readjustment, and even of sleep." Initially there may even be "nightmare-like confusion" before any harmony is obtained.[93] He expanded on the possibil-ity we are split personalities and hence might have multiple or "bilocate" reincarnations: "there is no such thing as a fixed and limited personality." "Our most intimate selves are related to a great number of bodies in *succes-sion* to each other in Time." Only the All-Self is fixed.[94]

The work ends with a Wagnerian *Tristan und Isolde* like vision of a merger of Love and Death: "even in the furthest spheres the poignant syllables 'I' and 'Thou' will surely still be heard: and a thousand deaths shall not avail to ex-haust their meaning and to make of love a pale and cold abstraction." But there will be moments of release for our reincarnated bodies when "we sometimes pass out of our little mundane dream into that other land where the great Voices sound and Visions dwell." This was possibly Carpenter's best shot at try-ing to evoke his apprehension that the mystical and the sexual were one.

Disciples

In 1883, at Millthorpe, "in a singularly beautiful Derbyshire valley," halfway between Sheffield and Chesterfield, close to Holmesfield with the nearest railway station four miles away, out of reach of those two worst aspects of Civilization "respectability and cheap intellectualism,"[95] Carpenter built the house, ashram if you like, to be home to all his causes till ill health drove him south to Guildford in 1922. Here was his experiment in mixing the classes: "architects, railway clerks, engine-drivers, signalmen, naval and military officers, Cambridge and Oxford dons, students, advanced women, suffragettes, professors and provision-merchants, came into touch in my little house and garden: parsons and positivists, printers and authors, scythesmiths and surgeons, bank managers and quarrymen, met with each other."[96] As a new age guru he attracted a wide clientele: "faddists of all sorts and kinds considered me their natural prey . . . Vegetarians, dress-reformers, temperance orators, spiritualists, secularists, anti-vivisectionists, socialists, anarchists . . . would call and insist in the most determined way on my joining their crusades." Carpenter's way was to buttonhole his visitors privately, "the politics of personal influence," "a sort of direct democracy in action" as Tsuzuki puts it.[97] How did the guru-disciple relationship work in practice? Carpenter's following was considerable and this account will be more exemplary and selective than extensive.

Henry and Kate Salt

Carpenter's relationship with the Salts betrays both the substance and the frailty of his role as guru.

Born 1851, not until an encounter with a follower of John Ruskin in Cumbria in 1879, one William Riley, a worker on Ruskin's experimental St. George's farm near Sheffield, and an encounter with Ruskin himself at Brantwood, did Henry Salt[98] begin to share Carpenter's outlook that Civilization was not what it claimed to be and that in fact he lived among meat-eating barbarians. He was to become a leading exponent of vegetarianism, an opponent of vivisection and blood sports, and one of the founders of the Humanitarian League, set up in 1891 and to survive till 1919. With the outbreak of war in 1914 the caveman, he believed, was on the loose again. He wrote of "the thoughtless infancy of our age," "the general lack of humanity." "The one and only talisman is love."[99] Humanitarianism was his mantra. If a close friend of the overbearing George Bernard Shaw he was always very much his own person.

It was out of a search for the simple life that he came into contact with Carpenter. Their paths had just failed to cross at Cambridge. Whilst at King's College, 1871 to 1875, Henry had attended F. D. Maurice's St. Edward's Church but Carpenter had just resigned as curate: "I have never been able quite to picture the author of *Towards Democracy* in the pulpit," he reminisced, "arrayed canonically in surplice or gown."[100] For many years both as pupil and teacher Henry had been content at Eton. But then he read the essays that made up Carpenter's *England's Ideal*. Those and a reading of Thoreau's *Walden*—"in my case an epoch, a revelation"[101]—did much to prompt his resignation from Eton as a teacher. This followed on from the dismissal of Jim Joynes, his brother-in-law and a fellow Etonian school teacher, for his friendship with the socialist, Henry George, and his publishing an account of their time together, *Adventures of a Tourist in Ireland*. He joined another experimental farm at Tilford in Surrey. It was Joynes who brought Carpenter on a visit and he was to become a frequent one, "'the tutelar deity of the place."[102] In time the Salts—by then he had married Joynes's sister Kate—visited Millthorpe though Henry was himself none too impressed by the house, "even thought it a blot on the landscape, with its slate roof and bare, hard exterior and its petty kitchen garden with the silly rows of tiny fruit trees."[103]

Henry was never a true acolyte. As Winsten put it: "Salt did not want to be a shadow of a great man, for though he deeply respected Carpenter and loved to listen to his experiences, spiritual or otherwise, he wanted to retain his own individuality."[104] Carpenter, he believed, lacked any talent for organization. But he recognized in him "one of the most influential writers and speakers in the socialist cause." He saw him at his best with people: "he seemed to be always master of the emergency, receiving the new-comers, however untimely their arrival with impenetrable urbanity . . . it was hospitality brought to a fine art."[105]

But his recollections of Carpenter following his death were less generous. In no way, he averred, was Carpenter a natural agricultural worker. Nor was he naturally at ease with local people, irritated by their slowness of speech: "he had a sort of affectation of coarseness." Revered as the hermit of Millthorpe, "he was very unlike a hermit." And with Carpenter the question has to be asked as for all gurus; who needed whom the more, the guru or the disciple?: "he seemed to need *personal* intercourse with friends to an extraordinary degree," observed Henry, so much so that he would exaggerate their merits. But Henry still ended on an upbeat note. Carpenter, certainly a reformer and idealist, "but to the deeper student the faculty which specially distinguished him is what may be called his mysticism or seership, the sense of a serene and illuminated wisdom which is felt throughout his written word." He brought together "the profound repose of Oriental thought with the reforming energy of the West; he was at once occultist and publicist, dreamer and reformer."[106]

There were interesting connections between India and Henry Salt. He was born there. His father, by and large absent in his life, served in the Indian army. On his mother's side, her brother-in-law was a chaplain who died at the siege of Lucknow. Famously, Gandhi found the answer to his culinary needs in a vegetarian restaurant in London and there he purchased Salt's pamphlet *Plea for Vegetarianism*. They met at the time, if passingly, Gandhi attending one of Salt's tea parties. Later GBS jokingly suggested to Ramsay Macdonald that, given the rapport between Gandhi and Salt, he should appoint him his Secretary of State for India. Certainly in 1931 Gandhi almost immediately visited Henry. Salt never ceased to be surprised at the way he, the rationalist, proved to be so attractive to the mystic.

Carpenter's relationship with Kate Salt was altogether a more troubled affair, and maybe predictably so, with one homosexual trying to overstep the accepted boundaries between them. Despite Joynes's warning to Henry that Kate was not as other women were, he had, in a very Victorian way, married his best friend's sister. Kate found the physical touch of heterosexual men repellent. Many, including GBS, believed her intellectual talents to be high and greater than those of both her brother and husband. But again in a Victorian way she was trapped by domestic duties. In the 1880s she found herself pulled between two gurus, Carpenter and Shaw, playing Beethoven piano duets with the former, Wagner with the latter. Alternating their ideals she tried to act out Carpenter's cult of manual labor by becoming a typesetter, but quite ineffectually, then acted as Shaw's secretary. But her deeper emotional tie, given their shared homosexuality, was always with Carpenter. She found Millthorpe "heaven itself, complete with a divinity."[107]

It was a two-way emotional exchange. In Kate, Carpenter had found that invaluable female confidante. He wrote: "you know you really have helped me very much, with all your tender mercies and goodness, quite cheered me up. So there is no need for you to thank me—else I should have to begin to do the same to you and so ad infinitum." She had listened to all his troubles with Hukin. But he also recognized the problematic of Kate's own affection for him and her lesbianism: "I am sure you suffer a good deal with your sympathies being constantly preyed upon—and from the hardened inhumanity of the world."[108]

But Kate's needs were far the greater. She had become the true disciple. "Don't you know what I really think of it?" (*Towards Democracy*). She confided:

> I think it is the most important book of our time but no words could say for me how, personally, I love and worship it and find in it my highest creed and hope and ideal—all that I have dumbly and feebly felt after—all that I have come close to in the best moments of my life, and I find it all expressed! written down.[109]

But there was unease in their relationship. "I wish Chips" (her nickname for him), she wrote later:

> I could quite get over being afraid of you—for I suppose it's really that. Then I should be much happier with you. I am always shamming and never really myself. And that is probably what disgusts you and makes you inclined to snap at me. I wonder if you well understand when I tell you that I feel nearer to you when you are away than when you are nearer. I do feel that apartness when you are near, but that all drops away when you are far off and then I feel myself hand in hand with the real you—the better you—which is hidden from me when you are here—because—well you know why (Was this a coded reference to both their homosexuality?). You don't mind my writing all this do you? Since you became my Master I feel I can say anything to you—that part of you at least which is my master.[110]

Carpenter and Kate continued to correspond over matters such as marriage and the woman question, issues all addressed in *Love's Coming of Age* but the strain of the relationship began to tell. In a letter frankly acknowledging that she pestered him she continued, movingly but in a rather hysterical vein:

> I find there's only you. You in all the world, so you see it's rather important for me—Edward! Don't leave me altogether if you can help it. I have really tried hard—but it is *so* hard—and sometimes I feel as if I shall go down. You know I don't want to torment you—but when I feel I am absolutely nothing to you it seems so impossible to go on. After all, why should I pretend and dissemble? Forgive me—and don't reject me utterly (inwardly I mean) and remember that all this time it has been blank darkness to me—and there's something in me that denies it all the time—denies that you can want to cut and lop me off altogether. I don't know why it is that I am cut off from you—perhaps somewhere there is some dreadful mistake—I think if you knew all about me you would not put me away. Edward I want your hand still.[111]

It required all of Carpenter's psychological skills to handle such emotional dependence, all too common in a disciple's relationship with a guru. Earlier he had encouraged her to practice meditation exercises: "turn all that fury and fire in your nature on them."[112] Later he enquired "if those black blues are departing and that you are trampling them underfoot. Don't blame yourself too much. You know how much these things arise from physical causes."[113] He continued, rather selfishly but it was a confidence she would have welcomed, to use her as a confidante, describing the handover as housekeeper from George Adams to George Merrill: "of course all these troubles arise from my outrageous temperament. If only I had a nice smug little wife etc."[114] But the crisis could not be staved off and by December 1899 Carpenter had to insist on a two-year break.

Two years later there was to be another of those harrowing letters, but half conceding that his discipline had been for the best: "I suppose it was the only thing to be done and I bless you increasingly for having caused me to do it." There followed an anguished expression of guilt at her having married Henry. But she did not give up hope that she and Carpenter would get back in touch; "it does seem so strange that my life should be so utterly apart from yours, for whatever you may feel about me (rage and scorn for my utter littleness and futility), I do know that those hands of yours belong to me by some unwritten elemental law, as no other hands that have ever touched. I felt it when we sat by your study fire and you told me my doom."[115]

And, indeed, they were to get ever closer in touch but at the price of Kate's final disillusionment. Shortly after Henry had been summoned north to stand by Carpenter in his hour of need to deal with the mad O'Brien, in 1910 they moved house to Holmesfield and were to be in almost daily contact. Kate then discovered, or so she believed, that Carpenter's claim to understand women was false: "he boasted at being one with them but Kate," judged Winsten, "soon discovered otherwise and even his writings on sex seemed rather obvious." And here there was to be a vicious circle for Henry's regard for Carpenter was related to Kate's, and with her loss of faith his own diminished, then his disaffection merely compounded Kate's own.[116]

Kate succumbed to a mysterious illness in 1914 though she was not to die of it till 16 February 1919. She could still rise to Carpenter's emotional needs, writing a strong letter of sympathy on Hukin's death: "he touched us all so much—I couldn't say which of us most. And I love him the more because of his understanding of the other two"[117] (viz. Carpenter and Merrill).

But personal relationships had always got in the way of the guru-disciple relationship between Carpenter and the Salts. They had taken to Hukin and the Adams's, especially Lucy, but fallen out with Merrill. Henry kept up with Carpenter after both had moved south, Henry to Hove, Carpenter to Guildford. As far as Henry was concerned Merrill was now nothing "but a commonplace inebriate and a humiliation."[118] Carpenter in old age he saw as "shaky and helpless, the giant of yesterday":[119] "music and meditation on Eastern religion now took up the whole of his days."[120] Carpenter died of a paralytic stroke, 28 June 1929. Henry lived on till 9 April 1939.

C. R. Ashbee

In C. R. Ashbee, Carpenter found his most committed disciple of comradeship, that ideal of a progressive alliance between the middle and working class, underpinned by homosexual attraction. In the words of his biographer, this was a romantic socialism, defined as "a mixture of angry youthful ideal-ism and of upper-class notions of duty tinged with panic: the important thing was to get in touch with the working class and to get at the common hu-manity below the differences of class."[121] Here was an ideal of class fraternity, prominent in the revolutions of 1848 but one that has over time been de-graded into a mere liking for rough trade. But Ashbee was little concerned with politics. His was a Gandhian idealism of the craftsman and an aversion for the machine-made. Next to William Morris his was to be the inspiration for the Arts and Crafts movement.

He was to reject a business career on offer in his father's firm in favor of training as an architect. Curiously his father was a great collector of erotica—Richard Burton had been a frequent guest—publishing under the pseudonym Pisanus Fraxi. And, ironically, his was to be one of the works Asbee could not gain access to when he joined in Carpenter's campaign against the British Museum, denied use of the catalogue of the Private Case in the Library. It was the Cambridge of the 1880s that shaped Ashbee's idealism. Lowes Dick-inson and Roger Fry were his closest friends. Lowes Dickinson was to prove even more important to him than Carpenter: "it mattered simply that Dick-inson was there."[122] Conversation in Cambridge exposed him to Plato, Henry George, Emerson, Carlyle, Transcendentalism, Swedenborg, Blavatsky; from Emerson "he came to look on all material things and the manifold details of experience as the revelation of a deeper spiritual reality."[123] He became a Practical Idealist.

But Carpenter at the time was the crucial influence. Lowes Dickinson acted as the intermediary. He visited Millthorpe in May 1885: "We (Goldie and I)," he recorded in his journal, "agree that it was being near Carpenter that had elated us out of ourselves into another world, another cycle of feel-ing."[124] In Carpenter's company he visited his first-ever steel mill: "great brawny men wheeling hither and thither molten ingots of steel . . . a whole epic is in one of those factories, a world of sorrow, beauty of ugliness, of power, of pathos, of heroism." On the farm at Millthorpe he had got to know rural workers: "if one could only shake off this devilish gentility." It was in Cambridge that Carpenter "unfolded to me a wonderful idea of his of a new free-masonry, of comradeship in the life of men which might be based on our little Cambridge circle of friendship." Carpenter had raised in Ashbee the question of "how he would respond to the illegality of his emotions."[125] Car-penter had advised him to bypass any professional training and reach out to the workers but it was advice he was partly to ignore, qualifying as an archi-tect. Only then did he embark on his experiment of Guild Socialism.

In enacting Carpenter's idealism Ashbee had both to address the nature of manufacture and the problematic of his personal life. He was not to be wholly successful in the former. Yet it was to be a bold experiment, with his Guild of Craftsmen initially attached to Toynbee Hall, but moving out to Mile End, the outer suburbs of the East End seen as more sympathetic to his craft ideal, and then with some 150 cockneys in all, the workmen and their families, transplanted to Chipping Campden in the Cotswolds, with some inevitable social problems in their assimilation. The Guild was "an idealized group of comrades banded together against the force of commercialism,"[126] or in Eric Gill's words, "a cell of good living."[127] But it was to fail as a business venture and to break up. Later Ashbee took up an alternative career as champion, inspired by Patrick Geddes, of garden cities, one that took him to Cairo during the war as teacher in a Training College—in Egypt he discovered that tradition of pre-industrial craftmanship he believed in—then invited by Ronald Storrs, Military Governor of Jerusalem, to advise on town planning and later under Herbert Samuel to become Secretary of the Jerusalem Town Planning committee. Although half-Jewish, Ashbee was to resign in protest at what he saw as the imposition of minority interests by force on the Palestinian people.

And how to resolve his personal life? Ashbee was something of a Puritan, maybe by way of reaction to his father, and it's quite probable that his homosexual affections were platonic. On the 8 September 1898 he was to marry the seventeen-year-old Janet Forbes. As he explained to her after she had accepted his proposal: "comradeship to me so far—an intensely close and all-absorbing personal attachment, 'love' if you prefer the word—for my men and boys, has been the one guiding principle in life, and has inspired anything I may have been vouchsafed to accomplish in the nature of the influencing or the building up of character."[128] One of the first persons he introduced her to was "the prince of comrades, sage and father figure," Edward Carpenter.[129] Prior to the move to the Cotswolds in 1901 they had lived in Chelsea, Ashbee acting the dandy, a Whistler look-a-like. For a long while it was a white marriage, forcing Janet eventually to seek emotional, if not physical, consolation in Gerald Bishop, another protagonist of the garden city. But in time they had children.

There are but a few Indian links in Ashbee's career. He was, if anything, pro-imperialist. He certainly had hopes that imperial preference might protect English craft industries. A sister of one of the workers in the Guild married the Anglo-Sinhalese art critic, Ananda Coomaraswamy. He had acquired a Carpenterish concern for the decline of traditional arts and crafts in Sri Lanka and India and found some consolation in the ambitions of the

Guild. Sister Nivedita lectured at the Guild in Chipping Camden. But the real connection with India lay in Ashbee's proto-Gandhian defense of craft industries.

The Neo-Pagans and D. H. Lawrence

The values of Carpenter the Victorian carried forward to a number of writers in a later Edwardian generation though in the strictest sense these were not his disciples. The response of Rupert Brooke and the neo-pagans, so christened by Virginia Woolf, was at most superficial. But there was an almost symbiotic link between the thought of D. H. Lawrence, forty-one years his junior, and Carpenter's, though Lawrence was never to acknowledge his indebtedness. All this was to do with covering his tracks as a bisexual. But if not disciples some commentary is forthcoming for in this later influence lies part of Carpenter's claim to guru status.

Carpenter is deemed the godfather (Whitman its spiritual grandfather) of neo-paganism. Here was another idealist Cambridge generation, loosely in thrall to Rupert Brooke—it included Justin Brooke, Jacques Raverat, Gwen and Frances Darwin, Ka Cox, and the Olivier sisters, aunts to the actor to be, Laurence Olivier—during their Cambridge years, 1908–1911 and beyond. Several were products of new public schools shaped by Carpenterish beliefs in the simple life. Jacques Raverat, the artist, and Noel and Daphne Olivier, had all been to Bedales, founded in 1893 by J. H. Badley, himself a follower of another of Carpenter's disciples, Cecil Reddie, who had set up the far less successful Abbotsholme. There was a cult of the open air and much work on the farm. Paul Delany hints at Carpenter's all-powerful influence: "total institutions (Victorian public schools and universities) have a way of begetting their own most ferocious adversaries; Luther the spoiled monk, Stalin the spoiled seminarian. One such adversary was, though a much gentler one, was Edward Carpenter."[130] But this rebel generation only took up part of Carpenter's message, that beyond Civilization lay an emancipated sexuality; they ignored his mysticism. And Carpenter's message proved as much inhibiting as liberating. Homosexual Carpenter had, after all, preached female chastity. Being in love was more important than making love. Brooke's personal neo-paganism is seen as "a willful sometimes desperate attempt to escape from his engrained puritanism."[131] Only in Tahiti in 1913 did he experience real happiness. In much the same way as Carpenter's rural Arcadian ideal turned its back on the present so the outlook of the neo-pagans was "nostalgic, anti-industrial, dedicated to leisure and personal freedom."[132] They attended Fabian summer schools but Beatrice Webb with her vision of Jesuit-style Young Fabians, found them quite unsuitable, too much influenced by Lowes

Dickinson and his anarchic ideas on sex. But, as Carpenter before him, Brooke rejected "the juiceless planned socialism of Shaw and the Webbs."[133] If the neo-pagans could be said to have escaped the incestuous intimacy of the Apostles and the preciousness of Bloomsbury there were no sustaining values here and neo-paganism had collapsed long before the 1st World War blew Arcadian Edwardianism away.

But D. H. Lawrence was a different proposition. John Bayley made a telling comparison between Brooke and Lawrence: "whereas Lawrence's genius, and sheer intelligence, brought him freedom, Brooke remained trapped inside not only sexual but class conditioning." Brooke was the perennial public schoolboy.[134] Emile Delevenay made a strong case for Lawrence being familiar with all of Carpenter's writings. Between 1906 and 1918 "Carpenter was consistently present in Lawrence's mental environment."[135] He may even have met Carpenter in his Eastwood days. In 1918 the Lawrences lived within a few miles of Millthorpe. Both, Delevenay generalized, shared "a common passionate desire to understand their own psychology. They hoped to do so by relating their inner conflicts to an absolute essence, to some eternal and unitary being."[136] Delevenay's is a literary study and he shows how close Lawrence in his novels, above all in *Women in Love*, was to Carpenter's ideas on marriage and homosexuality, demonstrating his indebtedness to *Love's Coming of Age* and *The Intermediate Sex*. Both were to be subject to police harassment for their views, and *The Rainbow* was banned, but arguably this had been a way of getting at their opposition to the war.

But a more significant influence was Carpenter's "erotic vitalistic mysticism." Lawrence learned as much from Carpenter the mystic as Carpenter the sexologist. By 1914 Delevenay sees Lawrence as already seeking "the recovery of organic consciousness, yoga command of the *chakras*, harmonization of the masculine and feminine elements in each individual, restoration of the relationship of the self with the cosmos."[137] He followed Carpenter's account of an evolution of consciousness toward the cosmic. He likewise shared Carpenter's idolization of Whitman and his idea of the superman.

But Lawrence is seen as a far more troubled and tortured personality than Carpenter and increasingly he drifted into darker territory. Influenced by Houston Chamberlain's racial mysticism, the occultism of J. M. Pryce's *Apocalypse Unsealed*, and the proto-fascist ideas of T. E. Hulme, he was to reject one version of elitism, Whitman's and Carpenter's, one, nevertheless, rooted in their concept of democracy and a cult of the average or common man, in favor of another, adopting the stance of the alienated artist and flirting with a Nietzschean totalitarianism. It is not always easy to see Carpenter's influence in this later period through all the accretions in Lawrence's mind of the ideas of Ouspensky (though he also was indebted to Carpenter), Madame Blavatsky and Lawrence's own readings in eastern religions. In the end Carpenter's *apologia pro vita sua* can be contrasted, Delevenay argued, with Lawrence's "tormented and sometimes horrified self-exploration haunted by ambition of leadership, of Messianic redemption of men."[138] It was an odd list of leaders, including Annie Besant, Gandhi and Mussolini. Both Carpenter and Lawrence had rated Eros over Civilization, "both were dreamers in love with a Golden Age."

It is worth quoting Delevenay's final assessment:

Robust good sense was mixed with the maddest speculations in both, inadaptation to an ordinary social life, sexual anomalies or frustrations, led both to try to forge for themselves total explanations of human nature embracing their own problems into a norm; they could not but fail as soon as this endeavor tried to encompass the social side of individual lives.[139]

The Maharajah of Chhatarpur and E. M. Forster

Carpenter's appeal for the Maharajah of Chhatarpur and his influence over E. M. Forster are the bridge to the next part of this text. The Maharajah became a close personal friend of Forster's but only corresponded with Carpenter and he will feature more fully below in that context.

Maharajah Vishnwarath Singh Bahadur, the Maharajah of Chhatarpur (1866–1932) dreamed of a companion who would speak to his pressing emotional and spiritual needs. The visit of Lowes Dickinson, Forster and Bob Trevelyan in November 1912 inspired the forlorn hope that Carpenter would fulfill this role and prompted his writing to Carpenter, Dickinson his means of access (Forster had yet to meet Carpenter): "his description of you has simply added fuel to fire and I am almost inclined to think that unless I have seen you my life will have lost its main object." It was a reading of *The Art of Creation* but even more a collection of homoerotic poetry *Iolaus* (1902) that led the Maharajah to sense "an inseparable affinity" and the greatly mistaken belief that Carpenter shared his pedophile tastes.[140] In a follow-up letter he was even more the fawning acolyte: "till now it had never occurred to me that there could be in this world of misery and trouble holy beings possessing such supreme and divine souls as yours undoubtedly is."[141] Would that they had met younger. Carpenter demurred (his replies are inevitably lost) but the Maharajah persisted: "I am like a man rolling in bed in agonies and you are the Messiah to say 'get up' and the life is saved."[142] Possibly Carpenter gave some grounds for hope for the correspondence did not flag. He wrote of his reading *The Intermediate Sex*: "the more do I feel my heart beating in sympathy with yours." By now he had appreciated the inappropriateness of sug-gesting that the old and frail Carpenter should be joined by a lady friend. Of course his male companion should accompany him. He requested copies of *Love's Coming of Age*, *Angel's Wings*, and *The Drama of Life and Death*. "You are the infinite Messiah. Do come and release me from my trouble." And a Vedantism lurked behind his plea: "I am in a myre (again, egoism) and I stand in great need of you." But he also fussed over the photos of the young actors in his Krishna troupe being too large to post; he had wanted Carpen-ter to adjudicate on their beauty.[143] Even as late as 1924 he still held out hope that if not Carpenter at least George Merrill should come on a visit. Clearly the Maharajah had the mentality of a disciple.

But this was not the case with Forster. The received wisdom is that he and Carpenter met in September 1913, following his return from India and with Dickinson once again the intermediary, fell under the spell of Carpenter's serenity, had his bottom touched by Merrill and, as Hindus might say, this was to release the power of the *kundalini*. All this proved the inspiration for his posthumous gay novel *Maurice*.[144]

Nicola Beauman has an alternative dating of July 1910. It came after a major trauma Forster had experienced in Cambridge the year before. He had met a friend of Malcolm Darling at dinner in King's, Ernest Merz, had briefly kept him company afterwards, but that night, 9 July, Merz had committed suicide. Was this out of guilt at his homosexuality? Could he have done more to help? Did Forster seek out Carpenter so as to come to terms with this trauma? Beauman believes the novel was begun after this visit and was in-spired by Merz's story.[145] Tariq Rahman has opened up the possibility of an even earlier familiarity with Carpenter's writings, once again at Dickinson's instigation, from 1905, though it was only in 1913 that "he became so to speak a disciple of the older man." After his second meeting in 1913 he con-fided to his diary: "Forward rather than back. Edward Carpenter! Edward Carpenter! Edward Carpenter!" It was an enthusiasm only to wane after 1922.[146]

In much the same way as Delevenay drew parallels between Carpenter's ideas and those in Lawrence's novels so Tariq Rahman does with Forster's fic-tion. He speculates that Mr. Emerson in *A Room with a View* (1908) and Mr. Failing in *The Longest Journey* (1907) are both modeled on Carpenter. In his revised version of the former, Mr. Emerson "has become a gentle mellowed old man who talks philosophically if a little fatuously—somewhat like Car-penter."[147] Mr. Failing expresses ideas akin to those in Carpenter's *England's Ideals and Other Essays*, his theory of exfoliation, that love will be the path-way to the brotherhood of man. More dubiously, Rahman proposes that the child of Helen Schlegel and Leonard Bast in *Howard's End* (1910) is Carpenter's uranian, one of those who will fashion a future utopia. Forster shared Carpenter's antipathy to a mechanized industrialized world. He likewise delighted in the anti-intellectual and a primitive spontaneity. By 1915 Forster had become so embattled on Carpenter's behalf that he broke off relationships with D. H. Lawrence because of his unacceptable criticism. But a deeper cause for acknowledging Carpenter lay in that "yogified mysticism" which, in its claim that we were all one, provided Forster with a means of overcoming his sense of alienation as a homosexual: if, in a Vedantist sense, we were all part of a whole then he himself was at one with all. Between 1913 and 1922 Forster kept in frequent contact by letter and undertook several visits to Millthorpe. Quite why the enthusiasm faded is not obvious: 11 May 1922 he recorded in his diary: "I like and admire E. C. as much as ever but he retains no mystery for me." In his Common Place book, "astonishing how he drains away."[148] In the bleak aftermath of war Carpenter's idealism began to look dated and naïve.

Conclusion

Does all this suggest Carpenter was a guru with "feet of clay"?[149] But even his latterday researchers cannot escape his appeal. In exploring that "broken revolutionary tradition" of the personal, the political, and the spiritual of the 1880s, centered on Carpenter and his circle, Sheila Rowbotham, his most perceptive biographer, writes of "the kind of closeness you have with old friends . . . having an address book of the past . . . this loving intimacy with ghosts." Here, fifty years on, is another quasi-disciple. She draws more attention to his socialist credentials, his response to the Commune and the 1st International, republicanism, land nationalization, links with the Leeds socialists, Alf Mattison and Tom Maguire, but all harnessed to his "democracy of feeling." She grasps well those labor saving aspects of the simple life: "how varnished floors upstairs and stone on the ground save housework." Such immediate practical gains would have appealed to Gandhi. However "vague" and "mystical" Carpenter addressed a real question: "how to connect the question of social control of the external world with the needs of human biology." His was an appeal to lofty sentiments: "he expected people to have the strength to will themselves into freedom." She writes of "his eclectic quest," his rummaging in anthropology, psychology, his own Broad Church Anglicanism, eastern religious thought as "something of a lucky dip": "it is easier to pull bits out than to understand the connection." These three chapters have sought to make those connections. Their focus has been on the inner connection between his views on sexuality and Hindu spirituality. Row-botham summarizes: "Eastern religious thought seemed to provide an alternative which avoided materialism and the Christian hierarchical dualism of spirit and matter. In the east they seemed to have found a place for pleasure without shame and a more easy relationship between mystical ecstasy and physical eroticism than the West." Her conclusion is as good as any and can stand: "But his struggle to make these connections was not merely theoretical, it was his whole life. The way he lived was a demonstration of what he thought and the two are inseparable. His influence, which was considerable, was less a matter of logic than a cultural stance."[150]

Notes

1. The text cannot open up any full discussion of Victorian and Edwardian moral codes. Introductory accounts include Samuel Hynes, *The Edwardian Turn of Mind* (Princeton: Princeton University Press, 1968); Michael Mason, *The Making of Victorian Sexuality* (Oxford: Oxford University Press, 1994); Eric Trudgill, *Madonnas and Magdalens* (London: Heinemann, 1976).

2. Wilde's role in the Dreyfus Affair is one of its curiosities. He knew Esterhazy and may indirectly have passed on the vital information that allowed Zola to blow open the cover-up of military intelligence. See J. Robert Maguire, "Oscar Wilde and the Dreyfus Affair," *Victorian Studies* 41, no. 1 (Autumn 1997).

3. Edward Carpenter, *My Days and Dreams* (London: Allen and Unwin, 1916), 302–3, 305.

4. This account is compiled largely from a personal memoir Carpenter composed 5 March 1913 on Merrill, Carpenter MSS 363/17, information in Carpenter, *My Days and Dreams*, 159–64 and C. Tsuzuki, *Edward Carpenter 1844–1929 Prophet of Human Fellowship* (Cambridge; Cambridge University Press, 1980).

5. Edith Lees to Carpenter, 4 October 1907, MSS 358/8.

6. For biographical information see Phyllis Grosskurth, *Havelock Ellis: A Biography* (London: Allen Lane, 1980). Amongst earlier biographies, see Arthur Calder-Marshall, *Havelock Ellis* (London: Rupert Hart-Davis, 1959). There are interesting arguments raised in Paul Robinson, *The Modernisation of Sex* (London: Elek, 1976), Chapter 1.

7. Havelock Ellis, *My Life* (Kingswood: Heinemann, 1940), 131.

8. Calder Marshall, *Havelock Ellis* 232–34.

9. Grosskurth writes of him"as an obscure messiah with a small but fervid following," 42.

10. Sheila Rowbotham and Jeffrey Weeks, *Socialism and the New Life: The Personal and Sexual Politics of Edward Carpenter and Havelock Ellis* (London: Pluto Press, 1977), 144.

11. Quoted Grosskurth, *Havelock Ellis*, 67.

12. Havelock Ellis, My Life, 162–63.

13. Carpenter, My Days and Dreams, 225.

14. Grosskurth, Havelock Ellis, 56.

15. Ellis to Carpenter, 13 January 1886, MSS 357 3(1).

16. Ellis to Carpenter, 12 March 1885, MSS 357/1.

17. Carpenter to Ellis, 7 July 1887, Carpenter Correspondence, Austin, Texas.

18. Carpenter to Ellis, 27 March 1890, Carpenter Correspondence. It seems a little odd that Carpenter had read no Tolstoy by that stage. And maybe just as strange to find George Adams so enjoying Ellis's translations of the poetry of Heine.

19. Carpenter to Ellis, 24 October 1885, Carpenter Correspondence.

20. Carpenter to Ellis, 27 March 1890, Carpenter Correspondence.

21. Carpenter to Ellis, 27 March 1890, Carpenter Correspondence.

22. Unfortunately this has to be another fascinating character that this text has to neglect. Art historian, married, with a penchant for Swiss peasants and Venetian gondoliers his was a considerable input into homosexual reform. See Phyliss Grosskurth, John Addington Symonds: A Biography (London: Longmans), 1965, and Phyliss Grosskurth, ed., The Memoirs of John Addington Symonds (London: Hutchinson, 1984).

23. Carpenter to Ellis, 18 October 1906, Carpenter Correspondence.

24. Carpenter to Ellis, 6 March 1885, Carpenter Correspondence.

25. Beverly Thiele, "Coming of Age: Edward Carpenter on Sex and Reproduction," in Edward Carpenter and Late Victorian Radicalism, ed. Tony Brown (London: Cass, 1990).

26. The text cannot do justice to Carpenter's friendship with Olive Shreiner (1855–1920). Ellis had recommended her novel The Story of an African Farm (1883) and they were to meet. Carpenter became a confidante of her troubled relationships with Havelock Ellis, Karl Pearson and Samuel Cronwright. But they drifted apart. See one recent biography Ruth First and Ann Scott, Olive Schreiner (London: Deutsch, 1980).

27. Edward Carpenter, Love's Coming of Age, 11th edition (London: George Allen and Unwin, 1919), 139–41.

28. Edward Carpenter, Love's Coming of Age, 144–45.

29. "Sagittarius A Review of Love's Coming of Age," The Adult 1898–1899, 12–16, Carpenter MSS C Per 1.

30. Edward Carpenter, The Drama of Love and Death (London: G. Allen and Company, 1912), 52.

31. Ellis to Carpenter, 17 December 1892, MSS 357/5.

32. Carpenter to Ellis, 25 January 1892? (the archive suggests 1896 but this feels wrong.), Carpenter Correspondence.

33. Carpenter to Ellis, 19 January 1894, Carpenter Correspondence.

34. Carpenter to Ellis, 28 November 1894?, Carpenter Correspondence.

35. Carpenter, Homogenic Love (Manchester: Labor Press Society, 1896), 43.

36. Carpenter, The Intermediate Sex (London: S. Sonnenschein, 1908), 128.

37. Carpenter to Ellis, 11 January 1909, Carpenter Correspondence.

38. Ellis to Carpenter, 8 April 1907, MSS 357/13.

39. Ellis to Carpenter, 17 January 1909, MSS 357/14.

40. Michel Foucault, *The History of Sexuality: An Introduction* (London: Allen Lane, 1979).

41. *British Medical Journal*, 26 June 1909.

42. Carpenter to the Editor, 6 July 1909, MSS.

43. *The Medical Times*, 27 February 1919.

44. Carpenter to Ellis, 7 May 1899, Carpenter Correspondence.

45. Edward Carpenter, *Freedom: A Journal of Anarchist Communism*, IX, no. 95 (July 1895), Carpenter MSS.

46. Carpenter to Ellis, 14 October 1895, Carpenter Correspondence.

47. It had a print run of 2,000 copies. Earlier John Addington Symonds had published fifty copies of an essay *A Problem in Modern Ethics*, but this was a privately circulated work. See Tony Brown, ed., *Edward Carpenter and Late Victorian Radicalism*, 388.

48. E. P. S. Haynes, "The Taboo of the British Museum Library," *English Review* (December 1913).

49. Carpenter to Ellis, 16 July 1913, Carpenter Correspondence.

50. As Carpenter described the incident in a letter to Ellis, 24 December 1915, Carpenter Correspondence.

51. See Michael Neve, "Sexual Politics," *London Review of Books* (5–18 February 1981). He interpreted Carpenter as standing for a specifically Northern agenda on sexuality.

52. Carpenter, *Intermediate Types Among Primitive Folk* (London: Allen, 1914), 80.

53. Carpenter, *Intermediate Types Among Primitive Folk*, 132.

54. Carpenter, *Intermediate Types Among Primitive Folk*, 57–62.

55. Carpenter, *Intermediate Types Among Primitive Folk*, 63.

56. Richard Maurice Bucke, *Cosmic Consciousness. A Study in the Evolution of the Human Mind* (New York: George Allen and Unwin, 1901), 11.

57. Richard Maurice Bucke, *Cosmic Consciousness*, 376–79.

58. Richard Maurice Bucke, *Cosmic Consciousness*, 17.

59. He referred to them in a footnote, p. 81 of *The Drama of Love and Death: A Study of Human Evolution and Transfiguration* (Edinburgh: 1912).

60. See his chapter, "Rest," in *The Teaching of the Upanishads* (London: Allen and Unwin, 1920).

61. Edward Carpenter, *The Art of Creation*, 3rd edition (London: G. Allen, 1912), 69.

62. Tony Brown, *The Personal and Social Ideals of E M Forster and Edward Carpenter* (Phd Bangor: 1982), 181–2.

63. Carpenter, *The Art of Creation*, 160–61.

64. Carpenter, *The Art of Creation*, 174–75.

65. Carpenter, *The Art of Creation*, 204.

66. See Chapter XIII, "Transformation," in Carpenter, *The Art of Creation*.

67. Carpenter, *The Art of Creation*, 230–31, 233.

68. Edward Carpenter, *Pagan and Christian Creeds: Their Origin and Meaning* (London: G. Allen and Unwin, 1920), 80.

69. Carpenter, *Pagan and Christian Creeds*, 208.

70. Carpenter, *Pagan and Christian Creeds*, 109.

71. Edward Carpenter, *The Teaching of the Upanishads* (London: Allen and Unwin, 1920), 19.

72. Carpenter, *Pagan and Christian Creeds*, 269.

73. Carpenter, *Pagan and Christian Creeds*, 23.

74. Carpenter, *Pagan and Christian Creeds*, 25.

75. Carpenter, *Pagan and Christian Creeds*, 27.

76. Carpenter *Pagan and Christian Creeds*, 250.

77. Carpenter, *Pagan and Christian Creeds*, 277.

78. In a footnote Carpenter, *Pagan and Christian Creeds*, 264.

79. Carpenter, *Pagan and Christian Creeds*, 273.

80. Carpenter, *Pagan and Christian Creeds*, 278.

81. Carpenter, *The Drama of Love and Death*, 30.

82. Carpenter, *The Drama of Love and Death*, 53.

83. Carpenter, *Pagan and Christian Creeds*, 186.

84. Carpenter, *The Drama of Life and Death*, 31.

85. Carpenter, *Light from the East* (London: Allen and Unwin, 1927), 103–4.

86. Edward Carpenter, *From Adam's Peak to Elephanta: Sketches in Ceylon and India* (London: S. Sonnenschein, 1910), 192.

87. Parminder Bakshi, "Homosexuality and Orientalism," in Tony Brown, ed., *Edward Carpenter and Late Victorian Radicalism*, 172.

88. Carpenter to Ellis, 27 September 1911, Carpenter Correspondence.

89. Carpenter, *The Drama of Love and Death*, 83.

90. Carpenter, *The Drama of Love and Death*, 101.

91. Carpenter, *The Drama of Love and Death*, 220. There is a recondite debate to be had as to whether or not Vedantism does endorse this survival of memory. Some would argue it also is shed in the process of absorption into the absolute. This is discussed below, Chapter 7.

92. Carpenter, *The Drama of Love and Death*, 233.

93. Carpenter, *The Drama of Love and Death*, 253.

94. Carpenter, *The Drama of Love and Death*, 282.

95. Carpenter, *My Days and Dreams*, 148.

96. Carpenter, *My Days and Dreams*, 164.

97. Tsuzuki, *Edward Carpenter 1944–1929*, 3.

98. Henry Salt wrote a number of autobiographical works, *Seventy Years Among the Savages* (London: George Allen and Unwin, 1921); *Company I Have Kept* (London: George Allen and Unwin, 1930). Stephen Winsten, *Salt and His Circle* (London: Hutchinson, 1951) is an intimate and perceptive portrait but relies heavily on personal recollection.

99. Salt, *Seventy Years Among Savages*, 243–43.

100. Salt, *Seventy Years Among Savages*, 45.

101. Salt, *Seventy Years Among Savages*, 78.

102. Salt, *Seventy Years Among Savages*, 75.

103. Winsten, *Salt and His Circle*, 85.

104. Winsten, *Salt and His Circle*, 94.

105. Salt, *Seventy Years Among the Savages*, 87–8.

106. Salt, *Company I Have Kept*, Chapter V.

107. Winsten, *Salt and His Circle*, 85.

108. Carpenter to Kate Salt, 23 February 1890, MSS 354?5?.

109. Kate Salt to Carpenter, 16 December 1890, MSS 355/3.

110. Kate Salt to Carpenter, 4 January 1892, MSS 355/6.

111. Kate Salt to Carpenter, 17 February 1897, MSS 355.

112. Carpenter to Kate Salt, 11 January 1897, MSS 354/45.

113. Carpenter to Kate Salt, 10 March 1897, MSS 354/46.

114. Carpenter to Kate Salt, 12 October 1897, MSS 354/50.

115. Kate Salt to Carpenter, 27 December 1901, MSS 355/23.

116. How Winsten explained it, *Salt and His Circle*, 126.

117. Kate Salt to Carpenter, 18 May 1927, MSS 355/58.

118. Winsten's account, *Salt and His Circle*, 155.

119. Quoted Winsten, *Salt and His Circle*, 155.

120. Winsten's account, *Salt and His Circle*, 147.

121. Alan Crawford, *C. R. Ashbee: Architect, Designer and Romantic Socialist* (New Haven and London: Yale University Press, 1984), 15. This is a highly perceptive account of the intellectual and psychological make-up of one of Carpenter's leading disciples.

122. Alan Crawford, *C. R. Ashbee*, 201.

123. Alan Crawford, *C. R. Ashbee*, 11.

124. Quoted Alan Crawford, *C. R. Ashbee*, 17.

125. Alan Crawford, *C. R. Ashbee*, 18–21.

126. Alan Crawford, *C. R. Ashbee*, 42.

127. Quoted Alan Crawford, *C. R. Ashbee*, 423.

128. Quoted Alan Crawford, *C. R. Ashbee*, 75.

129. How Crawford puts it in *C. R. Ashbee*, 83.

130. Paul Delany, *The Neo-Pagans: Friendship and Love in the Rupert Brooke Circle* (London: Macmillan, 1987), 9.

131. Paul Delany, *The Neo-Pagans*, 69.

132. Paul Delany, *The Neo-Pagans*, 97.

133. Paul Delany, *The Neo-Pagans*, .50

134. In his review of Delany's book, "Trapped in the Lower Fourth," *The Guardian* (31 July 1987).

135. Emile Delavenay, *D. H. Lawrence and Edward Carpenter: A Study in Edwardian Transition* (London: Heinemann, 1971). His research began in the early 1930s—

he befriended Jessie Chambers, Lawrence's first girlfriend and she assured him Lawrence was familiar with Carpenter's writings—so it is puzzling, unless this be a translation, why it took so long to appear. It is probably the best sustained attempt to date to expound Carpenter's philosophy.

136. Emile Delavenay, *D. H. Lawrence and Edward Carpenter*, 4.

137. Emile Delavenay, *D. H. Lawrence and Edward Carpenter*, 134.

138. Emile Delavenay, *D. H. Lawrence and Edward Carpenter*, 195.

139. Emile Delavenay, *D. H. Lawrence and Edward Carpenter*, 233–34.

140. The Maharajah of Chhatarpur to Carpenter, 4 December 1912, MSS 378/12.

141. Chhatarpur to Carpenter, 21 January 1913, MSS 378/14.

142. Chhatarpur to Carpenter, 27 January 1913, MSS 378/13.

143. Chhatarpur to Carpenter, 11 March 1913, MSS 375/15.

144. For an account along these lines see P. N. Furbank, *E. M. Forster: A Life* (Oxford: Oxford University Press, 1977), Chapter 14.

145. Nicola Beauman, Morgan: A Biography of E. M. Forster (London: Sceptre, 1993), Chapter 20.

146. Tariq Rahman, "Edward Carpenter and E. M. Forster," Durham University Journal LXXIX, no. 1 (New Series XLVIII, no. 1) (December 1986), 59–69.

147. Tariq Rahman, "Edward Carpenter and E. M. Forster," 61.

148. Quoted Tariq Rahman, "Edward Carpenter and E. M. Forster," 68.

149. Anthony Storr, *Feet of Clay: A Study of Gurus* (London: Harper Collins, 1996). One attempt at a taxonomy of gurus and an exposure of their frailties.

150. Sheila Rowbotham, "In Search of Carpenter," *History Workshop*, no. 3 (Spring 1977), 121–32k.

PART TWO

LOVE IN ABSENTIA

~

CHAPTER FOUR

Forster, Religion, and Sexuality

In an extraordinary interview[1] the Nobel laureate, Sir Vidia Naipaul, savaged E. M. Forster's imaginative engagement with Indian spirituality. He did so by making a quite explicit connection between the sexual and the mystical. Forster's vision of Indian religions was seen as heavily impaired through his visiting India out of a mere wish to indulge his homosexual tastes: "I know it might be liberally wonderful now to say it's OK, but I think it's awful. That's the background," he told his interviewer, "to all the mystery and lies." Often the reason for such outbursts is the Nobel Laureate's wish to pave the way for a new novel, to set aside any rival in its path and in a way his *Half A Life* (2001) is the inversion of *A Passage to India*; it is a passage to Britain. It is the story of an Indian whose father had been befriended by Somerset Maugham on a journey to India in the 1930s in search of Indian spirituality, naming his son Willy in honor of the friendship, and with the son traveling to England in the 1950s to exploit the connection. Here is yet another Naipaul story about exile. But such homophobia is inexcusable. It may be a matter of detail but Naipaul is just plain wrong in suggesting that Forster set out to seduce garden boys in India. Forster did indeed have a profound nostalgia for the innocent friendships of his childhood with garden boys and quite possibly much of his homosexuality was driven by a fantasy of return to such spontaneous affection. He wrote of his favorite, Ansell, he "probably did more than anyone toward armoring me against life."[2] But Naipaul is undertaking a far more serious criticism in challenging Forster's response to Indian religions. He sees himself as a realist, one who has stared Indian poverty in the face and any attempt at romanticizing Indian religions fills him with a profound distaste; in his words, "utter rubbish" and "a lying mystery." Naipaul is here of course expressing a personal sense of alienation from Hinduism. Only those writers whose imaginative powers enable people "to possess" and "to see their societies"—and interestingly he includes Kipling's Indian stories in this category—earn his admiration. The degree to which Forster achieved such a grasp in his Indian writings might well be disputed but it is strange that Naipaul wholly fails to see that with Forster there was an almost self-transcendent endeavor to come into some kind of relationship between his troubled sexuality and Indian spirituality. Can Naipaul not recognize that both he and Forster in their journeys to India were engaged in a critical attempt to work through a barrier in the content of their writing—Naipaul beyond his Caribbean past, Forster beyond Edwardian mores—and, more profoundly, to answer questions of identity? In the end, Naipaul came to accept himself as an exile, as an itinerant observer; Forster worked through to some much deeper acceptance of himself as a homosexual.[3]

But what was the nature of Forster's own insight into Indian spirituality? To answer that, there has first to be some examination of Forster's attitudes to religion and the problematic of his sexuality in an English context.

Liberal Humanism

Customarily Forster is seen as an exponent of liberal humanism, one who cherished the individual and personal relationships. There were certain absolute "goods": "sincerity, art, private freedom, diversity." In the novels, nations, classes, individuals must, in that leitmotif of *Howard's End*, "only connect": as Frederick Crews puts it, "overcome the artificial barriers of status and reach out to find their true brothers."[4] Here was Cambridge speaking through Forster and if he never actually read G. E. Moore's *Principia Ethica* it was his personalist philosophy that largely shaped Forster's emergent liberal humanism. This he shared with Bloomsbury even though he was to always remain on the fringe of that highly aesthetic movement. Following his giving a talk to The Memoir Club Forster confided to his diary: "I don't think these people are little but they belittle all who come into their power unless the comer is strong which I am not."[5] It might seem at the outset that Forster with his acceptance of a Greek ideal, defined as, "a reasonable and civilized acceptance of man's full nature," yet with his rejection of Platonism, "of any philosophy that smacks of other-worldliness,"[6] was a highly improbable convert to the values of Indian spirituality, to any outlook which questioned the integrity of the self. He was at the outset always more the Apollonian than the Dionysiac.[7] Yet this value system came under huge scrutiny through his involvement with India and in anticipation one could suggest that this approach became its opposite, "only disconnect," a process of unlearning, a shift from the moralistic to the metaphysical and mystical. And if Crews sees Forster as ultimately drawing back and remaining a defendant of liberalism, there had been a significant shift: "the victory belongs to reason but to reason defining the limits of reason."[8]

John Beer likewise sees Forster, despite the heady transition from the parochial conflicts within Victorian and Edwardian society into the vaster world of India, his "living in the universal," still retaining "a core of individual resistance,"[9] the basis for his almost eccentric, certainly lonely defense of liberalism in the 1930s in a world of conflicting totalitarian ideologies. He still saw the individual as separate and whole. But exposure to Hinduism had eroded the liberal humanism, there was a greater sense of irony, of man's impermanence.

Forster's own historical summary of shifts in the intellectual climate during his life-time, the story of three generations as he put it, reflects this troubled loyalty to liberal humanism.[10] If the pre-war generation were a gloomy one—"all thoughtful people tended to gloom—it was part of their prerogative, it was a tradition stretching back to Ruskin and Carlyle"—theirs was a faith in personal relationships. If individual needs could be met then the problems of the community would be resolved. This he had learnt at King's. But Forster came to recognize how "superficial" this was. It ignored, for a start, the economic: "we deified personal relationships and expected them to function outside their appropriate sphere." Then came the war-time and post-war generation, with the collapse of the League of Nations in 1930 as the cut-off point. If there was a flagging of idealism, with its attendant risk of world weariness, the mood was one of "disinterested curiosity," and Forster believed that "the man who is disillusioned and yet retains vitality represents in my judgment a very happy type of mind." Gerald Heard and Aldous Huxley were amongst its exemplars, Proust its literary mentor. Here was a scientific cast of mind but one which came to doubt Freud's account of the ego: "it doesn't do to regard the individual as if he is a solid and unaltered entity." But Forster's was a continuing commitment to liberalism: in Nicola Beauman's summary, "the liberal ideal inherited from Clapham, refined by Cambridge and defined throughout his novels would now become the nub of Morgan's existence."[11] Forster parts company with the next generation: "I'm sorry to have lived on into the 1930s—not because they are dangerous but because I am not equipped to understand them." Tolerance and the emphasis on the individual has gone, people are too busy to be curious and the hope without faith of the first generation, the curiosity of the second have been re-placed with the faith without hope of the third. In the third generation there was a religious belief that the world can be set to rights, "a forgetfulness of self, obedience to the movement, and the strength that comes from the masses." And if this be exhilarating, following the outbreak of war he fore-cast muddle and horror.

Another means of characterizing Forster's troubled liberal humanism lies in his response to other intellectuals and writers, past and present. If it is to take them out of that point of time at which Forster was their commentator, here they will be taken up chronologically. There is a tension revealed be-tween his commitment to the individual, rationalism and humanism and the attraction toward the mystical. Obviously this is a selective list. A 1941 talk on Voltaire reflected Forster's recovery of faith in humanism. Voltaire (1694–1778) he saw as dedicated to humanity, as "the complete anti-Nazi." He had expressed all those ideas that lesser men cannot say on their own be-half.[12] Walter Pater (1839–1894), if the supreme defendant of aestheticism, he still saw as moving beyond the sensations to a vision, one "that he never sees himself but that he surmises to be Divine Love."[13] Forster's friendship with D. H. Lawrence (1885–1930) was uneasy. They first met January 1915. Hostile remarks by Lawrence on Edward Carpenter,[14] with reference to his homosexuality, led Forster to record: "I cannot know him. He also makes me feel that I am in a bad state and have no friends."[15] Much of the tension lay in their attitudes to religion and mysticism. Lawrence warned Forster off In-dia, with its religion. The time had come, he preached, to throw off the past. Later, in his response to A Passage to India, he was to ridicule the boum or echo of the Marabar caves, whilst tartly pointing out to Forster the contra-diction of his doubting the importance of personal relationships whilst hing-ing the novel on the unsatisfactory friendship of two men.[16] But Forster in his obituary highlighted Lawrence's own mysticism. His was a genuine hatred of civilization, he wrote, with its making "human beings conscious and soci-ety mechanical": "he condemns the intellect with its barren claims of rea-soning and its dead weight of information, he even hated self-sacrifice and love." Lawrence's search had been "the forgotten wisdom, a Buddhist this-worldly mysticism." He concluded with a powerful evocation of the return of the Mexican gods in The Plumed Serpent.[17]

His tribute to Gide (1869–1949), discovered by the allies in Tunis in 1943, may be self-reflexive. Here was the paradigm humanist, "that is to say, he is curious about life, he has a free mind, he believes in good taste and he cares for the human race." Here was an individualist in an age of discipline, with a free mind, indifferent to authority yet not cynical about the human race. Forster conjured up a wonderful picture of Gide addressing the anti-fascist 1935 Congress of Writers in Paris—which he himself addressed—"full of airs and graces and inclined to watch his own effects. Then he forgot himself and made a magnificent oration . . . the individual will never develop his personality unless he forms part of a world society." If seen as a very complicated man "here was a light which the darkness could not put out: the light of humanism."[18] But he did not mention Gide's search out of sexual satiety for a mystical experience.

One early expression of doubt about the worth of personal relationships, and this is a sign of his disillusionment with liberal humanism, comes in a letter to his Indian friend Masood where they are seen as failing to redress life's sorrows; art, instead, is the way to find meaning.[19] Much later, by October 1948, his fears had become far more anguished: "I cannot speak to others of my worst trouble, which is that I have got tired of people . . . I feel scared. If human beings have failed me, what is left?"[20] Again, it was to be the experience of India that undermined this belief in friendship.

Clearly one should not exaggerate Forster's retreat from liberal humanism. John Colmer sees Forster in the 1930s as "the chief spokesman of a revived liberal humanist tradition."[21] Possibly his most famous affirmation of liberal belief came in his 1939 essay *What I Believe*, even if, true to a Cambridge and Bloomsbury tradition of skepticism, it was put over as a statement of non-belief: "my law-makers are Erasmus and Montaigne not Moses and St Paul."[22] In the 1950s he would still define himself as a humanist: "it expresses more nearly what I feel about myself and it is humanism that has been most fiercely threatened during the past ten years." Was it not being "elbowed out," denied by "the arbitrary theory of Original sin?"[23] But liberal humanism had been a fragile value system with which to survive the embattled ideological decade of the 1930s and the bleak prejudices of the post-war Cold War. P. N. Furbank concludes of Forster: "his mind was a vast breeding ground of judgments and discriminations."[24] One has to ask, did Forster seek strength from some alternative set of values in religion?

Religion

Forster summarized his religious life in a talk to the Cambridge Humanists in the summer of 1959 and this can usefully frame this inquiry.[25] Here he described the loss of his but tepid Christian faith. At his Eastbourne preparatory school the headmaster had once "with popping eyes" spoken of their neighbor, "a man who did not believe in God, a Mr. (T H) Huxley." At his public school, Tonbridge, he had been confirmed but this had merely complicated rather deepened any belief. Such faith as there was quickly withered on the vine in his second year at Cambridge. His friend, Hugh Meredith, was one catalyst of his disbelief, G. E. Moore another. The influence of the Apostles was to increase his agnosticism. First went the Trinity—"it kept falling apart like an unmanageable toy"—and this led to the unraveling of the incarnation. Contributory was a disaffection for Christ himself; as Forster put it, he proved to be no father figure, brother, or friend. All this helped him, as he phrased it in his Cambridge talk, "to cool off from Christianity." That Christ came to save sinners and not to address poverty furthered his alienation. If he conceded to being moved by the Christian birth and death narratives he interpreted early Christianity as becoming elitist, lacking in real intellectual power as opposed to insight and, above all, to be so humorless "that my blood chilled." It was this very lack of humor in Christianity but one he found in Hinduism that in time drew him to the Krishna cult. But the struggles of a previous generation in shedding their Christian beliefs had done much to facilitate Forster in jettisoning his own.[26] Not that this was the same as refusing to see the importance of religious experience. When one of Masood's Indian friends, hearing how Forster had lost his faith but expressing a supposition that Forster must at the least be a deist Forster riposted: "I have more sense of religion now than in the days of my orthodox Christianity. Do you say that unless one believes in God one has no religious sense?"[27] His became a distaste for powerful spiritual authorities: "I dread them all without exception as soon as they become powerful. All power corrupts. Absolute power which believes itself the instrument of absolute truth corrupts absolutely."[28] Nevertheless, John Beer can still make a claim for Forster's residual Christianity, above all through his sense of life as pilgrimage, "as a human exploration under the aegis of an unknown god."[29]

And Forster was subject to a profound religious inheritance. His paternal grandfather Charles Forster, an Anglican clergyman, by marrying Laura Thornton had married into the Clapham sect. Admittedly, Forster had no trouble discarding any religious legacy from the Revd Charles. He held his writings on Islam—and Mohammedanism Unveiled (1829) became quite well known in Orientalist circles—in contempt: "a worthless text," out of touch with such orientalist scholarship as existed and hostile to any progressive theology. His grandfather, he accused, "soon degenerated into a Hebrew prophet with nothing to prophecy about."[30] But the Clapham sect was another matter. Here was the moral conscience of a proto-Victorianism, William Wilberforce its greatest presence, Hannah More, "a bishop in petticoats," its moral inspiration and someone, indeed, that Forster still saw as a force in his lifetime. Interestingly, through their evangelicalism the Clapham sect had played a major part in the Indian story, opening up British India to missionaries in 1813. He accepted that theirs was a personalized faith, with little interest in ceremonial, was not self-punitively ascetic and was perfectly compatible with pleasurable living. Theirs was a life dedicated to God "without self-torture and torturing others."[31] But he was appalled by its character, all the same. "Solidly religious, they give one the impression," he wrote, "of having no sense whatever of the unseen."[32] Sardonically he wrote of the Thorntons, his great-grandparents, "he and she were to suffer but little from the onslaught of the imagination."[33] John Colmer suggests that Adela Quested is a latterday Hannah More, "deficient in emotion, imagination and beauty."[34]

But the Clapham legacy overshadowed his childhood, above all through his great aunt, Marianne Thornton, a spinster who took both his father Edward and the young E.M.F. under her wing. But for her bequest Forster would never have acquired the private means to be a writer. But this was to be a heavy burden on his conscience and do much to turn him into the moralist he became.

Admittedly, his family wore his loss of faith remarkably tolerantly: "they did not worry and when time went on they got used to my having no faith and so it has gone since," he told his Cambridge audience. "I have been spared the trials of Ernest in *The Way of All Flesh*." Samuel Butler's novel was a considerable influence in his religious emancipation. And there was rebellion here. Most obviously this expressed itself through his rejection of Christianity, but more pointedly in his increasing interest in the very area of the religious life in which Clapham was so deficient, the mystical.

It is instructive to compare Forster's religious life with that of Lowes Dickinson. He was probably the greatest influence of all in shaping Forster's liberal humanism. In time he was to be the King's College fellow he got to know and like the best. In India, from 1912 onwards, Forster claimed he began "to use him as a touchstone and to condemn those who failed to appreciate him."[35] Even so, Forster was no replica of Dickinson. As Crews puts it, "Dickinson's love of humanity is diminished to Forster's qualified trust in individuals, and Dickinson's quest for metaphysical truth becomes Forster's urbane curiosity."[36]

Dickinson had had to grapple with a far stronger family faith, with the morbid piety of his Christian Socialist parents. In his case it was to be Shelley, Plato, and Goethe who took the place of Christianity. But there was to be a period of considerable engagement with mysticism, looking into Esoteric Buddhism, and making a deep study of the neo-platonist, Plotinus. Dickinson claimed, indeed, to have enjoyed several mystical experiences or, at the least, a heightening of normal consciousness, once near San Francisco above the Yosemite falls, on another occasion climbing the sacred mountain of T'ai Shan, birthplace of Confucius. Dickinson brought a scientific inquiry to such experience, being an active member of the Society of Psychical Research. Forster saw in Dickinson "the chorus mysticus," "he was rare without being enigmatic, he was rare in the only direction which seems to be infinite."[37] "His mysticism always remained in his heart, folded up like a flower before the heat and brightness of a new day."[38] Yet, by the end, Dickinson had adopted the same position as the late Wittgenstein: "I feel now that we are all very ignorant and quite incredibly and unimaginably inadequate to deal with the kind of questions we ask about ultimate things."[39] In the end, their response to Indian mysticism was to be very different, Dickinson's antithetical, Forster's receptive.

Mysticism

Quite where Forster's response to mysticism came from is uncertain. Crews writes of Forster's "thwarted fascination with the absolute."[40] Forster is seen as "haunted by a feeling of ultimate despair," in search of an "elusive meaning."[41] If Clapham's inward spirituality can be linked to his own emphasis on the personal, it had stopped short at the imaginary and the mystical. Furbank suggests that Forster "though a rationalist was certainly by temperament a superstitious man."[42] Colmer sees in Forster that same fascination with the demonic in man, a need to cling to the visionary, of the Romantics.[43] In his response to mysticism, Colmer claims, Forster transcends the limitations of his liberal humanism. Here was his "final escape from the lapsed Protestantism of the Cambridge apostles and the preciousness of Bloomsbury."[44]

But a more personalized explanation lies in linking Forster's sexual frustration with the transcendent release made possible through the mystical and much can be made of his encounter with a kind of pagan mysticism in his visits to Italy in the early 1900s. The God Pan from then on became a metaphor for both sexual freedom and a somewhat dionysiac mysticism.[45] In the Mediterranean and the South the English were to throw away their inhibitions.[46] Even the British, Forster believed, could turn mystical: "there's such a thing as healthy mysticism," he wrote to Masood from Wiltshire, "and our race is capable of developing it, I think."[47] And Forster always had a mystical feel for the English landscape.

Once again Forster's opinions can be extrapolated from his commentary on other writers. In a talk to the Weybridge Literary Society on Kipling, predating his India trip of 1912–1913, Forster revealed his hand on the mystical. The Kipling that interested him was not the stories tied to action but the writing responding to Indian spirituality; he had particularly in mind the short story *The Bridge Builders* and the novel *Kim*. He commented:

> Mysticism may be a mistake, but no one will deny this—that if once a man shows traces of it, these traces must be carefully scanned by all who are trying to understand him. To have felt, if only for a moment, that this visible world is an illusion, to have even a passing desire for the One, is at once to be marked off from all who have not thus felt, thus conceived, thus desired. There is no explanation for this gift of mysticism; many criminals and outcasts have possessed it; many bishops, if the truth were known, are devoid of it; it pays no honor to rank, character or avocation (and as if to show its capriciousness) only one thing is certain; it is the peculiar gift of India and India has given it to Kipling as he gave it to his boy hero, Kim.[48]

In the 1920s Forster engaged with two writers, Gerald Heard and Aldous Huxley, both of whom were to be strongly drawn to mysticism. Heard was to be one intermediary between Isherwood and Forster. (And as he features much more strongly in Isherwood's life he is examined in greater detail below.) He and Heard had met just before the move from Weybridge to West Hackhurst: he reported to Masood "I am rather influenced for the time by a queer fellow called Heard."[49] Indeed, Heard must have seemed strange, dressed in purple suede shoes and with mascaraed eyes, but already seen as "a sort of Wellsian supermind."[50] And Forster was hesitant. To another newish friend, litterateur J. R. Ackerley, he confided: "he was disposed to intimacy but I held off, not being entirely advised whether he has a heart."[51] But a shared homosexuality was to break down the barriers. Forster became involved in Heard's love affair with Christopher Woods, though, unlike Isherwood for whom Wood became one of his closest friends in California, he rather disliked him. To Ackerley he wrote, 14 December 1928, of "Christopher's caddishness . . . we must try to part them for C cannot change." Masood was informed in a letter dated 31 December 1928: "Gerald is hysterical because of that shit Christopher Wood." They were brought even closer together through Heard being one of the most appreciative readers of the unpublished manuscript of *Maurice*, the as yet unpublished tale of homosexual love.

Forster came greatly to admire Heard's talent as an expositor of science on the radio. Here was the new scientific mind of the post-war generation in action at its best. On the radio himself 13 August 1931, Forster talked about Heard's *The Social Substance of Religion*. He began by praising Heard's fortnightly talks, supposing his audience had likewise "been thrilled and fascinated by his lucid account of scientific progress." In five years time Heard, he believed, would be recognized and for Forster he was already "one of the most remarkable thinkers of the younger generation." He took up the theme of the book, the way religion was essentially a communal affair, a way of attaining "spiritual refreshment" and not a quest for personal immortality. The problems of the day were psychological rather than economic.[52]

Heard was to turn pacifist and become ever more engaged with a kind of this-worldly mysticism in California. Forster kept abreast of his writings, though bemoaned their density and came to see any convoluted sentence of his own as "Geraldian." In a radio talk to India 3 February 1943 he responded to Heard's most recent book *Man the Master*. Heard's theme was once again man's instinctive interdependence. But by now his writings were saturated with the spirit of the Upanishads and he was preaching a theory of a new Brahmin elite of seers, visionaries who would advise the world's leaders and find solutions for peace. Forster's was a somewhat skeptical response. He found the analysis of the world's troubles impressive but the solution unconvincing:

> I believe with him that there is this 'seer' type with enhanced spiritual powers but I don't believe that Hitler or indeed a Cabinet Minister or indeed a civil servant would take the least notice of anything a seer said. They haven't in the past.[53]

Clearly, though, Forster was on Heard's wavelength and not unsympathetic to these mystical texts.

Forster likewise addressed his Indian audience on Huxley's ventures into mysticism. Huxley's was "the type of mind which desires to know God and to touch the Divine Reality." Huxley's *Grey Eminence* he saw "as a human book and a very wise one." This was the story of Father Joseph, the Capuchin friar who in 1624 under Richelieu became, as Huxley put it, an unofficial chief of staff for foreign affairs. This was Huxley's exploration of the saint or mystic in politics, a theme Forster saw as frequent in Indian culture from Arjuna onwards but rare in European. But Huxley doubted the belief of the *Bhagavad gita* that through denying the fruits of action one could engage in political life without corruption. Father Joseph was to plunge Europe into the Thirty Years War, out of some misguided belief this would lead to a crusade to free the holy land. Forster, however, was non-plussed by Huxley's pessimism:

> if the mystic oughtn't to turn politician, how can he help his fellows? Is he just to concentrate on union with God and to ignore the misery which spreads even more widely around him today than it did three hundred years ago? Is he to do nothing then?

He tantalized his Indian audience by eliciting that a text that did much to inspire Father Joseph, *Darlaam and Josephat*, was, in fact, a life of Buddha, Josephat a corruption of Bodhisattva. He commented:

> Is it not strange to reflect that the mystic who failed should at the opening of his life accidentally come across the mystic who succeeded, the great Indian who did not enter politics, who did not clamor for a crusade but found other and bloodless ways of promoting righteousness on earth?[54]

Forster was less happy with *Time Must Have a Stop*, Huxley's attempt to deal with a mystical sense of time, put off by his "remorseless" approach to physical suffering: "it has indeed a notable lack of tenderness, the tenderness which blurs our sense of fact and perhaps our sense of the spiritual but which certainly enables us to get on with one another while we remain under the dominion of time. I don't think his experience of earthly life at all resembles my own or most men's."

But here Forster's humanism returns. How, one wonders, did his Indian listeners respond to his question, "Are they like yours?"[55]

In 1943 Forster was also grappling with the mystical writings of Charles Mauron, a long-time friend since their meeting in 1925. He was the translator into French of *A Passage to India*. With Mauron by then blind, Forster became concerned for his safety and that of his wife, Marie, in occupied France. He made rather more sense, however, of Mauron's attempt, together with Chinese philosophy, to connect mysticism and esthetics than he did with Isherwood's attempt at the time to link mysticism and conduct.[56]

Forster's own deepest reading into mystical writings seems to have been into neo-Platonism and this raises the possibility that his whole response to Indian mysticism was refracted through his understanding of Plotinus rather than through any real grasp of Hindu mysticism itself. This resulted from his stay in Alexandria, 1915–1919, the city that had been home to Plotinus.[57] Earlier he had taken to the classical Greek poet, Theocritus, who had also lived in Alexandria. There was Lowes Dickinson's example of a deep study of Plotinus and Forster was to become more at ease with Indian spirituality after making a connection between Vaishnavism and Platonism. There is clear evidence that Forster drew on Stephen Mackenna's 1917 translation of the *Enneads* for his *Alexandria: a History and a Guide* (1922). Third century BC Alexandria had clearly been at the crossroads between Greek and Indian philosophy and no one doubts some inner connection between neo-Platonism and the later Advaita Vedanta of Sankara.

Any summary of Neo-Platonism will all too easily become garbled. Plotinus himself realized that the highest expression of God, the mystical experience of the One, was beyond language; there had to be its overflow into the intellectual principle to permit any description. It spilled over into the All-Soul, all of existence, matter and spirit, part of God. To anticipate, Godbole, the brahmin mystic of Forster's Indian novel, is seen as an attempt to portray Plotinus's ideal sage. John Drew bravely attempts one summary account: "the Ultimate Vision will not be achieved by conscious effort any more than by logic: it will come beyond image and idea, at that point where there can be no perception of, but only the existence of, Infinite Love."[58] You can never know if there has been a mystical experience. The only possibility lies through the imagination. And if this seemingly points to some Absolute, another critic, Shaheen, comes to the rather surprising conflicting conclusion that Forster's Alexandrian experience confirmed him in an essentially "shifting point of view."[59] Later Forster was to define the typically Alexandrian as a "mixture, a bastardy, an idea which I find congenial as opposed to that sterile idea of 100 percent in something or other."[60] Maybe Forster was always more drawn to the partial and contingent than to any absolute.

Did Forster share in this mystical experience? He told his Indian audience, that once in Cairo, visiting its most ancient but ruined mosque:

> there came over me an unusual sensation of peace and well-being and I was interested to read afterwards that a thirteenth century traveler had experienced the same situation in the same spot, that it was traditional in the mosque of Amr and that it was ascribed to the influence of the companions of the Prophet who had stood in the courtyard while the mosque was building.

But he then played down the experience: "a skeptic by temperament I don't take my experience seriously."[61] Entering mosques was one way Forster sought some kind of inner peace.

But this still falls short of any transcendent mystical moment and here Forster's still clinging to the integrity of the ego, the individual personality, provides an explanation. Discussing some Islamic writers he reflects:

> They do not seek to be God or even to see him. Their meditation, though it has the intensity and aloofness of mysticism, never leads to the abandonment of the personality. The self is precious because God who created it is Himself a personality; the Lord gave and only the Lord can take away.[62]

Significantly, the essay is dated 1923 and suggests that Forster the humanist, this clinging to the ego, represented the greatest barrier in the way of his grasping Vedantist mysticism. Even so, a case can be made, through the alchemy of the imagination, that Forster did get close to the mystical.

Forster is oddly muted in his reflections on death, the ultimate question that all religions address. Reflecting on Lowes Dickinson's—and mercifully it came before the true nightmare of the 1930s became apparent—he wrote: "one's own death is very little matter, it may become at any moment a great matter, but only when one is hysterical." In the nineteenth-century dying, he observed, had been taken much more seriously.[63] On a later occasion he doubted if death would lead to, as so often claimed, a rerun of one's whole life: "the interpretation gets made up as one goes along—not at the moment of death."[64] In that Cambridge talk he was to explain this indifference. If once, Forster admitted, he had been drawn to the theme of salvation, no more so; "I no longer wish to save or be saved." Nor did he wish to escape, for how, anyway, could one escape an expanding universe? (Forster did not often refer to modern physics.) All he sought was some improvement in himself and others: "Improve—such a dull word but it includes more sensitiveness, more realization of variety and more capacity for adventure." Possibly this humanism might fail him at the hour of death; "but I do not take the hour of death too seriously."[65]

The Maternal

If the theory that an unconstrained, loving relationship with one's mother, touched on in the discussion of Carpenter, enhances the possibility of some mystical engagement with Hinduism, itself so embedded in the eternal feminine, then clearly the nature of Forster's relationship with his mother is all important. And there seems little cause to doubt that this was the most formative relationship of his life, even though this is not to say it was the most important in Forster's eyes, let alone the most pleasurable.

He did not know his father, being but twenty-two months old at the time of his death from consumption, 30 October 1880. Little is known about his father, the youngest child but two of ten of the Reverend Charles Forster. He had trained as an architect. He married Lily Whichelo 2 January 1877 though had first met her in 1867 when he was twenty-one and she but thirteen. Through some muddle at his christening Forster acquired his father's Christian name of Edward rather than the one initially chosen of Henry. Nicola Beauman speculates that Forster was in fact named after his father's close friend and fellow architect, Ted Streatfield, that they were lovers and that Lily, reacting to Streatfield's joining them on a holiday in Paris, was aware of the fact.

Lily Whichelo was also from a family of ten, but she was the eldest and the responsibilities this engendered fashioned a more conventional character than that of the family as a whole. The Whichelos were more Bloomsbury than Clapham, with Forster's maternal grandfather a drawing master. Beauman sees Lily as "a kind of crystallized Victorian."[66] Forster was to enjoy a strong loving relationship with his maternal grandmother, Louisa, widowed young, far more spontaneous in its affection than that with his mother. On her death 15 January 1911 Forster recorded: "she knew how to love and to the end took it out of those who did not, like mother. M exalted sorrow. She may love me as much but she can do less for me."[67] Herself widowed young, Lily not only had to bear the social burden of her husband's familys snobbish belief that he had married beneath himself, but take on the role of a single mother. But for Forster the burden proved even heavier, for he had to bear all the hopes of this "lonely and unwanted widow."[68]

Looking back at their relationship after her death 11 March 1945 Forster reflected, "must clear up my relations with my mother which though never hostile or tragic did not go well after my grandmother's death, or even perhaps after Cambridge. I recall so few radiant moments . . . A little more ritual would have helped."[69] To Isherwood he wrote 9 May 1945 of "his terrible grief" though admitted "to no regret or remorse."[70] Later, 1 April 1946 from India, he wrote again: "my mother's death has been much more awful than expected. I am glad no one will miss me like that."

It is possible to track their relationship over time and point to a permanent state of tension, with Forster struggling to break away but seemingly held back by an even greater wish to stay. Beauman sees in this early dependence no love affair, just mutual devotion and a certain degree of laziness on Forster's part. Did he try to segregate his mother from his new Cambridge friends, the likes of Lytton Strachey and Hugh Meredith? There seem to be many possible turning points in their relationship. Beauman feels that traveling to Italy with his mother in 1901 was one: "by failing to break Lily's grip in the summer of 1901 it was likely that he now never would."[71] There were famous moments of uncontrollable rage, often brought on by a sense that his mother obstructed his love life. To his diary 1 November 1911 he confided: "last night alone. I had a satanic fit of rage against my mother for her grumbling and fault finding and figured a scene in which I swept the mantle-piece with my arm and then rushed out of doors and cut my throat, I was all red and trembling after."[72] When she doubted that his relationship with Masood could ever be the same were he to return from India Forster recorded: "mother freezes any depth in me."[73]

All the foreign travel without his mother were obviously attempts to break away. But even abroad he could not escape her: in India 1912–1913, "reachable only by letter the sap continued insidiously to drain out of him: 'the mother is waiting.'"[74] But their relationship could be at their warmest on his return. There was "a gasp of joy" at the presents he brought back from India in 1913. She read family prayers on his return from Egypt in 1919, something she had not done since his childhood. But manipulation continued. On his return from his first visit to India, after telling her "I seem worthless," he recorded: "Mother happier since I confided I felt done up, and couldn't work, but respects me less."[75] On his return from Egypt he confided to the diary; "I broke down at breakfast, very unwise as it puts me into mother's power. She is very sweet but it is never safe to be seen in pieces."[76] In 1923 he made a break of sorts, setting up a separate base in London but the emotional tie remained.

His mother was ambivalent about his success as a novelist, noticeably following the publication of Howard's End: "Mother bored by my literary successes."[77] "She turns everything to her own disadvantage and the sudden business of my life only makes her feel the emptiness of her own."[78] And whilst she grieved for her own mother Forster felt more distant: "am influenced very little by her now, for I cannot respect her as I used."[79] If it was awkward for her when dependency roles were reversed, for his Aunt Laura Forster in 1923 had left him Abinger Hammer, their home to be in West Hackhurst, in fact his seventy-year-old mother still took charge. 1925 was a particularly bad year, with his frequent loss of control, his mother sobbing, Forster throwing money onto the sitting room floor. But he had failed to break away. As Beauman puts it: "by now a complex mixture of inertia, masochism, guilt and anger at his father's death, an exaggerated sense of responsibility for Lily, and a deeply introverted streak would keep the forty-three-year-old Morgan for ever in the same cage in which he had been virtually all his life."[80] Earlier he had reported to Masood: "my mother keeps cheerful though increasingly still in body. To what extent satisfied with her odd son I know not: we are most of us sphinxes to each other."[81]

So how to assess the influence of this, clearly his most significant long-term relationship, on Forster? To a degree it infantalized him. His mother was so overprotective that Forster only late in life discovered that he was physically strong, his living into old age its visible proof. She also provincialized him and Forster became a kind of L. P. Hartley go-between of suburbia and Bloomsbury, neither fully one nor the other. At its worst he became like her: "living with his mother was bad, but worse he felt he was beginning to resemble her."[82]

Did her emotional demands inhibit his relationships with women? Forster in early manhood entertained the idea of his bisexuality and the prospect of marriage, his settling into some comfortable provincial existence.[83] But he was always on his guard with women. When a Violet Compton made approaches, "I was uneasy, fearing that she cared about me. She is in a nervous state and I wish she was married. She was most friendly and intimate and if I had felt safe I would have responded."[84] As an available bachelor Forster was inevitably faced with such encounters. There was a Mary Holmes: "she is only an excrescence, generally painless though twinging at times—wonder if I handled her properly and whether if the first meeting goes right—I should tell her the truth."[85] Probably she was the person he had in mind when he informed Masood, "a young lady has fallen in love with me. What an ill-considered world this is. Love is always being given where it is not required."[86] Any flaunting of female sexuality, as happened on the boat en route to India in 1912, was deeply repugnant. Not until well into manhood at the age of thirty did he understand the physical makeup of female sexuality.

Yet, by way of contrary evidence, Forster positively warmed to the dancers in a nautch that his Indian friends took him to in Delhi. He joined in discussing their merits. He was drawn to one with a "weak, but very charming face and very charming manners: I was never tired of looking at her," but was unattracted to another, more forward, seemingly arrogant. "One could easily lapse into the oriental," he ruminated: "I found myself discussing their points dispassionately."[87] There is more to be said on the way people of other cultures, other colors, will often intensify such positive or negative responses.

Did his fear of women turn him into an anti-feminist? One radio speech suggests so: "I believe there is a good deal of furtive anti-feminism about today, but it seldom comes out into the open, partly for a less reputable reason; cowardice. People who think women inferior to men often don't say so, because women have become so powerful."[88] And women were seen as curtailing his own sexual freedom. Beauman does not believe, however, that Forster was genuinely misogynist or anti-feminist; this was simply his way of keeping in with his misogynist homosexual friends. Women were to prove important to him as confidantes, a role his mother was never able to undertake on his homosexuality. To Edward Carpenter he confided: "when women do understand they are even better than men, but it doesn't so much as occur to them to start understanding."[89] Florence Barger and Josie Darling, amongst others, became confidantes, in a sense, surrogate mother figures.

And, of course, the most brutal question has to be, does his relationship with his mother explain his homosexuality? Beauman sees her as in some ways trying to protect her son from it, aware of his father's bisexuality, concerned at her son's lack of obvious manliness. To shield him from the revelations of the Wilde trials in 1895, she took him for a break to Paris. Maybe her repressive influence lay less in any emotional demands on her son, for she found it difficult to express her emotions, rather in her enforced domesticity, her being driven by her intense loneliness to keeping him under her control. Yet it all too easily fits an Oedipal paradigm, with a father who has been "killed" and a possessive mother. In the end Forster contrived to introduce his sexual partners to his mother, and if she found them all too often "common" she was always to be polite. Whether she fully imagined the true physical nature of these friendships is unclear. Forster clearly never ceased to need mother figures in his life and, fascinatingly, May Buckingham, wife of his longest-lasting boyfriend was, after some initial mutual animosity, increasingly, and certainly after his mother's death in 1945, to assume this role.

Possibly Forster should be given the last word. Here is an extraordinary summary of the relationship in a letter to Ackerley:

> Although my mother has been intermittently tiresome for the last thirty years, cramped and warped my genius, hindered my career, blocked and buggered up my house, and boycotted my beloved, I have to admit that she has provided a sort of rich subsoil where I have been able to rest and grow. That, rather than sex or wifiness, seems to be women's special gift to men.[90]

Whether there is a connection to be made between his mother's dominance and his capacity to respond to Hindu mysticism will be looked at elsewhere.

Sexuality

One should discount at the outset any sense of surprise at the none too physically attractive Forster investing so much of his life in the pursuit of sexual pleasure. As he wanly observed of himself: "my stoop must be appalling yet I don't think much of it . . . am surprised I don't repel more generally. I can still get to know anyone I want and have the illusion that I am charming and beautiful."[91] It is indisputable that his homosexual life became all important to Forster. It is often argued that he gave up writing fiction just because he could not write about homosexual love. It seems equally plausible that fiction had been a means of sublimating his emotional needs. Once he was able to realize them in the flesh, there was no further psychodynamic need to write fiction.

Virtually all his life, from the introduction of the Labouchere amendment in 1885, criminalizing love between men in private till its abolition in 1967, and, just as repressively, the prohibition of all expressions of homosexual love in public, Forster lived under the shadow of legal prosecution. For all his confessional writing, however, we do not know to what extent Forster lived in fear of blackmail or arrest.[92] It can be argued that the fears came as much from within as from without, and sprang from internalized guilt. But it took exceptional bravery to be open about one's homosexuality and there is no doubt that all his life Forster remained ill at ease, as much from shyness as secretiveness, at any self exposure. As far as possible he kept his homosexuality apart from all his other activities. Contemporary writers, Angus Wilson the most aggressively so, criticized him for this failure at openness. Forster was always concerned at the harm such disclosure might do to his policeman friend, Bob Buckingham. But posthumously, with access to the locked diary and the publication of *Maurice* (1971), Forster's private life has become very visible and there is no cause to doubt this is what he wanted.

Forster jotted down a sketch of his sexual history.[93] Interestingly, from the age of eleven he instinctively knew his orientation. Looking out of the window in a holiday hotel in Bournemouth he said to himself: "it all depends upon whether a man or a woman first passes. From the right came a gentleman with a brown moustache. I was much relieved and said he must be about twenty-eight. This is the first conscious preference that I recall." How serious was the damage of his mother's commenting on playing with himself as "dirty" he will not speculate, but he seems to have been troubled by masturbation. But, as he puts it, it ended the best chance of her becoming a confidante. There was a weird incident at his prep school when up on the downs at Eastbourne a 40–50-year-old man inveigled him into masturbating him. His mother should take some credit for this not proving to be a traumatic experience. Throughout his private schooling "stocky fair-headed older boys" attracted him but, as was often the case with genuine homosexuals, his schooldays passed without sexual activity despite its going on all around him. Maybe being a day-boy at Tonbridge kept him in ignorance. And ignorance and inexperience seem to have dogged his early life. "My instinct," he recognized, "has never given me true information about sex." Not until he got to Egypt was he to have in 1916 his first full sexual encounter with an English soldier on a beach.

Forster was not one for sustained enquiry into the etiology of his sexuality. He wondered if he had inherited it from his father. Early on, influenced by Samuel Butler's *Erewhon* he favored a Lamarckian view of evolution over Darwin's, the theory of the inheritance of acquired characteristics. He may have picked this up from Carpenter. This offered "a mystical sense of purpose to the world, something which Darwin had belatedly excluded."[94] Certainly homosexuality ran in his mother's side of the family, exemplified by Uncle Percy. Initially all he had to go on was Krafft-Ebing and this left him stranded between two demeaning accounts of the homosexual, the viciousness of someone who perversely chose to be homosexual or the disease of someone who was congenitally an invert. In time reading contemporary literature, A. E. Housman, J. A. Symonds,[95] Walt Whitman, and above all Edward Carpenter, he came to see that the homosexual had a place in the scheme of things and had a positive contribution to make to evolution. Maybe significantly, recognition of his homosexuality coincided with his agnosticism and this of course, if negatively, feeds the theme of there being a connection between his sexuality and his religious outlook.

Nor was Forster prone to any elaborate theorization of the nature of love. He rejected, for example, Proust's "gloomy" theory of love, that there is no mutuality and that all the lover experiences is the force of his own love reflected back on him from the beloved. Here is Forster's critique:

> He thought that the more deeply people fell in love the more they distorted one another, that passion is a certain prelude to misunderstanding. He thought too that jealousy is inevitable and that its arrival means the renewal of love which might otherwise mercifully have died.[96]

Clearly in his visits to Italy and Greece he found cultures seemingly more tolerant of homosexuality and, just as significantly, of friendships between the classes. As Parminder Bakshi wittily put it, in Forster's case "coming out" was replaced with "going away"; the further east, the more permissive.[97] An early, if resigned, acceptance of celibate love owed much to ancient Greece and Platonism. Much of his debates with the origins of homosexuality were rehearsed in the novel *Maurice*, written in 1913, though with many further amendments, but only published posthumously in 1971.

Forster was very much more concerned with the nature of the homosexual relationship itself and of the social background and appearance of his lovers. "Only connect," his great mantra, was of course a coded reference to such friendship. Once Forster had moved beyond the notion of a celibate affair, and this can be dated from about 1910, then arguably the choice became, should he invest all in one special friend, or was he to enjoy the more promiscuous life of numerous affairs? As is often the case with homosexuals Forster, in the end, settled for both, though there was always to be a search for that special friend. Nicola Beauman makes a case for Antinous, the youthful companion of Emperor Hadrian as Forster's physical ideal, large melancholy eyes, full mouth, broad swelling chest.[98] But Forster wrote of his "ideal male" in rather different terms, with reference to someone espied at his local post-office, December 1913: "he was what my brain had tried to make up. His expression was sweet and frank but not saint-like; full manhood of twenty; complexion fair, neck and cheek rather solid. He stood with his corduroy trousers clipped at the ankles."[99] Famously, Forster searched for love with a young man of the working classes, who might hurt him. There is a strange pessimistic passage in the locked diary where love and lust are contrasted. Love is for a particular person and "the purer the closer it keeps to the fact." Lust, however, idealizes, can be pure, can seek a unity of souls, "but in action it is disillusion and vanity, for souls like bodies can never merge."[100] Possibly one physical type met the needs of love, and the great affairs of the heart, Masood, Mohammed el Adl, and Bob Buckingham, conformed to the Antinous model, but there was a more earthy, coarser preference in his more casual affairs. Here was the paradigm "rough trade." They had a greater allure if bisexual and married. The effeminate held no attraction for Forster. Possibly only Buckingham was in the end to answer all these varying needs. But Forster's personal history was to be as much the quest for the freedom of the streets as the hunt for the ideal friend.

Forster's preference led him to the working class, soldiers, policemen. Their unselfconsciousness, as Carpenter interpreted it—and of course self-consciousness was a heavily loaded concept in Carpenter's philosophy—released his own inhibition. But the search for difference, a necessary stimulus in gay relationships, also lead Forster to men of color. Not that Forster ever relinquished the possibility that these encounters might flower into something more lasting. He always sought where possible to broaden out the relationship into one incorporating the whole of the lover's family, as if through some deep need Forster sought the father and the brother he had never known in his own family background. A case can be made that it was foreign travel that in the end overcame his inhibitions and it was not till he was over forty that he began to enjoy a more relaxed pursuit of pleasure. India clearly played a crucial part in Forster belatedly becoming more street-wise.

This is not a biography of Forster and it would be inappropriate to detail all his encounters. It is important though to see how Forster struggled toward acceptance of this license. It is around 1910 that Forster reveals these new sexual ambitions: "A vision of a khaki great coat has tormented me, of eyes so indifferent to mine; of manhood's hidden column."[101] In the days before railway carriages had corridors and were made up of separate compartments Forster looked for encounters on the train. There was a Norfolk pig farmer, intelligent and clear headed: "I felt he liked me very much and that if there were more of our sorts about modern England would be run more easily."[102] There was a sailor who regaled Forster with tales of officers and men dancing on board ship, if himself "too clumsy to dance."[103] But encounters on the train could be risky: "I raised suspicion and disgust in the carriage at Waterloo and was left with an angry growl."[104] He tried his luck in Hyde Park (Speaker's Corner became a well-known pick-up point) and even cottaging[105] but, pre-war, all this was still too emotionally disturbing: "I am afraid I must do this no more. I dislike good resolutions and am not ashamed in retrospect but find that lustful thoughts and glances leave a terrible depression behind them."[106] "It is a degrading moment when we admit people can't help their behavior."[107] And whatever the sexual nature of these encounters, a full sexual one was delayed till that anonymous one, October 1916, with a soldier on Montazah beach outside Alexandria: "I parted with my respectability."

The most active decade of his sexual history was in the 1920s. Post Egypt he confessed: "my mind is obsessed with sexual fancies and hopes: wasting much time. I am forty-one and inclined to a pot-belly, a red nose and baldness and I have become incapable of organizing anything or sticking to ideals."[108] But furtive transitory encounters, though these still occur, now gave way to experimental friendships. There was the ship's steward, Frank Vicary; the chauffeur, Tom Palmer, a sub-criminal type; twenty-four-year-old Harry Daley, the policeman, son of a Lowestoft fisherman, "plump, curly headed, genial, and rather cocky in manner."[109] But Daley was worryingly indiscreet. It was to be through Daley that he met Buckingham.

There is a particularly engaging account of his friendship with "pigsy-faced" Charlie Day, ship's stoker, he met in early 1926 on a boat trip to Bordeaux. "He radiated good temper and honesty, nothing more." Here is good evidence of another kind of physical preference: "he was shortish, very broad and strong, fair, face thick and pale with white teeth. When he talked he closed his little eyes and bars appeared over them as if speaking hurt him. A truculent air, really down to politeness. Tough and virile." In time Forster got to know his father and brother. It was, however, to be many months before Forster put to him the question: "at your school did boys ever do anything to each other?," prompting Charlie's wonderful reply:

When I was in Orstralia men asked me twice to sleep with them.
I suppose you said no Charlie.
I said yes.
Leaning towards him I murmured, I wish you'd do so with me.
YUS MORGAN'.[110]

Here is Charlie Day as good soldier Schweik, always ready to oblige. It's an account which makes the comparative loss of Forster as novelist of homosexual love all the sadder.

There was, of course, a specifically gay literature, but all published posthumously. The relevance of *Maurice* and the two short stories *The Life to Come* and *The Other Boat* will be discussed below when Forster's sexuality is discussed in an Indian context. But, of course, all of Forster's fiction has now been reinterpreted in the light of the new knowledge about his homosexuality and, again below, the homoerotic implications of the friendship between Fielding and Aziz will be discussed.[111]

Syed Ross Masood and Mohammed el Adl

Two of the most involving of Forster's love relationships were with men of color. They profoundly influenced his response to India. The first with Masood began in England but carried over into India. The second, with Mohammed, was in Egypt but here was to be an example of the way an experience in one place can be carried over into another. Memories of the Egyptian affair were to enflame Forster's sexual needs in India in 1922.

In many ways his love for the seventeen-year-old Masood was doomed from the start. Only Forster's inexperience in matters of the heart can explain his holding onto the possibility of a physical relationships with Masood as long as he did, right through till Masood's marriage in 1913. It was against all the odds, for Masood was wholly heterosexual, the wrong age and from the wrong class. It followed on from another unrequited passion, for Cambridge friend, Hugh Meredith, though at least here there was some physical contact, however innocent. At that point Forster was still in his Greek or Platonic phase. Masood was the grandson of the great Indian Islamic reformer, Syed Ahmed Khan and had been adopted as a ward by Sir Theodore Morison, first Principal of the Anglo-Oriental College at Aligarh and a neighbor in Weybridge. It was as his tutor in Latin for the Oxford entrance examination that they first met in the summer of 1906. "Large and magnificent looking," well over six feet, "with a sonorous and beautiful voice,"[112] the young Masood must have seemed to Forster an exotic version of his public school hero, of another Hugh Meredith, a type he still admired. The possibilities of misunderstanding were immense for Masood brought to the relationship his own very considerable idealization of friendship and it is hardly surprising that Forster read into his rhetoric the prospect of a deeper and sexual affair. There is some suspicion that early on Masood was simply playing with Forster though declarations of his friendship long after Forster's physical longings for Masood had subsided suggest otherwise.

Forster first resorted to a locked diary to record his passion for Masood. An early entry read: "Is the enigma him or his nationality? . . . Let me keep clear from criticism and scheming. Let me be him. You've stopped me. I can only think of you and not write I love you Syed Ross Masood, love."[113] Effusive language was exchanged by correspondence: "what a dear fellow you are and your letter shows me that you love me as much as I love you."[114] The diary complemented this: "I long to be out of London with him but this is self-indulgence. If I come in an unholy smash let me never forget that one man and possibly two have loved me"[115] (Hugh Meredith presumably the other). There were to be several occasions when Forster declared his physical passion, both in England and Italy, but each time Masood contrived somehow to steer round any personal embarrassment and without insult. In the Oxford and Cambridge Music Club, for example, it all came out, but Masood deflected the declaration "easily" with a "I know," Forster later writing to apologize and yet feeling "it will all be all right, that nothing can be wrong."[116] He consoled himself that in no way was his love unworthy. "If he goes away it will be with glory. It shall be my aim not to belittle him or pretend that I was well rid."[117] And after Masood had returned to India he wrote to him: "I can't describe how much I long to see you again. You have made me half an oriental and my soul is in the east long before my body reaches it. I don't understand the east or expect to understand it but I've learnt to love it for several years now."[118]

And that, of course, was the true reward of his love; Forster was already emotionally well disposed toward India even before his arrival. Much later he expressed his debt to Masood: "perhaps I owe more to him than any one individual, for he shook me out of my rather narrow academic and suburban outlook and revealed to me another way of looking at life—the oriental, and within the oriental, the Muslim. He prepared me for one aspect of India."[119]

Yet Forster never ceased to be the critical observer. In private he took issue with Masood's "eastern" character, "unreliable, not in heart but in action. Sensitive but not accurate . . . Probably touched by display of emotion. Probably touched by kindness but you can not be sure."[120] Whilst still in India he rather took Masood apart: "You seem to be getting infernally slack. You don't work at law, you don't write anyone letters, you can't even stop yourself getting fat by taking proper exercise. Soon you'll be too slack to trouble to keep your friends and will just drift about making acquaintances . . . You're damned selfish as we have often agreed and in the long run your selfishness may punish you." But then he tried to make it up: "you are such a fine chap at bottom."[121]

For all Masood's cult of friendship Forster was often to berate him for neglecting his true friends. Through his marriage and then the outbreak of war Masood had failed to keep in touch, prompting Forster's most bitter reflection: "he stands at the close of my youth. I wish very much he had felt, if only once, what I feel for him, for I should have no sense of wasted time. He and the continent he introduced have added little to my growth—not even a novel."[122] But, of course, in the end it did and Forster was to dedicate *A Passage to India*, the Indian novel that Masood had always believed Forster could write, to Masood. And Forster never relinquished his affection for Masood. There is a charming cameo of how they might end their days together in India, Masood celebrated and rather fat, Forster bald and obscure, "probably never read." Rather disingenuously at the time, October 1917, he confided: "I expect never to make a new Oriental friend now, never."[123] In fact, a new "oriental" friendship was taking shape.

The young Masood handled Forster's passion with considerable deftness if with a degree of mockery. Did he have his tongue in cheek when he wrote: "the day that sympathy that I know you have and that you feel for me diminishes ever so little will be a day which should be mourned by me during all my lifetime."[124] And was there still mockery in the invitation from Bankipore to Forster after he left India in 1913 to come and share his life with him: "the sooner the better and chuck up your land for a time. I promise to be very very nice to you."[125] This happened to coincide with Forster's writing of *Maurice* and it has strange echoes of the way the two lovers, Maurice and Scudder, escaped into the greenwood. But Masood only came to appreciate the friendship at its true worth when Forster's own passion had subsided. Masood's legal career never prospered. He was, however, to have an alternative career in education, initially as Director of Public Instruction in Hyderabad, closely linked to Sir Akbar Hydari and the foundation of Osmania University; in 1929, following the breakdown of his marriage, he became Vice-Chancellor of M. A. O. (Muslim-Anglo Oriental) University at Aligarh; but there was rupture here and he ended his career as Minister of Education in the princely state of Bhopal. He died of kidney disease 30 July 1937.

Here is Masood writing to Forster mid-1923:

> I have been thinking a very great deal about our friendship lately. I've read some of your letters recently and they made me realize most forcibly how very great your love is for me. You can have no idea my dearest how very much your love for me helps me to bear all of troubles. There are times when I feel as if my heart would break. On such occasions I say to myself 'But there is sweet Morgan who loves me' and a calm enters my soul and I feel my life has not been quite wasted.[126]

They kept in touch, met occasionally after Forster's return from India in 1922, and if Masood had not become his lover, he could at the least become the confidante of Forster's more successful affairs.

Beauman offers the tantalizing insight that it was following another hopeless declaration of love, with this time a more determined disclaimer by Masood, that Forster visited the Barabar caves near Bankipore January 1913, with the shattering consequences all too powerfully described in the novel.[127] But that is a part of Forster's experience of his sexuality in India itself and for later discussion.

One love affair Forster was to share with Masood was the second of his great affairs with men of color, Mohammed el Adl. He was an eighteen-year-old, "slightly negroid-looking Egyptian,"[128] a tram conductor, and the sexual excitement was all the greater as here Forster had to cross both the threshold of class and of color. It was the realization of an Edward Carpenterish working class affair and Carpenter was kept fully informed of its progress. Mohammed's marrying only made him the more attractive. Quite probably, though, this was to be yet another much embellished relationship. Was it all anyway colored by Forster's attempt to hold his own with the Greek poet, Cavafy, whom he had befriended in Alexandria?[129] Certainly Cavafy would have taunted Forster for his sexual inexperience. Beauman suspects Mohammed and Forster made love as few as a dozen times.[130]

Was Mohammed ever more than forbearing of Forster's love? He never sought to exploit Forster in any material way though Forster was to find him a better paid post with Military Intelligence in the Canal Zone. In his early letters to Forster he expressed some concern that Forster's "religious opinions do not put me off, as well as you respect mine as I do yours." He found it hard to comprehend Forster's emotional demands. If as Forster had reported he and his mother were well, what possibly had Forster to complain about? Forster's love letters from India in 1921, just struck him as "silly" and "foolish." But he did worry that Forster, through living in a palace in Dewas, might become too proud for the likes of himself. But at the very end, near death from tuberculosis, he wrote, thrice, "My love to you," followed by, "Do not forget your ever friend."[131] Writing over this letter Forster later recalled a haunting conversation when Mohammed had sought some explanation for Forster's befriending him, for was it not a disgrace, he wondered, his knowing a tram conductor: 'do you not only like me because I am a boy?' In fact Forster loved him because he was from the working-class but Mohammed's limited insight into their affair must always have hedged in Forster's own expectations.

Possibly for Forster this was some kind of symbolic rite of passage. He was anxious to share it with confidantes. To Carpenter, for example, shortly after Mohammed had moved to the canal, he wrote: "things grow better and better until I had nothing left to ask for and though it a terrible to be parted from him I am freed for ever from the burden of loneliness and failure that had oppressed me for so many years. I wish everyone would have my luck and come at last into the light."[132] If Forster delayed telling Masood of the actual nature of his friendship with Mohammed, for after all Masood was still a rival for his affection, in time Masood was to be drawn in and was even to write to Mohammed during his terminal illness. Almost apologetically Forster thanked Masood: "I think you have been wonderful in your acceptance of the affair—the more so since you belong to India, so undemocratic in its social structure. As for understanding the affair that you can only do by translating it into language you will scarcely wish to use."[133] Did he suppose Masood would be squeamish about homosexuality?

But Forster was already reconciled to his dying. Had he deceived himself, he asked, about any mutual love? Had Mahommed simply responded out of politeness, gratitude, even pity? How could he ever know now with his death what his true feelings had been? There was real despair: "not only he but all whom I love will disappear in a distortion when they die and then I shall die."[134] But by 1928 the anniversary of his death, 22 May, could pass without remembrance.

He made one final attempt to make sense of the friendship in an imaginary letter 27 December 1929. He accepted that theirs had never been a successful sexual relationship. Just sleeping together had been the real delight. "I have fallen in love through you but falling in love has obscured you. You have faded into being part of my development and will shrink to nothing unless I can recapture you in a dream." "I am close on fifty-one and can never love anyone so much and if there is the unlikely arrangement of a personal and pleasurable eternity I would like to share it with you."[135]

This was a love that profoundly affected his response to India in his second visit. Initially whilst in Alexandria Egypt came out poorly from any comparison with India. To Masood he reflected that it was "vastly inferior": "it is only at sunset that Egypt surpasses India—at all other times it is flat, unromantic, unmysterious and godless—the soul in mud. The inhabitants are of mud moving and exasperating in the extreme. I feel as instinctively not at home among them as feel instinctively at home with Indians."[136] Here are direct intimations of his description of Chandrapore in A Passage to India. Clearly the two travel experiences began to merge. Later, Egypt came out much more favorably from the comparison: "such Egyptians as I've seen are frankly anti-English. I retain my good opinion of them. They are men and possibly brothers and slave mentality has made fewer ravages here than in India. Their indifference to religion must also be remembered: there are no Hindus to set the pace."[137] The nationalist protest in Egypt in 1919 overlapped with the shocking events of Amritsar and Mohammed's arrest on a firearms charge and subsequent imprisonment enflamed Forster's aversion to imperialism. As Furbank puts it: "Egypt and India became more and more identified."[138]

The all important 1921 visit to India was sandwiched between a sexual rendezvous with Mohammed in Port Said en route and a longed for reunion on his return, with a fantasy of his playing for the first time the passive role, only to find him impotent through illness. It is surely significant that completing the novel is linked to memories of Mohammed: "finished A *Passage to India* and mark the fact with Mohammed's pencil."[139] Clearly the exceptional demands of his sexuality in India flowed from his thinking about Mohammed, this one relationship heightening his sexual response to the Indian experience. Here lies one crucial link between Forster's sexuality and mysticism in India.

The Three Indian Visits

Superimposed on these attitudes of Forster toward religion and sexuality were to be the three visits to India. How did these impact on Forster? In the aftermath of the first, 1912–1913 Forster was initially gloomy: "growing sense of my own futility doesn't sadden me though I shall grow queer and unpopular if I go on as I am now." The mood still did not lift: "India will not lose me. Thought it might but it reappears. . . . But it is a painful obsession rather—I get no pleasure, scarcely stimulus and my thoughts are tinged with politics." But then came a more assertive note: "India has made me more of a personage, more able to defend my sterility against criticism." And there was a breakthrough from provincialism: "Stevenage is dying at last for me and Cambridge may die too. India has obliterated and makes me careless of this suburban life."[140] In his letters to Masood he doubted if indeed he would ever be able to write about India. Let Indians write the great Indian novel. But through Masood India "had become part of my life" and he now felt "awfully cut off." But then there came once again a far more affirmative response:

> My own feeling for India and for what I conceive to be the Indian character is purely emotional and as soon as I try to justify it in words I fail. No doubt it is ridiculous to have fallen in love with a continent of 60,000,000 people but that is what I have done, and no doubt my emotions will seem ridiculous and worthless to the Indians themselves. However, there it is. They may not respect it but they must accept it.[141]

The response to the 1921 visit could be equally confused and tentative. Whilst still there he ruminated: "India not yet a success, dare not look at my unfinished novel. Can neither assimilate, remember or arrange." At home, prompted by Leonard Woolf, he forced himself to get back into the novel. He saw some benefit in the journey: "my practical experiences in Dewas have made me both cuter and stupider. I no longer make the emotional appeal that is necessary to call out the best from an oriental, real or imaginary."[142] There was some change in personality. "I think I am shaking off," he informed Masood, "the diffidence that is such a bore to my friends and such a provocation to any ill-natured acquaintance or stranger." "I am therefore drawing a hard line between the people who matter and those who don't."[143] This prompted the disturbing sentiment:

> When I began the book I thought of it as a little bridge between East and West; but that conception has had to go, my sense of truth forbids anything so comfortable. I think that most Indians, like most English people are shits and I'm not interested whether they sympathise with one another or not.[144]

Prior to the third visit he expressed a sense of a continuing tie: "my home is in England and I am conditioned by the west. But I still retain the notion of connection with India and shall continue to speculate where you (India) are sitting and what you are thinking about."[145] And the invitation to attend the P.E.N Conference in Jaipur, 20 October 1945, was greatly welcomed: "I have a romantic fantasy," he told Isherwood, "that I shall never come back." It was a journey, he later reflected, "that probably saved my mind." Grief over his mother's death had proved to be greater than expected. "In India I found food, warmth 'fame,' affection and space—the mere traveling about was exquisite. I can't tell you how happy I was."[146] Jamini Roy gave him a painting of Krishna.

Toward India

Clearly the first two visits to India were accompanied by a heightened sexuality. Love for Masood informed the first, love for Mohammed greatly colored the second. If in Christian terms an agnostic he was discovering a greater interest in religion prior to the first visit and out of some reaction against his Clapham inheritance, though also from some deeper need within himself, discovering an interest in mysticism. The second visit was clearly affected by his readings into Plotinus and neo-Platonism. The fascination lies in how two such strong forces, the sexuality and the mysticism, come together. Brooding in the background and always a potentially negative influence on his personal and religious life was a demanding and manipulative mother. The experience of India itself would show whether Forster could resolve his personal struggle with his homosexuality and reach out to a larger mystical awareness.

Notes

1. Farukh Dhondy, "Talks to V. S. Naipaul," *Literary Review* (August 2001), 28–35. It prompted considerable press attention. Geoffrey Wheatcroft for one, in *The Independent*, wrote of Naipaul, `this unlikely Wiltshire squire' as `a reactionary curmudgeon and scourge of liberal pieties', `the contrast between his literary genius and sheer bloody-mindedness. 'Frank Kermode sees his derogation of *A Passage to India* as 'out of crossness, out of a desire to insult.' Alternatively, out of a response to colonialism. See "The Tantrums of V. S. Naipaul," *The London Review of Books* 23, no. 17 (6 September 2001), 9–10.

2. E. M. Forster, *Marianne Thornton* (London: Edward Arnold, 1956), 275.

3. Jeffery Paine argues along these lines in his *Father India: How Encounters with an Ancient Culture Transformed the Modern West* (New York: Harper Collins, 1998).

4. Frederick Crews, *E. M. Forster: The Perils of Humanism* (Princeton: Princeton University Press, 1962), 37.

5. Locked diary, 4 February 1921, EMF Vol 4/4.

6. Crews, *E. M. Forster*, 43.

7. Terms made familiar by readings of Nietzsche. See particularly Walter Kaufmann, *Nietzche: Philosopher, Psychologist, AntiChrist* (London: Meridian Books, 1956).

8. Walter Kaufmann, *Nietzche*, 180.

9. John Beer, "Introduction. The Elusive Forster," in G. D. Das and John Beer, eds., *E. M. Forster: A Human Exploration* (New York: New York University Press, 1979), 5.

10. See his talk, Three Generations, given to both the Majlis at Cambridge 7 November 1937 and University College, Nottingham, 28 January 1939, published in *Cambridge Review* (12 November 1937). The Forster archive, King's College Cambridge, EMF/Vol 8/21.

11. Nicola Beauman, *Morgan: A Biography of E M Forster* (London: Sceptre, 1993) (references to the Sceptre 1994 edn), 337.

12. In "My Opinion" (17 January 1941), Broadcast talks 1930–1943, EMF Vo 6/7.

13. This talk on Pater, possibly given to the Theosophical Society in Alexandria in 1917, is one hint at the way Forster's own new religious enquiry, prompted by the Indian journey of 1912–1913, is beginning to influence the way he reads other writers. E.M.F. vi/32 A.

14. In fact Lawrence was profoundly influenced by Carpenter. See Emile Delavenay, already discussed above, *D. H. Lawrence and Edward Carpenter: A Study in Edwardian Transition* London: 1971.

15. Locked Diary E.M.F. Vol 4/4.

16. Letters of Lawrence to Forster, 30 May 1916 and 23 July 1924, E.M.F., Letters Book 1 Vol 8.

17. On the radio (16 April 1930), Broadcast Talks EMF Vol 6/7.

18. Broadcast talk (15 August 1943), E.M.F. Vol 6/7.

19. Forster to Masood, 25 May 1923, E.M.F. Correspondence, Masood Syed Ross xviii.

20. E.M.F. Locked Diary Vol 4/4.

21. John Colmer, *E M Forster: The Personal Voice* (London: Routledge and Kegan Paul, 1975), 211.

22. Beauman picks this up, *Morgan*, 92. For the essay, see E. M. Forster, *Two Cheers for Democracy* (London: Edward Arnold & Co., 1951).

23. A letter to, *Twentieth Century* (May 1955) E.M.F./Vol 5/4.

24. P. N. Furbank, *E M Forster: A Life* (1st published 1977, 1978 Oxford edition, Oxford University Press) 11, 297.

25. E. M. Forster, A Presidential Address to Cambridge Humanists (Summer 1959), Forster typescripts Series 11 Vol. 1, 137–42 E.M.F. Vol 8/22.

26. Crews explores this approach, looking in particular at Leslie Stephen, `typical of Clapham's second generation and his battle toward agnosticism, *E. M. Forster*, 10–11.

27. 5–7 April 1911, E.M.F. Locked Diary Vol 4/4.

28. In a letter to *The Twentieth Century* E.M.F./Vol 5/4.

29. Beer, "Introduction: the Elusive Forster," in G. D. Das and John Beer, eds., *E M Forster: A Human Exploration*, 9.

30. E. M. Forster, *Marianne Thornton* (London: Edward Arnold, 1956), 162.

31. E. M. Forster, *Marianne Thornton*, 59.

32. E. M. Forster, "Battersea Rise," *Abinger Harvest* (London: Edward Arnold & Co., 1936), 241.

33. E. M. Forster, *Marianne Thornton*, 65.

34. Colmer, *E. M. Forster*, 161.

35. E. M. Forster, *Goldsworthy Lowes Dickinson* (London: E. Arnold & Co., 1934), 138.

36. Crews, *E. M. Forster*, 48.

37. Crews, *E. M. Forster*, 241.

38. Crews, *E. M. Forster*, 84.

39. In a letter to an Indian enquirer, D. K. Roy, 18 January 1931 quoted Forster, *Goldsworthy Lowes Dickinson*, 229.

40. Crews, *E. M. Forster*, 7.

41. Crews, *E. M. Forster*, 14.

42. Furbank Vol 11, 131.

43. Colmer, *E. M. Forster*, 11–12.

44. Colmer, *E. M. Forster*, 167.

45. Beauman amongst others explores this, *Morgan*, Chapter 10. The god Pan featured in English writing of the period, Elizabeth Barrett Browning, Robert Louis Stevenson. Forster's most obvious reference was in his short story, *The Story of a Panic* (1902). As Norman Page puts it, here was Forster's seeing "the importance of the in-

stinctive and the impulsive as against the conscious and rational." Page, *E M Forster's Posthumous Fiction* (Victoria, BC: University of Victoria, 1977), 62.

46. Brilliantly explored in John Pemble, *The Mediterranean Passion: Victorians and Edwardians in the South* (Oxford: Oxford University Press, 1987).

47. In a letter, 18 August 1910, E.M.F., Correspondence Masood, Syed Ross xviii. See also Mary Lago and P. N. Furbank, eds., *Selected Letters of E M Forster Vol One 1879–1920* (London: Collins, 1983), 113.

48. "The Poems of Kipling," E.M.F. Vol 8/20, 52–81.

49. A letter dated 5 July 1925, E.M.F. Correspondence Masood Syed Ross xviii.

50. See Furbank's vivid description of him, Vol 11, 136.

51. A letter, 3 September 1925, E.M.F. Correspondence Ackerley.

52. E.M.F. Broadcast talks (1930–1943), Vol 6/7.

53. Some books, 3 February 1943, E.M.F. Broadcast talks (1930–1943) Vol 6/7.

54. We Speak to India: Some Books (11 February 1942), E.M.F. Broadcast talks (1930–1943), Vol 6/7.

55. We Speak to India: Some Books (c.1944–1945), E.M.F. Vol 8/21.

56. See Forster to Isherwood, 14 July 1943, Mary Lago and P. N. Furbank, eds., *Selected Letters of E. M. Forster*, Vol Two (1921–1970), 204–5.

57. I base this discussion on two essays, Mohammed Shaheen, "Forster's Alexandria: A Transitional Journey," and John Drew, "A Passage via Alexandria?," Chapters 8 and 9 in G. K. Das and John Beer, eds., *E. M. Forster: A Human Exploration*.

58. Drew, "A Passage via Alexandria?," 99.

59. Shaheen, "Forster's Alexandria," 87–88.

60. "The Lost Guide." A Talk to the Aldeburgh festival (17 June 1956), E.M.F. Typescripts Vol 8/22.

61. Some Books, A J Arberr,y ed., *Islam Today*, (28 April 1943), E.M.F. Broadcast talks 1930–1943 Vol 6/7.

62. E. M. Forster, "Salute to the Orient," *Abinger Harvest*, 61.

63. In a letter 30 October 1937 to Elizabeth Bessie Trevelyan E.M.F. Correspondence xviii.

64. "The Last Moment of Life," ca 1950? E.M.F. vi/14–A.

65. A Presidential Address to the Cambridge Humanists (Summer 1959), E.M.F. Forster Typesripts Series 11 Vol 1 Vol 8/2.

66. Beauman, *Morgan*, 28.

67. E.M.F. Locked Diary Vol 4/4.

68. P. N. Furbank, *E. M. Forster*, 11.

69. E.M.F. xi/11.

70. E.M.F. Correspondence to Isherwood (1932–1962).

71. Beauman, *Morgan*, 100.

72. E.M.F. Locked Diary Vol 4/4.

73. E.M.F. Locked Diary (5 March 1912).

74. Beauman, *Morgan*, 267.

75. E.M.F. Locked Diary Vol 4/4.

76. E.M.F. Locked Diary (24 April 1919).

77. E.M.F. Locked Diary (13 November 1910),

78. E.M.F. Locked Diary Vol 4/4 (11 December 1910).

79. E.M.F. Locked Diary (31 December 1912).

80. Beauman, *Morgan*, 321.

81. Letter to Masood, 23 October 1922, E.M.F Correspondence, Masood Syed Ross.

82. Jeffery Paine's insight. See *Father India: How Encounters with an Ancient Culture Transformed the Modern West* (New York: Harper Collins, 1998), 121.

83. So Beauman claims, *Morgan*, 115–16.

84. E.M.F. Locked Diary Vol 4/4 (13 November 1910). Neither Furbank nor Beauman shed any light on who she was.

85. E.M.F. Locked diary Vol 4/4 (31 December 1914). Again, neither biographer mentions her.

86. Letter to Masood, 5 December 1914. E.M.F. Correspondence, Masood xviii. Lago and Furbank, Vol One, 216.

87. Indian Journal 1912–1913 EMF Vol 3/3 (2 November 1912).

88. This was in response to a book on Coleridge by Walter Creswell. Forster congratulated him on having the courage of his anti-feminist convictions (13 August 1931), E.M.F. Broadcast Talks 1930–1943 Vol 6/7.

89. Letter 13 April 1916, E.M.F. Correspondence Edward Carpenter xviii.

90. I first came across this letter, undated but sometime in 1937, in a footnote G. D. Das and John Beer, eds., *E M Forster*, 305. Also quoted by Furbank Vol 11, *E. M. Forster*, 217.

91. E.M.F. Locked Diary Vol 4/4 (2 January 1925).

92. There is some suggestion he was at risk from blackmail in 1928. See Arthur Martland, *E M Forster: Passion and Prose* (Swaffham: GMP, 1999), 173.

93. E.M.F. Locked Diary Vol 4/4.

94. Arthur Martland, *Passion and Prose*, 68.

95. His influence on Forster may have been underestimated in comparison with Carpenter's. He confided: 'I feel closer to him than any other man I have read about. I am proud in some ways to be like him.' (12 January 1912), E.M.F. Locked Diary.

96. Some Books (31 March 1943), E.M.F. Broadcast talks 1930–1943 Vol 6/7.

97. Parminder Bakshi, "The Politics of Desire: E M Forster's Encounters with India," Tony Davies and Nigel Wood, eds., *A Passage to India* (Buckingham: Open University Press, 1994).

98. Beauman, *Morgan*, 127.

99. E.M.F. Locked Diary Vol 4/4.

100. E.M.F. Locked Diary Vol 4/4, (13 November 1910).

101. E.M.F. Locked Diary Vol 4/4, (29 January 1910).

102. E.M.F. Locked Diary Vol 4/4, (11 December 1910).

103. E.M.F. Locked Diary (15 May 1914).

104. E.M.F. Locked Diary (27 October 1924).

105. Argot for seeking sexual encounters in public toilets.

106. Post-India, late 1913 E.M.F. Locked Dairy.

107. E.M.F. Locked Diary (2 March 1911).

108. E.M.F. Locked Diary (2 November 1920).

109. Furbank's description, *E. M. Forster*, Vol 11, 140. Harry Daley was the only one of Forster's lovers to write a personal memoir, *This Small Cloud: A Personal Memoir* (London: Weidenfeld and Nicolson, 1986). In the end Forster's fussing over him and Daley's indiscretion led to the petering out of the affair. P. N. Furbank discusses their friendship in a preface to the memoir.

110. E.M.F. xi/3.

111. The most extensive analysis comes in Arthur Martland, *Passion and Prose*.

112. Furbank's description, *E. M. Forster*, Vol 1, 143.

113. E.M.F. Locked Diary (31 December 1909).

114. Letter 18 November 1910. E.M.F. Correspondence Masood xviii.

115. E.M.F. Locked Diary (8 December 1910).

116. E.M.F. Locked Diary (29 December 1910).

117. E.M.F. Locked Diary (1 January 1910).

118. Letter 19 August 1912 E.M.F. Correspondence Masood xviii.

119. "My Debt to India" (13/14 August 1942), E.M.F. Broadcast talks 1930–1943 Vol 6/7. One wonders how aware Forster was of the Quit India satyagraha then raging.

120. E.M.F. Locked Diary (10 January 1910).

121. Letter 1 March 1913, from Lahore, E.M.F. Correspondence Masood xviii.

122. EMF Locked Diary (31 December 1914).

123. In a letter from Alexandria, 8 October 1917, E.M.F. Correspondence Masood xviii.

124. Letter 22 November 1908, E.M.F. Correspondence Masood xviii.

125. Letter 25 September 1913, E.M.F. Correspondence Masood xviii.

126. Letter May to September 1923, E.M.F. Correspondence Masood xviii.

127. Beauman, *Morgan*, 274–77.

128. Furbank's phrase, *E. M. Forster*, Vol 11, 36.

129. They met early on in Alexandria and arguably he influenced Forster into accepting his sexual love for the working class even more than Carpenter, above all, doing something about it.

130. Beauman, *Morgan*, 316.

131. Letters 31 August 1917, 2 October 1918, 8 May 1922, E.M.F. Correspondence Mohammed el Adl Vol 3/1.

132. Letter late October 1917, E.M.F. Correspondence Edward Carpenter xviii.

133. Letter 26 January 1922, from the Isle of Wight E.M.F. Correspondence Masood xviii.

134. E.M.F. Locked Diary Vol 4/4, (25 March 1923).

135. To Mohammed el Adl, E.M.F. Vol 3/1.

136. Letter 29 December 1915, E.M.F. Correspondence Masood xviii.

137. Letter to Masood, 23 February 1922, E.M.F. Correspondence Masood xviii.

138. Furbank Vol 11, E. M. *Forster*, 62.

139. EMF Locked Diary Vol 4/4 (21 January 1924).

140. 26 January 1913, 31 December 1913, 10 August 1913, E.M.F. Locked Diary Vol 4/4.

141. Letters 20 April 1913, 15 August 1913, 20 November 1913, E.M.F. Correspondence Masood xviii.

142. 31 December 1921, 12 April 1922, E.M.F. Locked Diary Vol 4/4.

143. Letter 15 April 1922, E.M.F. Correspondence Masood xviii.

144. Letter 27 September 1922, E.M.F. Correspondence Masood xviii.

145. "India in Literature" (20 April 1942), E.M.F. Broadcast Talks 1930–1943 Vol 6/7.

146. Letters 9 May 1945, 1 April 1946, E.M.F. Correspondence Isherwood 1932–1962.

CHAPTER FIVE

~

Forster and the Krishna Cult

Orientalists, most influentially Max Müller, have given a distorted reading of Indian spirituality. They have emphasized the Sanskritic, Brahminical non-dualist Vedantism at the expense of the more popular, folk, Vaishnavite tradition. Maybe it was all too predictable that E. M. Forster, a liberal humanist with a strong sense of the integrity of the personality, would turn away from Vedantism, with its search to transcend the ego, in favor of a tradition of spirituality which sought communion rather than fusion with the divine, one which put love between humans and Krishna at its core. Forster was a natural dualist. In ways that he could not have foreseen, however, it was to be his visits to Madya Pradesh, to Chhatarpur, and Dewas, very much centers of Vaishnavism and the Krishna cult and one actively supported by both their Maharajahs, that led him in this direction. Prior to his first visit to India in 1912 Forster was beginning to discover in himself an interest in religion and India was to release an extraordinary attempt imaginatively to grasp Indian religions, both Islam and Hinduism, though Hinduism remains the focus of this study. Tourism was to be one way of learning about Hinduism and he also read reasonably widely. But it was exposure to the Krishna cult itself that forced the imagination. The first two visits were at times of still real confusion over his sexuality and it is worth speculating on the inner links between his problematic sexuality and his response to Indian spirituality and specifically to the Krishna cult. At the very least in both Forster saw muddle. To address this question one has to look in some detail at the Krishna cult itself and at the Maharashtrian saint, Tukaram, who featured prominently in the celebrations of Krishna at Dewas.

The Enormity of India

India stretched Forster to his limits. With reference to A *Passage to India* Frederick Crews writes of "a paralyzing vision of disorder," "a note of anti-meaning that reverberates throughout the book." Harmony with "the Indian earth means madness." Here the dionysiac had to be given free rein, entailing the eclipse of Forster's humanism. He had to move beyond the moral into the metaphysical, out of sheer recognition of "our drastic plight as human beings."[1] If Forster shares in Hinduism's ambition of trying "to tie, weld, fuse and join all the disparate elements of being and existence in a complete union," Benita Parry still feels that the novel itself "withdraws from the incalculable and unassimilable enormity of the enterprise."[2] Forster felt that "the arts of littleness are tragically lacking in India; there is scarcely anything in that tormented land that fills up the gap between the illimitable and the inane."[3] The state of Dewas "belongs to that broad region between reality and dreams where so much of the spiritual life of India proceeds."[4] Did India lie outside his imaginative powers?

Reading in advance did something to prepare him for the culture shock of India. Amongst other texts prior to departure in 1912 he read Ramsay Mac-Donald's *Awakening of India* and Lyall's *Asiatic Studies*, "abstruse but full of great beauties of style" as he informed his friend Masood.[5] Lyall impressed through his recognition of the importance of religion. In his poetry, above all, Forster found a response "to the primitive superstructure of Behar." (Masood was at the time working in its provincial capital.) Hinduism had caught him "as it has caught skeptics of all times and wrings cries of acquiescence and whispers of hope."[6] Other writers and personalities were to make India more accessible. There was Walt Whitman who provided the title for his Indian novel, a writer "I used to love unreservedly," with his "vastness, his warmth and his fearlessness": "no one who can so suddenly ravish us into communion with all humanity or with death."[7] There was Tagore whom he met in 1912 at Sir Wilmot Heringham's Harley Street dining room—his wife had published a book of her paintings of the Ajanta caves[8]—leaving a memory as vivid for Tagore's physical appearance as for anything he said though, as Forster later claimed, "I do myself the credit of realizing then and there that I was in the company of a great man."[9] Romain Rolland was another way into India, with his cult of heroes, above all of Gandhi. Oddly, Forster does not seem to have read his biographies of Ramakrishna and Vivekananda.[10] Another leading Indian poet he met and knew slightly was Iqbal: "I have always felt that of all great Indian contemporary Indian thinkers he has received the least attention over here."[11] And then there was Gandhi. If he clearly appreciated Rolland's portrait of Gandhi in which he came across as alone amongst the great prophets and mystics in having "no vision, no revelation and neither believes he has, nor wishes others to believe it" (mercifully so for Forster, with his dread of ideologies in that appalling totalitarian age) he seems to have warmed the more to Anand's picture of Gandhi in his novel *The Sword and the Sickle*: "I have read many accounts, fictitious and otherwise of interviews with Gandhi but this one is by far the most vivid and gives us a picture of the Mahatma which is partly admiring and partly critical."[12] Gandhi's assassination prompted a remarkable tribute:

> when the news came to me last week I realized intensely how small I was, how small those around me were, how impotent and circumscribed are the lives of most of us spiritually and how in comparison with that mature goodness the so-called great men of our age are no more than blustering school boys.[13]

Hinduism

Forster was an assiduous explorer of Hindu sites, both its pilgrimage centers and its temple complexes. Likewise he attended any festivals on his journeys. The Magha mela, which he witnessed at Allahabad, February 1913, if not on the scale of a Kumbh mela, was large enough, some million present. He gave a vivid description to his mother: "we saw whole villages enter the water at once in long chains, like the Tonbridge ladies at the Diamond Jubilee." "By the evening, dust and smoke cloud the whole plain. I have just been looking down into it from the embankment and it was like a pale blue sea with people crawling as shrimps on the bottom."[14] It took him a day or two to respond to Varanasi: "the energy of Hinduism—going ahead full steam." "The mess is unbelievable," he told his mother. William Rothenstein had given Forster an introduction to a fakir, one Nrusingh Sharma, and after one mistaken encounter with a gentleman on a bed of nails—"a terrible creature whose face was smeared with ashes and red paint. I fled like Hansel and Gretel from the witch"—they met. He spoke good English. Forster enjoyed a display of his sacred possessions, a lingam and a portrait of Siva and Lakshmi, the latter compared to Queen Victoria. They agreed to rechristen them George and Mary.[15] From Varanasi he went on an afternoon excursion to Sarnath. Staying with Masood at Bankipore he went to the more significant Buddhist site at Bodh Gaya. Looking down at it from the embankment he felt "there can't be anything like it in the world."[16] Forster also visited the Krishna pilgrimage center at Mathura, taking more to this center of Krishna worship than that of Siva at Varanasi, and preferring Mathura (Muttra) to Brindaban (Vrindavan).[17]

Temples were a major means for Forster's reading of Hinduism. First mention of a temple visit was at Kher, a village outside Aligarh: its "decorations of monkey's heads downwards was as wild and remote as I had expected."[18] There was the Hanuman temple near his guest-house in Chhatarpur whose priest "like a cheerful Christ skipped down the walls to greet us, dressed in a duster and smelling rather nasty—I suppose of ghee."[19] The temple complex at Mount Abu in Rajasthan was "magical" and if the mist and whistling wind was "alarming" it was "a wonderful place." But Forster grappled with its architecture, finding "cold splendor and elaborate emptiness" in the central shrine. "Were the decorative features of the temples bad or ill-arranged, he wondered; "the eye never dwells."[20] From Chhatarpur in December 1912 he visited the Khajuraho temples, still to be well-known, yet oddly they failed to please: "the temples are very wonderful but nightmares—all exactly alike and covered with sculptures from head to toe."[21] On his visit to Aurangabad in 1913 he only visited Ellora. Again there was a mixed response; if he found the astonishing Kailasa temple, sculpted directly into the rock, "more amazing than anything in a land which much amazes," with "the great mild face of a goddess, doing cruelty, fades into the pit-wall," the Buddhist temples struck him as less beautiful than those at Gaya or Sarnath and the Hindu "had no beauty either: the brute aroused instead of somnolent; that was all." In the end, after a further visit, he saw them as "satanic masterpieces."[22] To Masood at the time he reflected: "the caves are cruel, obscene things, the work of devils, but very wonderful."[23]

Only much later, following a visit to an exhibition in London on the Khajuraho temples introduced by Stella Kramrisch did Forster begin to read these temples. He now saw that the temples were symbols of the world mountain, "on the outside the universe in all its richness, striving upwards through all forms of life," whereas on the inside, the sanctum sanctorum, "the dark central cell was where the individual worshipper makes contact with the divine principle." Here were moral lessons for a west so tyrannized by totalitarianism: "we have also an inner war, a struggle by the individual towards the dark secret place where he may find reality." "Those who planned Khajuraho, Orissa and Madurai knew that the community cannot satisfy the human spirit."[24] It has to be said this is a surprising conclusion on Hindu temples, surely part of an intensely communal faith. But it meant that he visited the Ajanta caves in November 1945 with more informed eyes and preferred the Hindu there to the Buddhist at Ellora: "it is not congregational and leaves the individual alone with God. I do not like in either renunciation, and transmigration seems silly. Yet the Ajanta fusion convinces me and the freshness there is a part of the fusion."[25]

Caves were also temples but it seems it was the caves that left the darkest influence on Forster's imagination. Rather mysteriously it was to be the Barabar caves, near Bankipore, and really nothing out of the ordinary, that inspired the whole incident of the caves in his Indian novel. Nicola Beauman may well be right; it was the coincidence of the visit following Masood's final rejection of his physical advances that led to Forster's profoundly depressed, negative response to their visit.[26] And here could be telling evidence of how the sexuality and the mysticism are negatively related. But clearly the Ellora caves also underpin the story.

Interpretations of the cave sequence in *A Passage to India* might agree that the echo "boum" is simply Forster's way of evoking the sacred Hindu sound of "om." But otherwise they radically diverge. They alternate between those which see the cave experience, particularly given the breakdown of Mrs. Moore, as evidence of a glimpse of nihilism and those which see the positive implied by the negative and that here all along are the makings of a mystical experience. Clearly Forster's own individualism, his liberal humanism, is caught floundering within the maelstrom of Hinduism. But he approached Hinduism through a prism of neo-Platonism and there the platonic cave was a pointer to some ultimate truth. Ganguly suggests that Mrs. Moore has experience of this ultimate reality, that her own ego gives way to a glimpse of the atman, but she lacks the yogic skills for strengthening that insight and hence the breakdown. The ego has endured a terrifying sense of its limitations. She has only grasped the negative but not the indestructible lifeforce.[27] Colmer puts it neatly in terms of promise and withdrawal. There is an anti-vision but this "expresses the failure of the human mind to encompass negation, its incapacity to invest what is alien to itself with beauty and significance." Only the eastern mind has the ability "to accept absence as well as presence as an aspect of the divine." Withdrawal, that idea of "an endlessly vanishing sense of infinity" precedes fulfillment. Colmer concludes that in the novel "every positive has its counterbalancing negative or qualifying phrase."[28] But Crews will have nothing of these kinds of reading and doubts if Mrs. Moore had any glimpse of the atman. Hers is no wish to relinquish her sense of selfhood, that is to say, her own personality, and, to the contrary, far from reaching out to the "world-soul," "she reduces the world-soul to the scale of her own wearied ego."[29]

As critical interest turned from Part II of the novel to Part III, from *Caves* to *Temple*, ever more awkward questions are posed as to Forster's attitudes to Hinduism. Are we to go along with a view that the novel ends on a note of fulfillment, that the affirmative temple has absorbed the negative cave in much the same way as the Indian temple itself encloses the sanctum sanctorum? And did Forster betray his true feelings about Hinduism in his characterization of Godbole?[30]

Some critics have seen in the maddening mystification of Godbole Forster's way of displaying his exasperation almost to breaking point with Hinduism. Far from being a figure of reconciliation, Godbole is the trouble maker, one who failed to preempt, as it lay in his powers to do, the whole fiasco of the Marabar caves, who could have done more to bring Aziz and Fielding together: "Godbole has been bitten, possibly unconsciously by the worm of evil and has in turn planted his evil into the lives of other people."[31] Besides, he falls well short of his religious aspirations, standing on the edge of that carpet in the temple, able to encompass Mrs Moore's wasp but not the stone. Forster, the liberal humanist, has anyway far too strong a commitment to the self to sympathize with such Hindu attempts at transcendence.

But other critics, and maybe, significantly, Indian, reject this version of Godbole and see him instead as symbolizing "completeness." In Shahane's interpretation, Forster's is a double vision, a polarity of body and soul, of muddle and mystery, of negation and affirmation. In the Temple sequence the character of Godbole is seen as reaching out to some sense of ultimate reconciliation and harmony. Chaman Sahni emphasizes the social all inclusiveness of the worshippers at the temple, for were not the sweepers also present? This, of course, marvelously takes up Carpenter's idea of a spiritualized democracy. In Shahane's language "the mystically intuitive and visionary," Godbole "becomes the voice of affirmation, faith in God, belief in universal love"[32]: "his dance and his trance symbolize his attempt in the true spirit of Hinduism, at inclusion of the animate and inanimate in his ideal cosmos."[33] Sahni even tries to explain away that spiritual limitation of Godbole, the way the Vaishnavite Brahmin is unable to reach out to a Saivite symbol of the lingam in the stone. He has no doubt that Godbole has achieved *samadhi*. In Godbole Forster, he claims, has grasped "the core of Hindu culture, that the transrational faith and discursive intellect are not in conflict but progress hand in hand."[34] But, of course, of its nature this mystical experience cannot last; each synthesis breeds its anti-synthesis. Even so, the novel is seen by both as ending on a note of a potential final reconciliation: "no, not yet." But there is that continuing danger of reading Forster's sympathies into the novel and its characters, a failure to recognize the autonomy of a work of fiction. All one can safely say is that within the novel Forster entertained various metaphysical possibilities.

But all this does suggest that Forster tried to make some sense of the Vedantist dimension to Hinduism. Prior to departure he read some of the Hindu classics, much enjoying Kalidasa'a *Sakantula* and rereading the *Bha-*

gavad gita in Annie Besant's translation. At the time he interpreted this quite literally, as Arjuna's reluctance to kill his relatives in battle. He went through Krishna's justifications. Indifference to death, Forster argued, would be unappealing to any westerner and it made bravery pointless: "if to slay and be slain are the same, then to be fled from and to flee are the same and dishonor is as negligible as death." He merely reports the demands of duty (dharma) and sees it in terms of reincarnation (karma): were Arjuna "trivially to show mercy now, he might check the flow of his development and debar himself from showing mercy in some existence to come." But Forster saw the ambiguous legacy of the doctrine of renunciation, for even were this to lead to a glimpse of the divine it carries nemesis in its wake: "the fall of his enemies leads to his own, for the fortunes of men are all bound up together and it is impossible to inflict damage without receiving it."[35]

Benita Parry tries to extrapolate from Forster's summary of the text as Harmony Motion Inertia (Purity Passion Darkness) some larger triad, "consciousness and the present, the unconscious and the past, and the emergent metaconsciousness and the future." However, Forster's approach remains always "profoundly ambiguous, moving between responsiveness and rejection, making the myth and subverting it."[36]

But by 1915 Forster had acquired a sense of Hinduism. He recognized its transformation over time. From a belief system free of caste and priestly power it had become "complex, priestly, superstitious." Religion in India was all important, he recognized, and any Indian writer who failed to argue this "will never take us much beyond Bombay." The likes of Mrs. Besant had opened up for westerners a sense of the meaning of Hinduism. Forster drew significant distinctions between Protestantism, with its emphasis on conduct and Hinduism with its search for a vision of the divine. Hinduism was quite ready to dethrone even the Gods in its pursuit of the inconceivable: "the gods are but a stepping stone towards the eternal." In offering its sense of the whole it took on unwittingly a missionary role: "it gains proselytes, whatever its intentions, because it can give certain types of people what they want." Forster himself was hooked.[37]

Another if evasive strategy for defining Forster's involvement in Hinduism is to fall back on his recognition of the limits of language: maybe silence is the only way to penetrate eastern culture. As Michael Orange puts it: "as the novel progresses, the distrust of verbalization becomes absolute," though in the nature of writing some attempt has to be essayed and "language itself strives also to accommodate the twin sensations of flux and stasis."[38]

The critics are of course divided on Forster's acceptance of Hinduism. Crews poses the question, "is the novel a covert apology for Hinduism?" only to fall back on an argument of its, at best, endorsing its negative features, Forster's sharing its disbelief in providence, its verdict on man's ignorance of divine truth, its rejection of any idea of a man-centered universe.[39] And quite probably Forster could never share in the claims of Vedantism, that beyond *maya* lay reabsorption with the divine. As John Beer puts it, he fell back at most on an introspection: "he looked also to the inner life for liberation from self, for that artistic anonymity which is true freedom and which he could find best in the music of Beethoven and other romantics."[40]

But an equally strong opposite case can be made. The challenge of comprehending Hinduism to Forster was far too great for him simply to marginalize it. Maybe this contrary case has also to be seen in ambiguous terms. Such is Jeffrey Paine's approach. If religion, he argues, was handed to Forster at Dewas "on a silver platter but Forster whose appetite was not fastidious, for once refused to partake," nevertheless, "he treated his failure of understanding as a tunnel that might lead somewhere darkly in spite of himself."[41] The thesis is that Forster was driven by exceptional compulsions, that he saw in both his homosexuality and Hindu mysticism two powerfully subversive forces and in their common pursuit might lie the way for his own liberation and self-tolerance. But the way forward did not lie in Vedantism, it lay in the Krishna cult.

The Krishna Cult

If the approach be somewhat counterfactual, for it implies knowledge Forster did not have, there has first to be some account of the emergence of the Krishna cult and its nature before undertaking any analysis of Forster's response to it.[42]

History

Dating its emergence is a historical minefield but need not delay matters here. Was there a historical Krishna or was he in a Renanesque sense wholly mythological? In one conservative account he really existed: "but recent researches leave no doubt that Krsna-Vasudeva of Mathura was a human teacher, belonging to the republican Kshatriya clan known as Satvatas or Vrsnis, a branch of the Yadava tribe, which was famous in the age of the brahmanas."[43] The cult, it is claimed, can be dated from the fifth century BC. Here was the possible beginnings of the bhagavata (meaning the adorable) cult, together with Buddhism and Jainism part of a revolt against Vedism, with its cult of sacrifice and its strict social hierarchy, but not so rebellious that it could not be reincorporated into orthodoxy by the fourth century AD, Krishna being identified with Vishnu, and a cult to be adopted by the Gupta

dynasty, under Chandra Gupta II (378–414 AD). One neat chronological solution is to attribute different periods of time to the three major expressions
of Krisna; the warrior and chief of the yadavas of the *Mahabharata*, to a period prior to 300 BC; the god incarnate of the *Bhagavad gita* to sometime
thereafter and the child Krishna of Gokhul, to a period after 200 AD. But
Joseph Campbell would move the whole cult forward to the fifth century AD
and see it as part of that extraordinary efflorescence of brahminism. The confusion, he argues, lies in the way its exponents dated their own creative
achievement to a mythological past, "imaginatively projecting its perfection
far into the past, as though for millenniums India had known the voluptuous
grace and harmony of this moment of its apogee." In his account the Krishna
legend becomes "a final taste of the somewhat overripe late fruit of the tree
of India."[44]

But if the cult is reclaimed by orthodoxy, the "Vedic religion is," as
Thomas Hopkins puts it, "generally damned with faint praise."[45] For here
were the beginnings of the *bhakti* movement, with its emphasis on the emotional and the egalitarian, one wholly different from the ceremonial and hi-
eratic. It was, however, to be only in the south, in large part through the writings of the Vaishnavite Alvars, a group of Tamil saints, from the sixth to the
ninth centuries that the real working out of the Krishna cult took shape and
is given expression in the first of its great classic texts, seen by Milton Singer
as kind of New Testament, the *Bhagavata Purana*. Here was the canonical
scriptures of Vaishnavism. Another important early source is the *Narada-Su-
tra*. Possibly the *Bhagavata Purana* were composed, in the ninth or early tenth
centuries, in the great temple complex at Srirangam.[46]Not that the movement entirely distanced itself from abstract thought, for if it turned away
from the non-dualist Sankara it overlapped with Ramanuja's qualified non-
dualism and the path of knowledge was not wholly discounted.

Then the *bhakti* movement spread north. It was in Bengal that Vaishnavism took root and was to discover its most vigorous expression. At the twelfth
century court of Laksmana, of the Sena dynasty of East India, a former wandering ascetic turned professional poet, Jayadeva, wrote possibly the most influential of all the Krishna cult texts, the *Gitagovinda* (The Song of the
Cowherd, c 1175). Whereas southern Vaishnavism had ignored Radha, as
well as the cowherd background of Krishna, here Radha (translatable as perfection, success) took center stage.

There was to be a revival of the cult in the late fifteenth century by two of
the great figures in the movement, Caitanya (1485–1533) founder of the
gaudiya sampraday (it began in the Bengal province of Gauda)—and he was
to take the worship of Krishna to new extremes—and Vallabha, an Andhra

brahmin, (1478 or 1479–1531) founder of Pushti Marg or Path of Grace. He wrote the most influential commentary on the *Gitagovinda*, subsequently added to by his son, Vitthalanatha, the key text for interpreting the Krishna cult in terms of "mood." Gaudiya Vaishnavism took on some of the trappings of the Sahajiya cult, introducing a Tantric dimension.

Quite who should take the credit for setting up the pilgrimage center or *braj* around Mathura and Vrindaban is open to question. *Braj* can be translated as a place "where the senses can roam freely."[47] Did Vallabha visit Gokul 1492 or 1494? Certainly Gokhul was to become the center of the Pushti marg. Two Karnataka brahmins who worked in the court of Husain Shah, ruler of Bengal, converted by Caitanya and assuming the new names of Rupa and Sanatana and named *gosvamins* or theologians of the movement, arrived in Braj in 1517, settling in Vrindaban and founding a temple in 1533. But it was to be Akbar who gave a grant in 1565 to their nephew, Jiva Gosvami, to found a temple—so the Krishna cult owes much to the religious enlightenment of the Moghul emperor—this the Man Singh temple, opened in 1590. But it was a southerner from Madurai, though a follower of Gaudiya Vaishnavism, Narayan Bhatt, who, in a tract written in 1552, mapped out the pilgrimage route. This should properly be seen as a revival of the pilgrimage for its origins seem to have been a great deal earlier. In the seventeenth century the cult went into a decline, denied the lifeblood, according to Dimock, from the Caitanya-inspired Vaishnavism of Bengal.[48]

In the nineteenth century there was to be a major pressure group campaign to raise the profile of the Krishna cult, this led by Harischandra (1850–1885) in Varanasi, a follower of the Pushti Marg. Krishna was being harnessed to patriotism and nationalism. It had to face a claim by western orientalists for a Christian origin of the sect. If this was no semitised version of Hinduism, one that was to blight the twentieth century, Hariscandra made a successful bid to link all Vaisnava *sampradays* around Vaisnava *bhakti*. Vaisnavism became India's leading expression of Hinduism.[49]

Krishna

The blue-black-skinned boy (Krishna translates in fact as "black") is quite simply a love object for his worshippers. Krs translates as Being, na as Joy. It can also be translated as "one who attracts." Alternatively, he is *purusa* or pure consciousness. Here is an example of bhaktic worship:

Hari Hara Hari Hara Hari Hara Hari Hara
Murmur them with abundant faith

These names will ever support your life
They father you and mother you
Transforming these terrible times
Hari's gracious forms-let them suffuse your mind[50]

Krishna worship is seen as suitable for the kali yuga, the black age. Narayana, Vasudeva, Hari, Mukunda, Acyuta, Bhagavan are amongst his many names. Claims are made for Krishna as the high god. Not only did he displace the Vedic Indra—he did so by lifting the sacred mountain Govardhan and protecting Indra's former worshippers from his thunderous rain—but he also supplanted Siva. In the former case there is a break from Vedic sacrifice and ceremonial to *bhakti*; in the latter, a battle between two forms of worship, the ascetic path of yoga linked to Siva, and the bhaktic path of Krishna. There is a kind of ritual downgrading of Siva, the ascetic—though also the great lover—with his being both desperate to dance attendance on Krishna and having to do so dressed as a gopi (cowherd). If on the outside the hard ascetic, on the inside, Siva emerges in the Krishna story as soft and female. And if Krishna at one level is but one of several incarnations or avatars of Vishnu—an avatar means literally one who descends—at another he has become Vishnu. Yet, if part of his perfection lies in his being unborn, he is also completely human. As Hawley puts it: "indeed, though his form is human, his divine powers are available to him whenever he needs them and his divine beauty shines through the medium of his earthly form."[51] He has come a long way from being a minor deity near Mathura.

And if a love object, what was his appearance? This of course is the Krishna of the cowherd legend, with his childhood in Gokul. To quote Entwistle: "he is primarily a seductive figure and is usually represented with slender limbs and soft effeminate features." He lacks the muscular physique of a Hanuman. Krishna becomes, in Carstairs's analysis, "the thinly veiled longed for homosexual lover."[52] With his beauty the source of his appeal to his devotees and the crux of his divinity, accounts of his beauty become highly florid: "his eyes are like wag-tails birds at play; his ear-rings like suns; his hair, with flowers in it, is like a cloud streaked with moon-beams etc."[53] This can be endlessly glossed, e.g., his teeth "are like jasmine flowers . . . normally reddish . . . made white by his laugh."[54] Indeed, he is a positive paragon. "In him," we are told:

we find the ideal householder and the ideal *sannyasin*, the hero of a thousand battles, who knew no defeat, the terror of despots, sycophants, hypocrites, sophists and pretenders, the master statesman, the uncrowned monarch, the kingmaker who had no ambition for himself. He was a friend of the poor, the weak, and the distressed, the champion of the rights of women and of the social and spiritual enfranchisement of the sudra and even of the untouchables, and the perfect ideal of detachment.[55]

But this is a composite portrait of Krishna, hero, god, child. What is the story of the divine child?

One Kamsa, sired by a demon, has usurped his father's throne, King Ugrasena of the Yadavs, centered on Mathura, replacing the worship of Vishnu by that of Siva and imposing a reign of terror. But Vishnu engineers revenge through the children of Vasudeva and Devati: through her seventh child, Balaram, in part Vishnu, for he is sired by the white hair of Sesha, the great serpent, a Vishnu incarnation, and through her eighth child, Krishna, the incarnate Vishnu himself. To deceive Kamsa, who is aware that the eighth child will be his undoing, Vasudeva has entered into a conspiracy with his friend Nanda, a cowherd in neighboring Gokhul and married to Yasoda: he has already sent one of his wives, Rohini, to Nanda and it is she who actually gives birth to Balaram; Krishna, however, is born to Vasudeva and Devati, both by now imprisoned, but Vasudeva manages to escape and carry the young Krishna through the swollen waters of the Jumna and take him to Gokhul. Here he is exchanged for a daughter just born to Yashoda, Vasudeva returning to prison with this child, only for it to be slaughtered by Kamsa, followed by a massacre of the innocents. However, Krishna is safe, and so begins his idyllic childhood in and around Gokul with his foster parents. If the fulfillment of the story is Krishna's return to Mathura as a young man and his felling Kamsa with a mighty blow and so restoring justice, prior to his departure to study in Ujjain and future kingship in Dvarka, the thrust of the whole Krishna cult is surprisingly on his childhood, above all his flirtations with the gopis.[56]

Psychoanalytic interpretations can be applied to Krishna's childhood. Here in Jeffrey Masson's account can be diagnosed a kind of regression to the extreme dependence on the mother: "it is a world where all is in harmony and where the child is king." Endlessly gratified, the narcissistic child expects instant gratification, "his grasp is unending," and will not settle for one love object. Hence Krishna's pursuit of the gopis. The unpleasant is dealt with by projection so that, for example, Krishna projects a sense of the bad mother on to the demoness Putana.[57]

If Balarama plays little or no role in the childhood years of Krishna, as the elder brother and protector of Krishna he is a major figure in the Krishna legend. In contrast to Krishna he is of fair complexion. He is usually accompanied by his wife, Revati. As a serpent deity, and it is a serpent who aids Krishna's escape across the Jumna, he is likewise an avatar of Vishnu. It is suggested that he is also a precursor of Rama but in the Krishna legend is demoted and replaced by Arjuna.[58] He stands out for his strong physical presence, "somewhat pot-bellied," addicted to drink, the patron saint of bhang takers, prone to violence, a great wrestler and likewise their patron saint, as well as being an agricultural deity.[59] As a Rama precursor, in the long run, with the Hindu fundamentalist contemporary cult of Ram, he has displaced Krishna himself as the most popular Hindu god. Significantly in the Rama legend Rama is the elder brother to Lakshmana and is a far more respectable figure than either Krishna or Balarama. A more conventional morality reigns. For those attracted to a more solid physique Balarama makes an attractive alternative homoerotic figure.

The figure of Krishna takes on differing expressions in the literature of the legend. In the late nineteenth century Krishna could even become an exemplar of a Victorian and colonial morality, an ascetic, the love of the gopis deemed allegorical, "the embodiment of self-denial, self-control, self-sacrifice, and absolute purity of thought, word, and wish."[60] Maybe the most important point to make is that Krishna, whatever his self-sufficient divinity, needs others to enact his adventures. Only by taking human form, if in no way subject to its limitations, can he, as the language goes, enjoy his own sweetness. Between him and his devotees there is a similar kind of interdependence as there is between the guru and his disciples. If in the *Bhagavata Purana* he is the cynosure of all eyes, in the *Gitagovinda* he is as much the pursuer as the pursued; he is thoroughly love-sick for Radha. As Siegel puts it: "he is a man carnally loving a woman."[61] In Vallabha's commentary, however, he is once again wholly in charge: "for all souls are in Vallabha's system, completely determined in their thoughts, feelings, and actions by Krsna, who dwells within each soul in His aspect as 'Inner Controller.'"

In order to be on the same this-worldly wave-length as his devotees Krishna has, as Redington explains, to "constrain" himself: "Krsna must descend to their level to make them ascend." Krishna embodies all the moods. And here there is a soteriological purpose. By mirroring the activity of the devotee whilst displaying his superiority Krishna attracts the devotee to himself. "Krsna's Grace is not a matter of choice for its recipient, but of irresistible charm." And Krisna is powerfully innovative. He is "the bull elephant who bursts the dam of right conduct."

But Redington then seems to be taking the argument in a different direction, away from inter-dependence, when he accentuates Krishna's self-sufficiency. "He is all powerful: he depends on no one and nothing. He is the controller of time, actions and the natures of all individuals. He has absolutely no needs." He has no need of worshippers for they have nothing to add to him. But he changes direction once again: if Krishna has no need of others, then the only reason he could have for materializing himself is his quite gratuitously seeking to grant ultimate freedom.[62] Clearly the problematic lies in just how humans do relate to the divine.

A Theory of Love

Running through the Krishna legend is an endeavor to transcribe a love for the divine in terms of intense sexual love. It hovers continually on a borderline between the carnal and the spiritual. We return to a distinction between fusion and communion. Love depends on separation. Whereas there can be no love between *atman* and *brahma* in the Vedantist quest, for they are one and the same, in the Krishna quest love is of the essence, the only means by which humans can relate to a separate god. Admittedly the Krishna cult opens up numerous forms of love; the parental or filial of adults for the child Krishna; the friendship of the cowherd boys for their divine playmate; the love of the cowherd girls or gopis for their divine sweetheart. Entwistle writes of "the multi-valency" of Krishna's personality: "baby, boy, gigolo, trickster, hero and sermonizer;" this "allows people of different backgrounds, sexes and age-groups to select an appropriate model for their devotion."[63] The rich variety of relationships that the Krishna cult opens up makes it an attractive proposition for those of all sexual orientations. Here is an extreme expression of love: "tears, shivering, horripilation, perspiration, loss of color or complexion, loss of vigor, loss of voice and loss of consciousness constitute the eightfold pure signs of true devotion."[64]

But only the love of the gopis matches this extreme form and herein lies the conundrum. If the way to love Krishna is to identify with those who expressed the most extreme form of love then the gopis become the obvious role models and this raises an ambivalence as to how men identify with the female. Is not the Krishna cult for men self-evidently homoerotic?

The tension between the carnal and the spiritual is one continuing strand in the legend. For Joseph Campbell, so powerful is the expression of physical love in the *Gitagovinda* it is a text more akin to Shakespeare's *Venus and Adonis* than to Thomas à Kempis's *Imitation of Christ*. Siegel sees here "the sexualisation of the devotional, the sanctification of the erotic."[65] One obvious explanation for this convergence of the carnal with the spiritual lies in the emergence of this sacred literature out of the courtly love poetry of the classical age. Can it be argued, to look at it in a different way, that in a Gidean sense it is the satisfaction of desire, of *kama* that leads to a predisposition for spiritual enlightenment?[66] But the thrust is toward a sexual love that is not fulfilled. This is not procreative love but love for its own sake, love as play. In Vallabha's account, this is the story of *bhava*, of a total and obsessive love, one that sees Krishna everywhere, of a total surrender to Krishna and in the process to a loss of all ethical responsibility.

But here is also a very subtle account, elaborating on a theory of love for the divine in terms of mood, sustaining that mood as the means to the divine. Here a Hindu account of love comes into line with that of the French Utopian socialist, Charles Fourier, who likewise devised an idealized world based on love, but one in which love was postponed, a kind of continual foreplay, an endlessly deferred gratification, sustaining a constant mood of love.[67] And these Hindu exponents of divine love were shrewd psychologists for they sensed that the most intense longings of all came with rupture, the separation of the lover from the beloved, with those agonizing pains of sexual pleasure anticipated but denied. Separation would be the greatest possible spur to seek out the divine.

At the heart of this theory of love is the *rasa*, the great circle dance, the peacock or mating dance. Peacocks mated in the forests of Brindavan in the rainy season. In Campbell's account it became "an amplitude of dionysiac madness that is nowhere equaled—I believe—in the history of religious thought."[68] *Rasa* can be variously translated as relish, sentiment, juice or sap. Milk, an obvious liquid for a cowherd community, can also be a metaphor for semen. The idea of storing semen in the head relates the dance to Tantrism. Here is one description of the dance:

> The *gopis* formed a circle; in the center stood Krishna, playing on his flute while the *gopis* danced around him. Between every two *gopis* in the circle was to be seen a Krishna and there was a *gopi* between every two Krishnas. This dance against the background of the Yamuna, the river of life, on a beautiful moonlit night, has been a source of inspiration for many composers, poets, and painters and has enriched their works.[69]

Singer interprets this arrangement: Krishna's presence between two *gopis* symbolizes human interdependence; his presence alongside them God's constant protection.[70]

This is "the sea of *rasa*, the endless swelling ocean in which the empirical self is dissolved."[71] Here is an experience of community at its most intense. Gerald Heard's account of the caritism of the early Christian church reflects this love (see below). Joseph Campbell sees in the version of the dance in *Bhagavata Purana* a transition from *yoga* to *bhoga*, from introversion to physical enjoyment, an ecstatic dance of love. But when the women have been "excited to a pitch of frenzy beyond bounds, their god abruptly disappeared."[72] At the height of passion, there is separation. Krishna excused his cruelty thus: "when I refuse attachment to those devoted to me, my reason is to make their devotion more intense. I disappeared so that your hearts should be so absorbed in me that you would be unable to think of anything else."

Here a profound conflict is at work between liberation and order. A fundamental incompatibility is revealed between two forms of love, *kama* or sexual desire and *prem*, one that is pure and a world unto itself, one that "satisfies no desires of any who partake in it . . . it has no results in the natural world . . . it builds nothing . . . it is eternal."[73] Yet this is equally a battle with asceticism and renunciation. Yoga is seen as a running away from life. Krishna does not run away from the body. He is fully sensual. One has to look beyond the selfishness of physical love: "then one is set adrift from the sedimentation and pollution that inevitably attend the ever-recurrent process of procreation and death." One has "to recover one's true liquidity."[74] In the end the *gopis* exhibit a wholly selfless love of service to Krishna. Physical love leads to death, Krishna's to eternal life. This is not *moksha*, a mystical escapism. It is more of a return to the garden of Eden, love in an earthly paradise.

Just how subversive is this as a theory of love? There is the hugely awkward fact that at its center lies adultery. All the cow-girls are newly married. Radha, and with the *Gitagovinda* her privileged relationship with Krishna becomes center stage, is also married, to Abhimanyu, with a jealous mother-in-law to boot, Jatila, who does everything possible to prevent her meeting Krishna. Her immorality is compounded by her role as carer for Krishna in Nanda's household. Krishna is still a bachelor (though of course as avatar of Vishnu he is married to Lakshmi) but in time he is to drop Radha and marry Rukmini. Here the courtly tradition of adulterous love intrudes; marriage is seen as dull and only adultery is exciting, "on the edge" as it were: "whereas boredom can kill love in marriage a love affair with the unknown can never be boring."[75] Married love simply does not induce the right mood. Clearly Radha herself is exceptional: "she is neither a mother, creator or personification of wifely virtues, nor is she anything to do with fertility. She has no independent function outside of her relationship with Krishna in which she plays the role of a divine and fair-complexioned mistress with whom the dark Krishna can experience cosmic bliss."

But for so conservative a dharmic morality as Hinduism this is clearly unacceptable. The Pushti Marg, more conservative than Gaudiya Vaishnavism, simply have Radha and Krishna married. All kinds of exegetical devices have been resorted to, e.g., the *gopis* are not in fact married to their husbands, they are *saktis* of Krishna, his female energy, and through Krishna's powers of *maya* their husbands have been fooled into supposing that they are their wives.[76] Krishna, anyway, is a law unto himself, above conventional morality, and no charge of adultery would apply. Vallabha interestingly also turns the argument over adultery around. It is deemed "completely reprehensible." But more to the point, because of its high social risk, its indulgence breeds a fear and terror, wholly incompatible with being in the right "mood." There is nothing carnal about the love of the *gopis* or of Radha. We are back again to a distinction between *kama* and *prema*.[77]

Maybe the tension between the sacred and the profane cannot be reconciled. Can one square the circle as Siegel tries to do and suggest that the sexual love of Radha for Krishna is both deadly, for it ties her to *samsara*, but through Krishna's love she achieves liberation through joy? Siegel still concludes: "the *Gitagovinda* is unequivocally about the joy and sorrow of carnal love, about a god who is purely human, but it is also a work concentrated to that god as God."[78]

It is refreshing to come across Sudhir Kakar's account in which the adultery is frankly recognized—Radha is the personification of a *mahabhava*, of a great love which is heedless of all convention—and here is orgasmic love; "in the end and perhaps inevitably, the community's quest for pleasure triumphed over its theological scruples in firmly demanding that the mythical lovers be accepted as unambiguously adulterous." In adultery, he interprets, there is freedom from the sexual taboos of marriage, from woman's gendered inequality. Radha, for example, can adopt the masculine role in love-making.[79]

But the breaking of taboos goes deeper. Radha, significantly in Nanda's household acting in a maternal role toward the boy Krishna, takes on a role as a mother goddess. Here the legend confronts the incest taboo. Radha's dominating Krishna in the *Gitagovinda* reflects a Tantric-sakti cult tradition, a mother goddess cult influential in the North East. Joseph Campbell draws a connection with the ideas of the Tantric *vamacaris*, the Left Hand Path.[80] In a Kleinian sense here there is a conflict between the good and the bad mother figure, Krishna working through the negative image in his mastering the demoness Putana, sent by Kamsa to kill him, sucking out all the poison in her breast. In Freudian terms here is a regression to the level of the infantile dependence of the child on the all-powerful mother; as Siegel puts it, "the triumph of the infantile fantasy, the victory of the *id* over the external reality."[81]

But this unitive experience is also metaphor for the mystical. In terms of tantric yoga, a heightened sexual excitement is transposed, orgasmic feelings turn oceanic, "evoking fantasies of plunging into a sea of unlimited sexual experience, of becoming both the man and the woman in the mystic process of achieving union with the universe."[82] Whereas Fourier had believed it impossible to break through the incest taboo, the Krishna legend suggests not only can it be done but it is the means to mystical fulfillment.

But does the legend equally challenge another taboo, that of homosexuality? Here the evidence is far more ambiguous. Indeed, in the legend itself, there is no example of a self-conscious male sexually seeking out another. In the Indian religious tradition there is considerable evidence of a male fear of women. "Defensiveness and suspicion of the female sex are characteristics of Hinduism in general," claims Entwistle, "and there are many ascetics who will have nothing to do with women and even refrain from setting eyes on them."[83] Here the castration complex is at work. Then there is the widespread practice within Krishna cult devotees of cross-dressing. Does transvestism point to latent homosexuality or simply a way of reverencing women? Famously, both Caitanya and Ramakrishna assumed a female identity to worship Krishna. Jeffrey Kripal has suggested that in Ramakrishna's case this became overt homosexuality, with Ramakrishna the paramour of Mathur, the owner of the Dakshineswar temple, and the passive partner in a sexual relationship with his Vedantist instructor, the naked ascetic, Tota Puri.[84] In some cases Sudhir Kakar concedes that such cross-gendering reflects a homosexual libido, "a retreat from phallic masculinity into anal eroticism," but he favors as an explanation an attempt by the male, out of a wish for complete subservience to woman, of a reaching out for a female identity, the one thing denied him.[85]

And maybe here begins the unraveling of the mystery: a deep pursuit of androgyny. Once again this has mystical overtones. To quote Hawley: "the transferability of all sex roles between Radha and Krishna illustrates the extent to which they are themselves interchangeable, two aspects of a single reality . . . an undifferentiable nondual reality."[86] "In the Krishna cult," Entwistle analyses, "the sexual transformation is not a reaction to a feared threat but is more an adulation of the indivisibility of Krishna and Radha."[87]

It is tempting to read into the Krishna cult such contemporary interpretations as a defense of adultery and, if not of homosexual practice, at least of homoeroticism. But in the end the rhetoric seems to go in a different direction. And it has to be said any attempt to connect sexuality and mysticism is deeply offensive to some conservative Hindus: "there are no sexual relationships possible with God," asserts R. D. Ranade "and eroticism has no place in Mysticism."[88] Clearly all mystical writing is up against the barriers of language and it seems predictable that any attempt to describe a mystical experience will fall back, by way of analogy, on the most extreme experience open to humans, physical passion. But the legend is seeking to express some suprahuman and trans-gender experience. This mystical quest takes a different direction to that of Vedantism, with its search for *moksha*, an escape from *maya*; to the contrary, this is delight in a this-worldly experience, the experience of play in an earthly paradise.

Pilgrimage, Festivals, Plays

Over time the whole area around Mathura (Muttra) and Brindavan (Vrindaban) has become the *braj*, a pilgrimage center, a kind of theme park or Krishnaland. Maybe in a topographical sense this rather dry agricultural land is no longer at all like the sacred forest where Radha and Krishna once roamed. I felt on my journeys through the Panna forest near Khajuraho that here was a far more appropriate setting. This is a unique form of pilgrimage. In contrast to others, where there is a definite purpose, an end in sight, a linear model,[89] here there is mindless wandering, the need to cut loose from any fixed and stable center, a surrender to unpredictable play. Haberman also sees in the pilgrimage the opportunity for the illicit love affair. There are two kinds of pilgrimage, the braj-yatra, for the removal of sins, and the ban-yatra, "the realization of the ultimate meaning of things." Here is Haberman's rather portentous account of the latter in *braj*: "it does not aim for the orgasmic reduction of tensions but follows a path of unending curves and plays around all things on edge, enjoying the ongoing foreplay of the universe."[90] This is no search for renunciation but, as Entwistle puts it, "some kind of fulfillment in the here and now": "where Braj is concerned the ideal is not one of entering into and then returning from an experience, but of remaining totally immersed in love of Krishna."[91]

The pilgrimage in part gravitates around festivals. Holi is the most riotous, a spring festival, wholly subversive.[92] The Krishna festival occurs during the four rainy months of the monsoon, inverting those elsewhere where the gods at this time of year are seen to be asleep. There are many festivals, all marking aspects of the legend, the swing festival, the *rasa*, the bath festival, all celebrated at full moon. Somewhat paradoxically, having already celebrated so many aspects of his life, the climax comes with the birth of Krishna, the *janmastami*, this at the culmination of the rainy season, August–September. This also marks Vasudeva'a safely carrying the baby Krishna across the Jumna. If deemed a fast, it is in practice turned into a feast, for the requirement is to change one's diet rather than endure any penance and delicious sweet-meats are on offer. But one is required at the least to stay awake, songs of praise during the night a constant wake-up call. "As the night deepens, one sees," following Hawley's account, "streams of pilgrims threading their way through the twisting streets of Brindavan to gather at what is today the most popular temple in the town, that of Banke Bihari." If the public cannot attend the midnight birth, they do so the *darsana* (vision of deity) at 3 or 4am: "the lithe, flute-playing Krishna appears with a peculiar clarity at this early morning hour." At the following mid-day in the temple of Radha Raman, "a small, rhythmic, triply bent image of Krishna," dressed in simple white cloth offsetting his jet black skin, is ceremonially showered for hours on end with milk, curd, *ghi*, honey and crystallized sugar, only to retire for yet another bath. By then his symbolic birth is complete.[93]

Lilas or plays—it can also translate as sports or pastimes—likewise celebrate the Krishna legend. There are various ways in which they can be presented. At Brindavan there is a cycle of twenty-three plays. Each play takes up some episode in Krishna's pastoral story, much of the material drawn from the *puranas*. The content is highly metaphysical: "it is not easy for a foreigner to understand how widely philosophy has permeated the popular literature of India."[94] This is liturgy and is akin to temple worship; attending a play is the equivalent of sharing in a sacrament. For the Vaishnavites God is an actor. Krishna has descended to act in his own play. At Brindavan the *lilas* are performed on a stage. But there can be touring companies. Courts could have their own companies. Any group of friends can assemble to sing praises to Krishna.[95] Music plays a major part in the *lilas*. It can cover over the traces of sometimes not very distinguished verse.

Of particular relevance to Forster and the cult is the role of boy actors. Only those with unbroken voices can enact the roles of Krishna, Radha, and the gopis. These are the *rasdharis*. Older boys and adult males can act other roles. Appropriate for a drama celebrating "play," the essence of good acting is spontaneity and choice of plays is left to the mood of the *rasdharis*. Given the worship of children in Hindu culture it is not surprising that these boy actors are seen as themselves divine and for the duration worshipped as gods.

Forster and the Krishna Cult

How familiar would Forster have been with this material? Here a counterfactual approach has its difficulties. Can it be presumed that he did have insight into this philosophy, to the idea, for example, of mood? He certainly visited the Krishna sites in Mathura and Brindavan, though not Gokhul, and wondered if preference for Krishna over Siva explained his greater enjoyment of this visit over the one to Benares. In writing up his correspondence for *The Hill of Devi*, he did some homework, reading the *Bhagavad Purana* and *Vishnu Purana*. The narrative details of the Krishna legend he appropriated from W. G. Archer's *The Loves of Krishna*. Did he universalize the story and see in Dyer's massacre at Amritsar some analogue to Kamsa's massacre of the innocents?[96] Maybe the events at Dewas, with but a short procession through the town, did not require any familiarity with the specific content to the Krishna pilgrimage. But it is not clear how much he had read by the time of writing *A Passage to India* and here the knowledge gap had to be closed by Forster's intuitive imagination.

The Two Maharajahs

It was in large part through his visits to Chhatarpur, ruled by Maharaja Vishnwarath Singh Bahadur (1866–1932) and Dewas, ruled by Maharaja Tukoji Rao III, both minor princelings and best known because of their friendship with Forster, that Forster came into contact with the cult. Tukoji was an adopted heir. The royal house of Dewas often failed to reproduce itself and renewed its line by adoption from the Mahratta House of Stupa, a small jagir in the Presidency of Bombay. Conventionally the younger son should be chosen but on this occasion he had defective feet—all his toes were missing—and so it fell to the elder. Forster owed his introduction to their tutors, to Theodore Morison for the former, Malcolm Darling for the latter.[97] Dewas Senior, some 350 miles north west of Bombay in Madya Pradesh (there was a Dewas Junior), was some 450 square miles, with a population at the time of 83,000.

He was to make two visits to Chhatarpur, in December 1912, along with Lowes Dickinson and Bob Trevelyan and, briefly, in September 1922, on leave as it were from secretarial duties in Dewas. The Maharaja of Chhatarpur, but five foot tall, was unprepossessing in appearance, with his bridgeless nose, and a none too good advertisement for a western education, with his chaotic mix of ideas western and Hindu. But he was instantly attractive to Forster, with his recognizing their shared sexual tastes, if in the Maharajah's case this was evidently pederastic. In introducing him later to Jo Ackerley he wrote of him as "a truly strange and romantic character"; "indeed, he has many endearing qualities."[98] The second visit had been marred by a matter of protocol, when the Maharajah, after a quarrelsome day, instead of delivering Forster to the door of the guesthouse had dropped him off at the bottom of the small hill below and Forster, in a rare moment of vanity, had protested. But they parted friends.

He was a genuinely religious man, sought God and in honor of the gods supported a group of actors whose plays celebrated the gods, Krishna in particular. Oddly, it was Dickinson, in many ways alienated from Hinduism and India itself, who sensed a religious quality in the performance, equivalent in his eyes to the sacred dancing of classical Greece. It is possible to depreciate the seriousness of this quest and resort to the camp in describing the Maharajah's besotted admiration for his Krishna boy actors. And Ackerley has a rather unsavory account of the Maharajah's pursuit of a twelve-year-old boy, rather incongruously nicknamed Napoleon III, whom he wanted for his troupe, and who was indeed to be virtually kidnapped from his relatives in Kanpur.[99]

In his Indian journal Forster maintains a fairly straight face in describing the play he attended, all about a rishi attending the baby Krishna, being turned away by his mother despite Krishna's protests. In the end the rishi has to be welcomed back and turns out to be Vishnu in disguise. Significantly for the future novel this is the story of the birth of Krishna. If Forster was rather more taken by the acting of the fifty-five-year-old playing the hermit he was clearly moved by the performance of the boy actors playing Radha and Krishna. By the time he visited in 1922, such was the scandal of the Maharajah's tastes, the troupe had been much reduced.

The relationship with Tukoji III, or HH as Forster called him and after Masood his most important Indian friendship, was to be the more influential. His first encounter, Christmas 1912, with the then twenty-four-year-old Maharajah, "tiny, round-faced with a long weeping moustache,"[100] was none too happy, HH disparaging the sexual tastes of the Maharajah of Chhatarpur, but thereafter they became good friends. In mid 1916 he invited Forster, then in Egypt, to return to Dewas as his private secretary. When the invitation was repeated in 1921 Forster jumped at the chance, departing 4 March. Virginia Woolf wondered if he would ever return: "he will become a mystic, sit by the roadside and forget Europe."[101]

Forster had badly wanted to experience India in the monsoon climate, the seasonal background for the final section of his Indian novel. In fact Dewas is spared the worst of the heat, with some cool breezes. Even so, Forster wilted: "perhaps it is the heat but I feel so stupid, almost senile," he confided to Masood: "I cannot concentrate and I cannot remember."[102] His was a rather desultory day, working in the office about 8 to 11 am, "which included meddling with the garden, electric light, cars and guesthouse" and then the rest of the day, as he put it to Ackerley, "was without rhyme or reason."[103]

In fact Forster was present at a time of crisis for the princely states and the Maharajah was in a half-hearted way trying to get a constitution off the ground that would at least notionally appear more consultative. Forster was well aware that in Dewas he was back in the fourteenth century and living through the fag-end of a civilization. He liked it that the raj, if opportunistically, in its desperate search for any allies against the new challenge of Indian nationalism, was now treating the princes with greater respect. And, however despotic princely power, Forster felt "they reign over a people who have a natural feeling for royalty and for personal relationships and who emotionally can be swiftly yet permanently touched by a glimpse of the sacred figure."[104] But Forster was all too aware that without change a state such as Dewas was living on borrowed time. If Congress activists were unable to penetrate Dewas Senior they could shout abuse from the railway station of Dewas Junior. There were to be major domestic scandals, his son, Vikramsinha, accusing him in 1928 of trying to poison him and seduce his wife. If the predictable disaster was staved off till 1933, it was then, accused by the government of financial mismanagement, that he fled to Pondicherry, dying there December 1937. He was not yet fifty. The Times obituarist wrote of a potentiality betrayed: "he came from an ancient and renowned dynasty and in the earlier years his rule gave some promise of doing well, but an ungovernable temper and self-indulgence led to serious deterioration."[105]

However, saddened by his friend's decline, Forster was always his apologist: "my affection for him grows in remembrance," he wrote to Masood, "and is not influenced by anything he does. He is one of the most saintly of characters and the only human being who has ever made religion a reality to me. I can't stand piety and ecclesiasticism: but he had hold of something precious."[106] He saw him as saint. Such feelings were just as strong after HH's death: "he had a deeper sense of the nobilities and the delicacies of personal intercourse," he told his Indian audience, "than anyone I have ever met, whether English or Indian."[107] But here in large part was the explanation for the mismanagement of the state. HH would rather spend time on his religious duties than administrative affairs. At their heart lay the worship of Krishna.

Forster's Sexuality in India

Sexual needs, what Auden called "the intolerable neural itch," threatened to overwhelm Forster in India. Birje -Patel summarizes the drama: "his creativity was at its peak and his personal crisis was growing more acute day by day. The Temple section of A Passage to India was thus born of a need to impose order on a rage that his western puritan heritage could neither contain nor appease."[108] Might Forster, he speculates, find in the saturnalia of the Krishna cult some way of accommodating his deviation "as a variant of folly?" "In Dewas the greenwood might still flourish." Could, indeed, the fantasy of Maurice, when the lovers Maurice and Scudder disappear into the greenwood, be enacted? At the least, could he finally come to terms with his homosexuality?

We have already seen how his visits to India were overshadowed by his passion for Masood and Mohammed el Adl. By the time of his second visit in March 1921 Forster was a good deal more sexually experienced and hence less able to cope with frustration. However, out of respect to his host, HH, he initially resolved not to indulge. Not that Indians were particularly attractive to him. Parminder Bakshi suggests that "Forster depicts India primarily in terms of its men, observing in detail their physical qualities."[109] On being rowed ashore in Bombay in 22 October 1912 he observed of the oarsmen, "an ugly crew but beautiful skins."[110] The predominant physique of the students at Aligarh was "thin, dirty and bearded: I was not attracted to them."[111] It perked up a little in Benares: "the town is full of fat young men in blue blankets and black glossy hair—the Bengali at last."[112] In Hyderabad he observed: "Southern type; not much darker than the north but has an inky pigment in the skin. Male bust fatter with prominent nipples."[113] During his return from India 1921, on reaching Aden he noted: "black people with decent legs at last."[114] Here is an echo of Carpenter's bewailing the poor quality of the legs. It is odd that Forster, with his preference for men of a more sturdy physique, was unaware of the northern Jats and Sikhs. In the end he settled less for actual size and more for physical proportion.[115] On an excursion from Dewas to Bidar in November 1922 there were to be three days of great happiness: "I have forbidden my imagination to stray beyond the facts into licentiousness—there it was, two lads, one of whom recalled M(ohammed). Red fezes, knives at the waist."[116]

In the meanwhile life in Dewas had turned into nightmare. Forster knew that an earlier candidate for his post, a Mr. Thompson, had been caught *in flagrante delicto* with his Punjabi boy servant. But it was his earlier attempt to seduce HH's own Goanese butler that had upset the Maharajah the more: it "argued a coarseness of taste" to trespass on the servants of others. He should stick to his own. Thompson did not get the job though, even so, he was invited to return to Dewas in some other capacity.[117] In the end, and the story is now well known, Forster made approaches to one of the workmen constructing the new palace, feared he had been seen and become the subject of gossip and blurted it all out to the Maharajah. In fact HH claimed complete ignorance of these events. And here interpretations diverge. Either we accept Forster's own account, of how wonderfully tactful HH had been in accepting his sexual preferences, even though Forster resented his insinuations that it was all due to bad Mohammedan practices he had picked up in Egypt, and in time made arrangements for Forster to have as his lover, Kanaya, the court barber, or alternatively Richard Cronin's ingenious proposal that Forster was "the victim of a very unpleasant game devised by an accomplished sadist." This is in large part inspired by the character of Harry in Ruth Prawer Jhabvala's *Heat and Dust*, a rather pathetic attendant on the Naub and allegedly modeled on Forster and Ackerley in their capacities as personal secretaries. Cronin suggests that HH's manipulation of Forster, a European, is his way of getting back at colonial arrogance: in terms of Jhabvala's novel, the Naub "retains as his court buffoon a homosexual Englishman of weak character, a living exemplar of all the possibilities of Englishness that the British in India would rather deny existed. His patronage of Harry is a delicate racial affront. Racial hatred is the motive of much of his behavior."[118]

But only the most massive self-deception on Forster's part can sustain this interpretation—it would have been to undermine all his faith in personal relationships—and it is hard to see in the camp Harry, particularly as portrayed in the film, any real kinship with Forster. But it is true that the sexual liaison with Kanaya was fraught with embarrassment though again interpretations vary as to whether Forster could ever handle the almost total absence of privacy at Dewas or else reveled in a new experience. Nevertheless, for the first time in his life here was regular sex, if with someone far from being his preferred physical type, and with Forster to boot discovering in himself some pleasure at turning physical sadist.[119] But he was at the time far from sure of its benefit: "had K," he confided to his secret diary, "not been such a chatterbox I should have avoided feeling trivial and being lustful? brutal?. Great deterioration."[120]

In Forster's fiction on India strong links are made between sexuality and violence. In the short story, The Life to Come, the Indian prince, Vithobai, for one night the lover of a Protestant missionary, but then denied any furtherance of that love through the latter's priggish guilt, ends up by killing him, given a promise by the missionary that their love will be renewed in paradise. This was a story written in 1922, following the destruction of his erotic short stories but parallel to his attempt to complete A Passage to India. In The Other Boat, not completed till 1957–1958, the most erotic of all Forster's writings, a romance between an English officer en route to India and a half-caste Indian childhood friend, results in the murder of the half-caste and the suicide of the officer. Forster certainly had in mind as the homosexual officer Kenneth Searight, an army officer who had befriended both Forster and Dickinson and entertained them in his mess at Peshawar. Reading at the time Searight's accounts of his pederastic affairs, subsequently published as Paedikion, was for Forster a real awakening to the possibilities of sexual promiscuity. But one wonders if the relationships portrayed with Cocoanut, the half-caste, drew rather on Forster's own with Kanaya.[121]

How did Forster's homosexuality fit into the Hindu and Indian scheme of things? He would have been comforted in February 1913 by reading E. W. Knighton's Private Life of an Eastern King, an insider's revelations of the permissive court life of the King of Oudh in the 1830s.[122] Reading in July 1922 Emperor Babur's autobiography of his indifferent love for his wife, his belief in never betraying a friend and his preference for a lad, Babari, in the camp bazaar would also have been, if in retrospect, reassuring.

Major Puar, or Bhoj Maharaj, as he prefers to be called, a son by HH's second wife, Bai Saheba, suggested that Forster's embarrassment was more a consequence of his own feelings of guilt and that the court would have been quite unfazed by his sexuality. One leading courtier certainly shared his tastes. There was, he claimed, a strong tradition of homosexuality in the princely courts, Moghul, zamindari, above all, Sikh. Relationships between rulers and boys were of little real political significance and for sexual amusement only, and they were much safer than relationships with mistresses, who schemed and whose children could be the source of endless divisive rivalries.[123]

Masood chose to send him in January 1922 a tract on the Hijras or eunuchs, literally translated as neither male nor female. From this he would have learnt of the Hijra cult of a Hindu goddess, Bechara Matha (Besraji Mata) a mother goddess, near Surat (or Ahmedabad, accounts vary), details of the castration they underwent, and the fact that they would not be accepted into the sect should they betray any signs of manliness.[124] It is difficult to know if the *hijras* are the tip of some Indian iceberg of homosexuality or a wholly discrete expression of human sexuality, be it transvestism or transsexuality.[125] A case can be made that the term, intentionally pejorative, was used by a colonial regime, for all the tolerant orientalism of a Richard Burton, quite unable to face homosexuality, a prejudice shared by the religiously orthodox, both Hindu and Muslim, the better to categorize and brand a very much wider homosexual constituency. In the Indian Penal Code of 1884 cross-dressing in public was forbidden for the *hijras*, a means of driving any expression of sexual difference out of sight. There is the irony that those moral reactionaries in India today who reject homosexuality as a decadent western phenomenon are resorting to just that repressive foreign Victorian moral code which is in itself so alien to the Indian tradition.

Maybe paradoxically the virtue of the situation of homosexuality in India lies in just this very invisibility. There is evidence that in Vedic India apart from male and female a third sex was recognized, *tritiya-prakriti*, transgender citizens, who were encouraged to assimilate, either, if on the feminine side, as dancers, actors, singers, if masculine, as barbers, masseurs, house servants. What was unacceptable was for those who were deemed male to turn homosexual.[126] (Here was an anticipation of the contradictory response to an innate and an acquired homosexuality.) After all, the sexuality of the Indian gods was extremely various. Siva enjoyed a many faceted sexuality. And even Arjuna in exile had to spend time as a hermaphrodite. In one of the very few studies of homosexuality in India today[127] Jeremy Seabrook reports some fascinating conversations where claims are made that prior to the imposition of Victorian moral codes and in particular Article 371 of the Penal code which outlaws so called "acts against the order of nature," there was a culture which, whilst insisting on the demand for marriage and recognizing the absolute necessity of the family, turned a blind eye to a relatively widely expressed homosexual friendship: "'love between members of the same sex was portrayed as a higher form of attraction and was even considered divine by some."[128] Here is a valuable tradition, one of a more fluid, less formulaic male sexuality, not only at odds with a repressive colonial morality that independent India has inherited, but also with an alternative model of the gay movement from the west, with its often intolerant insistence on a politics of identity. And if the Indian middle class is showing signs of moving in the direction of a consumer-driven modern gay movement, might it not be the case, Seabrook speculates, that "globalization itself calls forth the recovery and reassertion of half-effaced indigenous sexualities?"[129] Was Forster, in fact, still in touch with some quite deeply engrained tradition of homosexual love?[130]

Worshipping Krishna

If in Dewas Forster found a Krishna cult flourishing "with a saturnalian gusto quite unlike anything he had known before," akin "to something which was fast disappearing from Europe,"[131] this was in large part the work of Maharajah Tukoji III. In childhood[132] he had accompanied his father, Anandrao, on pilgrimage to the Krishna center at Pandharpur. From an early age he had meditated on and studied the Vedas, the Puranas, and the writings of the poet-saint, Tukaram. He was well versed in Sanskrit and Marathi literature and the *Gita*. No one disputes that here was a highly religious man. In Supa the young HH had taken to the figure of Dolly, one of the household gods and the chosen family deity, and was to install it in the temple in the Old Palace in Dewas, probably after his marriage in March 1908. The figure that Forster compared to an ill-tempered pea in his letters, later modified to "a silver image, the size of a teaspoon" in the novel, does indeed, according to Bhoj Maharaj, look "like a wizened man, frowning upon the ways of the world."[133] If already a strong tradition in Dewas, Tukoji determined to put the great Krishna festival on the map, in part inspired by his attending the Ganapathi festival at Gwalior in 1907. It could become an advertisement for the royal house of Dewas. The first of the upgraded celebrations, incorporating the ceremonies at Pandharpur, occurred in August 1908. A craze became an infatuation. Costs spiraled in the 1920s, when—post Forster's visit—the ceremony was transferred to the new temple in the new palace. All the choirs and bands that had to be hired, mainly from Ujjain, the residential costs of some extra 100 folk in the palace, added up to an annual expenditure of some £6,000. If in fact it was as much the expense of his son's wedding in 1926 that broke the back of the states' finances, the running costs of the festival had much to do with it. When he fled in 1933, HH left Dolly's jewellery behind. In exile he went on hunger strike at the retrenchment imposed on the celebration of the birth of Krishna. If presently celebrated with less extravagance it remains "the most important thing in the life of the people of Dewas."[134]

Forster witnessed many other festivals at Dewas, the transgressive *Holi* on arrival, *Dussehra* close to departure but the major one was the twelve-day-long celebration of Krishna's birth, variously named the *Gokhul Ashtami* or the *Janmastami*. In the somewhat facetious account in his letters home, incorporated into *The Hill of Devi*, he is the participant; in the Indian novel he is both more present as author and yet more distant, for here, thrice over, there are characters who distance the festival, the atheist Fielding, the Muslim Aziz, and, in a way, the brahmin Godbole. Of its essence the Krishna celebration is caste free and turning the leading celebrant into a Chitpavin brahmin may have been a strategic error by Forster. After all, if Godbole is supposedly based on the two Maharajahs, Chhatarpur was a rajput, HH a Mahratta. However, Bhoj Maharaj suggests another possible model, the dewan of the court, Pandit Naraya Prasad, a great devotee of Krishna, so a brahmin identity may not be so out of place.

Forster struggled, not unsuccessfully, to capture the genuine religious rapture behind all the noise and muddle. Maybe he did not appreciate that the noise was functional, to keep the celebrants awake during the long reaches of the night. Forster himself never made the celebration of the morning after, when Krishna was once again put back in the temple. But he brilliantly grasped the element of play throughout, prompting his key insight that what was lacking in Christianity was just this "merriment." His is a vivid account of the pilgrimage of the image around the town, with that strange Barabbas-like release of one of the prisoners from the jail—of course for the Hindu this was a metaphor for release from the trammels of the ego—though he cannot maintain a sense of seriousness at the moment of immersion, when all the symbolic clay figures of Krishna's childhood in Gokhul slide off the tray into the lake or tank. In the novel Forster, again to maintain some ironic distance, resorts to comedy when one of the two boats carrying the European characters collides with the tray and they all, Aziz included, end up in the water.

One of the puzzling aspects of the novel is the coincidence of the festival with the death of the king. Was this a nodding gesture to Frazer's *The Golden Bough*, the rebirth of Krishna symbiotic with the death of the king? It is generally assumed that in the novel the mysterious vision of the king is Forster's referring to the sculptured images of Tukoji's royal ancestors by the lake side, but could another possible reference be to the small temple at the far side of the lake at Mau (today's Mausanias) and its inhabitant, the founding father of the royal house of Chhatarpur, the formidable Chaitanal?

Tukaram

After two hours of ecstatic dancing before the shrine to Dolly in the Old Palace, HH would unwind with readings from the poet-saint, Tukaram. If we see the history of Hinduism as a continual tension between the authority of canonical tradition and the innovatory role of charismatic saints then Tukaram, in much the same way as Caitanya and Ramakrishna, was clearly such a presence. Tukaram was one of five Maharashtrian poet saints, beginning with the Brahmin Jnanadeva and the tailor Nandeva in the thirteenth century, Ekanatha in the sixteenth, and Tukaram and Ramadasa in the seventeenth century. All are connected with the shrine to Vitthala or Vithoba at Pandharpur. Deleury[135] speculates that Vithoba may have been a historical figure, a twelfth-century Jain holy man who died by fasting to death. His son, Pundalika, founded a cult in his memory. By the thirteenth century the cult flourished and Pandharpur became a great pilgrimage center. It was at its height under the Yadav ruler, King Krsna (1247–1260). In time Vitthala became identified as an avatar of Vishnu and the cult bhaktic. Pandharpur, on the river Bhima, which flows into the river Krishna, is home to the shrine to Vithoba, an erect figure, arms akimbo, a naked small boy with his genitals visible, yet quite different from conventional images of Krishna, and in some ways the Krishna link is played down in the writings of the poet-saints. Yet here was a physique attractive to Forster and it can be no accident that he named the Indian prince in the erotically charged short story, *A Life to Come*, Vithobai. A sect or sampraday, the *varakari pantha,* centers on the shrine and given that the whole rationale of the sect was pilgrimage to Pandharpur and with the lack of any mention of HH's going on such a pilgrimage once Maharajah it has to be assumed he was not a member of the sect.

But HH held Tukaram in highest reverence. And if it is even more counterfactual, for there is little evidence that Forster had read much about him, there is good cause to see why Forster would have warmed to this strangely contemporary figure. He was born 1608, vanished 1649. He was born in Dehu, a village near Poona, to a shudra caste, *kunabis*, though his family were merchants, indeed held the office of *mahajan*, regulating the local trade, and he tried to run the family grocer's store. At an early age he became head of his extended family. His was to be a traumatized life, with his first wife and son dying in a famine c 1629. Tukaram felt less and less able to cope, became bankrupt, was stripped of his village office and became increasingly a social outcast. He turned to writing poetry, but this merely brought down on his head the wrath of the local orthodox brahmins, outraged that not only a low caste person should attempt to break into their literary world, but, even more sacrilegiously, that he wrote in the vernacular, Marathi, rather than in Sanskrit. All his poems were thrown into the local Indravani River. It was their miraculous recovery, unharmed, following Tukaram's fast, some thirteen days later, that proved the beginnings of his reputation as a saint. His life then centered on the shrine to Vithoba in his native village. At some point Tukaram met the young Sivaji, about to embark on his career as founder of Mahratta independence but, though tied by bonds of *bhakti*, he refused to act as his court chaplain. A more overtly political role fell to Ramadasa. Tukaram's reputation as a figure in Marathi vernacular literature, one of almost Shakespearean dimensions, rests on his 9,000 poems or *abhangs*—the number is open to question. These are the source for tracing his extraordinary religious quest.

These devotional lyrics can be categorized as advaita-bhakti-monistic. Either one can interpret his poetry unilinearly as a search, eventually rewarded, for God[136] or, dialectically, initially driven by a search for knowledge of the divine, then followed by a period of darkness, the mystic's proverbial dark night of the soul, only to be completed by a new affirmation, "the cancellation of the original determination and the middle negation into a final vision of the godhead."[137] The latter makes rather more sense. The modernity of Tukaram lies in his highly personalized and isolated search for God. Was he to blame for his failure, he asked himself? Had he been too attached to family and sex? Was he trying hard enough? He appealed to the saints for help. Might the way be through God's grace? In despair he taunts God himself with impotence, for God lacks the power to grant Tukaram his vision. Was not God anyway fashioned by his devotees? 'Now God and I are placed on an equality,' he mocked, "Thou art a thief and an adulterer. I know that Thou art an ass, and a dog, and an ox, and bear all sorts of burdens."[138] "To me God is dead. Let Him be for whomsoever thinks Him to be. I shall no longer speak about God. I shall not meditate on his name. Both God and I have perished."[139]

Only through the threat of suicide whilst seeking God in the hills above his village was there to be a breakthrough: "I see God's face and the vision gives me infinite bliss . . . I have now obtained limitless wealth and I have seen the feet of the formless Person."[140] Now followed the ecstatic: "my tongue has become uncontrollable and ceaselessly utters the name of God."[141] It was this mood that is reflected in Forster's references to Tukaram.

There is an apparent contradiction between Tukaram's Vedantism which speaks of the absorption of the Self in the Godhead, a personal death, one that lead to Tukaram's exceptional religious claims: "I possess the key of God's treasury and every kind of merchandise that may be asked for is with me,"[142] and the practice of *bhakti* which is premised on the separation of the worshipper from the divine. Dilip Chitre sees *bhakti* as a middle way between Brahminism and folk religion. Even so, this remains in Ranade's account a Personalistic Mysticism: "the humanistic and personalistic element in Tukaram is more predominant than in any other saint."[143] This is reinforced by Chitre. To quote: "he believed that the individual alone was ultimately re-sponsible for his own spiritual liberation. He was not an escapist. His mysti-cism was not rooted in the rejection of reality but rather in a spirited response to it after its total acceptance as a basic fact of life."[144] One can easily see why Forster would be attracted to such a personalist philosophy.

Only Connect

In what ways did Forster see connections between his sexuality and the Krishna legend? Clearly the legend opens up possibilities of some erotic iden-tification between the personalities in the Krishna story and Krishna himself and so through to some mystical experience of the divine. For many Indian devotees there is no difficulty in identifying with the *gopis*. Godbole does so. If there is something in Forster's sexual makeup to suggest that he could have identified with this passive and effeminate role—after all, his greatest wish was to be loved by some strong young working class male and possibly be hurt by him—his preference was for a love between two athletic, sturdy and mas-culine males. He would have been more drawn to the friendship between the cowherd boys and Krishna, maybe to Balarama, than to the androgynous Krishna but there is little on such love in the Krishna stories. There is of course a far stronger tradition of homoerotic love in Persian and Urdu poetry and there is frequent reference to this in the Indian novel. Sufi mystical writ-ing also embraces homoerotic love for the divine.

The friendship between Fielding and Aziz has now been extensively rein-terpreted as a search for homosexual love—Aziz translates as loved one in Urdu—and the discussion in part focuses on whether or not this might suc-ceed. Sandra Suleri, whilst acknowledging the strong homoerotic feelings running through the colonial encounter,—and she has a wonderful passage on the erotic implications of Aziz's fixing Fielding's collar stud—sees in colonialism itself the force denying such intimacy: "Aziz and Fielding function as signifiers of the abortiveness of colonial exchange."[145] Parminder Bakshi abstracts the friendship from its colonial context but in the end is even more pessimistic. Homosexual love is placed in a much larger sphere: "the whole universe is to blame for the rift between Aziz and Fielding—not politics *tout court*." It broke down through "the social and religious condemnation of homoerotic love."[146] If there is an attempted fulfillment through the orgiastic events at Mau it cannot succeed. "The religious allegories of love do not translate into relationships and India does not endorse homoerotic desire."[147] Forster is seen as having little hope that such love can succeed.

But more optimistic readings are feasible.

Forster's posthumously published novel on homosexual love *Maurice* was in fact written after abandoning his first attempt at his Indian novel in 1913 so it is not in the least disingenuous to draw parallels between the two. In ways highly evocative of the forest landscape in which Krishna and Radha play, the two lovers at the end retreat into the greenwood (they earn their living, it is supposed, as carpenters). There is a sylvan setting for Vithobai's love for the missionary, Pinmay. "Throughout Forster's work the 'woodland,'" as Martland puts it, "is presented as a free space where the homoerotic may flourish."[148] Pan and Krishna converge as symbols of unbridled love. The cry of Maurice from his bedroom window to his lover, Scudder, to "come" is surely directly echoed in Godbole's summons to Krishna, "come, come, come" except, of course that Scudder does climb through the window whereas Krishna refuses to come. Godbole has first to purge himself of selfish desire. Once in a more suitable frame of mind he again calls and this time successfully, in the ceremony at Mau.

There are many ways in which homosexuality is referred to in code. It is even suggested that naming the princely state Mau is a coded reference to *Maurice*. Twice, with the punkah wallah in the court, and the servitor who spills the contents of the tray into the lake, near naked Indian males are seen as being as handsome as Apollo and Apollo is the Greek god of homosexual love. More controversially, Martland speculates that the retreat to the greenwood in *Maurice* can lead to real change, "a promise of what, should the British nation be transformed along Carpenteresque lines, could reproduce itself throughout the whole of society"[149] and that in the Krishna legend of the Indian novel Forster has reconciled and resolved sexual and religious feeling. And if not now, then in a post-imperial future the love of Fielding and Aziz will triumph.

Conclusion

Clearly the Indian experience and the Krishna myth became a means whereby Forster could legitimize his homosexuality. In the very muddle—a favorite word of Forster's—of the Krishna ceremony Forster could surely find a way, as Birje-Patil puts it, of accommodating "his deviation as a variant of folly."[150] In another reading, the whole Dewas experience made it clear to Forster that he no longer had to see sexuality in terms of a committed love. Sexuality could be enjoyed for its own sake. It could just be fun.[151] Just as importantly, Forster had had to ride innuendo and scandal at Dewas and so acquire a far more assertive social acceptance of his sexuality. Jeffery Paine goes onto suggest, if this has to be guesswork, that the sexuality and the religion quite literally come together and that during the Gokhul Ashtami festival itself he and Kanaya met in the Old Palace and made love: "for that moment the partition of centuries that had kept sacred and profane experience separated was effaced." Forster had stumbled into "a new sexual-religious 'dispensation.'"[152]

But if India was a means to a greater self-tolerance, it still leaves begging the question the degree to which Forster entered into the mystical play of the Krishna cult itself. Colmer suggests that in the temple sequence Forster deliberately mixes the comic and the mystic and this is Forster's way of withholding total assent from Hinduism.[153] At the very end of his life in an interview with G. K. Das Forster stated that he was "not inclined to believe in Krishna not any more than anyone else," though added, "I like things about Krishna worship."[154]

It could of course be a psychological matter and that Forster was always inhibited from entering into this kind of emotional religiosity and that here comes into play the whole problematic of his negative relationship with his mother. Is this in large part the explanation of any limitations in his involvement? In very obvious ways the cult requires an instinctual capacity to share in the lovemaking of Radha and Krishna and to surrender to that sense of Radha as a mother goddess. It is very revealing how angry Forster still was at his mother in that final short story *The Other Boat*. It was "his mother, blind-eyed in the midst of the enormous web she had spun" who subverts Lionel's passion for Cocoanut.[155] Parminder Bakshi sees as a running theme of the novels the way women and marriage are the great obstacles to male love. Colmer, on the other hand, feels we are in danger of overplaying the homosexual in the novels, and that when Forster wrote about women they were not substitute men and that Forster had a real empathy for women.

Forster clearly withdrew from any expectation that immersion in the Krishna cult would entail the annihilation of the self. A deeply engrained humanism would explain that without any recourse to the dreaded feminine. Nor indeed does the cult expect this of its followers. Here instead is an opportunity to sport with the divine. Probably at some point Forster would part company with Tukaram but there again there would be much in the poet-saint's compassion that he could accept.

What is so extraordinary is the degree to which Forster the agnostic did open himself, emotionally and imaginatively, to the Krishna cult. The dictates of his sexuality took him a long way to experiencing its extraordinary vitality.

Notes

1. Frederick Crews, *E. M. Forster: The Perils of Humanism* (Princeton: Princeton University Press, 1962), 127–28.

2. Benita Parry, "'A Passage to India': Epitaph or Manifesto?" *E. M Forster: A Human Exploration*, ed., G. D. Das and John Beer (New York: New York University Press, 1979), 138.

3. E. M. Forster, "Adrift in India" (1922), in *Abinger Harvest* (London: 1936), 313.

4. E. M. Forster, "The Mind of the Indian State" (1922), in *Abinger Harvest*, 325.

5. Letter to Masood, 4 February 1911, E.M.F. Correspondence, Masood xviii.

6. See his review of Lyall's "Studies in Literature and History" (1915), in E. M. Forster, *Albergo Empedocle and Other Writings* (New York: Liveright, 1971), 211–15.

7. Some Books, 24 June 1942. E. M. F. Broadcast Talks 1930–1943 EMF Vol 6/7

8. She subsequently went mad which leads Furbank to speculate if she was the model for Mrs. Moore's breakdown P. N. Furbank, *E. M. Forster: A Life*, Vol 1 footnote, 216.

9. Tagore Broadcast, 7 May 1961, E.M.F. iv/21–6.

10. Romain Rolland Broadcast Talk, 16 January 1946, E.M.F. Vol 8/21.

11. Mentioned twice in broadcasts, Bookshelf, "On the Literature of 1938" (reporting Iqbal's death); India in Literature, 20 April 1942, E.M.F. Broadcast Talks, 1930–1943 Vol 6/7.

12. India in Literature, broadcast 20 April 1942, E.M.F. Broadcast Talks 1930–1943 Vol 6/7.

13. Mahatma Gandhi, "Forster Typescripts," Series II Vol 1, E.M.F. Vol 8/22.

14. A letter 5 February 1913, quoted in E. M. Forster, *The Hill of Devi and Other Indian Writings* (London: Edward Arnold, 1983), 194.

15. For his accounts of Varanasi see letter 9 January 1913. Quoted E. M. Forster, *The Hill of Devi*. 178 and Indian Journal 1912–1913 E.M.F. Vol 3/3.

16. A letter to his mother 29–31 January 1913, E. M. Forster, *The Hill of Devi*, 189.

17. See his letter to his mother 15 February 1913. Quoted in E. M. Forster, *Hill of Devi*, 197–98.

18. Indian Journal, 28 October 1912, E.M.F. Vol 3/3.

19. Indian Journal, 27 November 1912, E.M.F. Vol 3/3.

20. Indian Journal, 17 March 1913, E.M.F. Vol 3/3. See also E. M. Forster, *Hill of Devi*, 214.

21. In a journal-letter to his mother, 9 December 1912. Quoted E. M. Forster, *Hill of Devi*, 160.

22. Indian Journal, 28 and 29 March 1913, E.M.F. Vol 3/3; E. M. Forster, *Hill of Devi*, 225.

23. Letter 30 March 1913, E.M.F. Correspondence, Masood xviii.

24. E. M. Forster, "The Individual and His God." A Broadcast on the Eastern Service, 22 November 1940. E.M.F. Vol 6/11.

25. 23 November 1945, E. M. Forster, *Hill of Devi* 268.

26. Nicola Beauman, *Morgan: A Biography of E M Forster* (London: Sceptre, 1993), 274–75.

27. See Adwaita P. Ganguly, *India: Mystic, Complex and Real* (New Delhi: Motilal Banarsidass Publishers Private Limited, 1990), 152–65.

28. See his essay, "Promise and Withdrawal," in *A Passage to India*, in Das and Beer, eds., *E M Forster: A Human Exploration*, 121–28.

29. Crews, *The Perils of Humanism*, 158–59.

30. Here I am playing off the ideas of David Shusterman, "The Curious Case of Professor Godbole," in V. A. Shahane, ed., *Perspectives of E. M. Forster's A Passage to India: A Collection of Critical Essays* (New York: Barnes & Noble, 1968); V. A. Shahane, *E M Forster: A Study of Double Vision* (New Delhi: Arnold Heinemann, 1975); Chaman L. Sahni, *Forster's A Passage to India: The Religious Dimension* (New Delhi: Arnold Heinemann, 1981).

31. See Shusterman, "The Curious Case of Professor Godbole," in V. A. Shahane, ed., *Perspectives of E. M. Forster's A Passage to India*, 100.

32. Shahane, *E M Forster: A Study of Double Vision*, 118.

33. Ed., Shahane, *Perspectives of E. M. Forster's A Passage to India*, 10, xxiv.

34. Sahni, *Forster's A Passage to India: The Religious Dimension*, 146.

35. E. M. Forster, "Hymn before Action" (1912), in *Abinger Harvest* (London: 1936), 332–34.

36. Benita Parry, "A Passage to India: Epitaph or Manifesto?" in Das and Beer, eds., *E. M. Forster: A Human Exploration*, 136–37.

37. See further reviews in E. M. Forster, *Albergo Empedocle*, 220–27.

38. Michael Orange, "Language and Silence in *A Passage to India*," in Das and Beer, 142–60.

39. Crews, *E. M. Forster: The Perils of Humanism*, 151, 154.

40. John Beer, "Introduction: the Elusive Forster," in Das and Beer, eds., *E. M. Forster: A Human Exploration*, 9.

41. Jeffrey Paine, *Father India: How Encounters with an Ancient Culture Transformed the Modern West* (New York: Harper Collins, 1998), 142.

42. There are several spellings of Krishna, e.g., Krisna, Krsna. As Forster preferred Krishna that is the one adopted here.

43. Haridas Bhattacharyya, ed., *The Cultural Heritage of India Vol IV: The Religions* (Calcutta: The Ramakrishna Mission Institute of Culture, 1956), 37.

44. John Campbell, *The Masks of God Vol II: Oriental Mythology* (London: Oxford University Press, 1962), 323, 343.

45. Thomas Hopkins, "The Social Teaching of the Bhagavata Purana," in Milton Singer, ed., *Krishna: Myths, Rites and Attitudes* (Chicago: University of Chicago Press, 1966), 10.

46. So A. W. Entwistle speculates in *Braj: Centre of Krishna Pilgrimage* (Groningen: Forsten, 1987), 25.

47. David L. Haberman, *Journey through the Twelve Forests* (New York: Oxford University Press, 1994), 46.

48. Edward C. Dimock, Jr. "Doctrine and Practice among Vaishnavas of Bengal," in Milton Singer, ed., *Myths, Rites and Attitudes*, 46.

49. For a full account see Vasudha Dalmia, "The Only Real Religion of the Hindus: Vaisnava Self-representation in the late 19th Century," in Vasudha Dalmia and H. von Stietencron, eds., *Representing Hinduism: the Construction of Religious Traditions and National Identity* (New Delhi: Sage, 1995), Chapter 8.

50. Words from the last of the lilas cycle, "The Coming of Akrur," quoted John Stratton Hawley, *At Play with Krishna: Pilgrimage Dramas from Brindavan* (Yale: Princeton University Press, 1972), 243.

51. Hawley, *At Play with Krishna*, 60.

52. Entwistle, *Braj*, 92.

53. Siegel's paraphrase of descriptions of Krishna in the *Gitagovinda*. See Lee Siegel, *Sacred and Profane Dimensions in Love in Indian Traditions as Exemplified in Gitagovinda of Jayadeva* (Delhi: Oxford University Press, 1978), 97.

54. As in Vallabcharya's commentary see James Redington, *Vallabhacarya on the Love Games of Krsna* (Delhi: Motilal Banarsidass, 1983), 135.

55. Haridas Bhattacharyya, ed., *The Cultural Heritage of India Vol III The Philosophies* (Calcutta: 1937), 299.

56. Needless to say there are endless versions of the Krishna legend but a clear enough one is by W. G. Archer, *The Loves of Krishna in Indian Painting and Poetry* (New York: Grove Press, nd).

57. See J. L. Masson, "The Childhood of Krsna: Some Psychoanalytic Observations," *Journal of the American Oriental Society* 94, no. 3, 451–59.

58. D. F. Pocock makes this suggestion in, "Art and Theology in the Bhagavata Purana," in Veena Das, ed., *The Word and the World: Fantasy, Symbol and Record* (New Delhi; London: Sage, 1986).

59. See N. P. Joshi, *Iconography of Balarama* (New Delhi: Abhinav Publications, 1979).

60. Baba Jnanendranatha Mitra, *Sri Krishna: A Critical Biography Based on Original Sources* (Bankipore: 1900), 70.

61. Siegel, *Sacred and Profane Dimensions in Love*, 39.

62. See Redington, *Vallabcharya on the Love Games of Krsna*, 7–17, 32–37, 67–68.

63. Entwistle, *Braj*, 96.

64. In Vol 1V, *The Cultural Heritage of India*, 522.

65. Siegel, *Sacred and Profane Dimensions in Love*, 67.

66. The theme of Gide's early North African autobiographical novels.

67. Charles Fourier, *Le Nouveau Monde Amoureux* (First published 1849 Reprinted Geneva: Slatkine Reprints, 1979).

68. Campbell, *The Masks of God Vol II*, 361.

69. T. K. Venkateswaran, "*Radha-Krishna* Bhajanas of South India" in Milton Singer, ed., *Myths, Rites and Attitudes* (Chicago: University of Chicago Press, 1966), 155.

70. Singer, *Myths, Rites and Attitudes*, 155.

71. Siegel, *Sacred and Profane Dimensions in Love*, 54.

72. Campbell, *The Masks of God Vol II*, 347.

73. See Hawley's brilliant analysis, *At Play with Khrisna*, 157–58.

74. Hawley, *At Play with Khrisna*, 163.

75. Haberman, *Journey Through the Twelve Forests*, 184.

76. Edward C. Dimock Jr. explores these debates. See "Doctrine and Practice among Vaisnavas of Bengal," in Singer, ed., *Myths, Rites and Attitudes*, 56.

77. See Redington, *Vallabcharya on the Love Games of Krsna*, 95–96.

78. Siegel, *Sacred and Profane Dimensions in Love*, 200–5.

79. Sudhir Kakar "Erotic Fantasy: the Secret Passion of Radha and Krishna," in Veena Das, ed.,*The Word and the World*.

80. Campbell, *The Masks of God Vol II*, 359–60.

81. Siegel, *Sacred and Profane Dimensions in Love*, 120.

82. Entwistle, *Braj*, 68–69.

83. Entwistle, *Braj*, 95.

84. Jeffrey Kripal, *Kali's Child: The Mystical and the Erotic in the Life and Teachings of Ramakrishna* (Chicago: University of Chicago Press, 1995). This has proved a highly controversial account but so scholarly a work cannot be ignored.

85. Kakar, *The Indian Psyche*, 90–92.

86. Hawley, *At Play with Khrisna*, 111.

87. Entwistle, *Braj*, 196.

88. R. D. Ranade, *Mysticism in India: the Poet-Saints of Maharashtra* (Albany: State University of New York Press, 1983), 12.

89. See for example Ann Grodzins Gold's account of Rajasthani pilgrimage to Benares. This is a way of coping with death and is in pursuit of *moksha. Fruitful Journeys: the Ways of Rajasthani Pilgrims* (Delhi: Oxford University Press, 1989).

90. Haberman, *Journey Through the Twelve Forests*, 69.

91. Entwistle, *Braj*, 104–6.

92. See McKim Marriott's marvellously evocative personal account of its experience, "The Feast of Love," Chapter VIII in Milton Singer, ed., *Myths, Rites and Attitudes.*

93. Hawley, *At Play with Khrisna*, 62–67.

94. "Cultural Heritage of India Vol IV," 521.

95. See Milton Singer's account of such worship by the *radha-krishna* bhajanas in Madras, devotional *bhakti* groups, products over generations of a guru-disciple relationship and at least in the course of worship socially egalitarian. Milton Singer, ed., *Myths, Rites and Attitudes.*

96. Ganguly's idea, *India*, 307.

97. For a brilliant account of Malcolm Darling and Dewas, see Clive Dewey, *Anglo-Indian Attitudes: The Mind of the Indian Civil Service* (London: Hambledon Press, 1993).

98. Letters to Ackerley, 21 January 1921, 15 March 1921, E.M.F. Correspondence.

99. Described in J. R. Ackerley, *Hindoo Holiday: An Indian Journal* (London: Chatto and Windus, 1932).

100. Furbank Vol 1, 238.

101. In her diary, 1 March 1921. Quoted Furbank Vol 2, 66.

102. Letter 10 May 1921, E.M.F. Correspondence Masood xviii.

103. Letter 12 March 1923, E.M.F. Correspondence Ackerley.

104. E. M. Forster, "The Native Rulers of India are having a very pleasant time," printed in *Nation and Athenaeum* (April–May 1921), E.M.F. Vol 6/11.

105. Obit of Highness Maharaja Sir Tukoji Puar, E.M.F. xxix/3.

106. Letter 11 November 1924, E.M.F. Correspondence Masood xviii.

107. "My Debt to India" (13/14 August 1942), E.M.F. Broadcast Talks 1930–1943 Vol 6/7.

108. J. Birje-Patil, Forster and Dewas, Chapter 10 in Das and Beer, eds., *Centenary Essays: E M Forster*, 105.

109. Parminder Bakshi, "The Politics of Desire: E. M. Forster's Encounters with India," in Tony Davies and Nigel Wood, eds., *A Passage to India* (Buckingham: Open University Press, 1994), 53.

110. Indian Journal (1912–1913,) E.M.F. Vol 3/3.

111. Indian Journal, 25 October 1912.

112. 9 January 1913, Indian Journal (1912–1913).

113. 21 March 1913, Indian Journal (1912–1913).

114. 21 January 1922, E.M.F. Locked Diary, Vol 4/4.

115. Did Forster in fact borrow from a colonial way of looking at the body, off-setting a derogatory account of the Indian body with an idealised colonial European one? See E. M. Collingham's intriguing *Imperial Bodies: The Physical Experience of the Raj c 1800–1947* (Cambridge: Cambridge University Press, 2001).

116. 18 November, E.M.F. Locked Diary.

117. Colonel Leslie, E.M.F. xi/4.

118. Richard Cronin, *Imagining India* (London: Macmillan, 1989). See Chapter 11 *The Hill of Devi*, and *Heat and Dust*, 173, 175.

119. His account of his relationship with Kanaya is published as Appendix D, in E. M. Forster, *The Hill of Devi and Other Indian writings* (London: Edward Arnold, 1983).

120. Hyderabad. 31 December 1921, E.M.F. Locked Diary.

121. E. M. Forster, *The Life to Come and Other stories* (London: W. W. Norton, 1972). See also Norman Page, *E. M. Forster's Posthumous Fiction* (Victoria B.C.: University of Victoria, 1977), 14. He suggests that 'external violence can be a metaphor for sexual union.' Cocoanut looks on sexual passion as also a means of attaining mystical insight.

122. For a recent account of this text which accepts its historicity see Janet Dewan, "The Barber, the Narrator, and *The Private Life of an Eastern King*," in *Indo-British Review* XXIII no. 2, 1–11.

123. Personal conversation, Dewas, 30 November 1999.

124. Eunuchs or Hijdas. Acquired for E.M.F. by S. R. Masood, E.M.F. Corr. u/i.

125. In a very lively piece of reportage, *The Invisibles: A Tale of the Eunuchs of India* (London: Weidenfeld and Nicolson, 1997), Zia Jaffrey points out that one of the subgroups within the *hijras*, a group that are not castrated but are simply transvestites, the *zenanas*, do practise homosexuality. If still organized on a pan-Indian scale, and particularly strong in Hyderabad and Jaipur, and their numbers, if officially 50,000, may be as many as a million, as a social presence they are a pale shadow of what they once were.

126. Here I am indebted to a paper, entitled, "Tritiya-prakriti: People of the Third sex," but alas, anonymous.

127. Jeremy Seabrook, *Love in a Different Climate: Men Who Have Sex with Men in India* (London, New York: Verso, 1999). See also his essay, "It's What You Do in Out South. Sexual Minorities in the Majority World," *New Internationalist* 328 (October 2000). This reveals a pretty bleak picture of oppression in so called third-world societies. In the research he undertook in Delhi Seabrook discovered that men resorted to homosexual acts out of a search for a different form of sexual pleasure, rather than out of any sense of a gay identity and here his research confirms Foucault's understanding of the nature of homosexuality.

128. Seabrook, *Love in a Different Climate*, 139.

129. Seabrook, *Love in a Different Climate*, 181.

130. The love between Maan and Firoz in Vikram Seth's, *A Suitable Boy* (London: Phoenix House, 1993), exemplifies this tradition.

131. Birje-Patil, Forster and Dewas, Chapter 10 in Das and Beer, eds., *Centenary Essays*, 104.

132. And here I am largely following Bhoj Maharaj.

133. Bhojsinharao Tukojirao Pawar, *Aspects of a Passage to the Hill of Devi* (Kolhapur: Privately published, 1993), 96.

134. Pawar, *Aspects of a Passage to the Hill of Devi*, 91.

135. G. A. Deleury, *The Cult of Vithoba* (Poona: Deccan College Postgraduate and Research Institute, 1960), is a clear account of the cult and its pilgrimage. In that there is a definite, objective, darshan at Vithoba's shrine, and listening to the gurus en route, this has a far more linear feel to it than the braj Krishna pilgrimage.

136. The approach of Dilip Chitre in, *Says Tuka: Selected Poetry of Tukaram*, Penguin: 1991).

137. The approach of R. D. Ranade, *Mysticism in India: the Poet-Saints of Maharashtra* (Albany: State University of New York Press, 1983) and endorsed by Shankar Gopal Tulpule, *A History of Indian Literature: Classical Marathi Literature* (Wiesbaden: Harrassowitz, 1979).

138. Ranade, *Mysticism in India*, 296–97.

139. Ranade, *Mysticism in India*, 299.

140. Ranade, *Mysticism in India*, 300.

141. Ranade, *Mysticism in India*, 301.

142. Ranade, *Mysticism in India*, 308.

143. Ranade, *Mysticism in India*, 355.

144. Chitre, *Says Tuka*, xvi.

145. Sara Suleri, *The Rhetoric of English India: Forster's Imperial Erotic* (Chicago: University of Chicago Press, 1992), 148.

146. Bakshi, "The Politics of Desire," 51–52.

147. Bakshi, "The Politics of Desire," 59.

148. Arthur Martland, *E. M. Forster: Passion and Prose* (Swaffham: GMP), 149.

149. Martland, *Passion and Prose*, 157.

150. Birje-Patil, Forster and Dewas, Chapter 10 in Das and Beer, eds., *Centenary Essays*, 105.

151. This is Jeffery Paine's approach in *Father India*, 125–28. Forster was freed from his rose-tinted beliefs in romantic friendship.

152. Jeffery Paine, *Father India*, 144. It has to be said, however attractive a proposition, this is purely guess work.

153. John Colmer, *E. M. Forster: The Personal Voice*, 160.

154. Quoted in Ganguly, *India: Mystic, Complex and Real*, 288.

155. Quoted Martland, *Passion and Prose*, 179.

PART THREE

THE ATMAN DENIED

CHAPTER SIX

~

Isherwood and
Swami Prabhavananda:
The Guru-Disciple Relationship

It is still little known that the author of the novel *Goodbye to Berlin* which inspired the play *I Am a Camera* and the film *Cabaret* became a trainee Ramakrishna monk and a serious student of Vedantism. And it is indeed more than a little surprising that a writer and intellectual like Isherwood, so caught up in the post-war cynicism of the 1920s and the radical idealism of the 1930s should have become so involved with this expression of a reformed Hinduism. It stands as out as one intriguing aspect of its universalism. For Isherwood, true to the values of E. M. Forster, personal relationships came first and the initial question that has to be asked, what was the nature of his encounter with his Hollywood Indian guru, Swami Prabhavananda? For Isherwood the guru-disciple relationship was central to his Vedantist quest. So important was it that this chapter will focus entirely on this one theme. To do justice to this particular guru-disciple relationship, one has to pay an equal attention to the *sadhana* (spiritual quest) of Swami Prabhavananda as to Isherwood's own. Isherwood indeed found himself as a consequence of the spiritual journey of his guru in a direct line of descent to Ramakrishna, for Prabhavananda's guru had been Brahmananda and Brahmananda's, Ramakrishna himself. To make sense of the world from which Prabhavananda himself came and hence the kind of spiritual force he was to exercise over Isherwood, it is germane to look at the *sadhanas* of two of Prabhavananda's contemporaries, though this will take us quite some way from Isherwood. To see Isherwood's own quest in some comparativist perspective, the sadhanas of other contemporary Europeans will also be portrayed. This will help in answering a number of questions about the specific guru-discipleship of Prabhavananda and Isherwood. To what extent did Prabhavananda himself have, in taking on the traditional role of guru and through having to operate in an American context, have to adjust its character? To what extent did Isherwood bring specifically western needs to the relationship so that it became subtly transformed into something different from that in an Indian context?

The purpose of this relationship was to train Isherwood in Vedantism but Isherwood's seeming obsession with himself, the constant presence in his earlier writing of Christopher as observer made him an implausible candidate for the kind of self-transcendence required of Vedantism, and we will have to ask if, in the end, he was capable of non-duality. But there can be no doubting the seriousness of the endeavor, nor its deep influence over his later writing.

Toward a Conversion to Vedantism

Family and Education

Isherwood's earliest experience of religion was the expected one of his class but with some hints of the more esoteric to come. He was born 26 August 1904 into the English upper middle class but with the possibility of joining the landed gentry. His father, Frank, was an army officer, his mother, to be much the stronger presence in his life, was the daughter of the Marshall-Smiths who ran a wine business in Bury St. Edmunds. But until his paternal uncle, Henry got married in October 1907, Christopher stood to inherit the almost stately home of Marple Hall on the edge of the Peak district. To a limited degree this religious quest ran in the blood. His father took an interest in Buddhism and theosophy, drawn to their emphasis on silent meditation and his younger brother, Jack Isherwood, a good-looking uncle that the young Isherwood much admired, shared this interest in the esoteric, taking up hatha yoga, spiritualism, and vegetarianism. As one biographer has put it; "it is not surprising Christopher Isherwood turned to Vedanta."[1]

But his mother stood for a conventional loyalty to the Church of England and another biographer would see in Isherwood's rejection of his Anglican upbringing one aspect of his almost pathological hostility to his mother.[2] In April 1914 he joined St. Edmund's School, Hindhead, in Surrey, Wystan Auden to join him there the following year. Isherwood, despite an early rejection of the Church of England, won the school Divinity prize. Auden at the time defended his own mother's High Anglicanism. In January 1919 he went to Repton, where the future Archbishop of Canterbury, Geoffrey Fisher, was Headmaster. Although to be confirmed Isherwood saw this as a shameful surrender to the establishment. "Soon after my confirmation," he wrote later, "I began to discover that as they say I 'lost my faith' or, to be more exact, I discovered that I never had any."[3] If Auden was only to become a real influence on his life later—they were not to meet again till December 1925—Isherwood fell immediately under the influence of Edward Upward—still a little unbelievably alive today—a fellow schoolboy at Repton, and much of his rejection of formal Christianity owed a great deal to their shared adolescent rebellion. He became an avowed atheist: "I said privately and publicly that I loathed religion, that it was vile, superstitious, reactionary nonsense." "I assumed," he later admitted, "quite arbitrarily that every Christian was secretly longing to indulge in forbidden pleasures and that he was only prevented from doing so by his cowardice, ugliness and impotence."[4] Yet maybe for both Isherwood and Upward the rejection was not total. At Cambridge in 1924 Upward was writing a poem on Buddha. As a private tutor Isherwood chose to teach divinity.

And quite how strong an affect stuck to Isherwood's hostile attitudes to religion from his leaving Cambridge and his arrival in America in 1939 is a matter of guess-work. How entangled was it anyway with his embattled confrontation with his homosexuality and his later involvement with the politics of the left? Isherwood's moral debate in the interwar period was framed in terms of what he and Auden called the Test. This was substantially to do with two versions of his father. There was his mother's attempt to set him up as a heroic role model, symbolized by his death in the war 8 May 1915, a version which Isherwood came to see as neurotic and based an a self-centered conflict and a doomed search for personal fulfillment by the truly weak man, and the alternative version he came to defend, that of the truly strong man, who had nothing to prove, but unassumingly got on with his life. If this was a running theme of much of his writing it was probably given most explicit expression in *The Ascent of F6*, a play about a kind of mystical quest, the climbing of a mountain, where the would-be hero, Ransome, modeled on T. E. Lawrence, only comes to terms with his neurotic quest in death, preceded by a meeting both with an Abbot and his mother. This play opened in London 26 February 1937.

One very clear indication that the religious debate had been but buried and was coming to the surface again were the exchanges between Isherwood and Auden over religion during their visit to China in 1938: "my dear," Auden observed, "one of these days you're going to have such a conversion."[5]

In a sense, robbed of his father whilst still at prep school, Isherwood never let up in a search for a father surrogate and in consequence never ceased to be an adolescent. In an obvious way his search for a guru was part of this quest and of this retardedness. It is, of course, that very oedipal character of his quest that situates him in such a western context and raises questions as to how altered or distorted was his search for a guru from any Hindu model. Not that father-son relationships are absent in an Indian context and the word guru can translate as elder.[6] There were to be many preliminary gurus before Swami Prabhavananda.

Earlier Mentors; E. M. Forster and Gerald Heard

A line was drawn between the role of influential friends and of gurus. It would not be correct to see either Upward or Auden as gurus. But E. M. Forster, for long Isherwood's role model as a writer and, just as significantly, as a person—he became a leading example of the truly strong man—was a kind of a guru, though Forster would have declined the very idea of acting in such a role. As early as 1925 both Upward and Isherwood saw Forster as a literary model. William Plomer introduced them in September 1932 and they became friends. Auden shared in this cult of Forster. Earlier gurus included his history master at Repton, G. B. Smith, John Layard, disciple of Homer Lane, the psychologist—crucial as a liberating factor for both Isherwood and Auden in coming to terms with their homosexuality—and the Viennese film director, Berthold Viertel, whom Isherwood worked with for the film *Little Friend* in 1933 and again in Hollywood and whom he was to transform into a guru figure as Friedrich Bergmann in his first Vedantist novel, *Prater Violet*. But none were to influence Isherwood's spiritual life so greatly as Gerald Heard.

They first met through Auden in 1930. Auden and Heard shared an interest in science. Isherwood got on better with Heard's wealthy and younger friend, Christopher Wood. Another link, as already described, was Heard's friendship with Forster. At this stage, apart from a shared homosexuality—though Heard was to become a celibate—there was little cause for Isherwood to turn to Heard. Heard remains a shadowy figure and significantly no biography has yet appeared. His adopted son, Jay Michael Barrie, has abandoned his attempt. But he was always an appealing personality and by all accounts a charismatic speaker. Jonathan Fryer sums him up well: "the rather dry tone of his books does not do justice to the man himself; he was a brilliant talker, witty, playful and scintillating—a true exotic, if occasionally theatrical in a pleasing Irish way."[7] He would have crept into Isherwood's fiction anyway as an engaging eccentric but it as a guru, August Parr, that he appears in *Down There on a Visit*. (But Huxley was also an influence here.) Heard and Huxley became good friends in 1929 and together were to work out a pacifist position in the 1930s prior to their departure to America in 1937. It was Isherwood's discovery of his own pacifism in 1938 that led him to seek out Heard shortly after his arrival in America in 1939. By then both Heard and Huxley had made a link between their pacifism and Hinduism and both of them, though Heard the more so, had become disciples of Prabhavananda.

Here was a new Heard, no longer as in London, to quote Isherwood's description, "essentially an agnostic, a liberal and cautious investigator" but a new Gerald, "disconcertingly, almost theatrically Christlike." Fortunately from Isherwood's point of view Heard was going through an anti-Christian phase, for such were Isherwood's deep prejudices against organized Christianity only a new vocabulary, in this case Sanskrit, permitted any engagement with questions of spirituality. Nevertheless, real hostilities had to be broken down. "I had always regarded Vedantic philosophy and yoga as the ultimate in mystery-mongering nonsense," he wrote in his diaries. So Heard needed several months to work a change. "I suppose," Isherwood reflected, "I shall never again in my life have moments of such intense excitement and revelation as I had then." Heard had opened his eyes to "what life is for"; awareness of our real nature and our actual salvation.[8]

There is very much more to be said on Heard's place in Isherwood's spiritual life and this will be discussed more fully in the context of Isherwood's Vedantism, and quite probably his was always the greater intellectual influence, but Isherwood was so structured that personality counted for more than intellect and it was here that Prabhavananda, the Ramakrishna monk, was to be the deeper force in his life. Interestingly, Isherwood was grateful that Heard never tried to make him one of his disciples. They were too alike and "it would have ended in absurdity." But he had a great regard for Heard's evaluation of others and it was Heard's acceptance of Prabhavananda which "made me willing to accept him, at any rate until I was able to form an opinion of my own." It seems that Heard was himself so dazzling at the first meeting that Isherwood retained little memory of Prabhavananda himself. It was to be their second meeting, 4 August 1940, in the small study that formed part of the temple complex of the Vedanta center, that was to change his life.[9]

Swami Prabhavananda as the Disciple

One of the problematics of analyzing the guru-disciple relationship between Swami Prabhavananda and Isherwood is Isherwood himself being to such a degree its extensive and persuasive interpreter. What else is there to add? Looking back in 1963 he had this to say. Only through a relationship would he be able to approach religion at all. Only an individual "can give you a dim glimpse of the Atman within him, simply by being what he is." He does not have to be perfect. "But he must have no pretences; he must be, at all times, neither more nor less than himself." Through this clarity you can get a glimpse of "the element which is not he, not his personality, not his individual nature." You can then believe in him. "You can feel that he is holding you, like a rock-climber on a rope, just as he himself is being held by the rope that goes on up above him. That is what the disciple demands of the guru. It is a tremendous demand."[10] So who was Prabhavananda and how to explain his own spiritual development or sadhana in India, his own role as disciple?

He was born 26 December 1893 in the village of Surmanagar, his mother's hamlet, two to three miles from the family village of Bishnapur, itself near Bankura, and, as it happened, but twenty miles from Ramakrishna's own birthplace of Kamarpukur and Sarada Devi's, Ramakrishna's wife, of Jayrambati. Bishnupur was a market size town and later the railway link from Calcutta and it was here Sarada would get down en route to her village. Subsequently, the house in Surmanagar was pulled down and a medical dispensary, a small prayer hall, a library and a dedication stone erected in its place, all in honor of Prabhavananda.[11]

And what influence did his family exert over the young Abindra Nath Ghosh as he then was? His mother, Jnanada Sarkar, was conventionally pious. His father, Kumud Behari Ghosh, was a lawyer. Prabhavananda described him as "very tender-hearted and charitable in his way," feckless with money, but an ethically minded lawyer; "he would not represent anyone in matters involving falsehood." It was not a strict upbringing. On the second occasion that his mother scolded him, "I wanted to commit suicide. My parents never scolded me after that." "They knew I was very sensitive." At the age of seven he went to a school in Bishnupur. When a teacher hit him with a cane, his maternal grandfather came and threatened litigation if he hit him again. The family do not seem to have made strong claims on him nor is it likely that here was any strong preconditioning explanation for his conversion.[12]

Might he have gone in another direction? Isherwood saw him "as a lively young man, fond of sports and a bit of a dandy."[13] Later he told Isherwood that his friends were amazed at his joining the monastery: "They thought I was just a dandy boy. I parted my hair and wore rings and a gold chain. I liked to play practical jokes. I was known as the best dressed boy in Calcutta."[14] Sister Nivedita, who met him in autumn 1910 at the home of Vivekananda's disciple, Swami Sadananda, saw him as a sissy;[15] not at all one of Vivekananda's muscular young men. (Vivekananda was very keen on physical fitness.) At the age of sixteen he came to Calcutta to be a student at the Calcutta City College. At the age of twenty, after graduation—he studied general philosophy, mathematics, psychology, ethics and theology, "all from a western perspective"[16]—he entered Calcutta University College to take an MA in Philosophy, working under Professor Brajendra Seal. Clearly he belonged to the Bengali intelligentsia. We can form some idea of alternative career choices from those of his siblings; his elder brother, Amulya, became a West Bengal MLA, his younger brother, Gokul, principal of Bishnupur high school, and the youngest, Auraabindo, a lawyer in the village of Khatra, some fifty miles away. There were two sisters. But they all shared the same religious feelings. All the family became devotees of Ramakrishna, a "bhakta family," "clinging to God and his dispensations."[17]

Was he ever seriously drawn to Bengal revolutionary politics? Isherwood would have us believe that he joined a revolutionary organization, wrote subversive pamphlets and "hid revolvers under his bed, without being quite sure how to shoot with them." He was allocated this role "because of his youthfully innocent appearance. But this was no child's play. He and his friends were literally risking their lives."[18] His friend, Rash Behari Bose, December 1912, threw the bomb at the Viceroy, Lord Hardinge. He had earlier invited him to his father's house. The principal of his college, a Mr Maitra, got him to destroy incriminating evidence. On another occasion, in 1914, he was awoken to be confronted by six or seven bullock loads of weapons outside his window; he told them to ship them onto Chandernagore.[19] Interestingly, at his first meeting with Brahmananda he was quizzed if he belonged to a revolutionary organization led by one Yogin Thakur.[20] But one is tempted to see in Isherwood's account some glamorization, for he needed to see in the young Prabhavananda something of a political rebel, the better to add to his attractiveness, though it is true that Prabhavananda remained an Indian nationalist.

Quite probably the wish to escape marriage in 1914 was as strong a factor as any in shaping his decision to become a monk, but the influence of the Ramakrishna Mission was there from early on. Was he indeed fated to join the Mission? There was that odd early connection through his maternal grandfather, Ishwar Sarkar, his once being involved in a legal suit in which Ramakrishna himself had been called as a witness. It was this same grandfather that the young Prabhavananda used to tease when he cried at religious plays: "grandpa, have you put chillies under your eyes?" A private tutor, the blind Rama Akshay Vidyabhusan, had introduced him to the *Gospel of Sri Ramakrishna*. In Bishnupur at the time there was a chance meeting with Sarada Devi. In Calcutta he became a fan of the playwright, Girish Ghosh, and saw him perform. Here was also of course a further attractive association for Isherwood, himself to be so much taken by the once philandering, drunken but regenerate writer. And probably here is the explanation for Prabhavananda's first meeting with Brahmananda, for it was at nearby Balaram's house that he met him in 1911. "Suddenly I felt such an attraction drawing me to Maharaj that I wanted to sit on his lap." But it was only at a second meeting at Belur that they came into physical contact, where he was privileged to massage his feet. "My feeling at the time was something I had never felt before in my life; a complete fulfillment in his presence. I cannot express it in any other way. You see, he was like a magnet."[21] But early religious instruction came instead from another of Vivekananda's followers, Swami Atmananda. But he got permission from the Brahmo College where he was staying as a student to visit Belur the weekends. In the autumn of 1912 he followed Brahmananda to the Kankhal ashram at Hardwar, though the Ramakrishna monks at the Advaita ashram in Varanasi en route were reluctant to accommodate him, fearing he was a revolutionary. Brahmananda already saw him as a brahmachari. Here he expressed a wish to join the monastery but Brahmananda told him first to complete his studies. But he was informally initiated. He went on to Vrindaban where there was another influential encounter, this time with a holy man. There was to be another meeting with Sarada Devi in Jayrambati. He was becoming increasingly drawn into the movement, frequenting the company of Swamis Premananda and Turiyananda.

So was there at this stage a real tussle between his political sympathies and joining the monastery? The crucial decision was taken during a brief stay at Belur in December 1914 to study Vedanta philosophy. At the time he claimed he still resisted the monastic vocation; he felt it bred laziness and he wanted to devote himself to political activities. An old man also staying in the math asked Brahmananda: "when is this boy going to become a monk?":

Maharaj looked at me and his eyes had an unforgettable sweetness as he answered quietly: 'when God wills'. That was the end of my political plans and ambitions. I remained in the math.[22]

It was only then that Brahmananda initiated him into brahmachari with the name of Bhakti Chaitanya. (All trainee monks have to have a second name.) At this stage his parents expressed their dismay and he was granted leave to visit them at Bishnupur. At one point he tried to leave his home secretly but his brother, Amulya, came to the station and persuaded him to return for a few more days. And so he did and so parental resistance was eventually broken down. Prabhavananda later told Isherwood: "I would *never* have been a monk if I hadn't met Brahmananda."[23]

In some ways the interesting question to put to Prabhavananda's life in India prior to leaving for America is the extent to which it fits the pattern of a conventional swami's life. To what extent was the monastic routine broken, for example, by periods of isolation or pilgrimage? He undertook in 1915, together with an American, Gurudas Maharaj, a pilgrimage to Badrinath and Kedarnath, going onto to visit Swami Turiyananda at Almora prior to his stay at Mayavati. He became an assistant editor of an English medium journal *Prabudha Bharata*. After his return and his joining Brahmananda at Puri he was given special leave to attend his father's funeral. Then there was to be a four-year stay at the math in Madras, where he took on other editorial duties as editor of the monthly *Vedanta Kesari*.

But his memories of Madras were centered on visits by Brahmananda. In 1921 during observances for the Durga and Kali pujas Prabhavananda received sannyas from Brahmananda, then acquiring his monastic name, meaning "he whose bliss is the source" or "in the creator of the universe." After parting in Madras they were not to meet again. By the time he arrived at Bhubaneswar after going on pilgrimage in South India Brahmananda had already departed for Belur. There he died 10 April 1922. Prabhavananda stayed on a year at Bhubaneswar, then returned to Belur. He was scheduled to go to Singapore. Turiyananda, however, when they met in Varanasi for the last time—he died in 1922—opposed the idea. He preference was for his going to America where he had himself worked. And in the end the new President, Swami Shivananda, likewise opted, despite Prabhavananda's youth, for America. Prabhavanada's own response was one of dismay: "But I can't teach. 'Nonsense' replied one of the elder monks, severely; "You have seen the son of god, and you *dare* to say you cannot teach?"[24] To familiarize him with the company of women, seen, and rightly, as vital for teaching in America, he was sent to the Gadadhar ashram near Kalighat, attended by high society ladies. In April he departed.

It is tempting to speculate how far he had been prepared for a western discipleship through his friendship with the Dutchman, Cornelius Heyblom. Working in New York in the 1890s he had been won over to the Ramakrishna Mission through the sheer force of Vivekananda'a personality. It was to take him several attempts to adjust to the Indian way of life but here was a rare European Ramakrishna monk who did acclimatize to the Indian situation. The first five-year experiment had been from 1906. It was during his second attempt at acclimatization, as Garudas Maharaj, that he and Prabhavananda had become friends at Belur and been on pilgrimage to Kedrinath and Badrinath together in 1916. His third and successful adjustment came after 1922. But he was always clear that European capabilities for the monastic life were of a different order. Westerners, he told John Yale (to be a friend of Isherwood), himself on a visit to India in 1952 to receive sannyas at Belur when they met in Hardwar, should not fool themselves that they can become Indian. They needed a better diet and a private income.[25] Prabhavananda during that visit to Kedranath and on other occasions may have acquired some insight into these limitations. If so, Isherwood, to be very spoilt by the Mission, was to be the beneficiary.[26]

The Brahmananda Prabhavananda Guru-Disciple Relationship

As a monk in the Ramakrishna Mission Prabhavananda emerged from an emotional hothouse, another kind of spiritual Bloomsbury. Human relationships were central to this spiritual training and, most important of all, was his relationship as disciple with his guru, Brahmananda. To understand Isherwood's analogous relationship with Prabhavananda and to place it in context, we have initially not only to describe Prabhavananda's involvement with Brahmananda but Brahmananda's with his own guru, Ramakrishna as well, for there is a kind of apostolic succession in these dependencies. Of course, what was extraordinary here was the proximity in time of Ramakrishna as avatar, Isherwood being so curiously near to this source of spiritual enlightenment.

Brahmananda was born 21 January 1863 in Sikra Kulingram, a village thirty-six miles north east of Calcutta, son of a wealthy landowner and trader in salt and mustard seed. He was kshatriya by birth. His pre-monastic name was Rakhal Chandra Ghosh. Rakhal translates as cowherd boy. This link to Krishna proved very important to Ramakrishna. His mother died when he was five and he acquired a stepmother, but a loving one. He stayed with her family on coming to Calcutta for his education in 1875. He was an energetic and good-looking boy, fond both of sport and music. It was in a gymnasium near his college, Metropolitan School that he encountered Narendra, the future Vivekananda, and it was he who persuaded him to join the Brahma Samaj. Both fell under the influence of Keshub Chunder Sen. Anxious at his son's religious predilections his father arranged a marriage with the eleven-year-old Viswewari but this turned out to be a strategic error, for both her mother, Shama Sindari and brother, Manomohan Mitra, were already disciples of Ramakrishna and it was the brother who introduced him in June or July 1881—so he was already eighteen at the time—to Ramakrishna, to prove a fateful encounter.

Ramakrishna had already been forewarned in a dream that he was to become mother to a son, to play the role of Yasoda to Krishna. Here was the
pure-hearted, the eternal companion Ramakrishna had always sought. It was
clearly love at first sight and Rakhal played the role of the childlike son. He
was to experience a "boyish jealousy" at Ramakrishna having other beloved
disciples but came to recognize "that the guru belonged to all as the moon
shines equally upon all; and his jealousy left him forever by the grace of his
guru."[27] An attempt to break away in a fit of pique at Ramakrishna's failing
to provide him with immediate access to samadhi was frustrated. He was almost literally tied to his guru. It is, however, quite difficult to imagine the
large and strongly built man that Brahmananda was to become in this physically dependent role on the quite frail Ramakrishna.

There was the awkward fact of his marriage but, cleverly, Ramakrishna
steered the young bride into the arms of Sarada Devi, and nor did he entirely
prohibit contact between the young married couple, though Rakhal begged
Ramakrishna to free him from sexual desire. The wife was to die in 1891 and
their son, aged ten, in 1896. There is of course no prohibition on householders becoming monks, providing they take a vow of celibacy and this
Rakhal was to do under Vivekananda's guidance in January 1887 in the initiation of the monastic order at Baranagore.

Vivekananda saw Brahmananda as an organizer of men, as a king—hence
his name of Maharaj—and tended always to devolve the running of the
monastery onto him. In 1897 he was elected President of the Calcutta center and in 1902 took over as head of the order until his death. But Brahmananda always insisted on his subordinate status. There is that marvelous
exchange on Vivekananda's return from America in 1897, with Brahmananda's riposte to Vivekanananda's address "the son of a guru is to regarded as the guru himself," "one's elder brother is to be respected as the guru
himself."[28] But Brahmananda initially fought against these responsibilities
and was to spend years away from Calcutta on spiritual pilgrimages in a
search for samadhi. Even whilst President he would invariably absent himself
to visit other Ramakrishna centers. His favorite places were Varanasi,
Kankhal, near Hardwar—this he himself founded—Vrindaban and Puri.

But he was an exceptional spiritual director. He could see into the mind
and soul of the disciple. At first he severely limited the number he would
take on and insisted on long periods of probation but Sarada Devi persuaded
him to be more generous. His emphasis was always on the spiritual life within
rather than on any efficiency in work: "it is utterly impossible to annihilate
the ego simply by work."[28] Not that the interior life need be a struggle; he
promoted a simple form of yoga, sahaja yoga, the constant recitation of one's

mantra or japa. He was clearly no pedagogue but exercised influence by his sheer spiritual make-up; Swami Ramakrisnananda said of him: "the self in Brahmananda is entirely annihilated. Whatever he says or does comes directly from the divine source."[30] There was one occasion when Prabhavananda found him in a state of samadhi in the library of the math in Madras but felt too intimidated to accept an offered embrace: "I did not consider myself pure enough to touch Maharaj while he was in such a lofty mood."[31]

But even if Brahmananda prioritized meditation and the life within he also impressed on Prabhavanada during his stay in Madras the importance of ritual, his resistance to observances a stumbling block he had to overcome. Later he was to help Isherwood to do the same. Evidently, Brahmananda had his feet on the ground. As Prabhavananda put it: "Maharaj did not want his disciples to be credulous or superstitious. By his attitude he taught me to rely upon natural explanations rather than look for supernatural phenomena."[32]

There were all kinds of emotional games gurus could play with their disciples and Brahmananda was no exception. He could be apparently cruel, faulting disciples for quite minor blemishes, but in justification these were seen as certain tendencies which might well play havoc in the future and were best dealt with at an early stage. On one occasion, when Prabhavananda had felt spurned and had decided to leave the monastery, Brahmananda switched from criticism to affection: "never before had I been so deeply aware of his love and protection." Brahmananda sort of explained: "our love is so deep that we do not let you know how much we love you."[33] When Prabhavananda sought freedom from lust he replied: "I could do that for you, but then, my child, you would lose all the joy of struggle. Life would be insipid."[34] Here he was not as kind to his disciple as Ramakrishna had been to him. Sexual desire was, of course, to be the key issue for Isherwood. But Brahmananda clearly needed his companionship and at one point dissuaded him from going off to meditate by the river Narmada. Shortly before they parted for the last time in Madras in 1921 he whispered to Prabhavananda: "it makes me feel so bad, having to leave you. I shall miss you very much." Earlier he had "whispered into my ear: 'lovest thou me?'"[35] But it was not always so intense. Brahmananda had a rich sense of humor: "often he would make us roar with laughter."[36]

For Prabhavananda the guru-disciple relationship was to be for life and to extend beyond the grave: "after the teacher has passed away, he still continues to watch over his disciples in spirit. He will not accept his own liberation until all are liberated."[37] Clearly Prabhavananda was to feel his presence throughout his time in America. He came to look on Brahmananda and his personal god or ishtam as one and the same, likewise on Ramakrishna and Brahmananda as one and the same. "Maharaj gave me everything. All the excitement is on the surface. Underneath I am a speck of dust on Maharaj's feet. That is my real nature."[38]

Other first generation Ramakrishna monks also influenced his development. Swami Premananda, born Baburam Ghosh, 10 December 1861, was one. His being a class-mate of Brahmananda at Metropolitan College strengthens the idea of this monastic community as a kind of spiritual Bloomsbury. Together with Brahmananda he was to be the physically closest to Ramakrishna, "an extraordinarily handsome child with a fair complexion," the reincarnation, it was thought, of the feminine nature of Radha. He succeeded Brahmananda on Vivekananda's death as Manager of Belur, though he was not allowed to initiate monks. If not a learned man he was devoted to the life of Ramakrishna; "day and night he read the living Upanishads, that is the life and teaching of Ramakrishna." He was a stern taskmaster of monks: "he could not bear the monks to be even slightly indifferent or careless towards their work."[39] Prabhavananda first encountered him at the Ramakrishna Advaita ashram in Varanasi in 1914. He accompanied him everywhere in the city, to the temples and to the bathing ghats: "I used to follow Swami Premananda and would take the mud from his footprints and put it on my body." "Those were the days. To walk with gods." There is an extraordinary account of Premananda going into samadhi at the Vishwanath temple and returning, still in a trance, to the ashram.[40]

Another influential monk from this early generation was Swami Turiyananda, born Harinath Chattopadhya, 3 January 1863. He accompanied Vivekananda and Sister Nivedita to America in 1899, there to prove himself another tough teacher, for which he was often misunderstood: "the guru," he would justify himself to his western students, "is the physician and once the disease is diagnosed he must not fear to apply the lancet."[41] But he was seen as "a spiritual dynamo."[42] Prabhavananda discounted his reputation for toughness: "in all my years of association with him, I saw him as only loving. Such affection and such love as we saw in these disciples of Sri Ramakrishna I have not seen anywhere else."[43] He died from diabetes 21 July 1922.

Prabhavananda had skills as a masseur. He used to massage the feet of both Brahmananda and Turiyananda. One could speculate on any homoerotic implications in such physical contact but in Hindu culture touching feet is always a mark of respect. Turiyananda told him the last time that they met in Varanasi in June 1922 that it was during his first massage that he recognized Prabhavananda's powers.

Comparative Sadhanas in India

Another way of getting Prabhavananda's personal sadhana in India into perspective is through a comparison with those of two of his contemporaries, Swami Purushottamananda[44] and Swami Yogananda.[45] Both are convergent, the first intriguingly through their both being monks of the Ramakrishna mission and both disciples of Brahmananda, the second through Yogananda's likewise going to be a teacher in America. But the differences are more telling.

Purushottamananda was born Neelakantam, 23 November 1879, in the village of Tiruyvalla, near Kottayam, Kerala. His father, Narayanan Nair was a temple servant, maintaining the lamps in the Tiruvalla temple, though the family had land through his mother. His was to be an English medium education, attending the CMS College School at Kottayam—there is surprisingly little on Christianity in his memoir—but it was there, before taking up his place in Form V, that he was struck down with rheumatism and paralysis and confined to a sick bed for five years. Clearly always of a religious disposition that enabled him to cope with this setback, he was to slip away one day from the family and with the aid of "a tall, hefty person" got himself to the temple of Guruvayur. There, the poet and author of the poem *Narayaneeyam*, inspired by the Krishna classic, the *Bhagavatham*, one Sri Nanarayana Battachiri had been cured of paralysis, and he was himself to be temporarily cured, staying in the temple precincts for some six months. On his return it became impossible for him to renew his studies and he had to earn his keep as a teacher to boys of Sanskrit. Both his parents died and he was isolated but independent.

By dint of impressing the local munsiff with a reading of the *Bhagavatham* to his local Ramakrishna sangh in 1910 he became its president and it was this chance association with the Mission that took him to Hariapad to have darshan of Swami Nirmalanda, on a visit to another center there. He overcame his stage fright and had intended to prostate himself at his feet; "in actual fact, what I had done was not to prostrate at his feet but to repose my head on his lap, and with that act I had unconsciously transferred all my burdens and problems to him."[46] It was the beginnings of a lifetime guru-disciple relationship.

It is clear that Nirmalanda was a highly-strung and awkward guru figure. Reflecting on their relationship he admitted:

> If one could serve such great ones with total sincerity, then there is nothing one cannot achieve. I too have behaved towards Swamiji without the least

trait of insincerity. But to stay with Swamiji is in itself a terrible penance. Whenever there used to be a conflict in my mind and I used to suffer, I too used to leave the Swamiji and get away. I did not least desire ever to serve Swamiji even with a little bit of unwillingness.[47]

Once again there was to be that trial of all those emotional games. Nirmalanda got angry at any display of impracticality though the disciple exonerated such scoldings as his way "to eradicate completely my ego and my incompetence."[48] "Swamiji's heart," he conceded, "was at once harder than diamond and softer than a flower. Whenever he observes any defect or lapse on anybody's part, he would use the first available opportunity of berating him harshly." He could become violently angry and slapped him several times.[49] But there were rewards. Enjoying meditation with him "constituted the seventh heaven of happiness, the greatest of blessings to me."[50] Any shared experience or proximity was sought out: being give some food from his plate was to enjoy "nectar;" once in the ashram at Bangalore "I have been fortunate to sleep beside him in his own room."[51] He had conferred on him the name of Bhakta. In the end, though, he broke away, abandoning his ashram to make another visit to Guruvayur to seek a cure for malaria; Nirmalanda surrendered: "I have made Bhakta free."[52]

In fact Nirmalanda was to prove himself one of the more recalcitrant members of the Ramakrishna Mission. Its official historian, Swami Gambhirananda, denied that he was ever a personal disciple of Ramakrishna but clearly he had emerged early on as one of the math's foundation members. He was later sent to help out in New York, arriving 25 November 1903 where he set up a Vedanta center in Brooklyn, but was recalled, returning to Belur in January 1906. Then he was dispatched south to help Ramakrishnananda in setting up new mission centers. The Bangalore Ramakrishna ashram was opened 30 January 1909. Nirmalanda was particularly active in Kerala and it is there with the new foundations in Tiruvala, October 1912, Hariapad, August 1913 and Quilandy in North Malabar in May 1915 that he drew Purushottamananda into his administrative ambitions. Maybe these successes went to his head for he was to become involved in that major conflict back at Belur—a conflict somewhat hushed up—between Ganendra Nath, with his power base in the *udbodhan* offices and the Belur authorities, only resolved with their forcible occupation 13 December 1929 by the Belur monks. Nirmalanda then declared a kind of UDI for the southern centers. When the law courts declared later in favor of the Mission 13 August 1935, he walked out of the Bangalore ashram. If not all his followers remained loyal, Purushottamananda was to do so to the very end.

There is a particularly interesting convergence between the sadhana of Prabhavananda and Purushottamananda in their mutual love of Brahmananda. On one of his visits south in 1916 Brahmananda was scheduled to visit Tiruvala. Nirmilanda himself greeted the President though Brahmananda said of him: "he is a terrible man. But he is a great devotee as well."[53] One wonders if Prabhavananda might have been one of the brahmacharis accompanying Brahmananda on this visit but his name is not mentioned in the autobiography and it seems on this visit Brahmananda was especially close instead, anyway, to his personal secretary, Swami Sankarananda. Purushottamananda confirms the sense of Brahmananda as a silent man, often in meditation. The climax of this visit was to be a week-long stay at Kanyakumari. He was in awe of "the physical beauty of Maharaj's body."[54] He did everything possible to get close to him, begging him for his leather chappals; he promised to send him some wooden ones from Belur. He had to be ticked off for washing his cook's clothes. Brahmananda was to confer on him his mantra. But when he later received sannyas it was to be at the hands of his successor, Sivananda, in October 1923.

Although Purushottamanda was thereafter to keep in touch with Ramakrishna centers, mainly Kankhal and Belur, from then on he was far more the loner, seeking out pilgrim sites in North India and eventually coming to rest in 1928 in the cave at Vasitha Guha, an idyllic site upstream on the Ganges from Rishikesh. Maybe his independence was compounded by the split between his guru and the Mission. It is now that his sadhana so markedly diverges from Prabhavananda's. He continued to itinerate, often in dire poverty, inevitably falling foul of illnesses such as dysentery and malaria. Such mountain caves he saw as aids to meditation. "All this solitary life," he wrote, "is for the purpose of attaining complete and total detachment from the senses and the sense objects."[55] It was only at this stage that he undertook a serious study of Vedanta. In time he became a guru in his own right. One of his disciples whom I met will feature below. He died 13 February 1961.

Yogananda's Autobiography is probably the most widely read of any such accounts of the life of a modern-day yogi. He was born Mukunda Lal Ghosh, 5 January 1893, in Gorakhpur, a kshatriya and Bengali. His father, Bhagabati Charan Ghosh, worked for the Bengal-Nagpur railway, which accounts for the unsettled nature of his early days, though his upbringing was largely in Calcutta. His father was that paradigmatic Indian one, kind, grave but distant, something of a disciplinarian. Only much later with the premature death of his elder brother did he betray a softer side: "outwardly the grave father, inwardly he possessed the melting heart of a mother. In all family matters he played this dual parental role."[56] Both parents were pious. Sexual relationships were solely for reproduction. It took Yogananda years to come to terms with the early death of his mother when he was but eleven.

One early expression of his religious temperament was a wish to escape to the Himalayas and there were several if frustrated attempts to do so. There were to be a number of precursors to his guru and maybe here the most interesting one was Mahendra Nath Gupta, author of *The Gospel of Sri Ramakrishna*. Oddly, at the time Mahendra lived in their old family home, 50 Amherst Street, where his mother had died. "I am not your guru," he told him, "he shall come a little later."[57] But he did take him on many occasions to visit Dakshineswar. On getting away from Calcutta to an ashram in Varanasi after narrowly passing his school exams, it was to be there, in the Bengali streets of the city, that he encountered his guru. Yogananda claimed: "with an antenna of irrefragable insight I sensed my guru knew God and would lead me to Him." This echoes that encounter between Carpenter's guru, Ramaswamy and his guru, Tilleneithan. His guru's response was: "o my own, you have come to me . . . I give you my unconditional love." This was Sri Yukteswar Giri, "tall, erect, about fifty-five at the time," who ran an ashram in Serampore.[58]

Yogananda put the highest possible premium on the need for a guru. As he puts it in the opening words of his book: "the characteristic features of Indian culture has long been a search for ultimate verities and the concomitant disciple-guru relationship."[59] The autobiography is as much an account of an apostolic succession of gurus, from the deathless one, Babaji, guru to Lahiri Mahasaya, from Lahiri Mahasaya, guru both to his father and to Yukteswar and so from Yukteswar to Yogananda. Babaji appears to be wholly supernatural and, as with the Masters of Theosophy this recourse to the magical somewhat detracts from the appeal of an otherwise engaging text. From Babaji came the kriya yoga, older than Patanjali's, indeed as old as Krishna and Arjuna, and that forms the link between all three.

Lahiri claimed to have met Yogananda in the Himalayas in Ranikhet, near Almora, in 1861, when working as an accountant for the Military Engineering Department: "he bore a remarkable resemblance to myself." It turned out that he had been his guru in a previous incarnation. At the age of thirty-three, Lahiri, married with one child, became the ideal householder. In 1886 he retired from government service. He died 26 September 1895. It was this man who had been his father's guru, whose portrait had been part of Yogananda's childhood and which, he claimed, had cured him of cholera. Lahari Mahasaya was born Prya Nath Kerar, in Serampore, son of a wealthy businessman whose family home became the venue for his ashram. He himself had little formal education. He married and had a daughter. Only on his wife's death did he become a swami. He dressed as a babu: "himself an exec-utive Occidental in outer habits, inwardly he was the spiritual oriental."[60]

The Yukteswar-Yogananda relationship was to be another that hinged on strictness. "This flattening to the ego treatment was hard to endure but my unchangeable resolve was to allow Sri Yukteswar to iron out all my psycho-logical kinks."[61] This discipline, it seems, allowed him to overcome his sex-ual drives. But Yogananda interestingly saw such a discipline would not work in the west; there would have to patience and forbearance. There was no need now to escape to the mountains; enlightenment was to hand in the guru. Yukteswar in time, after a period in yoga training, granted him an ex-perience of samadhi, though, it has to be said, this reads rather like an ac-count of a mescalin trip.[62] His training had been in jnana yoga, somewhat against the grain, for his was instinctively a bhaktic approach. Again, this ac-count is weakened by claims of the supernatural, with Yukteswar allegedly once appearing out of his body in Serampore whilst still in Calcutta. He was to confer sannyas on him in an informal ceremony on an inner balcony of the ashram in Serampore. Yogananda chose his own name. He had joined the giri branch of the swami order, one that descends from Sankaracharya him-self. Yukteswar he came to see as a yogi-christ, someone who could in the manner of the atonement take on the karma of others.

Meanwhile Yogananda had struggled through his university education. He had attended Scottish Church college. He himself turned educationist. Through the generosity of the Maharajah of Kasimbazar a school was set up at Ranchi in Bihar, with a broad syllabus and a closeness to nature, but with kriya yoga at its heart. Through contact with C. F. Andrews he met Ra-bindranath Tagore and exchanged thoughts on education.

Yukteswar claimed to have received a message from Babaji at a Kumbh Mela that a disciple would come to him who was to take kriya yoga to Amer-ica. In fact, Yogananda was invited by the American Unitarian Association to address an international Congress of Religious Liberals in Chicago. He left for America in August 1920 and addressed the Congress 6 October. He turned missionary, setting up the HQ of the Self-Realization Society, the American name for the Yagoda Satsanga Society in 1925 in Mount Wash-ington Estates, Los Angeles. All this throws up interesting parallels with Prabhavanda's career in America.

He did not return to India till August 1935. Yukteswar was still alive. There was a moving encounter. Only then did Yogananda have the nerve to ask him what all along he had really meant to him. "In you I have found my son," he replied. "Yogananda I love you always." Had he craved such an open expression of love all his life? "I felt a weight lift from my heart, dissolved forever at his words. I knew he was unemotional and self-contained, yet often I had wondered at his silence."[63] Yukteswar conferred on him the title of *paramahansa*. "My task on earth is now finished. You must carry on."[64] He died soon afterwards, Yogananda absent at the time at the kumbh mela in Allahabad. Needless to say, he was to be vouchsafed a supernatural experience of him later, his materializing in a Bombay hotel bedroom: "for the first time in my life I did not kneel at his feet in greeting but instantly advanced to gather him hungrily in my arms."[65] It is difficult not to see a kind of running parallel in this guru-disciple relationship to that between Ramakrishna and Vivekananda, except that increasingly Yogananda himself seems to become both rolled into one. He died in Los Angeles 7 March 1952.

Prabhavananda's American Challenge

The Prabhavananda who went to America was less the loner than Purushot-tamamanda, less inclined to go on pilgrimage and seek out isolated places, more the obedient monk, and if he and Yogananda were both to fulfill themselves in America, in contrast he was the less credulous, little inclined to fall back on the supernatural and occult. But here we have to ask, how ready was he to adapt to a radically different mental climate in America and what, indeed, was required of a swami in America? Did the Ramakrishna Mission have to, and could it anyway, adjust to new cultural demands?

This is not the place for any detailed account of the Mission in America to date.[66] If Vivekananda's impact at Chicago in 1893 can be exaggerated and his own contribution to the emergence of the movement in America proved ephemeral—he was little interested in organization—he did impose a lasting influence on its character: "his decision not to emphasize Rama-krishna but to dwell on philosophic Hinduism as embodied in the Vedanta has largely dominated down to the present."[67]

The prima donna role of swamis became apparent from the beginnings. In New York the Vedanta center divided, the American trustees unhappy at the frequent absence of Swami Abhedananda; they turned instead to Swami Paramananda, and Abhedananda broke away to found his own center in West Cornwall, Connecticut. Were the centers indeed, the question was raised, just to meet the needs of its members or was the role of the swami to seek a wider audience? In the west coast at the Shanti Ashrama in Santa Clara County the replacement of Turiyananda by Swami Trigunatita led to all kinds of confused loyalties for its members. Miss Ida Ansell, for example, could not transfer her devotion to a new swami and Trigunatita had to lay down the law: "have faith in me. I know better than you what is right and what is wrong for you. If you do not believe in me like that, you will have to suffer for that. And if you believe in me fully then you will have all the time to be gaining and improving."[68] With Turiyananda's blessing she came into line. If an old-fashioned monk, and one who never mastered English, he put the San Francisco center on its feet. Unusually he tried to create more of a role for women and also gave a political dimension to the Mission, supporting socialism. He died 27 December 1914 from injuries after a bomb was let off in the center by "a demented one-time follower." Jackson argues that centers, nevertheless, tended to be more alike, though he comments; "in the end a swami either possessed the qualities and flexibility to lead a Vedanta society or did not."[69]

It was his successor, Swami Prakashananda whom Prabhavananda was sent to assist in April 1923. Maybe he became something of a role model, his dressing in stylish western clothes, playing tennis passionately: "though Hindu on the inside, he could be western on the outside." His was a successful balancing act "between transmitting Hinduism's authentic message and adopting its teaching for American audiences."[70] He died of a heart attack in 1940, still aged only fifty-six.

On arrival in America Prabhavananda had to make the transition from disciple to guru. He gave lectures and took classes on the *Gita*. But he was proving more attractive than Prakashananda—a familiar rivalry of swami personalities—so it was agreed that he should work instead, September 1925, in Portland, Oregon. It was in December 1929 that, thanks to the generosity of Mrs Carrie Mead Wyckoff—she had heard Vivekananda lecture in America and had never forgotten—who bequeathed her home, 1946 Ivar Avenue, to the Mission and it was here that Prabhavananda opened the Hollywood Vedanta center in Los Angeles. Even if he was now his own master, it remained an uphill struggle. Sister Amiya, the same Ida Ansell, recalled; "the growth was slow and painful; on many occasions Swami would stand and lecture for the full hour before a mere handful of people scattered among the empty seats." In the end he gave up lecturing in rented halls and just held meetings in the home. He recognized that all he was attracting were "mainly mystery mongers and metaphysical shoppers."[71] But these were the years of the depression. In 1931 he began initiation.

The threshold or take-off came following a visit to India August 1935 to March (?)1936. Here he was able to recharge his spiritual batteries with visits to the birthplaces of Ramakrishna and Sarada Devi, Kampukur and Jayrambati, to Vrindaban, Varanasi and its Vishwanath temple, and to Puri. No doubt meeting up with two of Ramakrishna's disciples still alive, Swami Abhedananda and Vijnanananda, also renewed his enthusiasm. The former,

Vice-president of the mission since 1922, its president in 1934, had made his mark in famine relief work in the 1890s in the districts of Mahula and Murshidabad, and had set up a Ramakrishna center at Sargacchi near Behrampur. Seen as a self-made man, "he preferred worshipping the poor living gods in the village rather than preaching Vedanta."[72] He had chosen not to go to America. He died at Belur from diabetes, to be the curse of so many of the monks, 7 February 1937.

The latter, Vijnanananda succeeded him as President. He was a formidable character, a great wrestler, qualifying as an engineer prior to joining the Mission at Alambazar in 1896, "truly a karma yoga."[73] It will have been as a reflection of conversations with Prabhavananda at this time that he later stated: "the Americans respect Swamiji more than the Master." He died at Allahabad 25 April 1938.

Slowly the movement in the 1930s began to gain influence. Swami Nikhilananda, who opened the Ramakrishna-Vivekananda center in New York in 1933, raised the literary and scholarly profile of the Mission. Prabhavananda made his mark as translator and popularizer. He is seen "as one of the Ramakrishna movements most successful workers."[74] The Hollywood center began to expand. On July 7 1938 the new Temple was dedicated. An Italian visitor gave the center a ten-acre site near Santa Barbara—but Spencer Kellogg is also named as donor—to become later the Sarada Devi convent. It was dedicated as the Sri Rashada Math 13 February 1956. In 1942 Gerald Heard had opened the Trabuco College, near Laguna Beach, but was unable to sustain the experiment and had it transferred to the Mission; it was dedicated 7 September 1949 as the Ramakrishna ashram.

Prabhavananda was all the while imposing his house style on these institutions. Sister Amiya put it this way: "Swami Prabhavananda's guiding principle is and always has been impartial love and each monastic member is made to feel that honor and self-discipline are the rules for a truly spiritual life." "This honor system is a radical departure from the orthodox training usually enforced by religious organizations in the west, yet it is by this very system that there is maintained the steady, relentless sifting process—a process that leaves little question as to the sincerity and determination of those that remain."[75] The historians of the Hollywood Center put it another way. Prabhavananda's idea was of "a constant recollectedness of the lord. The cultivation of devotion is at once very simple and very difficult. It demands continued inner check or control of the mind and a constant turning toward God. It is a matter of experience that the more a person's heart and mind are attracted to God, the less he will be interested in satisfying his material sensual cravings."[76] His was a policy "that freedom is necessary for growth." The historians recognized; "this wisdom has attracted many individuals to Vedanta thankful at last to find a religion in which it is possible to think for oneself and to progress according to one's own temperament."[77]

But these were now serious enquirers after the truth who had only came to Vedanta "after a period of intense and sometimes prolonged soul-searching among various alternatives." Protestants found "Vedanta's universal message especially liberating."[78] Their backgrounds were marvelously diverse: sailor, musician, engineer, college student, radio technician, interior decorator. Correspondingly, it was never made difficult for those who were unsuited to leave: "it is not easy to give up the habits, the sensitivities and desires that make up such a large part of one's unregenerate self." Numbers should not be exaggerated. In 1936 the entire Mission in America only contained 365 women and 163 men. By 1956 in the various centers attached to the Hollywood center there were but fourteen brahmacharinis, twelve brahmacharis, and two swamis. But the real turning point in the history of the Hollywood center came when Prabhavananda "by chance"[79] met Gerald Heard in 1939. This brought a group of internationally known writers into its orbit.

Isherwood the Disciple

Isherwood's own accounts of his conversion to Vedantism stand out as some of the most engaging and searching religious literature of our times. My Guru and his Disciple completed a trilogy of autobiographical writings, Kathleen and Frank, on his parents and upbringing, Christopher and his Kind, largely on the 1930s and the first open admission of his homosexuality. It drew heavily on his diaries, to be published posthumously. One early published account of his discovery of Vedanta was an article entitled, "What Vedanta Means to Me," in Vedanta and the West Volume 14, 1951. Probably the fullest account, however, came in an essay An Approach to Vedanta, originally conceived as an introduction to his biography of Ramakrishna but published separately by Vedanta Press, Hollywood in 1963. It is impossible to separate out discretely the theme of the guru-disciple relationship from the Vedantic quest, they are so inextricably linked. But Isherwood placed so much emphasis on this relationship that it makes sense to try to do so.

Oddly, considering his homosexual makeup, sexual feelings do not seem at the time to have influenced his response to Prabhavananda. Isherwood, indeed, seems rarely to have experienced any homosexual attraction to Indians (he was attracted to some of the younger monks at Belur on his visits in 1963) and indeed Prabhavananda's somewhat Mongolian and non-Indian features were seen to be to his advantage. But he accepted that he would have been attracted to him with his "lithe, athletic body" as a youth. Isherwood's being taller "made me love him in a special protective way, as I loved my childhood nanny, and as I should love Stravinsky."[80] Even in a dream where he encountered Prabhavananda in a homosexual brothel—and there were several similar dreams—their relationship remained chaste. This was how others described him: "a short moon-faced little man, with the kindest expression we have ever known."[81]

This is Isherwood recalling that initial encounter:

> The swami I found to be small and impressive. Not formidable. Not in the least severe or hypnotic or dignified. But very definitely and unobtrusively one who had the authority of personal experience. Outwardly he was a Bengali in his middle forties who looked at least fifteen years younger, charming and boyish in manner, with bold straight eyebrows and dark wide-set eyes. He talked in a gentle, persuasive voice. His smile was extraordinary—so open, so brilliant with joy it had a strange kind of poignancy which could make your eyes fill suddenly with tears. Later I got to know another look of his—an introspective look which seemed to withdraw all life from the surface of his face, leaving it quite bare and lonely, like the face of a mountain.[82]

Isherwood speculated whether his Britishness was in any way a barrier, with all the baggage of Indo-British political antagonisms. Maybe it did get in the way with Prabhavananda's nephew, Asit, also a resident in the Hollywood center, but not with Prabhavananda himself. Yet for Prabhavananda imperialism did remain an issue: "at heart he's still a flaming Indian nationalist," Isherwood noted, "and gets very heated when British policy is discussed."[83]

Their age difference was critical, thirty-five to forty-six, a gap which just opened up the possibility of a father-son relationship, one that proved impossible for both Huxley and Heard in their relationship with Prabhavananda, given their comparable ages. And as Katherine Bucknell puts it, the swami had "'in addition to his subtle personal attributes, the ultimate dimension in any father figure—a relationship with God.'"[84]

Questions of sexuality were always decisive. Isherwood remained deeply troubled by his homosexuality and there could have been no future in this relationship had Prabhavananda suggested any hostility. But he did not show "the least shadow of distaste on hearing me admit to my homosexuality."[85] It is indicative though of how repressed Isherwood still was that he failed to confide to his diary this admission of his homosexuality at their first meeting. Prabhavananda suggested that he try to worship Krishna as a beautiful youth, a pleasing indication of how untroubled Hinduism can be about homosexuality, and that in time feelings of lust would go away. Isherwood detected in Prabhavananda himself "a strong sexuality which seemed to be controlled rather than repressed or concealed."[86] But this whole theme of sexuality and spirituality will be treated in the following chapter.

Isherwood was always conscious of Prabhavananda's own continuing dependence on his guru. This was not only a powerful example of the guru-disciple relationship, invaluable for Isherwood as disciple, but it took Prabhavananda off any pedestal: "it meant I needn't expect him to be perfect and try to explain away any weaknesses."[87] It was a continuing dependence which leant him "the air of a second-in command," that "firm refusal to try to make an impression on those who met him." Would a guru without weaknesses he queried have been more attractive? Isherwood acknowledged "the Hindu idea that you should subject your prospective guru to every kind of test, until you are entirely convinced of his honesty. Then and only then should you submit your will to him and obey him absolutely."[88] But if all this made for a greater accessibility Isherwood was still left with the problematic of his having acquired too many gurus.

The awkward conflict of loyalties for Isherwood lay between Heard and Prabhavananda. There may always have been a touch of jealousy here between the two, for Heard was the more charismatic lecturer and attracted larger audiences. Isherwood came to see their differences brilliantly: "Gerald offered me discipline, method, intellectual conviction. But the swami offered me love." It all seemed summed up by the old-maidish tidiness of Heard's apartment compared to the disordered bohemianism of the Hollywood center. Tellingly, Isherwood felt Forster would have preferred the swami.[89] A real break between Heard and Prabhavananda came in February 1941 after Prabhavananda, always choosy over his initiates, had turned down Danny Fouts, ever the trouble-maker, a friend of both Heard and Isherwood, only for Heard to take him under his own wing. Heard found Prabhavananda insufficiently ascetic, what with his chain-smoking and his companionship with women.

Isherwood found himself torn between Heard's new college at Trabuco and the Hollywood center. Huxley had also undermined his faith in Prabhavananda by quoting Krishnamurti's doubts over his method of meditation. But Isherwood early on grasped the need to make a choice; "if I sit at the feet of a lot of different masters I shall be aware only of their mannerisms, and waste my time in an Athenian craze for novelty. I had better stick to yoga and the swami and not attempt too big a synthesis."[90]

Isherwood was never to advance beyond being a probationer monk at the Center and his monastic quest was always to be a struggle. But the attempt is in itself sufficiently amazing. On 8 November 1940 he was initiated, receiv-

ing his mantra—seen as the most important gift a guru can give to his disciple—and in return he gave him a white rose. But Isherwood was still in a
deeply confused state and even this degree of commitment was quickly followed by appalling doubt, "terrible attacks, storms of rajasic fury sweep over
me, until I begin to wonder how long I shall stay even outwardly sane."[91]
Prabhavananda then appointed him Assistant Editor of the journal launched
in January 1938, *Vedanta and the West*. Securing his literary services may have
been Prabhavananda's intentions all along. Yet in Fryer's estimate, "asking
Swami Prabhavananda to be his guru was one of the most important, positive decisions, if not the most important, of Christopher's entire life."[92]

But he still did not feel ready for the monastic life and there followed a period of working for the Quakers with German refugees. Prabhavananda advised him against joining the Quakers, feeling they would never agree to
share him with Ramakrishna. The problem of the draft hovered over Isherwood. Prabhavananda recommended his registering as a theology student
and so have himself classified as 4-D; Prabhavananda was by then very anxious to recruit Isherwood's special services as a translator. With the age of
conscription raised, however, the problem went away and, once again, Isherwood found himself facing the possibility of entering the Center as a trainee
monk. Meanwhile Prabhavananda had made contact with Heard and Trabuco and something of a reconciliation between them took place in the college, 23 September 1942, though there were "embarrassing silences" and
Prabhavananda persisted, despite Trabuco's house rules, in smoking.[93]

It remained for Prabhavananda to allay Isherwoood's doubts as to his capacity to become a monk: "I wouldn't be asked to do things that I wasn't fitted for or wasn't inclined to do."[94] Isherwood felt that only the problematic
of his joining the Civilian public service camp had led to this decision anyway. But there were in fact profound personal imperatives: "I'm feeling increasingly the misery of not being all of a piece, of living my life in a number
of compartments with connecting doors which are narrow and hard to open."
"I've just got to belong to the Ramakrishna order with as few reservations as
I can manage."[95] So on 6 February 1943 he moved into a newly acquired
property, 1942 Ivar Avenue, Brahmananda cottage as it was to be called, and
more familiarly, the swamitage. Isherwood reflected: "but good or bad, this is
the place for me. It will be tough here, but easier than anywhere else."[96]

The troubled experiment lasted till 25 August 1945, though the break
could easily have come a good deal earlier. He was never to be initiated as a
brahmachari. This could only come after a five-year probation. He was required to take a conditional three-year vow of celibacy; a lifelong one would
only follow after ten years. Inability, in the end, to sustain this vow was one

major reason for leaving, though not till later on, and it was to be of a piece with the privileged status that he was to enjoy in the community that a boyfriend had been allowed to join both the Center and Trabuco. Isherwood often speculated, had there been someone else present inside the Mission on his wavelength, like Danny Fouts, would he have persevered? He accepted that he was always free to go: "whatever else the spiritual life, it isn't tragic, because every effort and discomfort is purely voluntary; you can stop whenever you wish."[97]

And he was in a very permissive regime as far as Ramakrishna centers went. There was a bad moment when Belur insisted on the Hollywood center tightening up its discipline, but here Prabhavananda himself turned rebel. Such rules, he replied to Belur, could not possibly apply to western probationers; "If they refuse to change" he said, "I shall leave the order." "What a little rock of safety he is," Isherwood added.[98] And he had chosen his guru well. Prabhavananda had the imagination to grasp that different rules would have to apply to westerners. Isherwood was to visit other centers at Portland, Seattle, and San Francisco and came to appreciate just how relaxed the Hollywood one was and how well it fitted his needs. So Isherwood could come and go. He spent almost every Sunday, for example, with his friends Dodie Smith and Alec.[99]

But the demands nevertheless were considerable. Adjusting to the other residents was a struggle. Increasingly Isherwood found real relief in meditation in the shrine room. The one rule that the Center insisted on was a daily three-hour period of meditation. Prabhavananda also helped him to come to terms with temple ritual. Isherwood, indeed, had to make some quite considerable cultural adjustments, though he never ceased to feel a degree of alienation from the Hindu and the Indian. But he persisted: "to live this synthesis of East and West is the most valuable kind of pioneer work I can imagine—never mind who approves or disapproves."[100] Isherwood always felt his friends outside sneered at his monastic life. Prabhavananda, on the other hand, assured him of Brahmananda's continuing supportive presence though Isherwood took this on board with some skepticism: "I can accept this in a way—but only as a kind of symbolic truth."[101]

But the key to his staying at all lay in his relationship with his guru. It was only on his joining that Prabhavananda switched from calling him Mr. Isherwood to Chris. Early on Isherwood recorded: "I feel such a deep relationship with him. 'Love' is too possessive a word to describe it. It's really absence of demand, lack of strain, entire reassurance."[102] There could be doubts: "what exactly *was* Prabhavananda? Could he be simultaneously Abanindra Ghosh and Brahmananda's instrument? Could he be combining the mannerisms of his immature persona with the insight of a saint?"[103] When Prabhavananda left for India in June 1943 he slept in his room: "I was extraordinarily conscious of swami's presence there, almost as though I was sharing it with him."[104] There is almost a sense that Isherwood was in a very non-Forsterian way transcending personal relationship. "If there's anything I'm sick of," he recorded, "it's personal relationships, on which I and the rest of my friends used to expend a positively horticultural energy."[105] Something new was taking its place. After Prabhavananda had been ill, Isherwood reflected:

> we lay, unmindful like children, in the completely uninteresting certainty of their father's love. . . . It isn't a relationship, because there's no element of surprise, no possibility of change. He would not cease to care for us. Our demand on him is total and quite merciless. *Of course* he is and will be there—now, tomorrow, whenever we decide we want him.[106]

Had their relationship indeed moved into non-duality?

Prabhavananda was to try very hard to dissuade Isherwood from abandoning his vocation: "I don't want you to leave here Chris. I want you to stay with me as long as I am alive. I think you'd be all right, even if you left. I think you have the makings of a saint."[107] And that promise of a lifetime commitment was important. Prabhavananda had no intention of ceasing to be his guru should he leave, however badly he felt "when he seems to lose control over people."[108]

But by December 1944 Isherwood felt the situation had become "impossible," his love for a new friend, Bill Caskey, bringing the crisis to a head. Significantly, at that point the diary stops. Even so, he deferred his leaving till August 1945.

But it would be wrong to argue as Brian Finney does that Isherwood had "finally decided that his true vocation or *dharma* was that of a writer and not as a monk."[109] There were two ways Isherwood could declare his discipleship to Ramakrishna, as a monk and as a householder. He kept open for a while the possibility of returning to the Hollywood center but then came his meeting with Don Bachardy. At that point he chose, instead, through his partnership with Bachardy, a householder relationship. He was never to give up the work of translation.

Prabhavananda did not surrender easily. In May 1951 he had suggested Trabuco, by then a Ramakrishna monastery, as an alternative. And after mulling this over with him Prabhavananda had taken "it for granted I'm coming," but Isherwood dreaded "the boredom and the isolation, of the place." He also felt he had to move beyond "categorical" relationships: "trying to fix a situation and ensure security by involving yourself is no good."[110]

It was not enough just to be a monk. Yet he found himself brooding: "am I still a monk at heart? Ramakrishna will hound you, Swami said."[111] But he had come to recognize "the monastery is here wherever I am."[112] Still he reflected: "But I mustn't lose touch with Swami—I've hardly seen anything of him—and with Gerald. That's more important than anything else, including my writing."[113] And Prabhavananda was to respond in kind: "it's as if he were exposing me to stronger and stronger vibrations of his love—yet all the while making almost no personal demand . . . I don't feel he is altogether a person any longer."[114] Isherwood saw himself in his visits to the Center as the prodigal son, "always uncritically welcomed by a Father.[115] But he had by then himself become a father figure to Bachardy. Prabhavananda blessed the friendship. Isherwood through his domestic life with Bachardy had become the Ramakrishna householder disciple.

Comparative Discipleships

How did other contemporary Europeans and Americans search for a guru? The distinctiveness of Isherwood's quest will emerge more clearly by looking at the way Europeans approached Ramana Maharshi, the Indian South's answer to Ramakrishna, off-setting an Indian-based search with Isherwood's American West Coast. Two will be looked at, Paul Brunton, who was to discover Ramana Maharshi for a western audience, and S. S. Cohen.

Half-Jewish, but five foot in height, born 21 October 1898 as Raphael Hurst, and just a little older than Isherwood—he died 27 July 1981—his quest came at a roughly similar age. It was described in A *Search in Secret India*, published in 1935. A chance encounter with an Indian in a London bookshop inspired this Indian journey, one to sort out the fake from the genuine Indian holymen, anticipating in a way Tahir Shah's much more recent sardonic account of his search for the makers of magic. This later study is a useful way of maintaining some wry detachment at the improbable character of so many of India's spurious exponents of spirituality.[116]

Brunton's own skepticism likewise helped to sort out the rogue from the genuine. He was not to be taken in, for example, by the would-be Parsi messiah, Meher Baba, even if later he was to enjoy a cult following in Hollywood. Alienated from India's backwardness he took to a modernizer like Sahabji Maharaj, leader of the Radha Soami society, in his efforts to fashion a westernized society yet one inspired by his version of yoga, sound yoga, at Dayalbagh near Agra. He assured Brunton that "a sincere, fully determined seeker will eventually be brought to his real master," magnetically.[117]

Interestingly, he met Ramakrishna's Boswell, Mahendranath Gupta, "a venerable patriarch" out of the Old Testament: "I began to understand how potent must have been the influence of the teacher when the pupil exercised such a fascination upon me."[118]

Both an ex-sepoy turned yogin he had encountered in Madras and Shri Sankara of Kumbakonam, 66th in direct descent from Sankara, whom the soldier had led him to in Chingleput, were to steer him toward Ramana Maharshi. It was the Sankara who instructed Brunton, after he had done the round of his possible gurus, "to pick out the one which makes most appeal to you. Return to him and he will surely bestow his initiation upon you."[119]

Ramana was clearly a quite exceptional religious teacher. In essence his was a very simple message; know yourself. Maybe just because he discouraged discipleship and left no body of apostles as Ramakrishna did, he is the less well known; the Christian story is another example of how the human tapestry of apostleship lends a greater attractiveness to a religious movement. He was born Venkataraman in 1879, brahmin, his father a lawyer of sorts, in a village some thirty miles from Madurai. There were to be no early signs of a religious temperament, though educated at a mission school. At the age of sixteen, however, he underwent a transforming experience, an acute awareness of death, leaving him with a sense of the radical apartness of body and spirit. He had already heard of the sacred hill of Arunachala, or sacred red mountain, home to Siva, and in 1896 he simply set aside family, any thought of a career and headed for Tiruvannamalai. Initially, he practiced extreme austerities in the Aruncheleswara temple but after three years moved to a cave in the Hill of the Holy Beacon. Here a brahmin pandit, Ganapati Shastri, was to discover him and bestow on him the title of Maharishi or great sage. In time his full designation became Bhagavan (meaning Lord or God) Sri Ramana (a shortened version of Venkataraman) Maharshi. He was persuaded to turn teacher and in time the Ramana ashram grew up around him. The presence of Siva in the hill held him captive and from 1925 till his death from cancer in 1950 he was never to move more than a few miles from base. Significantly, as a spiritually enlightened person he was entirely self-taught. And it seems probable that his reading of sanskrit[120] texts came late in life.

Brunton came to interpret this decisive encounter in anti-intellectual terms. He initially discovered Ramana in *samadhi* or trance. The experience of "this mysterious telepathic process" drove away all his prepared questions: "I perceive with sudden clarity that the intellect creates its own problems and then makes itself miserable trying to solve them."[121] Is it indicative that Brunton, who refused to turn native in India, judged Ramana's appearance "more European than Indian?" It took him two weeks to summon up the nerve to ask Ramana the question that had brought him to India: "forgive me for saying so, but I am not religious. Is there anything beyond man's religious existence? If so, how can I realize it for myself?" The answer given, as it was always to be: "know first that *I* and then you shall know that truth."

He was discouraged from adopting Ramana as guru: "I receive a queer feeling that the sage dislikes to discuss the subject of masters and their methods."[122] "It became perfectly obvious that he has no wish to convert anyone to his own ideas, whatever they may be, and no desire to add a single person to his following." It is as if the "impersonal, impenetrable quality of all Nature," the very rock of the Holy Mountain itself, had been absorbed by Ramana. But with Ramana in samadhi Brunton felt he was somehow known: "I feel that he understands also what mind-devastating quest has impelled me to leave the common way and seek out such men as he."[123] So when Brunton, back in Bombay and ready to depart, became aware that his quest had failed and that he would be leaving India a pilgrim without a God, he felt impelled to return to South India and once again seek Ramana as guru. The answer was to be the same: "you must find the master within you, within your own spiritual self." And, indeed, Brunton came to recognize "somewhere within me there is a well of certitude which can provide me with all the waters of truth I require."[124] Brunton was then himself to experience samadhi: "I find myself outside the rim of world consciousness."[125] But he was also to sense a mingling of himself with Ramana.

But David Godman's interpretation of Ramana's ideas suggests Brunton may have misunderstood his account of the guru-disciple relationship. It is true that Ramana identified the concepts of God, guru and the self and in that sense the self is its own guru. But Ramana recognized how difficult it was for most of those who came for his advice to put themselves in touch with their own self and saw how essential it was for there to be a guru, externalized as it were, who could guide them.[126]

Nor does Ramana come across as quite so distant in other accounts. S. S. Cohen, who joined the ashram in 1936, portrays a quite different almost family atmosphere, with the members of the ashram gathered around Ramana, speaking to him "as intimately to a beloved father." Nothing gave Ramana more pleasure "than to listen attentively to his devotees' spiritual difficulties and give his advice."[127] But both Brunton and Cohen concur on the relatively relaxed character of the ashram and here their experience does compare with Isherwood's. "The Maharishee," Brunton wrote, "is the last person in the world to place his followers in the chains of servile obedience and allows everyone the utmost freedom of action."[128] In Cohen's account of ashram life there were "no compulsions," no program to be followed: "realization surges up from within by free impulse."[129]

Brunton saw the potential dangers of this deification of the self, its leading to a messiah complex. Anthony Storr doubts if it was a lesson he properly learnt. Yet his "calm, untroubled certainty" suggests that he had found an answer to his questions through Ramana.[130]

In his turn Brunton, in much the same way as Carpenter had done, became the guru. In Jeffrey Masson's memoir, My Father's Guru, the story of Brunton's guru relationship with his father Jacques, his uncle, Bernard and himself we encounter all the anger of the disciple betrayed. Intriguingly, we learn that Brunton's relationship with Ramana broke down. Ramana's brother and Ramana himself were angry at interviews Brunton gave on the Maharishee to the Indian press. "The guru-disciple relationship, like most romances," Masson sourly observes, "tends to end badly, with both sides feeling aggrieved, hurt, misunderstood and misused."[131] Brunton made out he himself was a reluctant guru. In much the same way as Hindus believe husbands and wives are remarried in each reincarnation so Brunton saw disciples ineluctably drawn to the same guru each time round.

This was heady stuff for Masson's father who had met up with Brunton in Mysore in December 1945 and was to remain a follower for decades in the forlorn hope that Brunton would confer on him certain occult powers, especially the capacity to read other people's minds at a glance. Brunton played all kinds of games with the brothers, exploiting their sibling rivalry the better to keep them under his spell.

Throughout his childhood Jeffrey saw himself as the companion of a sage in a guru-disciple relationship. In all that insistence on sexual abstinence and obsession with purification Masson, in retrospect, saw some form of sexual exploitation or abuse: "purification and sexuality were not just opposites; they were fused in a dance of denial."[132]

There were curious convergences with Isherwood's story. When the family lived in Hollywood they visited the Vedanta center in lieu of synagogue or Sunday school, and there they met the chain-smoking Swami Prabhavananda. Jeffrey was more impressed by his junior colleague, not named, who "had a sweet, almost melancholy way of speaking about Vedanta that made me wonder a few years later if he really believed what he was saying."[133] Masson rather disparagingly writes of "the somewhat watered down version" of Hinduism being taught in the American Vedanta centers. There was an encounter in a lift with Aldous Huxley but he seemed to have little knowledge of Brunton and that led Masson to wonder if after all he was a "gigantic hoax."[134] When driving past Somerset Maugham's house outside Cannes

Brunton made out he was the model for Larry in *The Razor's Edge*, a role often attributed to Isherwood.

It was extraordinary for how long Brunton was able to keep up his front as guru but disillusionment came in the end. Jacques and Bernard were both outraged that Brunton did not join them in Montevideo where they had fled, a city Brunton had selected as the safest place to escape the nuclear fall-out from World War III, only for himself to opt instead for Australia. Was there something he had not told them? Jacques then fell under the spell of another guru, Krishna Menon from Trivandrum, though he never ceased searching for a guru and never lost his respect for Brunton.

But Jeffrey's was to be a radical break. As all of Brunton's claims became exposed, as a Sanskrit scholar, as a visitor to Tibet, as a Phd, and finally, and most embarrassingly, in the summer of 1967, as a medium, so anger set in and he saw him as "a phony, a charlatan, a mountebank, a quack": "he was just a hodge-podge of misread and misunderstood ideas from an ancient culture he did not know or understand."[135] His is a final devastating verdict on the guru-disciple relationship:

> Every guru inflicts tyranny upon his disciples, every guru exploits his chelas, every guru dominates the student. Abuse is part of the definition, whether it is financial, emotional, sexual, physical or intellectual. Once in, there is no escape. The best way out is never to go in.[136]

He branded it a totalitarian relationship.

Maybe now we have to stand back and explore the divergent claims made in a more general sense for this relationship.

The Problematic of the Guru-Disciple Relationship

Here I am relying on conversations in India, in Calcutta, Delhi and Rishikesh and Chennai, backed up by relevant literature of the interviewees, not just on the problematic but on other issues to be discussed below, the interrelationship of ego and the self in the Vedantist quest, on the dynamic between sexuality and spirituality, on the dominant role of the feminine in Indian culture and the problem this might pose to western visitors, especially homosexual. Here was a wide spectrum of opinion, from secular-minded intellectuals, like the psychoanalyst, Sudhir Kakar, and the cultural historian, Ashis Nandy, to the religious minded but academic, Professor Das Gupta, to Europeans who had turned Vedantist in India, like the Swiss, Swami Vishveshwarananda, President of Omkarananda ashram in Rishiskesh, to several wholly committed Vedantist swamis, such as Swami Chidananda, President of the Divine Life Society. Others I will introduce as I go along.

I met Sudhir Kakar in his office and consulting room, 8 November 1999, in New Delhi. He saw the guru-disciple relationship as of relatively recent vintage—eighth to eleventh centuries—catching on through its offering greater moral support to Hindus at a time of considerable cultural anxiety, with Hinduism on the defensive from both Buddhism—though arguably it had won this battle—and from Islam. He confirmed that deeply held Hindu notion that semen could be stored in the brain as a source of spiritual strength and the imperative of chastity for the spiritual quest. But this led onto the astonishing comment that what a disciple would most like from his guru would be his semen and this would be acquired by fellatio or sucking. Given that even the dirt washed from the feet of a guru is sacred—as Jeffrey Masson had discovered at great cost to his health—how much more valuable would a drop of semen be? We have already seen how important it was to disciples to own personal items of clothing of the guru or to share his food or to sleep in the same bed as the guru. Even Isherwood was clearly moved to have been allowed to sleep in Prabhavananda's bed when he was absent in India.

For Kakar the need for this relationship is deeply rooted in the frailties of the psychological moorings of the Indian extended family. Indian children are given a far longer period of unconditional maternal love than in western cultures, with the consequence that the withdrawing of this love at the time of the second birth is a traumatic loss, "a narcissistic injury of the first magnitude." For the Indian male this prompts "an unconscious tendency to 'submit' to an idealized omnipotent figure," "the lifelong search for someone, a charismatic leader or a *guru*, who will provide mentorship and a guiding world-view, thereby restoring intimacy and authority to individual life."[137] The loss of maternal love is compounded by the emotional coldness or distance of the father, a built in requirement of the complicated emotional demands of the extended family. It encourages in the son a "non-partisan feminine submission towards all elder men in the family," "a passive receptive attitude towards authority figures of all kinds." This leads to a weakened superego: "Indian men tend to search for external figures to provide that approval and leadership not forthcoming from their own insufficiently idealized superegos."[138]

He is very interesting on suggesting why a community of disciples should be so attractive to both Indians and Europeans. Here is a kind of "non-binding brotherhood" which offers Indians an escape from oppressive communities, both of the extended family and of caste and Europeans an escape from an isolationist, competitive and over-individualized society. One of his case studies is the Radha Soami cult. Here he sees in the relationship between disciple and guru a recapitulation of that same process of hurt in childhood, a willful submission of the disciple's self to the guru, but with a compensating self-esteem acquired through dynamic association with the leader. Such is the logic of the relationship that the guru takes on the status of a God. It is vital that the disciple entertains no doubts as to the perfection of the guru. In Kakar's analysis the guru, far from being an "apparently quiescent . . . locked in his meditative stillness" is, instead, "a veritable psychological powerhouse." It adds up to a surrender of adulthood "to a hankering after absolute mental states free of ambiguity and contradiction in which the onerousness of responsibility is renounced together with the burdens of self-criticism and doubt."[139] The guru has a vital role to play in controlling the forces of the *chitta*, a kind of sexualized unconscious, steering it to the "one-pointed" or focused, but guarding "against the danger of psychotic breakdown."[140] Many of Kakar's patients are those who have broken down in this Vedantist quest. It is a veritable valley of death and only for an exceptional few.

Interestingly, Kakar analyses his own guru-disciple relationship with the psychoanalyst, Erik Erikson: "he was the guru my Indian self was searching for." They had met by chance when Erikson had rented his aunt's house in Delhi whilst working on his Gandhi project; "I could therefore approach him naturally without any inhibiting awe."[141]

The opinions of those associated with the Ramakrishna Mission itself have a more religious framework. An authority on Vivekananda and Indian spirituality, Professor Das Gupta[142] was curiously skeptical of the guru-disciple relationship. He sees it as encouraging a dependency culture, and with its stifling of initiative as a bane for India. He argued, for example, regarding Gandhi as guru had emasculated Congress. He saw it as having an exaggerated place in the Ramakrishna mission and wondered if this was for self-interested reasons: it was one means of creating support for the older generation. It worried him that respect for the guru was compatible with indifference to fellow gurubhais. In his view, Isherwood through his sensibility and imagination got close to Indian spirituality, but became too dependent on his guru, failed to break free from Prabhavananda and this was to limit his creative response to Indian spirituality.

Bernard Cicerone[143] is a youngish Catholic American who had been a brahmachari in Chicago, both at the Vivekananda center there and its off-shoot, the Vivekananda Monastery and retreat, Ganges, Michigan 1984–1986. He had become a free probationer on a visit to Belur in 1985. He tended to downplay the significance of the disciple-guru relationship but then the guru who had initiated him had died, he had not been a Ramakrishna man anyway, and he seems never to have recreated the relationship in the Mission. Indeed, Bernard felt Indian swamis were rather condescending to Americans, had never felt personally able to discuss his doubts with the Indian swami, and was more likely to have done so with his peer group. In his view the Isherwood-Prabhavananda relationship was an exceptional one and only the permissive climate of the Hollywood Center had made Isherwood's stab at being a monk possible at all. At both Belur and Ganges Bernard had come up against tiresome regulations, e.g., in Belur, swamis ticked him off for going outside Belur to buy soft drinks, in this way betraying a kind of negative attitude to the outside world; at Ganges, it was held against him he had gone out for meal with a visiting friend. But at a deeper level, himself an amateur artist, he found that the Mission did not share his aesthetic enjoyment of the world outside as filled with God, quite apart from his worrying at the grandiose ambitions of the center in building a major meditation center. And so his vocation lapsed. Interestingly, in comparing the relationships between psychoanalyst and patient and between guru and disciple he stressed their difference, for did not psychotherapy encourage an excessive dwelling on the self?

Out at Narendrapur I met Swami Ashaktananda,[144] who had been a swami at the Hollywood center and had known both Prabhavananda and Isherwood, and found him one of the toughest intelligences I encountered in the Mission at Calcutta. He thought it predictable that as people put the question, "what is the meaning of existence?" and as several "churches" failed to come up with an answer, they would seek out a guru. The role of the guru was to be a good listener and if he himself had read nothing on psychotherapy, still felt that the guru should engage with the emotions of the enquirer. His own approach, however, had been to send people away with particularized reading lists. Both he and Prabhavananda had laid emphasis on ritual deeds. Prabhavananda had always been happy to take on the role of guru and this became more pronounced as he got older. Ashaktananda had taken to Isherwood more than Huxley and Heard, though disliking his homosexuality. He felt Prabhavananda had got through to Isherwood by the strength of his personality rather than of his intellect and that Isherwood was drawn to Vedantism through his love of Prabhavanada and a search for a personal God. Prabhavananda he saw as a gentle man, a quiet speaker but clear, always able to make a point but, at the end, his mental balance faltered, he became jealous at Ashaktananda' greater appeal to disciples—the old problem of the swami as prima donna—and maybe incipient Alzheimer's bred paranoid delusions.

In Rishikesh and its environs I had numerous opportunities for conversations with swamis. The more I met with them and discussed the whole theme of Vedantism and the psycho-sexual nature of the attraction of Hinduism the less I sensed I was discussing a closed conformist culture. To the contrary, I felt the Vedantic quest was always highly individualized and this put the whole guru-disciple relationship into an increasingly paradoxical context.

The President of Parmath Niketan ashram, Swami Chidanand Saraswati, youngish, bearded, elegantly clothed, the very conventional image of the cosmopolitan holy man, presented an account of the spiritual search in which each individual simply extracted whatever met his own *sadhana* needs. This was combined with a laid back view of the role of the guru. They do not choose to be such but are chosen. There's no inherent reason why gurus should have disciples. Disciples seek him out and by implication use them for their own purposes. We extract anyway what we need from those around us, from people, from books. Why not the same for gurus? The important thing is to pursue our own spiritual growth.[145]

The Swiss President of the Omkarananda ashram was less opportunist. He rated the relationship very highly and that his own with Swami Omkarananda, an Andhra whose main ashram is in Zurich, was still crucial. However, you grow into being a guru in your own turn.[146]

But my favorite conversation was with Swami Shantananda Puri Maharaj, Tanjore brahmin and disciple of Swami Purushottomandaji—a nice connection for this text—an avuncular figure and now an ashramite of that same Vasitha Guha ashram, on the banks of the Ganges upstream from Rishiskesh. Here was another of Brahmananda's spiritual grandchildren.

Back in the 1950s he had been drawn by the reputation for saintliness of the occupant of the cave and had sought sannyas from Purushottamandaji, only to be told that he had too much of the householder in him and was sent away to get married and have a worldly career. Only in the 1980s did he feel free to relinquish these ties and become initiated. He often stays and lectures at the Ramana Maharshi ashram. He admitted that the guru-disciple relationship was crucial and intense but it can become idolatrous and one should always endeavor to become one's own guru. This has the feel of Ramana's teaching. One of his favorite metaphors was of being a character in a play. We are all programmed. Our own meeting was predetermined. But we still want to get out of the play and escape. He was opposed to all organization. It spelled the death of the spiritual life and he felt the Ramakrishna mission had lost its way. Even so, Ramakrishna had been the starting point of his own sadhana. But here was another highly individualized quest if one that was wholly otherworldly.[147]

But the most exceptional of my conversations in Rishikesh was with Swami Chidananda, President of the Divine Life Society. A study of its attitudes is as good a way as any in defining traditional Indian approaches to the guru-disciple relationship. It is an organization which always emphasizes the more permissive nature of its work over that of the Ramakrishna mission: there is an almost Fourierist stress on the variety of tasks undertaken, the need to be in control of your own work and yet to retain a sense of the whole. Here, seemingly, is the possibility of a more individualized sadhana. Not that the Ramakrishna mission and the Divine Life Society should be seen as rivals; it was Swami Ranganathananda, its President, who especially recommended that I try to meet Swami Chidananda.

The society can be dated from the setting up by its founder, Sivananda, of his own ashram on the right bank of the Ganges in Rishikesh March 1934, the establishment of the Divine Life Trust 13 January 1936 and the Divine Life Society itself 16 April 1939. Swami Sivananda was clearly a charismatic leader. Born 8 September at Pattamadai, near Tirunelveli, son of a revenue official of a large estate, he had aimed at a medical career but his father's death interrupted his studies at Tanjore Medical Institute. But the passion to serve was there and this was to take him to Malaya where, despite his lack of formal qualifications, he was virtually to run the hospitals on the rubber plantations at Seremban and at Johore Bahru, near Singapore. In 1923 he surrendered all of this, driven by a spiritual quest that took him back to India, the adoption of a sanyassin life-style, the conferment of sannyas 1 June 1934 by an elderly sannyasin, Viswananda in Rishikesh and to an extraordinary career of dedication to social service and spreading the gospel of Vedantism. A major feature of the Sivananda ashram was its Yoga Vedanta Forest Academy.

But there is a quandary in assessing the nature of the guru-disciple relationship in the Divine Life Society. Just how authoritative was the guru to be? As with so many gurus, Sivananda himself would disown any wish to be a guru. He saw himself as the perennial student. Everyone else was his guru. And experience was deemed his own greatest guru. But inevitably as a man of god he attracted disciples, though at the beginning he was all too happy on demand to surrender these to other swamis. Initially he was careful in his choice of disciples but thereafter was ready to welcome all and sundry. There was never to be any inner coterie of disciples. He claimed to look on disciples not as chelas but as co-workers in his spiritualized social service project. He reached out to each individual's needs. His biographer claimed: "he never converted; he only led." "He coaxed, cajoled, argued bribed but never compelled. His was the rule of love."[148]

He offered a relatively simple sadhana, though its simplicity was seen as transformed by his personality, the so-called guru kripa or grace of the guru.

Tough requirements were laid down for the disciples. To benefit from the guru they had already to be purified. The emphasis was on obedience. To quote Sivananda himself; "the disciple who has faith in the guru argues not, thinks not, reasons not and cogitates not. He simply obeys, obeys, obeys." But only out of such obedience could come the capacity to command: "learn how to be a disciple. Then alone you can become a guru."[149] The guru's spiritual advice or *upadesha* is strictly private and should not be discussed amongst other disciples for this will undermine the guru's authority. Yet Sivananda always seems to have recognized the limitations on the guru's influence. "The guru," he wrote, "is a help, but the actual task of practical sadhana falls to the aspirant himself."[150] All the guru can undertake is to steer the disciple in such directions as lay within their range, indeed "to follow only those of his teachings which suited their fancy."[151] He always wrote and taught in English, given his peculiar concern to win back westernized Indians to their own cultural heritage, but of course, this meant he was also open to Europeans. His was an attractive style of spiritual leadership. He died 14 July 1963.

It was to be his successor, Swami Chidananda I was to be privileged to interview.[152] A slight but quite tall man, in his eighties, he had the night before been in formidable voice as he led the evening worship, and song is central to the Society. We met in the Society's administrative offices, Guru Niwas, on the riverside. Once he had sat down and this was a rather elaborate procedure, "I am at your disposal" he said, and for an hour and a half he was and I was certainly to be the more fatigued by this astonishing conversation. He dealt with the role of gurus by analogy. What can you learn on your own? Who teaches you to read and write, to make shoes, to cook? All skills have to be learnt, so why should it be any different for the spiritual life? He also addressed that growing sense of paradox I was beginning to experience, that on the one hand the Vedantist quest seemingly pointed all in one direction and this pointed toward conformity, and yet on the other I was continually being confronted by a sense of highly individualized quests. His reply was again by analogy. In climbing a mountain the aim is the same but climbers approach by different routes; there are as many different routes as there are climbers. But then he back-pedaled and stated that, in fact, only a certain number of routes were laid down. I will refer to other features of this conversation elsewhere.

I also had the privilege of a meeting with Swami Krishnananda, No 2 in the Society. A short squat man, his legs so miraculously tucked under him as he sat lotus-style on his bed, I wondered if he was paraplegic. In one of his essays he addresses this paradox of the guru's role with a more cunning apologetics. How can anyone hope by their own efforts alone to escape their subjectivity, to escape the confines of space and time, and hence to seek the at-man? He does not see the role of guru as "an old-fashioned story or dogma. It is the only way by which the mind can be purified." The mistake lies in see-ing the guru as a person and failing to see, instead, that "he is a principle which represents a power behind the visible framework which you call the body of the guru." In his words: "To look upon the guru as a person and then to judge him as you judge anybody else in the world and to take his word or not to take it from your own point of view, would be to cut the ground from under your own feet." There are philosophical complexities in the search for self-realization that only a competent master can unravel. Again, to quote: "There is no other way than to be submissive and humble before the might of this tremendous mystery we call God, we call the self." "Humility is the hallmark of the spiritual seeker, and the guidance of a master is essential."[153] So is the position of the Divine Life Society ultimately dirigiste?

Conclusion

If only a building block for a sadhana or spiritual quest the guru-disciple rela-tionship can threaten to become an end in itself. In an Indian context, through the psychodynamics of the extended family, its programming an Indian for such submission, it can deteriorate into a psychologically crippling dependency. But it need not be that way and examples of such relationships within the Ra-makrishna Mission, under Ramana Maharshi and within the Divine Life Soci-ety point to a more liberal outcome. But to anyone preconditioned to a greater individualization and prone to Oedipal conflict with authority such constraints would be intolerable. In the most moving of his autobiographical writings *The Guru and His Disciple* and in his last Vedantist novel *A Meeting by the River* (1967) Isherwood portrays how a European can manage the demands of disci-pleship. Isherwood in fiction here compensates for his own failure to become a monk. In many ways Isherwood succumbed too much to its spell—maybe the still guilty side of him needed such dependency—and in the process he lost his way in the quest for non-duality. Yet it is highly improbable that the relation-ship would have worked as well as it did had Swami Prabhavananda not made such considerable adjustments to his own experience of the relationship, had not made exceptional allowances for Isherwood, above all in respecting the dic-tates of his sexuality, and indeed he entered more into a kind of platonic love-affair than into the more strictly moral and spiritual encounter laid down by tradition. Here was a highly individualized guru-disciple relationship. But its role is also essentially instrumental, a means rather than an end, and its ra-tionale lies in whether or not it facilitates the search for the divine.

Notes

1. Jonathan Fryer, *Isherwood: a Biography of Christopher Isherwood* (London: New English Library, 1977), 28.

2. Brian Finney puts it this way; "Her growing tendency to mourn the past rather than live in the present is to be matched by her son's subsequent determination to turn his back on the past in all its forms—the ancestral home, class distinctions, the study of history, Cambridge and finally England itself." See his *Christopher Isherwood. A Critical Biography* (London: Faber, 1979), 24.

3. Christopher Isherwood, "What Vedanta Means to Me," *Vedanta and the West* 14, (1951): 153.

4. Isherwood, "What Vedanta Means to Me," 154

5. Quoted Fryer, *Isherwood: a Biography*, 180.

6. Jeffrey Masson makes this point. See *My Father's Guru* (London: D. Reidel, 1993), 20.

7. Fryer, *Isherwood: a Biography*, 137.

8. Christopher Isherwood, *Diaries Volume One: 1939–1960* ed. Katharine Bucknell (London: Methuen, 1996). Entry May 1939, 22–30.

9. See Isherwood's account in *My Guru and His Disciple* (London: 1980), 22–30.

10. Isherwood, *An Approach to Vedanta* (Hollywood: Vedanta Press, 1963), 71.

11. Another member of the Hollywood Vedanta Center who went on a pilgrimage to see his guru's birthplace. See John Yale, *A Yankee among the Swamis* (London: Allen and Unwin, 1961), 188.

12. These family details are in Pravajika Anandaprana ed., *A Historical Record: from Conversations with Swami Prabhavananda* (Hollywood; nd). I am very grateful for her sending me a copy of this memoir.

13. Swami Prabhavananda, *Religion in Practice* (London; Allen and Unwin, 1968), Isherwood Introduction, 19.

14. Quoted Katherine Bucknell, ed., *Christopher Isherwood Diaries Volume One*, 363.

15. Pravajika Anandaprana, ed., *A Historical Record*, 8.

16. Pravajika Anandaprana, ed., *A Historical Record*, 10.

17. See John Yale, *A Yankee Among the Swamis*, 175.

18. Isherwood, Introduction to Prabhavananda, 20.

19. Anandaprana, *A Historical Record*, 21–22.

20. Pravajika Anandaprana, ed., *A Historical Record*, 11.

21. Pravajika Anandaprana, ed., *A Historical Record*, 10–11.

22. Prabhavananda, *The Eternal Companion: Life and Teachings of Swami Brahmananda* (Mylapore: Vedanta Press), 12th edition, 78–79.

23. Isherwood, *Diaries*, 18 April 1944, 344.

24. Isherwood, *Diaries*, 12 October 1942, 254.

25. See John Yale, *A Yankee and the Swamis*, 169–71.

26. See Swami Atulananda, *Atman Alone Abides* (Madras: Sri Ramakrishna Math, 1978).

27. Swami Chetanananda, *God Lived with Them: Life Stories of Monastic Disciples of Sri Ramakrishna* (Mayavati: Advirta Ashrama, 1997), 84.

28. Quoted in Prabhavananda, *The Eternal Companion*, 56.

29. Prabhavananda, *The Eternal Companion*, Prabhavananda's paraphrase.

30. Quoted Chetanananda, *God Lived with Them*, 103.

31. Chetanananda, *God Lived with Them*, 116.

32. Chetanananda, *God Lived with Them*, 81.

33. Chetanananda, *God Lived with Them*, 85.

34. Chetanananda, *God Lived with Them*, 82.

35. Chetanananda, *God Lived with Them*, 92.

36. Chetanananda, *God Lived with Them*, 93.

37. Chetanananda, *God Lived with Them*, 97.

38. Anandaprana, *A Historical Record*, 122–23.

39. Chetanananda, *God Lived with Them*, 201, 203.

40. Anandaprana, *A Historical Record*, 25–26.

41 Quoted Chetanananda, *God Lived with Them*, 371.

42. Chetanananda, *God Lived with Them*, 388.

43. Anandaprana, *A Historical Record*, 74.

44. The source here is Sri Purushottamanda Swamiji, *Autobiography or the Story of Divine Compassion*, Malayalam edn (Tehri Garwhal: Private publication, 1956). English edition, translated Sri J. Padmanbha Iyer (New Delhi: 1994). Unfortunately the copy I was so generously given on my visit to the ashram, Vasithha Guha, in November 1999, is missing pages 149–80.

45. The source here is Paramhansa Yogananda, *Autobiography of a Yogi* (New York: Philosophical Library, 1946). I am referring to the paperback edition (Mumbai: Jaico Publishing House, 1998).

46. Purushottamananda, *Autobiography or the Story of Divine Compassion*, 43.

47. Purushottamananda, *Autobiography or the Story of Divine Compassion*, 211.

48. Purushottamananda, *Autobiography or the Story of Divine Compassion*, 51.

49. Purushottamananda, *Autobiography or the Story of Divine Compassion*, 210.

50. Purushottamananda, *Autobiography or the Story of Divine Compassion*, 56.

51. Purushottamananda, *Autobiography or the Story of Divine Compassion*, 87.

52. Purushottamananda, *Autobiography or the Story of Divine Compassion*, 99.

53. Quoted in Purushottamananda, *Autobiography or the Story of Divine Compassion*, 88.

54. Purushottamananda, *Autobiography or the Story of Divine Compassion*, 65.

55. Purushottamananda, *Autobiography or the Story of Divine Compassion*, 224.

56. Yogananda, *Autobiography of a Yoga*, 230.

57. Yogananda, *Autobiography of a Yoga*, 76.

58. Yogananda, *Autobiography of a Yoga*, 89.

59. Yogananda, *Autobiography of a Yoga*, 1.

60. Yogananda, *Autobiography of a Yoga*, 118.

61. Yogananda, *Autobiography of a Yoga*, 119.

62. See the account on page 141.

63. Yogananda, *Autobiography of a Yoga*, 392.

64. Yogananda, *Autobiography of a Yoga*, 394.

65. Yogananda, *Autobiography of a Yoga*, 407.

66. There are two accounts. Harold W. French, *The Swan's Wide Waters: Ramakrishna and Western Culture* (Port Washington; London: Kennikat Press, 1974) and Carl T. Jackson, *Vedanta for the West: the Ramakrishna Movement in the United States* (Bloomington and Indianapolis: Indiana University Press, 1994).

67. Jackson, *Vedanta for the West*, 36.

68. Quoted French, *The Swan's Wide Waters*, 108.

69. Jackson, *Vedanta for the West*, 61.

70. Jackson, *Vedanta for the West*, 64.

71. Sister Amiya, "Vedanta in Southern California," *Vedanta and the West* 14 (1951).

72. Chetanananda, *God Lived with Them*, 583.

73. Chetanananda, *God Lived with Them*, 612.

74. Jackson, *Vedanta for the West*, 102.

75. Amiya, "Vedanta in Southern California," 146.

76. *Vedanta and the West* Issue 120, 35.

77. See Vedanta in Southern California. Special number *Vedanta and the West* 120, 55.

78. Jackson, *Vedanta for the West*, 98.

79. Anandaprana, *A Historical Record*, 112.

80. Isherwood, *My Guru and his Disciple*, 39.

81. Robert Joseph and James Felton, *Hollywood Swami Script Magazine* (Feb 1948). Quoted French, *The Swan's Wide Waters*, 130.

82. Isherwood, *An Approach to Vedanta* (Hollywood: Vedanta Press, 1963), 26–27.

83. Isherwood, *Diaries*, 24 May 1943, 294.

84. Introduction to Isherwood, *Diaries*, xiv.

85. Isherwood, *My Guru and his Disciple*, 26.

86. Isherwood, *My Guru and his Disciple*, 39.

87. Isherwood, *My Guru and his Disciple*, 42.

88. Isherwood, *An Approach to Vedanta*, 44.

89. See Isherwood, *Diaries*, March 1941, 151.

90. Isherwood, *Diaries*, 28 July 1940, 113.

91. Isherwood, *Diaries*, 30 November 1940, 129.

92. Fryer, *Isherwood: a Biography*, 206.

93. Isherwood, *Diaries*, 23 September 1942, 240.

94. Isherwood, *Diaries*, 23 September 1942, 250.

95. Isherwood, *Diaries*, 30 December 1942, 261–22.

96. Isherwood, *Diaries*, 11 February 1943, 271.

97. Isherwood, *Diaries*, 6 April 1943, 279.

98. Isherwood, *Diaries*, 22 July 1943, 305.

99. See Finney, *Christopher Isherwood: a Critical Biography*, 182.

100. Isherwood, *Diaries*, 6 August 1943, 308.

101. Isherwood, *Diaries*, 26 February 1943, 272.

102. Isherwood, *Diaries*, 16 July 1943, 303.

103. Isherwood, *My Guru and His Disciple*, 111–12.

104. Isherwood, *My Guru and His Disciple*, 128.

105. Isherwood, *Diaries*, 6 April 1943, 280.

106. Isherwood, *Diaries*, 28 February 1944, 335.

107. Isherwood, *Diaries*, 23 June 1944, 352.

108. Isherwood, *Diaries*, 8 July 1944, 353.

109. Finney, *Christopher Isherwood: a Critical Biography*, 184.

110. Isherwood, *Diaries*, 23, 28 August 1951, 439–40.

111. Isherwood, *Diaries*, 21 April 1953, 456.

112. Isherwood, *Diaries*, 27 April 1951, 434.

113. Isherwood, *Diaries*, 2 November 1954, 470.

114. Isherwood, *Diaries*, 21 February 1957, 683.

115. Isherwood, *My Guru and His Disciple*, 216.

116. Tahir Shah, *Sorcerer's Apprentice* (London: Weidenfeld and Nicholson, 1998).

117. Shah, *Sorcerer's Apprentice*, 242.

118. Paul Brunton, *A Search in Secret India* (Ind edition, New Delhi: 1998), 184.

119. Paul Brunton, *A Search in Secret India*, 129.

120. Paul Brunton, *A Search in Secret India*, 153–54.

121. Paul Brunton, *A Search in Secret India*, 141.

122. Paul Brunton, *A Search in Secret India*, 144–45.

123. Paul Brunton, *A Search in Secret India*, 162.

124. Paul Brunton, *A Search in Secret India*, 278, 280.

125. Paul Brunton, *A Search in Secret India*, 305.

126. See in particular Chapter 8, David Godman, ed., *Be As You Are: the Teachings of Sri Ramana Maharshi* (Penguin Books, 1992)

127. S. S. Cohen, *Guru Ramana* (Tirunannamalai: Sri Ramanasraman, 1998), 8, 21.

128. Brunton, *In Search of Secret India*, 292.

129. Cohen, *Guru Ramana*, 7.

130. See Anthony Storr, *Feet of Clay: a Study of Gurus* (London: Harper Collins, 1996), 162–66.

131. Jeffrey Masson, *My Father's Guru* (London; Harper Collins, 1993), 25.

132. Masson, *My Father's Guru*, 64.

133. Masson, *My Father's Guru*, 31.

134. Masson, *My Father's Guru*, 48.

135. Masson, *My Father's Guru*, 160.

136. Masson, *My Father's Guru*, 173.

137. I have relied on Sudhir Kakar's compendium volume, *The Indian Psyche* (Oxford; Oxford University Press, 1996). This contains both his "The Inner World" and "Shamans, Mystics and Doctors. From The Inner World," 128.

138. Kakar, *The Indian Psyche*, 134, 138.

139. Kakar, "Shamans, Mystics and Doctors," *The Indian Psyche*, 146–47.

140. Kakar, "The Inner Childhood," *The Indian Psyche*, 25.

141. A Personal Introduction in Kakar, *The Indian Psyche*, 15, 17.

142. I had two wonderfully full and pleasing conversations with Das Gupta, 8 October, 27 October 1999 in his office in the Ramakrishna Mission Center of Culture, Calcutta. If today physically frail, he remains mentally very strong and capable of tellingly honest and questioning thought.

143. Our visits coincided at the Ramakrishna Mission Center of Culture. We talked formally 20 October and 21 October 1999. Here was a good opportunity to get inside an experience of the Mission that was in several ways quite close to Isherwood's own.

144. He ran Narendrapur and has recently received a Schweitzer prize for his work. This meeting was on 16 October 1999.

145. I met him in the pleasing garden of the ashram, 9 November 1999. My guide, Swastik, had visited the ashram in the hope of meeting a doctor who was attached to it but he was away in London and we met Chidinand instead.

146. A quite tall, well-preserved man, with half-moon spectacles, of a benign appearance, we met at his ashram, 12 November 1999.

147. Our meeting was 11 November 1999.

148. N. Ananthanarayanan, *From Man to Godman. The Inspiring Life-Story of Swami Sivananda* (Erode: Private publication, 1970), 148, 127.

149. Swami Sivananda, *Bliss Divine. A Book of Spiritual Essays on the Lofty Purpose of Human Life and the Means of Its Achievements* (Delhi: The Divine Life Society, 1991), 4th edition, 113, 111.

150. Sivananda, *Bliss Divine*, 173.

151. Ananthanarayanan, *From Man to Godman*, 133.

152. Interview with Swami Chidinanda, Sivananda ashram, Rishikesh, 12 November 1999.

153. Swami Krishnananda, *Self-realization. Its Meaning and Method* (Tehri-Garwhal: The Divine Life Society, 1987), 14–20.

~

CHAPTER SEVEN

Isherwood's Vedantist Quest:
Transcending the Ego

Once embarked upon Isherwood was not to abandon his Vedantist quest whether or not he stayed on in the Hollywood Vedanta center. Isherwood's role as translator and commentator on Vedantist texts and as biographer of Ramakrishna long outlived his stay. If it would be too simplistic to read this quest as a battle between a would-be spirituality and sexuality, clearly Isherwood's sexual needs had proved a major obstacle in his vocation as a monk. Making sense of both Prabhavananda's Vedantism and Isherwood's is to take drastic short-cuts through ancient Indian traditions and centuries of European ideas on the nature of personality but these are inescapable. There are extremely awkward issues of nomenclature, for wholly contrasting intellectual beliefs lay claim to ownership of the concept of the self or self-realization. Carpenter's exegesis, of course, had run into similar problems of nomenclature. If it be to take a massive liberty, it will make for comprehension if it is conceded that where in European thought we might well use the concept of the self we agree to use, instead, the concept of the ego and restrict the use of the concept of the Self to the Vedantist, its word for the Atman and the Brahman.

After a brief account of their joint roles as translators the way into this Vedantist quest is probably best by a discussion of yoga, the ancient means by which the ego attains the atman, and only then to explore the whole problematic of what this might possibly mean. As Isherwood's guru, Prabhavananda's account of Vedantism will be given center stage. Quite why Isherwood felt driven intellectually—we have already explored its psychological dimension—to this quest in the first place and whether he attained in any real degree to non-duality follows. Are there peculiar barriers to this quest in the Vedantist insistence on a sublimated sexuality and did the role of the eternal feminine in Hinduism pose particular problems for Isherwood, especially in the light of his lifetime struggle with his mother? This particular quest will have all the time to be contextualized in the light of a wider debate on all these issues.

Isherwood as Translator

Isherwood was not an indispensable co-translator. Prabhavananda was the sole translator of Vyasa's *Srimad Bhagavatnam* (*The Wisdom of God*), the story of Krishna, published in 1947, and Frederick Manchester acted as co-translator for *The Upanishads*. But they were fellow translators of Vyasa's *Bhagavad gita*, first published in America in August 1944 by Marcel Rodd, a rather dubious publisher of pornography but trying to turn respectable,[1] and in England in 1947 under the title *The Song of God*. There followed Sankara's *Crest Jewel of Discrimination* in 1947 and Patanjali's *Yoga Sutras* in 1953. This had first appeared piecemeal in *Vedanta and the West*.

There could, of course, be no better way forward for Isherwood in his quest than immersing himself in the classical Vedantist literature. Quite clearly Prabhavananda had angled to get Isherwood reclassified for the draft in September 1942 so as to secure his services as translator of The *Gita*. But even prior to joining the Hollywood Center they were hard at work, with Isherwood's almost daily visits to the Center as they struggled to turn the Sanskrit into a more flexible English. But oddly it was Prabhavananda who flinched at literal translations: he had "practically to be psychoanalyzed before he'll admit to the literal translation."[2] Isherwood was all too aware that "translated literally, it would have been a poem written in telegrams." But they were stuck. The breakthrough came in November 1943 when a close friend, Peggy Kiskadden, with Huxley in agreement, saw it as dull and clumsy and reeking of Sanskrit: Isherwood "felt a wave of depression sweep over me"; "Prabhavananda suddenly turned very small and grey and shriveled, a bird on a winter bough."[3] The answer, as Isherwood saw in a flash, was to turn large sections into blank verse, anticipating just the way Tony Harrison was to translate the Iliad. As a practiced scriptwriter it was then easy for Isherwood to make headway, though the effort drove him back to smoking. They became chain smokers together.

Yet even so this could have been a hard decision for Prabhavananda to accept for by adopting a dual style of translation, both poetry and prose, it raised the specter that this was a corrupt text, one with accretions.[4] They went to some lengths to justify this decision in the English edition. This is an epic, they argued, and "the shouting of warriors, the neighing of horses and the outlandish names of chieftains are still sounding in our ears as the dialogue between Krishna and Arjuna begins." It would have been wholly ahistorical, they reasoned, to translate these military scenes in the same prose style as the philosophical discourse. But they conceded: "there is of course no justification for this experiment in the text itself." But, veering in the other direction, they defended the use of Sanskrit terms: "the translator who uses 'reassuring' topical equivalents and twists the meaning of Sanskrit terms, may think he is building a bridge between two systems of thought when actually he is reducing them to nonsense." Clearly there was a compromise between the translators. This is Isherwood speaking: "extremely literal translations of the Gita already exist. We have aimed rather at an interpretation. Here is one of the greatest religious documents of the world; let us not approach it too pedantically, as an archaic text which should be jealously preserved by university professors. It has something to say, urgently, to everyone of us." And this is probably Prabhavananda's balancing act; "nevertheless our work is not a paraphrase. Except in a very few difficult passages, it faithfully follows the original."[5] At least one critic recognized their good intentions: "the translators have presented a version of the great dialogue that does some violence to the original flavor of the poem, but makes it easily understandable to the common reader."[6] One of my conversationalists in Rishiskesh, a new member of Parmath Niketan ashram, Majaji Pratiba, a highly intelligent and, I assumed, an ex-academic person, pronounced it her favorite translation.

This gives a flavor of the translation, Arjuna questioning why we do evil:

Smoke hides fire
Dust hides a mirror
The womb hides the embryo
By lust the Atman is hidden

Maybe the translation of Krishna's revelation of his true self to Arjuna does not quite match Robert Oppenheimer's quotation to evoke the blasting of the Atomic bomb in the New Mexico desert: "suppose a thousand suns should rise together into the sky: such is the glory of the shape of the Infinite God."[7]

In their translation of Sankara's *Crest Jewel of Discrimination* they stressed their going for simplicity with no attempt to imitate Sankara's meter: "Sankara's message is infinitely more important than its literary form." Even so, here is language of real intensity:

I am burning with blaze of the world forest, which no man can extinguish. Evil deeds out of the past drive me like huge winds, hither and thither. I am full of fear. I have taken refuge in you. Save me from death. I have no other shelter.

One wonders how Isherwood would have coped with its language of physical disgust:

The body is a bundle of bones held together by the flesh. It is very dirty and full of filth. The body can never be the same as the self-existent atman, the knower.

But then Isherwood was to evoke just such a sense of physical disgust in his later novels, in particular in *Down There on a Visit*.[8]

In their translation of and commentary on Patanjali's *Yoga Sutras* they were at their most effective. Here they were drawing on direct, practical experience. They had to loosen up Patanjali's highly cryptic, aphoristic style, off-putting, as they rightly believed, to readers. Isherwood incorporates his own urban life-style to lend a contemporaneity to an ancient text. There are references to theatre and film, to a writer's block. Analogies are drawn with working out in a gym. City metaphors permit a greater immediacy, viz:

The truly helpful man is like a public trolley car, available to all who care to use it, but traveling, nevertheless, along a fixed route to its destination

Or again, there is only one lifeforce:

just as in a department store, the same elevator takes you to women's hats, the sports department, the furniture and the restaurant on the roof.

Isherwood is also clearly aware how words are overlaid with cultural associations, the way puritanism, for example, has colored our sense of language:

Discipline for most of us suggests a drill sergeant; mortification, a horrible gangrene; austerity, a cabinet minister telling the public to eat less butter

And some of the satire is quintessential Isherwood:

A community of degenerated yogis, using psychic powers for business and political ends, would be even more unpleasant to live in than our own atom-wielding world

Or again:

So with the mind—that yelling parliament of conflicting interests. It is nothing but a madhouse until it is "called to order."[9]

Here is language that anticipates the best of his novellas *A Single Man*.

This text on yoga is our best way into an exposition of the Vedantic quest.

Yoga

Here is an ancient practice, possibly as old as the most ancient Vedic texts, some 4,000 years old. It features strongly in both the Upanishads and the Gita. Clearly Patanjali, and no one knows who he be—was he a grammarian?—or when he lived—the text is variously dated from the fourth century BC to the fourth century AD—was no innovator, but his text has come down as the best summary statement on yoga from classical Hinduism. Whether its very antiquity has allowed such an enormous amount of commentary to accumulate or some essentialist trait in the Hindu mind, one of the dominant aspects of commentary on yoga is an off-puttingly Ockhamite tendency to endless differentiation. Processes which other cultures might see as relatively close-knit, e.g., thinking, are here endlessly fragmented. It all leads to endless enumeration and catalogues. This may, of course, derive from the needs in a largely oral culture to provide easy means of mnemonics. Yoga is not necessarily a practice that sought the divine; it could just as well meet purely personal and secular needs. Yet it all builds up into a meta-psychology equally as all encompassing and as provocative as the Freudian. Just because psychoanalysis at the time did not recognize the Atman, or supra-consciousness, Prabhavananda and Isherwood chose largely to keep their distance from this rival system. They did not present yoga as a matter of faith: for "true faith is provisional, flexible, undogmatic, open to doubt and reason." The key to its success lay in enthusiasm: "luckily for us energy is like a muscle; it grows stronger through being used."[10] But how exciting an account of it could they manage?

Initially we have to describe its component structure. In the beginning was *prakriti*, "the elemental, undifferentiated stuff of mind and matter," yet this is itself but a projection of Brahman. Their's is something of a cop-out in attempting its definition: "for the human intellect is itself within Prakriti and therefore cannot comprehend its nature."[11] This basic matter is composed of the three *gunas*, *sattwa*, *rajas*, *tamas*, and a great deal of the fascination of the way yoga explains human nature lies in the endless capacity of these three elements for realignments. Isherwood came to use them much as medieval writers did the four humors. *Tamas* was torpor, sloth, despair, all those forces that tied us down; *rajas* was the energy that allowed us to break free, but it could take the form of destructive anger and desire; *sattwas* is our idealism, inspiration, our spiritual side and through yoga we can realize this side of our makeup. Of course, as is often the case with the good, this can often seem a little dull compared to the more lurid aspects of our personalities. And as their commentary emphasizes, the worst sin is indifference; it is better to hate God than to ignore him: "by way of rajas we may find sattwa; by way of hatred we may find love."[12] If this is unexplained, it presumably has some analogies with Dostoyevsky's belief that through sin we discover God.

So what is the ego? A less plausible part of the whole system is the concept of sheaths, encasements of the ego. There is the physical, or gross matter; the subtle, the stuff of the spirit world; the causal, the web of karmas. Just because the first two are in abeyance in dreamless sleep, the third is seen as the real constraint on the emancipation of the ego: "the causal sheath is the ego-sense which makes us see ourselves and the phenomena of the universe as separate entities."[13] All this hinges on our accepting the implications of *karma* or reincarnation. We are battling with liberation not just from the influences of this life but inherited traits from previous lives. Isherwood seems to have had no difficulty in accepting the theory of reincarnation.

Then comes their epistemological account of how the ego is trapped by sense experience and how to escape this imprisonment. All our sense experiences have left a kind of deposit in the mind, *samskaras*. It is not a question of just making the mind blank: if this were really desirable, it could be "much more easily achieved by asking a friend to hit you over the head with a hammer."[14] Initially we have to experience non-painful thoughts, those that do not cut us off from the divine through our ignorance, the better to negate the painful ones, but, in the end, these good ones must also be escaped, as they all constitute disturbances of the mind. We have to offset waves that lead us toward the objective world, the will to desire, with thoughts that lead us to self-knowledge, the will to liberate. This is in no way a form of self-torture: "we are renouncing nothing that we really need or want, we are only freeing ourselves from imaginary needs and desires."[15] And here, if little is made of it but it is a real difficulty with this whole psychology, we have also to escape memory, seen as yet another thought wave.

Then comes an account of how yoga will achieve this transcendence. There is the battle with distractions. This is the challenge of concentration, or, in its more advanced nature, meditation. There is a very Isherwood account of how unfocused our minds usually be:

Consecutive thought about any one problem occupies a very small proportion of our waking lives. More usually, we are in a state of reverie—a mental fog of disconnected sense-impressions, irrelevant memories, nonsensical scraps of sentences from books and newspapers, little darting fears and resentments, physical sensations of discomfort, excitement or ease. [16]

"You never realize how much rubbish has accumulated in the sub-conscious region of your mind, until you make the attempt to concentrate."[17]

This prompts some very prim, Mrs. Grundyish advice, that we should avoid "gossip, 'light' entertainment, ephemeral journalism, popular fiction, radio-romancing. They encourage us to drift into a relaxed reverie, neutral at first but soon colored by anxieties, aversions, so that the mind becomes dark and impure."[18]

All the customary aids to concentration are examined, e.g., the frequent recitation of one's mantra, *japam*—there is no aversion here to ritual—or *prana*, breath control, making clear that this is really energy. They are scathing of *hatha yoga*, branded a degenerate form of yoga, "a cult of physical beauty and prolonged youth."[19]

But the really serious side comes with the account of how the ego can transcend itself and identify with the Atman within. An initial quest is to reach out to Ishwara, and in a sense they mean here what is customarily meant by God, but, in Hindu terms, is defined as "brahma seen within prakriti; Ishwara is all that we can know of the Reality until we pass beyond prakriti."[20] But slowly we can attain to higher forms of consciousness, to *savitarka samadhi*, where we are identified with the object, and to *nivitarka samadhi*, where we are beyond the object, this the highest form of transcendence and indeed we have achieved *moksha* or liberation. Clearly, they recognize the weight of skepticism on the matter, Kant's conviction, for example, that we can never know the thing-in-itself. All they can do here is fall back on the defense that Hinduism is above all an experiential faith: "Religion is in fact a severely practical and empirical kind of research." "Each one has to find it for himself."[21] But there is also a reference to grace that suggests Isherwood had not wholly thrown off his Christian inheritance.

They contrive to dramatize this quest by stressing its dangers, both public and personal. Concentration, whilst still focused on this world, can have disastrous consequences, as the abuse of atomic power by the scientists has revealed. The danger lies, however, "not in fission of the atom, it is in the human mind."[22] Austerities are open to abuse: "the body is not to be brutally beaten and broken," but handled in the same way as a man breaks in a horse.[23] Exercises in breath control have special dangers and can only be undertaken with the guidance of a guru and whilst chaste; "otherwise they may easily lead to mental disturbances of the most dangerous kind."[24] The oxygen jag can lead to insanity. One is reminded of Sudhir Kakar's warning that the Vedantic quest can lead to psychosis.

Alternative Accounts of Yoga

Yoga has, of course, in the twentieth century become an international phenomenon. It was one talisman of the 1960s liberation movements. But the merely physical side to yoga, hatha yoga, was to the forefront. Can we see the Isherwood-Prabhavananda approach in a larger context?

In Krishnananda's *An Introduction to the Philosophy of Yoga* we have a kind of orthodox textbook, though one with western audiences in mind. It begins with semantic questions of a philosophical and psychological nature, rather tiresome in nature, but all to do with the relationship of mind to body and epistemology. His is the theme of transcending space and time. The ego is defined as "the faculty of self-assertiveness or self-affirmation. As a matter of fact it precedes all other functions." He is rather engaging in his recognizing how intolerable we all find one another's egos and the need to be socially isolated if we are to practice meditation. Mrs. Grundy also surfaces. Hindus believe that our thoughts at the time of our death can shape our future chances of reincarnation:

> therefore it is important that people should not spend the last hours of the day in clubs, hotels, cinemas, etc. It is a bad habit, highly distractive, very injurious to psychic health. One should never go out of one's room after sunset, as far as this is practicable.

The last hours of the day should be engaged with "lofty thoughts." Our bodies do not belong to ourselves but to everybody; "literally we are the property of all things." Here is a mortal blow to the ego's complacency. If Krisnananda differentiates his version of yoga from what he sees as Patanjali's introversion—for what is inside, what is outside?—in fact his methods are identical. Yoga and God are one and the same and if undertaken with "ardor" it is bound to succeed. The aim is a loss of a sense of separate identity: "you see yourself in me and I see myself in you."[25] This brings to mind that scary image in Bergmann's film *Persona* when uncannily the two leading female characters become one and are interchangeable.

Gopi Krishna'a *Kundalini—The Secret of Yoga* is an altogether more critical text and one that did much to make yoga more attractive outside India. Here there is an appealing relativism. There are a huge variety of ways in which the mind achieves transcendence. The likes of Wordsworth, Tennyson, Charlotte Bronte, Nietzche all are seen as having achieved it without undergoing the grind of yoga. Patanjali's "unfluctuating unmodified state of consciousness is not for all." Even the state of *nirvakalpi samadhi*—and significantly he denies that the mystic is seeing God, for that would be impossible, there is just "a highly enhanced supersensory form of awareness, in contact with the subtle universe of consciousness that was previously impervious to his inner vision"—is itself subject to cultural conditioning. His is an approach which emphasizes the role of *kundalini*, that extraordinary reserve of psychic energy coiled at the base of the spine, but he tried to explain this in modern or scientific concepts. He did so in terms of a psychosomatic approach, the *kundalini* a kind of metaphor for our central nervous system, the means of spreading *prana* or energy, from the base of the spine through the spinal cord to the brain. He equally stressed the dangers, the *kali* element in *kundalini*: a morbid awakening of *kundalini* can lead to insanity. But he saw immense advantages in drawing on this energy: "the most pressing need of our age is to widen the inner horizons of consciousness." And there have been and can still be accomplished yogis, often men of action, marked by attributes of ecstasy, moral elevation, psychic powers, and genius.[26]

And the attempt to bring spirituality into line with modern science is a strong feature in the present-day study of yoga. This is certainly the aim of Professor Anantharaman in a pleasingly lucid exposition of the scope of yoga. "Further progress," he believes:

> towards a harmonious integration of Science and Spirituality may prove easy if one looks for and documents directly measurable or detectable changes or even scientifically interpretable subjective experiences at the intellectual, mental, vital and physical levels in man caused by transcendental, mystical and supramental processes and phenomena.

He draws particular attention to the work of Gopi Krishna and C. F. von Weizaecker, brother of West Germany's post-war President. He wants to restore the role of the intellect to the quest, though "purified and refined" by the techniques of yoga.[27]

The ashram, Shantikunj, at Hardwar, likewise has as one of its objectives the scientific testing of yoga. Its founder, Shriram Sharma Acharya (1926–1991) in his Autobiography prioritized the spiritual uplift of the Indian people, and the aim of the movement is primarily educational, but when he shifted the center of his operations from Mathura to Hardwar in 1971 he set up the Brahmavarchas Research Institute, to conduct, as he put it, "research on synthesis of science and spirituality." "Research," he continued, "is being conducted specifically in the science of *yagcha*. Its results have been found to be encouraging with regard to its healing impact on physical and mental diseases, on animals and vegetation and in refining environment and atmosphere."[28]

One of my more extraordinary conversations during a visit to Rishikesh and Hardwar was with the Bengali, Doctor Datta, in charge of this scientific laboratory. He has great faith in these machines for measuring the efficacy of singing the *gayatri* and for registering the benefits of meditation. Those who come to the ashram for a three or four week spiritual training are measured before and after to discover its impact on their physical well-being. And no-one would dispute that yoga helps to control stress. There is also serious research into ayurvedic medicine, with substantial greenhouses of plants and chemical laboratories. At the end of our meeting he shouted into one of these machines, in the shape of the human body, laying out all its *chakras*, designed to establish the connection between the volume of one's voice and one's capacity for focus and concentration. Dr. Datta himself had a formidable voice. But even he conceded you could not measure those virtues such as truthfulness and compassion which go to make up a spiritual society.

Arthur Koestler, who made a thorough study of yoga during a visit to India in 1959, was unconvinced by any of these claims. He went with an open mind and met several leading practitioners, including Masson Senior's new guru, Krishna Menon in Trivandrum, as well as visiting centers of research into yoga, "medical, miraculous and mystical." He saw Patanjali's *Sutras* "as a profoundly seductive if somewhat obscure treatise on mystic philosophy of much earlier origin." His attention was drawn just as much to hatha yoga, whose ultimate aim, he saw, as the release of the *kundalini* and the sublimation of the libido, and to the siddhic aspects of yoga: "all disclaimers notwithstanding," he asserted, "the siddhi are an integral part of yoga." India, he averred, had never passed through a scientific revolution and had still not severed itself from the world of magic.

But his commentary on its mystical dimension, on samadhi, was equally damning. He saw this as an act of annihilation of the mind, a homage to the death instinct, to Thanatos: "it is a systematic conditioning of the body to conniving in its own destruction, at the command of the will, by a series of graduated series—from a suspension of vital breath, through the temporary suspension of consciousness, to the ultimate step." And where did this act of annihilation lead?: "Only the Real self is waiting whose attributes are all negative . . . the ultimate void—compressed in the reverberations of the single syllable *Om*." The *kundalini* and Siva the destroyer become one. Clearly Koestler had come up against an account of consciousness which he found utterly alien, one in which the external world has no separate existence and only exists in consciousness: "the result of this stepwise dismantling of reality is that consciousness alone remains, and as the only object of consciousness, consciousness itself—the fullness of the void, the brahma or atma."[29]

Clearly Isherwood, through his own belief in Vedantism, was opening up a gap with his intellectual contemporaries. That he could in consequence make himself a laughing stock was always an anxiety.

Prabhavananda's Vedantism

His guru's experience of Vedantism was the closest version he was to encounter and hence the one most likely to influence his own and has at the outset to be explored.

Intellectual biographies presuppose adaptability and evolution yet the story of devotees of this Indian religious tradition often seem hemmed in by the sheer difficulty of coming to terms with such an ancient and complex tradition: does the very act of comprehension permit any space for personal reinterpretation? It takes the unique personality of a Ramakrishna to break through to new existentialist insights. But even his originality is in danger of being stifled by attempts to bend his highly personalized response to the dictates of the tradition. Prabhavananda was, of course, exposed, by dint of serving in America, to western ideas and his writings quote figures as various as Aristotle, Kant, Schopenhauer, Nietzche, and Freud. One might reasonably expect some adjustment in the way he read the tradition. He attempted two summary statements, one in 1937, *Vedic Religion and Philosophy* and one in 1962, *The Spiritual Heritage of India*. Another text, with an introduction by Isherwood, *Religion in Practice*, published in 1968, is a collection of his ideas over time. There was also, of course, the translations of sacred texts. It is interesting that the 1962 volume contained information on Tantrism and Buddhism absent from the first and points to a widening of interest. But exposure to the west seems, on the whole, to have driven Prabhavananda back into assertions of the unique claims for the truths of Indian philosophy. Maybe, with the example of Vivekananda the patriot, there was something of the cultural patriot lurking in all Ramakrishna monks. But he was always lucid and has many virtues as an expositor. He would have been a helpful teacher. And Isherwood was himself to lay increasing stress on clarity in his own prose style. But did he really address Isherwood's needs?

The 1937 text best indicates the kind of approach Isherwood would have encountered following their meeting in 1939. For a culture so overwhelmed by the sheer scale of its religious literature Prabhavananda takes a common short cut in insisting that experience be the judge of faith rather than abstract reasoning; the truth "must be universally understandable and must be communicable to us in terms of known experience." He defined the central problem of Indian philosophy as "an overpowering sense of the evil of physical existence, combined with a search for the release from pain and sorrow." Here there was to be a glancing aside at Freud, stressing how Indian philosophy goes beyond the limited Freudian focus on the conscious and unconscious to the realm of the superconscious, "which no school of Western psychology has yet taken into account." As part of an existential approach, he freely admitted that the Upanishads put forward no systematic body of ideas but were 'rather revelations and outpourings from inspired souls.' He neatly summarized the two central concepts of Brahman and the Atman as, respectively, the objective and subjective views of the reality behind the world of appearances. He met western dualism part of the way by accepting that *maya* was not complete illusionism and that the world of phenomena possessed some empirical reality. But he made the rather semantic point that the very fact of change necessarily pointed to the changeless or the atman, "the eternal witness, the eternal subject." If the west is subject to the constraints of seeking the infinite through the finite, "with all the limitations of a purely sensational and sense-bound philosophy," Vedantism sees the knowledge of the Self or Atman as the highest purpose of man. He drew most heavily on the *Gita*, seeing here no ideal of a Nietzchean superman, rather an Aristotelian ideal man, "one who is active as well as meditative, who is devotional and at the same time possesses the knowledge of the self."

But Prabhavananda immediately gives the lie to any expectation that this leaves open any kind of romantic individualism, any existentialist assertion of one's own moral agenda. Underpinning the Vedantic quest is a stern moral code: "ethical conduct is the very basis of spiritual life." Fleshly desires had to be given up: "renunciation is indeed the beginning, the middle and the end of the spiritual life." But this implied no fatalism, no passivity, no subservience to *karma*: "you combine a life of intense activity in the world of flux and multiplay whilst seeking the Kingdom of Heaven." It was down to a case of self-exertion. Whatever tolerance Prabhavananda was to show for Isherwood's sexuality, here were uncomfortable recommendations for an explicitly ascetic way of life.[30]

In the updated summary account of 1962 more space is given to the heterodox whilst trying to incorporate them within the orthodox. He saw the teachings of the Tantras as compatible with those of the Upanishads. Here the role of the eternal feminine is introduced; the power of *sakti*, of God the mother, inseparable from the Absolute, from Siva and Brahma, itself "the power of the Absolute." He quoted Sir John Woodroffe: "the concept Mother takes many forms, has many aspects and what is experienced as terror and death and destruction is included in her play. These three, terror, death, and destruction are but the obverse of bliss, life and creation." Of course, all this addressed those fears of castration and, in the case of homosexuals, of misogynism, a strong component in Isherwood's make-up, deriving from his life-long conflict with Kathleen, his mother. Buddhism is likewise rescued from heterodoxy, Prabhavananda insisting that here was no denial of God, Buddha's acceptance of the world as belonging to the non-self wrongly interpreted as a denial of the Self: "if it had any foundation, the whole teaching of nirvana—the idea of Buddhahood—would fall to pieces."

He also here sets out more fully an account of the psychology of yoga. Intriguingly, he tries to demonstrate that Freud's two basic instincts, Eros and Thanatos, translated here as the will to live and the will to death—and quite clearly in America with its cult of psychoanalysis Prabhavananda could not continue to ignore Freud—can be incorporated into yoga psychology; Thanatos is in fact the same as that central element in Patanjali's system, the will to freedom. He states: "it is the principal purpose of Yoga psychology to show us how the will to freedom, the higher will, may be strengthened and the will to live overcome." But as psychologies, the western and the Indian are still markedly differentiated; the west sees mind and consciousness as one and the same, India separates them out. The western has no idea of this *cit*, or the supreme unconditional consciousness.[31]

It is difficult to know in their joint translations where Prabhavananda leaves off and Isherwood begins. A great deal of these concern mysticism and here Prabhavananda was the teacher, Isherwood, the learner. In many ways the translation of Sankara's *Crest Jewel of Discrimination* comes across as a more revealing text of attitudes than those of the *Gita* or of Prabhavananda's solo translation of Vyasa's *Srimad Bhagavatnam*, The Wisdom of God. In the last, in discussing Krishna in human guise, Prabhavananda introduces a greater social dimension into his writing. This leads to a commentary on Krishna's sense of equality: "none is hateful to him; none is dearer to him than others. Neither father, nor mother, nor wife, nor son has he." He exists "as the innermost self in all beings."[32] But however human he becomes, Krishna is in no way subject to *maya*. Prabhavananda tends always to skate over the surface of such awkward questions as caste.

In the interpretation of Sankara there is a sharper definition of concepts. Here Brahman and Atman are defined as the "that" and "thou" of "that are thou." They may seem opposites: "Brahman may refer to God, the rule of Maya and creator of the universe. The Atman may refer to the individual soul, associated with the five coverings which are effects of maya . . . But this apparent opposition is caused by Maya and her effects. It is not real but superimposed."[33] But it is in this text that the greatest horror is expressed of human desire and the demands of the body: "the heavenly fragrance of the Atman is overpowered by the foul odor of countless evil desires, which are like mud within us. The more a man satisfies his cravings in the objective world the more his cravings will increase."[34] One has to suppose that the intensity of these translations drew on Isherwood's experience rather than Prabhavananda's.

Given the Christian background of his American devotees Prabhavananda had to reach out to Jesus but he did so in a way which betrayed less his oecumenicism and more the strength of his Vedantism. His guru, Brahmananda, had experienced a vision of Christ shortly before he joined Belur in December 1914 and this greatly reinforced Prabhavananda' readiness to see Jesus, following Ramakrishna's own vision of Christ, as avatar, an illumined soul, who voluntarily takes human form to restore religion to mankind. But he refused to see any uniqueness in Christ as avatar and denied that he was both wholly human and wholly divine. He reads the beatitudes in Vedantist terms. The pure in heart, for example, are those who are in yoga terms free from distractions. There are overtones of Isherwood's fear of the Test in the admonition not to kill: "when the test comes, if our minds are full of hatred, then hatred will express itself in acts of violence and destruction and murder." The Christian requirement to love our neighbors as ourselves is turned into a Vedantist belief: "when we love god we must love our neighbor as ourself because our neighbor is our very self." The Lord's prayer is subject to a similar process of Vedantist reinterpretation, e.g., "to be in heaven is to realize God in our own consciousness," to forgive us our trespasses is read as removing the debts of karma. One wonders if any of this did anything to persuade Isherwood to relent in his distaste for Christianity.

Yet along the way he has learned to recommend asceticism in positive rather than negative ways. Continence should not be advocated as a "don't: in this way for the great majority of people, who instinctively hate 'don'ts,' the idea of continence has become unattractive and associated with repression, gloom and cowardice; whilst the idea of incontinence becomes more and more attractive and is associated with freedom, fun, and courage. This terrible and destructive misunderstanding, if not corrected will eventually poison the whole national life." He stood for a sexuality sublimated into spirituality: "true self-mastery or inner control is gained only if man make themselves eunuchs 'for the kingdom of heaven's sake.'" There is also a relativism: the way we resist evil is determined by the nature of our moral strength and some are better equipped than others to practice non-violence.[35] This might have allayed Isherwood's concern to defend his sexuality.

But the major thrust of Prabhavananda's Vedantist outlook was mysticism. If he recognized that the *jnana* way was difficult and that instead the *Gita* recommended the *bhakti* way, this was his own preferred route. Religion was "primarily mysticism." He was ready to go on a wide circuit to come back to this central truth:

> If we recognize our brotherhood with our fellow men; if we try to deal honestly, truthfully, charitably with them; if, politically and economically, we work for equal rights, equal justice, and the abolition of barriers of race and class and creed, then we are in fact giving the lie to the ego-idea and moving toward awareness of the universal, non-individual existence.[36]

There has to be a certain restlessness of the mind if you are to find God. But distractions have to be removed and there has to be "a complete house cleaning of the dirt and dust that have accumulated in the mind." "The great psychologist of India,"[37] Patanjali, had showed the way. There are many accounts of his sutras in Prabhavananda's writings. He makes use of one of those very Vedantist metaphors of the inkwell: "we must keep pouring crystal clear pure thoughts of god into our mind, then we can renew the subconscious and unconscious mind and find eternal life."[38] The ultimate aim is *samadhi*, an experience beyond verbal communication, one that can best be communicated through silence.

In one of his last published talks, catching up with the mores of the 1960s, he warned against recourse to drugs to attain this mystical experience. Drugs lead to no permanent change of awareness, reinforce the ego and are dangerous. He was afraid that "at the present moment youth appears to be moving toward chaos by their rebellion." Only through a genuine mystical experience will there be change: "true mysticism is the conviction that God can be seen; that he can be directly known and realized; and that to have this realization is the only purpose of life."[39]

Prabhavananda's Vedantist world-view is shot through with moral ambiguity. At one level there is a certain moral relativism, a distaste for the language of guilt and sin, but underneath is the all powerful Hindu moral code of *dharma*, an ethical code which set exceptionally tough standards of moral behavior. Here was a twentieth-century version of the perennial philosophy, but one still steeped in the moral expectations of a Hindu tradition and in the end making few allowances for western libertarianism. But it held out the dizzying prospect through meditation of a transcendence of the ego and a discovery of identity with God. Could Isherwood meet this challenge?

The Vedantist Problematic Explored

A search for non-duality is clearly an extreme solution to the crisis of identity. It is also a dangerous one, threatening, as it does, psychosis. At one level, in Isherwood's case, it is no more than a further attempt to break through his as yet unresolved adolescent crisis of identity. Together with Gerald Heard and Aldous Huxley he belonged to an inter-war generation coming to terms with the civilizational breakdown of the Great War, breeding a period of moral nihilism, together with feelings of self-loathing and despair. Here was a situation where Vedantism could very well offer a way out. But the old ego ideals of imperialism and of the upper middle class had not gone away and the requirement to match up to those standards—and this is at the heart of Isherwood's endless circling around the idea of the Test—were additional incentives for flight into an alternative persona. In Isherwood's case there was the further intolerable demand of heterosexuality.

Yet it is a very mysterious quest. It is, seemingly any way, much easier to work with a dualist model. Seemingly, for even definitions of the ego/self run up against multiple definitions. As the Buddhist, Urygen Sanghararakshita, summarizing this confusion, puts it: "there is no self, that it is a fiction, a matter of brain processes, a sociological locus, a center of narratives . . . an ineffable category all its own."[40] But what it might actually mean to throw off this ego for a transcendent self or atman is surely to pose an even more elusive problem of definition.

If psychoanalysis offered the latest way into a definition of the ego/self, then this group of would-be mystics were confronted by two highly complex metahistories of the ego/self, a Freudian which encouraged some accommodation with the ego, strengthening it against the destructive forces of the id and the superego, and the Vedantist, which requires a sloughing off of a maya-ensnared ego for the atman or transcendent Self.

So, encircling this strange story of Isherwood's search for the Atman are questions of why, how, and the extent of its success. The "why" requires a greater contextualization; what were the influences on Isherwood's decision by 1939 to explore Vedantism? In particular, a connection has to be made in this religious quest, this *sadhana*, between Isherwood's pacifism and Vedantism. Here it will be enough to look at the influence of Auden and Gerald Heard. The "how" will lead back to Isherwood's wartime struggle and his period as a trainee Ramakrishna monk. The extent of success opens up a discussion of more intimate matters; to what extent was his sexuality the explanation for his limited success? Whatever the playing down of the concept of guilt, asceticism is evidently a major requirement for the Vedantist path.

And, more speculatively, did his often negative relationship with his mother raise barriers in his coming to terms with a mother-dominated Hinduism?

Auden and Isherwood

In December 1925 Isherwood, down from Cambridge, met up again with Auden, in his first year at Oxford, taking up a friendship where it had broken off on their leaving their preparatory school, St. Edmunds. At one level, their's was always to be a prep school friendship. They even fell into a prep school sexual relationship, though possibly Auden's was a genuine love for Isherwood. If Isherwood was the elder, and Auden was to place great faith in his literary judgment, it was Auden who was the stronger influence in the relationship and who, indeed, did much to shape the mental outlook of a whole generation of 1930s intellectuals. It was Auden who had a talent for assimilating new ideas and, as Samuel Hynes puts it, "transforming them into parabolic forms."[41] Hynes also makes the point that this was not so much a generation as a circle of friends, more, in other words, in the Bloomsbury mode. Here was a post neo-pagan generation for whom sexuality remained a problem. It was Auden who discovered Homer Lane and preached the doctrine of healthy living through the expression of instinct, even if he was never himself to be free from a feeling of guilt at his homosexuality.

The dilemma for the 1930s writers was all along the connection to be made between the private and the public. How were they to come to terms with the threats of public events, the clash of ideologies, the menace of war? In fact, Auden never quite escaped the sense that his taking on the mantle of Kipling as a public writer, "that civil tradition of poetry"[42] as Edward Mendelson puts it, was a form of betrayal of those more enduring personal demands. Maybe he was always play acting: "he was not so much *engagé* as anxious to become *engagé*, and he was searching as much for the will to act as for actions to perform."[43] In his 1935 essay *Psychology and Art Today* Auden is seen to be "what he always essentially was: an individualist, inclined more to Christianity than to any other system."[44] Both his grandparents were clergymen, his mother was a High Anglican and had planned to be a protestant missionary. Probably Auden was always destined to become that "avuncular, domestic, conservative, Horatian, High Anglican priest of civilization."[45]

He was friends with Gerald Heard in the early 1930s and it was Heard who led him away from a romantic individualism to a sense of the primacy of the group—though Freud's concept of the primal horde was also a factor—and

Heard's *Social Substance of Religion* almost certainly does much to explain Auden's mystical experience one summer's evening in June 1933 whilst a prep-schoolmaster at Downs School near Malvern. Two matrons and a fellow teacher were sitting out on the lawn after dinner "when, quite suddenly and unexpectedly, something happened. I felt myself invaded by a power which though I consented to it, was irresistible and certainly not mine." He knew that "it would be literally impossible for me deliberately to injure another human being." He knew what it meant "to love one's neighbor as oneself." Here was a vision of Agape, revealing the uniqueness of each individual. It was a mystical feeling that lasted with this intensity for two hours and was to linger on for two days and it was an experience that ultimately shaped his sense of the priority of religious values.[46] It was very close in character to Heard's account of the caritism of primitive Christianity but they were to differ over the primacy of the group or of the individual.

But these feelings were buried or kept quiet till his visit to Spain during the civil war. Auden's response to his very brief visit to Barcelona and Valencia— ostensibly he went out as an ambulance driver—was highly idiosyncratic: he was above all struck by the fact that all the churches were shut. Again, he kept quiet and it was only in an essay in 1955 that he later explained: "I could not escape acknowledging that, however I had consciously ignored and rejected the church for sixteen years, the existence of churches and what went on in them had all the time been very important for me."[47] His verse cycle *In Time of War*, inspired by his visit as a journalist with Isherwood to China in 1938, is seen as a religious response and when he came to write the epitaph of the 1930s in his poem *1939* he did so, in Hynes's analysis,[48] in terms of man's "original sin and of war as a justified punishment."

At the time Isherwood resented Auden's Christian dogmatism, his own "wooly mindedness" tangling with Auden's "wooziness," his grandiloquence, his obscurantism. Isherwood would declare passionately that he did not have a soul. Auden, in China, warned him of his religious conversion to come.[49]

It is impossible not to suppose, given their close companionship during the late 1920s and 1930s, that Auden's rediscovery of his religious beliefs did not have a real influence on Isherwood's own religious outlook.

Heardism

But Auden's faith was his mother's High Anglicanism and he did not share Isherwood's attraction to Vedantism. Here Gerald Heard led the way. Auden had introduced them in 1932. But only from their meeting in Los Angeles in 1939 did he take on a role as guru. The tussle, as we have already seen, was to be between Heard and Prabhavananda as gurus and Isherwood could just as easily have ended up in Trabuco College as the Hollywood Vedanta center. So the question posed is, how convergent were Heard's ideas with Vedantic ideals?

Heardism has rightly been seen as more a "path" than as any systematic philosophy.[50] He wrote prolifically but in an ungainly style, with little concern for lucidity, yet with a desperate attempt at persuasion. A kind of history shaped his theories, one steeped in anthropology, and with a Toynbeesque reference to past cultures. The thrust of his ideas lay in an attack on the ego and on the need to reabsorb the individual within society and to see the way forward—he was an evolutionist but in the mental and psychological fields rather than biological—in an expansion of consciousness. In the writings of contemporary Marxists, above all Gramsci, consciousness was a vogue concept but Heard was anti-Marxist and sought a spiritual progress. Yet the direction was this-worldly. Man, in Heard's views, to quote John Coates paraphrase, had lost "that spontaneous identification of himself with the common good."[51] Here Heard was breaking away from an orthodox transcendent Vedantism, though, alternatively, it was to bring him into line with a more this-worldly Vedantism of Vivekananda and Aurobindo. Rather than trying to do justice to the full scope of Heard's thoughts, here those insights that fed into Isherwood's own concerns will alone be highlighted.

Born 1889, from a clerical background, Cambridge educated, in his time an extra-mural lecturer for Oxford University and a giver of talks on science to the BBC—from 1920 to 1927 he had worked for Horace Plunkett, Irish politician and agrarian reformer—he was to join the ranks of the spiritual gurus of the 1930s. "Said to be the cleverest person in the world," Evelyn Waugh recorded in his diary though found him "personally unattractive."[52] If hard to read, Heard was a gifted speaker and above all a brilliant spiritual counselor. A lapsed Catholic priest, Donald Hayne, who met him at Laguna beach in 1943, described him as "thin and slight, with his pointed beard and his striking memorable eyes, and his seemingly almost anguished intensity about the things that matter most."[53] It was obviously important for Isherwood that he was likewise homosexual. He had formed a long-term partnership with Christopher Woods, ten years his junior, though in time, to be consistent with his neo-Vedantist ideals, Heard turned celibate.

In *The Social Substance of Religion* (1931) Heard set out his critique of individualism and his credo for the recreation of the group. Falling back on anthropology he pictured an earlier group culture, one which was to break down through the pressure of individual self-consciousness, with a matriarchy and the family coming into existence to meet the needs of a consequent intense loneliness. In language resonant of Carpenter's, though he always referred to Carpenter somewhat derogatorily as something of windbag, he wrote of history itself as being driven by man's intensified self-consciousness. Rationalization was a consequence rather than a cause of this individualism and this is a crucial concession by Heard, for he was not opposed to science and was no proto-post-modernist in any rejection of the Enlightenment project.

Heard sets out to describe moments when attempts were made to restore this original group existence. There is a powerful account of what he calls the charistic character of primitive Christianity. The gospel had abolished the individual. "It is," he discerned, "a communism so profound that economic communism beside it is but a symptom. It goes below any equal sharing between each, to the only possible settlement, the fusing in a common love of all separate selves into a common being." But this is not merely "the recovery of the old group sense:" "the individual fissure of consciousness is healed, the subjective and objective minds come together, for the threshold is fused by the common love of the group." He goes on: "a new being is being created, as intensely as the individual has ever been, and as widely aware as the subconscious."[54] But its lifetime proved but brief, a sense was lost of the proper scale of communities, and Agape gave way to the Mass or Eucharist. St. Paul in the end endorsed a salvationist, ascetic, and individualist faith.

Interestingly, Heard did not see India as capable of contributing to any rediscovery of the charistic community. It was locked into an ascetic approach, the fakir rather than the guru its emblematic figure. Medieval mysticism had also failed through its emphasis on individualism, with an all too predictable consequent spiritual aridity, that dark night of the soul. The next real breakthrough came with the Moravians under Count Zinzendorf. Once again, "the individual is being broken down by making the subconscious free to flood across the limen and swamp self-consciousness, while the spirit is to be drawn out through affection into self-forgetfulness."[55] And another breakthrough came with George Fox and the Quakers. "With unerring intuition," Heard claimed, "he felt his way to the essentials of worship—the small group of like minds, the charging meditative silence, together with the absolute freedom to discharge in utterance when the charging was complete."[56] But both movements went astray through their obsessive fears of sex, failing to sense the wider role that the libido played in making these communities work.

So Heard ended with a passionate appeal for the recreation of such groups today, to save mankind from the inherent destructiveness of individualism. He wrote rather elliptically of "a hierarchy of wholes, a real feudal system of intense loyalties,"[57] and on the need for compassion.

Together with Aldous Huxley—he had taken over from D. H. Lawrence as Huxley's intellectual sparring partner—Heard was an early supporter of Dick Sheppard's Peace Movement. Launched at an Albert Hall rally in July 1935 it crystallized as the Peace Pledge Union 22 May 1936. Hitler's remilitarization of the Rhineland in March had acted as the spur. Heard and Huxley were both sponsors and were in due course appointed Chairman and Vice-Chairman of its Research and Thinking Committee. Heard had given a lunch-time talk on the new pacifism 26 November 1935. He and Huxley had come under the influence of an American pacifist and admirer of Gandhi, Richard Gregg, whose pamphlet *The Power of Non-Violence* introduced Gandhian ideas on the need for cadres of an ashram trained, nonviolent, elite. Heard was immediately enthused by such thoughts of "intensive training." "One trained man," he wrote to Sheppard, "is worth 100 untrained."[58]

But all this was but grist to Heard's mill of specialized spiritual groups. If war was a product of a "diseased individualized civilization," the answer lay in pacifists joining such groups: "what is clear beyond a doubt is that in the 'field' of a small like-minded group trained in meditation are the powers essential to curing conflict in the self, in society and between humanity."[59] Sheppard was rather relieved when both Huxley and Heard departed for America 7 April 1937, taking these rather faddish Greggist ideas with them. From there, Heard informed him, he could do little until he had himself become more spiritually enlightened; "I feel increasingly sure that the spirit is calling one to a life of very much more thorough devotion."[60] If here a link is already established between Heard's ideas and through his rapport with Gandhi with India, it is still going to need his encounter with Prabhavananda to draw him into Vedantist Hinduism.

Once settled in America Heard, whilst continuing to explore the theme of a superconsciouness, became increasingly obsessed about how to organize these utopian communities. He had both to show from whence the extra consciousness could come from and how it could then be harnessed for the salvation of the world. In particular, he had to work out a training schedule for the new spiritual elite, the seers or neo-Brahmins, as he came to name them, the visionaries who could forecast the future. Throughout, Heard never doubted that world leaders would see the advantages of consulting this new elite. He was not put off by Forster's skepticism. The whole language in which these ideas were presented took on an increasingly Hindu tinge, with yoga now seen as the key technique for realizing these spiritual powers.

In his most striking work, *Pain, Sex and Time* Heard argued that the evidence for the surplus psychic energy for a heightened consciousness lay in man's capacity to endure pain and to sublimate sex. If man was to transcend his ego and to master this new mystical outlook he had also to move into a new sense of time. But this posed the question of means and quite specifically yoga was selected, though he also referred to Radakrishnan's integral approach. This was his first reference to the powers of the *kundalini*. He rambled on in one of those long historical circuits to make his point, discerning early approximations to yoga in the old testament, interpreting Elisha as the yogin as opposed to Elijah, the fakir; then the Essenes, indebted he believed to the laws of Manu and with evidence of "a fairly complete extension into the Levant of Brahminic teaching and techniques;"[61] the mystery religions of the Greeks, with the mediumships of the Delphic oracle; the medieval text *The Cloud of Unknowing*. But after the Renaissance, with the rise of individualism and of analysis, he felt that, "the spontaneous Yogic effort declines and maybe vanishes."[62] But there was an exception: "yoga and Quakerism must be blended in an original synthesis."[63]

India's contribution is further emphasized, drawing attention to shakti yoga and the tantric means of harnessing the power of coitus reservatus. He looked to the example of Sankara and believed, had he been living today, he would have seen in man's psycho-physical make-up hope for spiritual advance. He now referred to *samadhi*, that "intent alert passivity and vigilant openness."[64] In Buddha's eight-fold path Heard saw a set of rules for the new monastic communities. Clearly he passionately believed that in this neo-monastic movement lay the answer to the crisis of a new Dark Age, to the "strangulated consciousness"[65] of the ego.

With plans for Trabuco College, set up in 1941, there had to be clear guidelines for these new communities. Heard was by now deep into the perennial philosophy and using precise Vedantist language; the spirituality sought was to be "the conscious realization of union with *That* from which it has sprung."[66] The old Benedictine vows of poverty, chastity, and obedience were to be updated to anonymity, frugality, and dedication of the mind-body. Mortification of the flesh was to give way to "psychophysical athleticism."[67] But this was still advocacy of sexual sublimation. Significantly, a second pamphlet came back to the problematic of sex: "if it is not mastered then the life of virtue is impossible." Rather unconvincingly, tenderness was held out as an answer to lust.[68]

All this was to be an experiment in intentional living. There was a positively Gandhian emphasis on the need for a regulated diet. These communities would be in an economic sense largely self-supporting, though the real burden would be born by their psychological and spiritual reserves; the economic and social self-sufficiency would follow. The role of the guru was stressed. The problematic lay in the fate of the ego. It could not be transcended by the will. The ego had to be developed rather than annihilated. But this left open the persistent Vedantist question, would there be continuity or hiatus with the past? Heard wrote: "for what it aims at doing is no more or less than to expose the ego-deformed consciousness to the light of the complete consciousness, the eternal Life to whom it belongs." "Our dwarfed spirit mutates." "If you stay in God's presence you will become, you must become Godlike."[69]

So how would a society be formed to sustain this spiritual elite and, indeed, where were the seers to come from? Heard begins to move between an account of these intimate communities as never more than a dozen or so in membership, and some larger community. Rather disturbingly, he rejects what he calls atomistic democracy, based on misguided, as he believed, concepts of social equality, in favor of an organic democracy. Here he recruited Indian caste categories. India itself had become stultified through caste and though it had produced philosopher-saints "had remained socially squalid."[70] But Heard still conceived of a society with caste rankings. Neo-sudras would make up its routine workers, neo-Vaishas its technicians, neo-Kshatriyas its administrative cadres and neo-Brahmins the spiritual elite. The neo-Brahmin could not afford to take on social work or administration; it would cut him off from access to the ultimate good. Indeed, the neo-Brahmins were at risk both from an inflated sense of individualism, the very disease they were there to transcend, and the risk of despair, surrendering to a sense of the world as *maya*. Their's had to be an extensive training; Heard drew a parallel with that of the musician.

He now came up with an extraordinary proposition. He was drawing heavily on Jungian ideas of maturation, of adults in their forties entering on a second adolescence, persons seeking a new spiritual vision. And where might these people be found? Heard suggested they could come from the 4.5 percent of America's population in mental hospitals. "Our mentally broken population" were in fact "our greatest asset": "in our asylums are lying the raw stuff of a new and real service."[71] He reasserted the need for the two sides of the mind to be united, the self-conscious and the subconscious, giving rise to "new integral, comprehensive consciousness."[72] Without acknowledgement, much of this had overtones of Aurobindo's supramental consciousness. Heard's text looks back to Huxley's *Brave New World* and forward to Hermann Hesse's *The Glass Bead Game*. Would it work?

There is a hint of defeatism. May be "there is no other way of carrying on, any constructive power" and mankind will continue to resort to violence, to his "uncoordinated specialization." But his final note was optimistic: "there is then an even chance that the neo-Brahmin might be called upon and might succeed."[73]

All this was heady stuff and will have worked its way into Isherwood's guilt complex over his homosexuality, his pacifism, his Quakerism and ultimately his Vedantism. Maybe Isherwood saw himself as entering a second adolescence, though, arguably, he had yet to outgrow his first. Even so, it was to be Prabhavananda's path he chose. Maybe Heard threatened to smother too much his own independent train of thought.

Pacifism

Isherwood, ever the chameleon, on his arrival in America was to undertake a yet further redefinition of himself. Jonathan Fryer puts it this way; "he had turned against his dominant ego, was sickened by his own ambition, by Christopher Isherwood the public manifestation."[74] But the Isherwood who faced the challenge of non-duality retained a very strong sense of his own identity. For all his guilt at his sexuality and the moral confusion he was in by 1939 he never lost a sense of his own worth, a natural arrogance that may have stemmed from a mutual love between father and son. But it makes all the more problematic any understanding of his attempt to transcend this ego. Does a person who has a strong capacity to look at himself from outside, to write of "Christopher," the observer, in the third person, have a greater or lesser chance of seeking out the atman within? It certainly requires both a very strong motivation to seek a change of persona and, if this is not contradictory, a degree of self-loathing. Is the prognosis for non-duality indeed the stronger with self-love or self-hatred? The way into this interpretation lies in the means Isherwood himself adopted. Can he meet this new version of the Test? The first question to be raised is, what is the inner connection between his newly discovered pacifism in 1939 and the Vedantist quest?

Isherwood was haunted by the question, would he have met the frightening demand of being a soldier in the Great War? In the novel *The Memorial* he suggested that he fantasized about the possibility of volunteering underage. This overbearing legacy of the war was hugely inflated by his father's death at Ypres in May 1915 and the consequent burden of having to live with the memory of his father as a war hero. Isherwood had an ingenious solution to this burden of the father figure. He split it into the cultist one of his mother's and of "the others" who pedestalized his father as war hero, the one he violently rejected, and his own recollection of his father as someone who saw through the flummeries of the military life and took war lightly.

Yet the legacy of the father could not be so easily resolved. Isherwood loved his father but had to live with the knowledge that his father had, indeed, displayed exceptional courage and was a war hero. There was no embarrassment about that love. For all his latent homosexuality, he had not fantasized about his father as a sexual partner; the sight of his father exercising naked, however erotic, had not excited any sexual fantasies.[75] Yet whatever the sang-froid his father had displayed under fire—and he fought both in the Boer War and the Great War—here was an awesome example of physical courage.

Significantly, the young Isherwood had seen some of the letters that at the time his father has dispatched from the front to his wife. In a letter of 9 April 1915 he had initially written of the decision to send Christopher to a preparatory school as a boarder in terms of flattening him out, of making him like other boys, but then doubted the decision: "when all is said and done, I don't know that it is at all desirable or necessary, and I for one would much rather have him as he is."[76] Isherwood was too honest to suppose his father, had he lived, would easily have been reconciled to his homosexuality, pacifism and Vedantism, but here was an affirmation of himself that must have signally contributed to his sense of self-esteem. In the test Isherwood invented, between defining oneself as the Truly Weak Man, the neurotic who would out of fear go to elaborate lengths to prove himself, the route as he described it of the North West Passage, and the Truly Strong Man, a person of real courage, who unfussily just got on with the matter, his father became a key example of the latter.

If war was the ultimate test the challenge could be endlessly transposed. In many ways he continually failed the test. He failed Oxbridge by failing in the Cambridge tripos examination. He failed the test of the General Strike, tamely, in the end, becoming a volunteer in a sewerage farm. The various personae he adopted, Isherwood the artist, Isherwood the socially concerned Marxist, were all flights from confronting the real test of courage. He admitted:

> I knew what was inside it now—just plain, cold, uninteresting funk. Funk of getting too deeply involved with other people, sex-funk, funk of the future. I was eternally worrying about what was going to happen to me—in 1930, in 1940, in 1950; eternally building up defenses against attacks which were never launched.[77]

At some level his homosexuality must also have been experienced as a failure of the test of manhood.

Throughout the 1930s it is hard to see Isherwood, for all his flirtation with the radical causes of the decade, as politically committed. The demands of the private ego/self always prevailed over the public. His talent was as an observer at best, as a documentarist rather than as an activist. If a brilliant portraitist of a city in moral decline, of Berlin on the eve of the rise of Nazism, he failed to fight in Spain. It was to be his visit to China in 1938, together with Auden, as a war correspondent that forced him to face himself.

Isherwood then belatedly faced the test of war. At the outset he found his entry into a war-zone "dreamlike, unreal"; he felt "an irresponsible, schoolboyish feeling of excitement." For Auden and Isherwood their trip had the feel of a schoolboy prank. As they set off from Hankow they saw themselves as "a couple of characters in one of Jules Verne's stories about lunatic English explorers." Auden had already, if very briefly, experienced war at first hand in Spain. But for Isherwood this was new and he admitted; "I don't know if I was frightened. Something inside me was flapping about like a fish." Whilst Isherwood slept fitfully, Auden slept deeply "with the long calm snores of the truly strong." From Hankow they journeyed by train to Chang-Chow and onto Suchow, the Japanese but thirty miles away. By rickshaw and horse they got to the front line. After returning to Hanchow they set off for the south east front, only to be stranded for a while in the hotel, Journey's End, in Kiukiang: "why not stay? why bother about the Fourth army? It could take care of itself. What was this journey? It was an illusion." But they persevered to Nanchang and Kin-wha, reaching the front on foot, Isherwood with sorely blistered feet, only to find the Fourth army in strategic retreat from Meiki. Eventually by boat they reached Japanese-occupied Shanghai. They came away with a sense of helplessness at Chinese poverty: "oh dear, things are so awful here—so complicated. One doesn't know where to start." But about war they were clear: "war is bombing an already disused arsenal, missing it and killing a few old women. War is lying in a stable with a gangrenous leg . . . War is untidy, inefficient, obscure and largely a matter of chance."[78] But Isherwood had survived the test. He could now look on war in a different way. He could in all conscience become a pacifist.

Isherwood suggested his conversion to pacifism came on the trans-Atlantic crossing in 1939 but he recognized it was a position long in the making. Maybe his failure to become fully involved in the political struggles of the 1930s lay rooted in a recognition that the anti-fascist movement ineluctably led to war. The journey to China had not only "reduced my neurotic fear of war in the abstract"; it had brought him back "from a world of political principles to a world of human values which I had temporarily lost."[79] Can we fit Isherwood into any typology of pacifism?

If we accept Martin Ceadel's distinction between pacifism and pacificism, the former a religious belief, the latter a readiness to accommodate to actual circumstance and to seek a solution to conflict by any strategy short of war, then Isherwood falls clearly into the first. He showed no interest in the pacificist support for the League of Nations, for disarmament, for sanctions, for internationalism generally. But nor did he come at it from any religious standpoint. So we have to ask another question: Could becoming a pacifist in fact lead to religion?

One of the new strands in pacifism in the interwar period was a humanitarian one and in some of its expressions, above all the writings of Huxley and Heard, this could indeed lead into a religious outlook. The character Anthony Beavis in *Eyeless in Gaza* makes a connection between peace and the perennial philosophy:

> in peace there is unity . . . Dark peace, immeasurably deep . . . Peace through liberation, for peace is achieved freedom. Freedom and at the same time truth. The truth of unity actually experienced.[80]

Huxley had been drawn to the ideal of non-attachment in Buddhist, Confucian, and Hindu philosophy.

In some ways Isherwood's own pacifism echoed the "facetiousness" of the Bloomsbury intellectuals in the Great War. Lytton Strachey famously replied to the Tribunal when he was asked what he would do were a German soldier to attack his sister: "I should try and come between them."[81] For Isherwood it would be absolutely impossible to fight the Germans for to do so might lead to his having to kill his German lover, Heinz. But then for Isherwood, if there was one cause for which he was ready to go to the stake, as he would say, it was his queerness.

Interestingly, as all attempts to stave off war failed and the pacificists were forced to recognize they were not pacifists after all, a new kind of pacifist appeared, more libertarian, more cussedly minority-minded, often Bohemian in outlook: "its inspiration," Ceardel claims, "was a conception not of morally correct behavior, but of individual liberation from unjust restraints."[82] Often individuals were drawn to pacifism through personal problems, emotional, sexual. Isherwood as pacifist readily falls into this category.

In America all Isherwood's defenses were down. He had lost his moral bearings. He was "paralyzed by apprehension," "desperately needed anonymity."[83] In this mood he renewed his acquaintance with Heard in Los Angeles. They had first met through Auden in 1932. It was Heard's pacifism that he wanted to discuss: he reported to John Lehmann that he might "flatly disagree" with the views of Huxley and Heard "but I have to hear their case, stated as expertly as possible."[84] It was therefore to be by an indirect route that Isherwood alighted on yoga and meditation.

But Ceardel also establishes that pacifists were drawn at the time into forming specialized communities as a way of spreading the ideal of pacifism. In gravitating into Heard's experiments in intentional living Isherwood was once again following a pattern. And in taking up social work with the Quakers—he worked in a Quaker refugee center for Germans, mainly Jews, in Haverford, Pennsylvania from October 1941 to July 1942—Isherwood did likewise; as Ceardel puts it: "for most pacifists social service was a means of atoning for being a tolerated sect without a political solution to offer."[85] Interestingly, the Quakers are seen as inherently pacificist, ready to work as far as possible within the system, and this suggests Isherwood himself was not an out and out pacifist rebel. He had, nevertheless, to go through all the procedures as a conscientious objector. He volunteered to undertake public service in a forestry-camp. But by the time his age had excused him from military service, Isherwood was deeply embroiled in another kind of test altogether.

The fit between his pacifism and his Vedantism was in fact tenuous. It depended on a reading of the *Bhagavad gita*. It is far from clear that the admonition by Krishna to the warrior, Arjuna, to accept his caste *dharma* and be ready to fight his relatives to the death is any kind of a critique of war and a defense of non-violence. Isherwood saw the dilemma: "if its teachings do not seem to agree with those of other gospels and scriptures, then my own system of values would be thrown into confusion, and I should feel completely bewildered." Somehow the text had to be made to endorse his pacifism. But all he could come up with was the hope that with the world as *maya* all killing is illusory anyway and an argument on the sacramentalism of all decisions and action: "the pacifist must respect Arjuna. Arjuna must respect the pacifist." He accepted that "the *Gita* neither sanctioned war nor condemned it. Regarding no action as of absolute value, either for good or evil, it cannot possibly adopt either position."[86] This was surely cold comfort.

Beyond Christopher

In many ways Isherwood had reached a crisis in just the ways Jung discerned. Not quite turned forty he was morally at sea. Jung saw this as a crisis of a second adolescence, with the way forward via a maturation process, acquiring a new sense of spiritual purpose. But whereas Jung saw this in terms of a renewal of the ego, Isherwood was taking up a Vedantist endeavor in which the ego, on the contrary, had to be transcended and there would have to be a search for the Atman or the true Self within. The Atman within was one and the same as the Brahman without: this was the ultimate reality. The Atman could be characterized as "God immanent," the Brahman as "God transcendent," though Isherwood feared such definitions had the feel of a dry Victorian theology.[87] And he was ready to take on the whole Vedantist vision. He accepted the concept of *karma*: "the ego-sense which is the basis of individuality will continue to work its way upward, through inanimate matter, through plant life, through the lower animals, into human form and consciousness." This both explained social inequality and induced a sense of mutual responsibility.[88]

But for someone always obsessed by questions of identity, the real issue was, what should replace the person called Christopher Isherwood? How could one cease to be oneself? As he put it, and in a long quotation:

> For the Vedantist that personality is an illusion.
>
> Christopher Isherwood is only an appearance, a part of an apparent universe. He is a constellation of desires and impulses. He reflects his environment. He repeats what he has been taught. He mimics the social behavior of his community. He copies gestures like a monkey and intonations like a parrot. He is changing all the time. He has no essential reality.

We are simply products of our egotism:

> an egotism which is asserted and reinforced by hundreds of your daily actions. Every time you desire or fear or hate; every time you boast or indulge your vanity; every time you struggle to get something for yourself you are really asserting 'I'm a separate unique individual. I stand apart from everything else in the universe.'

But this is mistaken. According to Vedantism we are all interrelated through our common sharing in the Atman. If you love Christopher Isherwood "then you ought to love your real self much more. The atman is perfect."[89]

This was not to be self-centered; you will become far more community-minded. This is not to blaspheme and say Christopher Isherwood is God. These are the standard jibes against Vedantism. This pursuit of non-duality was to be by far the greatest test Isherwood had to undertake. How did he go about it?

There were two gurus giving him direction, Gerald Heard and Swami Prabhavananda, and both proposed a praxis of meditation and yoga. If convergent on means, and here Heard had learned from Prabhavananda, their ultimate purposes were apart, Heard looking for some spiritual solution to the problem of war and social breakdown, Prabhavananda a mystical encounter with Brahman. It makes sense to try and track their separate influence on Isherwood.

Heard soon wore down Isherwood's scorn for yoga and Vedantism. Initially he undertook but short "sits," ten to fifteen minutes twice a day and found this "sort of flirtation with the unconscious"[90] very exciting. Heard won him over to a more serious way of looking at life: "awareness of our real nature and our actual situation." "Here was a sort of mystical algebra in terms of which every type of religious experience, from that of St. Francis to that of Charles Kingsley could be tersely and adequately expressed."[91] And even if in the lotus position he heard his ego say, "look at me . . . aren't I extraordinary," he felt these periods of meditation "produced some kind of beneficial effect on my behavior."[92] "The ego shivers. It smells the wind of its destruction."[93] But it was a struggle: "part of me wants to wallow in black lazy misery, like a pig in filth."[94]

Heard was a remarkable spiritual counselor. He chaired a four-week experiment in community living at La Verne, a Quaker venue east of Los Angeles, between the San Gabriel mountain and the sea. He kept this group of eighteen men and women together. "When at the general request he himself spoke on some metaphysical or historical theme, his listeners had an experience which none of us will easily forget." Half stayed on for an extra week, stepping up the hours of meditation to four a day.[95] Heard himself routinely managed six. He drew a distinction between meditation, struggling to bring the mind into focus, and contemplation, an effortless process when time stood still. "For the first time," Isherwood recorded, "I understood the basic appeal of a monastery."[96] To a degree Isherwood shared Heard's faith that a spiritual community could by meditation actually influence the course of events and this was the best way forward for pacifism: "you can't make propaganda for the spiritual values. You can only demonstrate them by *being*."[97]

Yet he was not to follow Heard to Trabuco College but to enter the Vedanta center and clearly, in the end, a search for a new identity prevailed over his pacifist convictions. Even so, he must at some level have shared Heard's belief in the Vedantist quest as contributing to peace.

When they first met Prabhavananda laid down a number of non-dualist ground rules. Firstly, imagine an all pervading Existence all around one; secondly, transmit thoughts of peace and good will in all directions; thirdly, "think of your own body as a temple which contains all knowledge;" fourthly, accept "that the reality in yourself is the reality within all other beings."[98] Isherwood was encountering a person for whom "spiritual truths are unanswerable, like the facts of geography. You don't get excited about them, or argue, or defend. You just state them."[99] Prabhavananda scorned Isherwood's attraction to *hatha* yoga: "what is the matter with you, Mr. Isherwood, surely you don't want eternal youth?"[100] Isherwood was always to be drawn to *jnana* yoga over *bhakti* and Prabhavananda had to win him over to the need for ritual worship in the temple. He was to do his stint of chanting Jaya Sri Ramakrishna an hour at a time. The shrine room took on a new character during the chanting: "the atmosphere seems to be tremendously charged with energy and excitement."[101] Early on in his stay Isherwood recognized, "I've got to convince myself practically that the shrine can give me strength to do what I could never do alone."[102] "Sometimes it's as if the whole shrine room becomes your brain and is filled with thought."[103] Reflecting on prayer, Isherwood came to see: "instead of thinking of my life as journey and myself as a traveler, I should think of the real self, the Atman, as essentially static, perpetually contemplative within the shrine, always in the presence of God."[104] Isherwood got into the habit of *japam*, the recitation of his mantra, with the aid of his rosary, five to ten thousand times a day. He contemplated on the word OM. Three hours per day of meditation was a Center rule. But the reading—Vivekananda, Aurobindo, Jan van Ruysbroeck—and the translating—the Gita—was also crucial.

In this ultimately indefinable process of attaining non-duality, did Isherwood make any headway? Isherwood fell back on the argument that the mystical cannot be put into words: "there is only one way to find put what samadhi is like: you must have it yourself."[105] Experience was all. Was there early on a glimpse of the Atman when he uncannily recalled himself sitting in a park with Gerald Hamilton, one of his dubious Berlin cronies, back in 1936 in Amsterdam, the observing and observed selves wholly separate, catching "the faintest glimpse of something else—that part of my consciousness which has not changed, which will never change, because it is a part of reality?"[106] On another occasion, looking at some fish, he became aware of their utter uniqueness: "I seemed to open a crack of consciousness within myself."[107] He had a vision of his own face, "very distinguished, rather like a Red Indian;"[108] according to Prabhavananda, a vision of his own subtle body. Isherwood believed that he was making progress: "despite all my failures, I'm surprised what a long way I've come already. There is no longer any question now that this 'thing' works as far as I am concerned."[109]

But the real battle was with the Ego: "goodness this thing is difficult. The ego like a lazy collaborator steps in when it's time to claim credit."[110] "The death of the ego," he commiserated with himself, "was never supposed to be pleasant; and this misery may really mean that we are getting ahead."[111] "How can the ego improve? It can't. It can only wear thin, and let more of the light in."[112] But Isherwood was locked into a losing struggle with his sexuality. On the one hand, he recognized, "I've simply got to strike my own roots. After all, what's the alternative," but, on the other, there was his unreasoning body, "it wants to get out and break all the rules. For a weekend, for a single night it would trade eternity—until next morning, when a hangover transforms it into the nastiest little puritan of them all."[113]

Looking back at it all in the aftermath of leaving the Center he still recognized the value of the endeavor: "prayer, meditation, thought, creation are the *only* refuge and stronghold. Without them I am nothing."[114] "I can't find any answer to the proposition that man's aim here is to know the Atman."[115] But he had ceased to practice meditation. His alienation from God, his sense that he had betrayed the opportunity the Center had offered him, left him with a profound sense of guilt. What had gone wrong?

In the Way of the Atman

Is there any kind of temperament that is more compatible with the quest for non-duality? Were there parts of Isherwood's personality which handicapped him in his quest? Clearly all sexual demands could be a barrier to spiritual achievement—although the Tantric path suggests otherwise—and it would be absurd to suggest that in his homosexuality lay some essentialist reason for his failure. But the way to spiritual insight must lie in a particular kind of openness and all internal conflict, all hostility, would act as a barrier. There are two possible explanations in Isherwood's case. One lies in his adversarial attitude to his homosexuality. The other was a lifetime conflict with his mother. The latter would have brought him up against the feminine side of Hinduism, with the cult of the Mother in the forefront of the Ramakrishna mission. Learning to love the feminine, coming to terms with the incest taboo, may lie at the heart of non-duality.

Isherwood addressed his homosexuality in terms of acceptance rather than analysis. He seems curiously uninterested in questions of etiology. Even though arguably his be a reverse Oedipus complex, with a love of the father and hatred of the mother, he was indifferent to Freudian explanation. Indeed, in their biography he writes about his parents with a curious detachment. His only speculation here was to wonder, had his parents allowed him to stay in coeducational schools, might not his heterosexual side have dominated? And he did enjoy at least one heterosexual experience though felt it was not for him: girls he felt lacked romance. In fact Isherwood experienced, as Katherine Bucknell puts it, "a passionate uneasiness about mature female sexuality."[116] He was always rather disgusted by his bisexual friends who married. It was to desert the cause. And, typically, he rejoiced that he had become homosexual: "despite the humiliations of living under a heterosexual dictatorship and the fury he has often felt about it, Christopher has never regretted being as he is."[117] He gives the impression that he had chosen to become a homosexual as an act of will, his way of snubbing the establishment.

But there was to be a prolonged struggle with guilt. Auden's introducing him to the ideas of Homer Lane, that all illness derives from blocking the expression of one's natural instincts, proved a moment of liberation. They spoke of the need to be "pure in heart."[118] He also took up D. H. Lawrence's *Fantasia of the Unconscious*, another polemic on being true to one's instincts. This took Isherwood to Berlin and to its more libertarian climate. He wrote little about the repressive character of English society. But even in Germany Paragraph 175 of the Criminal Code legislated against homosexual acts and if a debate was imminent in 1929 in the Reichstag on its abolition it was not to be and homosexuals remained on sufferance, fatally so once the Nazis came to power. Isherwood, somewhat reluctantly, came to recognize that Magnus Hirschfeld's reform campaign was his own though he was not, at that stage, wholly prepared to identify himself with gay causes and with the homosexual "tribe." He was anxious to let it be known that his haunts were not the "decadent" bars of smart Berlin but working class clubs with "normal" boys.

If Isherwood was later to show a readiness for casual sex with older men, indeed with the one-legged and the deaf and mute, his preference was for younger men, from sixteen or seventeen to early twenties. These were his lovers. He had an obsession with blondes. He saw his sexual experiences in both Germany and America as a way of coming to possess these two countries. One of his American lovers was for him Walt Whitman's all-American country boy. As he matured, the need for those from a different class seemed to wane. In much the same way as English middle class gays are drawn to regional accents, Isherwood felt that the German language was "irradiated with sex."[119] His was the experience of all those who live abroad, that the constraints of life in Britain were lifted and that as a foreigner in Germany he was at last liberated. Hirschfeld felt that his cult of the working class sprang from a kind of infantilism, but Isherwood turned this round into saying he was "boyish" and hence masculine, rather than being queeny or "nicely-nice third sexism."[120] He enjoyed wrestling with his young working class lovers.

If promiscuous, Isherwood was driven by a hatred of loneliness and always sought a more lasting partnership. In time he found this in Heinz, and in their long-term relationship throughout the 1930s they lived together as all but "the most ordinary married heterosexual couple."[121] From an early stage

Isherwood betrayed his aspirations to become a householder. But he wore a mask and in those days he had no other choice. In *The Memorial* the leading homosexual character, Edward Blake, masquerades as a heterosexual, if with a sympathetic female partner, attempts suicide in Berlin, and if, by the end, he is living with a boyfriend in Paris, he deserts him. Isherwood seemed unable to make a case for a gay life style and studiously refused to identify the Christopher of his writings as gay. But his position was always embattled and his reasons for breaking with the left in the 1930s was its failure to defend homosexuality, most notoriously in Stalin's reversal of the initial, liberal legislation of the Revolution.

It makes more sense to see the whole period in America till he settled down into a householder relationship with Don Bachardy as a continuum, as an attempt finally to come to terms with his homosexuality and to overcome his guilt. Until he did so, he could not pursue the Vedantist way. Equally important, he could not be honest as a writer. Bucknell sees "a kind of apartheid in his work between the writer and the man, and it was stopping all progress."[122] As he faced the possibility of a monastic life he thought he could cheerfully give up sex "if it could be managed without too much difficulty."[123] He had to take a conditional vow of celibacy for three years; after ten years it would be lifelong. But it was not to be; as early as 24 August 1943 "quite unexpectedly, irrelevantly and insanely" there was a sexual adventure.[124] Isherwood felt ill at ease in the Center: "I hate the present set-up, because my chief motive for abstaining from sex is merely guilt; and this is hypocritical, even when my conscience is clear."[125] Prabhavananda went to considerable lengths to accommodate Isherwood's needs, encouraging Vernon, the first of his American boyfriends, to join the community. He always angrily rejected the idea that it was his love for Bill Caskey, his first serious attempt to recreate another Heinz-like relationship, though this time with an older and middle-class person, that explained his leaving the Center; the decision had been taken before meeting him.[126] This was a widely recognized relationship amongst his friends and Isherwood found himself for the first time, and ill at ease about it, having publicly to acknowledge his homosexuality. He regretted, however, not coming out with his gayness when questioned by the police for visiting a gay bar with Caskey.

But their's was an open relationship and Isherwood embarked on a period of exuberant sexuality. Heard disapproved of the friendship with Caskey, a betrayal in his eyes of Prabhavananda, and Isherwood was as much embarrassed as guilty that his guru should learn of his promiscuity. As an act of appeasement he persevered with the translations of Patanjali. It is a sign of self-acceptance, however, that he was unattracted to guilt as a literary theme: "to a writer of my temperament, prolonged guilt is distasteful and boring as a theme for fiction."[127] Isherwood persevered with the relationship with Caskey despite their constant conflict of wills. He began to recognize that being a householder was every bit as real a challenge as being a monk. If the so-called lost years of 1945 to 1951 are marked, at the end, by the parting from Caskey, a new Isherwood is signaled with his love for Don Bachardy. As Katherine Bucknell puts it: "falling in love with Bachardy triggered such a powerful sensation in him of the numinous richness of life that Isherwood was at first overawed by the richness of his own emotions."[128] His obligation to Bachardy came together with a renewed sense of his religious commitment. It was this new Isherwood who was to be Ramakrishna's biographer. Overcoming guilt, discovering love, made for a greater chance of success in the Vedantist path, even if its essential expression from now on was to be in his householder relationship with Bachardy and in his writing.

Isherwood would argue that his homosexuality was to spite his mother, with all her conventional expectations of his having a career and producing grandchildren. Overcoming his resentment against his mother probably constituted an even greater psychological barrier to openness than his combative attitude toward his homosexuality. Both Auden and Isherwood were conscious of mothers, to quote Hynes, as "female carnivores."[129] Isherwood's relationship with his mother, Kathleen, runs like a leitmotif throughout his diaries and fiction, resentment alternating with attempts to be fair to her. They were at their worst in the aftermath of his father's death in 1915, her role as war-widow a constant galling reminder of his father's heroism, together with his financial dependence on her. An allowance later from gay Uncle Henry, his father's elder brother, did much to alleviate the latter. Of course, it may all well have been Oedipal, for in childhood his had been a cloying mother love and with his father's death he had won his mother. In the character of Mrs. Lindsay in *All the Conspirators* and Mrs. Vernon in *The Memorial* Isherwood gave two pretty savage portraits of his mother. In the latter the son figure, Eric, is seen as detecting in his mother:

> a certain hardening and blunting of her sensibilities. She could give a sharp answer without realizing that she was quarrelling. And this reflection of himself in her gave him more pain than any other aspect of their relationship.[130]

And if his mother here fell victim to projection she could also be scapegoated: "so there were bitter sessions in which he revenged himself on the tired tearful woman for all the humiliations he had endured at the hand of others."[131] And there was an underlying guilt; what if his father were after all to return and find mother and son locked in this humiliating conflict? He loathed her ancestor worship, her cult of the past, as he saw it, and they argued over religion, his mother's conventional Anglicanism against his atheism. He was to take his brother Richard's side in his own quarrel with his mother.

But in many ways Kathleen became the tougher of the two and Isherwood the loser, and with his instinct for self-preservation he saw the wisdom of a truce: "she was a passive fortress and he had stopped attacking her. What was the use? She was impregnable anyway."[132] He challenged her with his homosexuality but she proved unshockable. He was always indeed tempted to use her as a confidante. She even visited the gay ménage with Heinz in Portugal in 1936, though she treated his boyfriend as a servant. Isherwood looked to her to act as his literary agent whilst he was in Berlin and evidently she did take a pride in his literary success.

There is a wonderful contrast between Mrs Auden and his mother at the opening night of *The Ascent of F6*: "beside this solemn intense woman with her austere nose, Kathleen seemed frivolously feminine."[133] Probably his mother's continuing youthfulness and feminine good looks compounded any Oedipal struggle. Did she have any realization that the play was all about the hero, Michael Ransom's attempt to compensate for the lack of his mother's love in childhood by seeking the admiration of the masses?[134]

Occasionally Isherwood recognized the psychological gains to be made from this conflict. Reflecting on his rows with Vernon he observed:

> What if he is priggish and humorless sometimes? Can't I supply enough humor and understanding for both of us? If I can't, what is the use of having been through all those quarrels with M?[135]

After the war he was a dutiful son and always visited his mother. He was struck by her continuing strength and there was to be no let up in her loyalty to her core values. He even accompanied her on a visit to church in London, only to be confronted by T. S. Eliot as a sidesman. After her stroke in 1959 he answered her enquiry, did Vedantism offer an after life, with a half-truth, yes, but he did not go on to explain, only for those parts of the ego which had overlapped with the atman. She died 15 June 1960.

As he tried to make sense of his mother's influence in his life, he came to see that her astonishing vitality, her very obstinacy, was essential to his own growth: without it "he would have lost the counter-force which gave him strength."[136] But the Vedantist quest insists on a love of the mother and discounts this negative confrontational image. Maybe Isherwood was in the end incapable of a positive love for his mother. But this was an insight into the nature of Vedantism he seems never to have grasped.

The Eternal Feminine

The role of the feminine in Hindu culture is a huge issue and here the commentary can be but suggestive. As Sudhir Kakar puts it: "Hindu cosmology is feminine to an extent rarely found in other civilizations."[137] Mother goddesses are reservoirs of constructive and destructive energy, *sakti*, and the male Gods, Siva, Brahma and Vishnu have to be energized by their female consorts. Swami Chidananda put this in our conversation in an arresting way; the self-sufficient but static Absolute is masculine and needs *sakti* or female energy to give it movement.[138] Maybe all goddesses are ambivalent, but some are deemed good, for example, Parvati, Sarasvati, Lakshmi, Durga, others bad, for example, Kali.

Not all would subscribe to this generalization. Ashis Nandy suggested to me not only should we differentiate between the maternal and the conjugal in the goddesses and he sees an increasing evolution in Hinduism today toward the latter, with its promise of a feminist agenda, but the emphasis should rather be on the androgynous.[139] Chidananda agreed that at the heart of Hindu spirituality is a being who is both male and female and concurred that the idea of androgyny would work for Indian religions though not for Indian philosophy. The latter he saw as beyond gender. The revulsion of some European writers, James Mill and Kipling, for example, against Hinduism may lie in their own inner fears of latent homosexuality and hence a revulsion to an androgyny branded as effeminacy. Ashis Nandy, however, was anxious to point out that acceptance of androgyny, as, for example in Gandhi's acceptance of his feminine side, is in no way to accept any homosexual makeup.

The profound ambivalence toward the mother goddess is best explained by seeing that the Indian pantheon as in some way a projection of the social norms of Indian society. Women in Hindu society are both idealized and subjugated. A woman's status is only won by the birth of sons. Consequently she both invests an enormous amount of herself in the nurturing of the son but will also at some subconscious level, and here I am following Kakar's analysis, experiences murderous feelings toward a son on whom so much of her own worth depends. The son experiences a dependency on the mother "of an intensity and devotion that differentiates it from the experience of infancy in western world,"[140] but, correspondingly, fears abandonment. The mother can seem both "aggressively destroying and sexually demanding." Swami Shantananda suggested more commonsensical explanations, that the emotional distance of fathers from their children self-evidently led the son into a greater dependence on the mother and didn't they, anyway, always grant his wishes, but he did not rule out the fear of a ferocious female sexuality.[141] We are here into the Melanie Klein syndrome of a child's response to the smothering love of a mother, to the good and the bad breast. Here is the source of a castration complex.

Nowhere is the cult of the mother goddess stronger than in Bengal. Each year in November there is the hugely popular Durga festival, followed by the Kali, with the Lakshmi sandwiched in between. The Kali figure is the most terrifying of all. She originated from mountain tribal societies.[142] In her left hand she clutches the sword to decapitate the demon king, but, as the head is symbolic of the penis, also to castrate. This is symbolic both of death and asceticism. Death becomes the ultimate erotic experience, union with Kali. Without shame, she stands in a reversed sex role over Shiva, her tongue stuck out in ecstasy. But all this can be interpreted positively. In her right-handed self Kali is there to slay the forces of the ego and to strengthen spirituality.

As a Bengali-inspired movement, the cult of the Mother dominates the Ramakrishna Mission. Ramakrishna's wife, Sarada Devi (and, needless to say, the marriage was not to be consummated), was revered as the Mother. Jeffrey Kripal[143] has a controversial but compelling account of Ramakrishna himself as a failed Tantric, one who could only accommodate his latent homosexuality by reverting to childhood and treating Kali in all her demanding sexuality as Mother. The celebration by the Mission of the Kumari festival, Vivekananda's favorite, during the Durga festival, with its worship of a prepubescent virgin, is self-evidently Ruskineque. Chidananda pointed out that the Ramakrishna Mission is exceptional in insisting on celibacy—other religious orders allow entry to those who have been married—and Swami Shantananda felt anyway that the monastic would always have greater trouble coming to terms with female sexuality than the householder. It is possible that in Bengali culture more incestuous practices prevail between mother and son and Kripal invites comment on how Ramakrisna related to the village women.

But for all their awesome power, these Mother goddesses are the path to spirituality. There are obvious parallels with the Marian cult. There is a voluminous literature on the need for such mother worship, the texts by Andrew Harvey amongst the most recent.[144] How would a European homosexual respond to this demand in the Vedantist quest?

In Isherwood's earlier writings and during this spiritual quest there is little mention of Mother goddesses. Yet it would have been all around him in the Vedanta Center. Isherwood was more drawn to *jnana* than to *bhakti* and in his translations the focus was on Krishna and the metaphysical rather than on

Durga and the mother goddess. But as misogynist and homosexual Isherwood would have felt hostility and aversion toward such mother goddess figures. This would have mixed with hostility to his own mother. Maybe, and even more so with a homosexual, there is a need for such a figure as Kali to come to terms with the castration complex. Maybe all would-be non-dualist mystics have to come to terms with this incest taboo. Is there here a depth explanation for Isherwood's failure in the Vedantist test?

The Problematic of the Atman Quest

Beyond putting it to the test of experience, any attempt to describe what is actually happening in this search for the Atman meets the mysterious and elusive. What is the relationship between the ego and this higher Self? Is there continuity or hiatus? And what happens to memory? For Proustians, memory is the key to identity.

These are questions I put to all those I met in India. Sudhir Kakar argued strongly for hiatus. He did so, I assume, through his fear as a psychiatrist that the quest is intrinsically dangerous and that for many it can but lead to psychosis. But for those already on the path the answer was rather for continuity, or, at the least, for a gradual shedding of the ego. Swami Vishveshwarananda spoke of the former ego as fading away, though also warmly recommended the intense activity of karma yoga as a means of escaping its demands. Swami Shantananda likewise saw our egos as falling away. With regard to memory, he stated we would retain memories of our former ego but they would be without affect. But his prospect was of an eventual complete dissolution in the Absolute, ego, memory and all, a return to zero. And Swami Chidananda's account was the same. He saw continuity rather than hiatus, but still spoke of a moment when, and here he resorted to metaphor, after climbing step by step, you have to make a bold leap onto the balcony above. If he conceded that memory was crucial to the ego and is held onto to the last, it has to be surrendered if there is to be absorption into the Absolute. It is worth quoting his own guru's account of the experience of the Atman: "It is pure self-awareness beyond the reach of sense, mind, and intellect. The ego-sense is absolutely dead here." For this to happen, "the intellect and the senses must cease functioning."[145]

Yet for me an enigma remained, that in a quest for some impersonal Absolute, which would seemingly point to some standardized impersonal quest, to the contrary, in practice, all those on the path seem to be adopting some highly individualized approach. Did this not shore up the ego rather than guarantee its dissolution? Swami Shantananda fell back on his metaphor that we were all characters in a play. A Canadian Buddhist I met in a *hatha* yoga center in Rishiskesh could only explain this paradox in terms of language: there are so many resonances to the concept of "self" that to speak of offsetting a lower self against a higher may fail to convey the right meaning. Only practice can reveal the truth.

Others have tried to make sense of this epistemology of the ego/self by placing the Vedantist quest in the context of psychoanalyis and in a contrast with Christian dualist mysticism. Vedantism, in tracing the origins of the ego, begins with a concept of descent. Initially, the individual is in *avyakta*, an original causal undifferentiated state, where all rationality is suspended: "there were no moral or logical standards. Opposites could exist together without marring the sense of rest." In other words, the nascent ego is locked into a world akin to Freud's *id*. Out of this a sense of individuality or *ahamkara* is born: "the not-Self gave rise, while in compact with the Self, to the feeling of self-hood or egoism." Freud's failure was, whilst giving a sense of the dynamic to the unconscious, failing to do so for the conscious: "this conception of mind as a subtle substance having a spatial existence and capable of taking on shape is so basic in Eastern psychology and so foreign to the West that it constitutes a real barrier to mutual understanding." The ego has then to reverse, and here one might speak of an evolution, all the stages of its materiality to return to the Atman. It can do so through the *karmashaya* "a repository of potential passions."[146]

The contrast between a non-dualist and a dualist mysticism comes down to one between fusion and communion. Dr. Cuttat compares the yogin and the saint, the former liberated from the ego and evil and living in a state of "non-duality," "without a second, beyond relation" and the latter, only freed from evil, face to face with God, "in interpersonal communion, in extreme reciprocity." He plays on the contrasting concepts of *en-stasis* an "abiding within," with *ekstasis* an "abiding without," the former, "transcendent pure interiority, impersonal self-transcendence, supreme identity," the latter, "transcendent reciprocal interiority, inter-personal self-transcendence, supreme communion." But in his analysis the yogin is seen as "ultimately solitary." He contrasts Hindu *bhakti*, which aims at fusion, with Christian *agape*, which maintains a dualist distance between man and God. Cuttat is clear that the Christian cannot fuse with Christ: "two historically individualized persons cannot fuse or merge." And if he seeks to reconcile these two positions, it is clear that in the concept of interpersonal encounter it is a good deal easier to explain what is happening to the ego than in one of absorption. In the case of the Saint, the ego remains, whatever the degree of transcendence.[147]

Conclusion

If one does not accept the very existence of the Atman than Isherwood's religious quest can take on the character of the absurd. It is of course perfectly possible to comment on his Vedantism without sharing its premise. Isherwood's spiritual activity could be interpreted as yet another attempt at self-invention. At most, Isherwood gains a greater insight into the nature of self-consciousness.[148] He came to see that his attempt to be a monk would not work until he had come to terms with his homosexuality. It was not enough that Prabhavananda turned a blind eye. Hence the emotional and spiritual turmoil of the so-called lost years. Without self-tolerance there could be no further pursuit of a higher self. But Isherwood would have been unhappy with any account of his Vedantist quest as but another form of self-invention. We might treat with some skepticism his belief that in his moments of heightened consciousness he had fleeting glimpses of the Atman, though yoga will lead to such a heightened awareness. Given that these occurred before he entered the Hollywood center they may have owed more to Heardism than to Vedantism. Even so, Swami Prabhavananda was convinced Isherwood had in him the makings of a monk, even a saint, and there is no cause to doubt the seriousness of the endeavor. Both Das Gupta and Swami Ashaktananda expressed a greater liking for Isherwood, if demurring over his homosexuality, over Heard and Huxley, seeing in his intuitive powers as opposed to their rational intelligence a greater sympathy for Indian spirituality. This made him to them the more attractive personality.

But the pursuit of non-duality is an extraordinarily demanding one and only for a spiritual elite. And for someone from a dualist background and with such a strong sense of his own ego this was always going to be a tall order. Probably Isherwood never obtained non-duality, whether through his too great a dependence on his guru or for the reasons suggested, of his adversarial attitude toward both his homosexuality and his mother. Nevertheless, the quest profoundly altered him both as a person and a writer. His already considerable capacity for self-detachment was greatly heightened. He became a far more scrupulous and mordant observer of human vanity. Almost despite himself he became a Forsterian moralist. And if this was to reveal itself more in his role as writer, as Prabhavananda had warned him, Ramakrishna was to hound him to the end.

Notes

1. As Christopher Isherwood portrays him in his *Diaries*, 20 June 1944, 350.
2. Isherwood, *Diaries*, 12 October 1942, 252.

3. Isherwood, *Diaries*, 22 November 1943, 328–29.

4. This fear he points out in *My Guru and His Disciple* (London: Methuen paperback edition, 1981), 152–53.

5. See their introduction to the English edition (London: 1947), 1–4.

6. Anon, *Time*, 12 February 1945. Quoted Robert W. Funk, *Christopher Isherwood. a Reference Guide* (Boston: Hall: 1979), 40.

7. Funk, *Christopher Isherwood. a Reference Guide*, 58, 119.

8. See their translation of *Crest Jewel of Discrimination* (Hollywood: Vedanta Press, 1947), 7, 45, 68.

9. Although the translation and commentary first appeared in *Vedanta and the West*, 1950–1953, here the references are to the Ramakrishna Mission's Indian edition, Swami Prabhavananda, *Patanjali Yoga Sutras* (Mylapore: nd). (Isherwood for some reason has been dropped from the title.), 97, 116, 62, 129, 161.

10. Prabhavananda, *Patanjali Yoga Sutras*, 28.

11. Prabhavananda, *Patanjali Yoga Sutras*, 16.

12. Prabhavananda, *Patanjali Yoga Sutras*, 153.

13. Prabhavananda, *Patanjali Yoga Sutras*, 46.

14. Prabhavananda, *Patanjali Yoga Sutras*, 4.

15. Prabhavananda, *Patanjali Yoga Sutras*, 12.

16. Prabhavananda, *Patanjali Yoga Sutras*, 34.

17. Prabhavananda, *Patanjali Yoga Sutras*, 48.

18. Prabhavananda, *Patanjali Yoga Sutras*, 100.

19. Prabhavananda, *Patanjali Yoga Sutras*, 42.

20. Prabhavananda, *Patanjali Yoga Sutras*, 30.

21. Prabhavananda, *Patanjali Yoga Sutras*, 55.

22. Prabhavananda, *Patanjali Yoga Sutras*, 58.

23. Prabhavananda, *Patanjali Yoga Sutras*, 64.

24. Prabhavananda, *Patanjali Yoga Sutras*, 118.

25. Swami Krishnananda, *An Introduction to the Philosophy of Yoga* (Delhi: The Divine Life Society, nd), 67, 95, 143, 189.

26. Gopi Krishna, *Kundalini: the Secret of Yoga* (Indian edition: U.B.S. Publishers Distributors Ltd., 1992), 8, 41, 182.

27. T. R. Anantharanam, *Ancient Yoga and Modern Science* (Delhi: Mushiram Manoharlal Publishers, 1996), 34. I had the pleasure of meeting him in the Theosophical Society, Adyar in December 1999, where he was delivering three lectures to the School of Wisdom.

28. Shriram Sharma Acharya, *My Life. Its Legacy and Message* (Revised edition. Hardwar: Yugtirth Shantikunj, 1998), 87.

29. Arthur Koestler, *The Lotus and the Robot* (first published 1960, Paperback Edition, London: Hutchinson, 1964), 90, 121, 142–43, 43–44.

30. Swami Prabhavananda, *Vedic Religion and Philosophy* (Mylapore: Sri Ramakrishna Math, 1937), 3, 9–10, 18, 45, 55, 93, 109–10, 111, 142.

31. Swami Prabhavananda, *The Spiritual Heritage of India* (London: Allen and Unwin, 1962), 144, 149, 181, 237.

32. Swami Prabhavananda trans., Vyasa *Srimad Bhagavatam (The Wisdom of God)* (Mylapore: 1947), 191.

33. Swami Prabhavananda and C. Isherwood trans., *Crest Jewel of Discrimination*, 85.

34. Swami Prabhavananda and C. Isherwood trans., *Crest Jewel of Discrimination*, 92, 99.

35. Swami Prabhavananda, *The Sermon on the Mount According to Vedantism* (Madras: Allen and Unwin, 1964), 50, 49, 86, 55, 57.

36. Swami Prabhavananda, *Religion in Practice* (London: Allen and Unwin, 1968), 45.

37. Swami Prabhavananda, *Religion in Practice*, 67.

38. Swami Prabhavananda, *Religion in Practice*, 69.

39. Swami Prabhavananda, *Yoga and Mysticism* (Hollywood: Vedanta Press, 1969), 43, 39.

40. See his review of S. Gallagher and J. Shear, eds., "Models of the Self, Searching for me, Me or I?," *The Times Higher Educational Supplement*, 17 March 2000, 28.

41. Samuel Hynes, *The Auden Generation. Literature and Politics in England in the 1930s* (London: Bodley Head, 1976), 55.

42. Edward Mendelson, *Early Auden* (London: Faber, 1981), xx–xxi.

43. Mendelson, *Early Auden*, 181.

44. Hynes, *The Auden Generation*, 169.

45. Mendelson, *Early Auden*, 20.

46. See Mendelson, *Early Auden*, 160–61 and further. His account of this experience was not to appear till Anne Fremantle's anthology, *The Protestant Mystics* (1964), but appeared at the time as a poem, "A Summer Night."

47. Quoted Hynes, *The Auden Generation*, 251.

48. Quoted Hynes, *The Auden Generation*, 383–84.

49. See Christopher Isherwood, *Christopher and His Kind 1929–1939* (London: 1970), 216–17, 271–72.

50. Richard Chase made this point. "The Huxley-Heard Paradise," *Partisan Review* 10 (March/April 1943): Footnote on 146.

51. J. B. Coates, *Ten Modern Prophets* (London: F. Muller, 1944), 25.

52. Quoted Martin Ceadel, *Pacifism in Britain 1914–1945* (Oxford: Oxford University Press, 1980), 16.

53. Donald Hayne, *Batter My Heart* (London: Hutchinson, 1963), 199.

54. Gerald Heard, *Social Substance of Religion* (London: Allen and Unwin, 1931), 204, 209, 210.

55. Heard, *Social Substance of Religion*, 291.

56. Heard, *Social Substance of Religion*, 307.

57. Heard, *Social Substance of Religion*, 310.

58. Heard to Sheppard, 1 October 1935. Quoted in David Bradshaw, "The Flight from Gaza: Aldous Huxley's Involvement with the Peace Pledge Union in the Context

of His Overall Intellectual Development," in *Now More than Ever: Proceedings of the Aldous Huxley Centenary Symposium, Munster 1994*, ed. Bernfried Nugel (Frankfurt: Peter Lang, 1994), 13.

59. Gerald Heard, "The Significance of the New Pacifism," in *The New Pacifism*, ed. Gerald K. Hibbert (London: Allenson and Co., 1936), 17, 21.

60. Heard to Sheppard, 29 October 1937. Quoted Bradshaw, "The Flight from Gaza," 25.

61. Gerald Heard, *Pain, Sex and Time* (London: Harper and Brothers, 1939), 137.

62. Heard, *Pain, Sex and Time*, 180.

63. Heard, *Pain, Sex and Time*, 226.

64. Heard, *Pain, Sex and Time*, 221.

65. Heard, *Pain, Sex and Time*, 266.

66. Gerald Heard, *Training for the Life of the Spirit* (London: Cassell, 1941), 11.

67. Heard, *Training for the Life of the Spirit*, 27.

68. Gerald Heard, *Training for the Life of the Spirit. Pamphlet Two* (London: Cassell, 1944), 37.

69. Heard, *Training for the Life of the Spirit. Pamphlet Two*, 42.

70. Gerald Heard, *Man the Master* (London: Faber and Faber, 1942), 113.

71. Heard, *Man the Master*, 202.

72. Heard, *Man the Master*, 103.

73. Heard, *Man the Master*, 241–42.

74. Jonathan Fryer, *Isherwood: a Biography of Christopher Isherwood* (London: New English Library, 1977), 196.

75. A point he makes in his biography of his parents, *Kathleen and Frank* (London: Methuen, 1971), 252.

76. Quoted in Isherwood, *Kathleen and Frank*, 321.

77. Christopher Isherwood, *Lions and Shadows* (first published 1938. London; Magnum Books, 1979), 187.

78. W. H. Auden and Christopher Isherwood, *Journey to a War* (London: Faber and Faber, 1939), 28–29, 104, 75, 182, 202, 253.

79. Christopher Isherwood, *An Approach to Vedanta* (Hollywood: Vedanta Press, 1963), 8.

80. Quoted Martin Ceadel, *Pacifism in Britain 1914–1945* (Oxford: Oxford University Press, 1980), 185.

81. Quoted in Ceadel, *Pacifism in Britain*, 45.

82. Ceadel, *Pacifism in Britain*, 229.

83. Isherwood, *An Approach to Vedanta*, 14–15.

84. Quoted in Fryer, *Isherwood: a Biography*, 194.

85. Ceadel, *Pacifism in Britain*, 307.

86. See his essay "The Gita and War," reprinted from *Vedanta and the West* in *Exhumations* (first published 1966, London: 1968), 123, 130–31. There is a fuller version in C. Isherwood, ed., *Vedanta for the Western World* (London: Allen and Unwin, 1948).

87. Isherwood, *An Approach to Vedanta*, 47.

88. Isherwood, ed., *Vedanta for the Western World*, 20.

89. Isherwood, ed., *Vedanta for the Western World*, 11–13.

90. Isherwood, *Approach*, 21.

91. Bucknell, ed., "Isherwood" (May 1939), in *Diaries*, 26, 29.

92. Bucknell, ed., "Isherwood" (July 1939), 38–39.

93. Bucknell, ed., "Isherwood" (November 1939), 48.

94. Bucknell, ed., "Isherwood" (January 1940), 82.

95. Christopher Isherwood, "The Day at La Verne," *Penguin New Writing*, no. 14 (1942), 12–14.

96. Isherwood, *Diaries* (July 1941), 169–70.

97. Isherwood, *Diaries* (January 1941), 133.

98. Isherwood, *An Approach to Vedanta*, 28.

99. Isherwood, *Diaries* (July 1940), 108.

100. Isherwood, *Diaries* (July 1940), 156.

101. Isherwood, *Diaries* (May 1943), 293.

102. Isherwood, *Diaries* (March 1943), 272.

103. Isherwood, *Diaries* (26 October 1940), 122.

104. Isherwood, *Diaries* (September 1942), 247.

105. Isherwood, ed., *Vedanta for the Western World*, 9.

106. Isherwood, *Diaries* (February 1940), 91.

107. Isherwood, *Diaries* (Sepetmber 1940), 121.

108. Isherwood, *Diaries* (December 1940), 129.

109. Isherwood, *Diaries* (September 1940), 122.

110. Isherwood, *Diaries* (July 1940), 105–6.

111. Isherwood, *Diaries* (September 1943), 314.

112. Isherwood, *Diaries* (February 1944), 335.

113. Isherwood, *Diaries* (18 February 1944), 335.

114. Isherwood, *Diaries* (17 August 1949), 414.

115. Isherwood, *Diaries* (22 August 1951), 438.

116. Katherine Bucknell, ed., *Diaries*, xxxii.

117. Isherwood, *Kathleen and Frank*, 273.

118. See Isherwood, *Lions and Shadows*, 185–88.

119. Isherwood, *Christopher and His Kind*, 24.

120. Isherwood, *Christopher and His Kind*, 30.

121. Isherwood, *Christopher and His Kind*, 88.

122. Bucknell, *Lost Years*, xxv.

123. Isherwood, *Diaries* (July 1941), 164.

124. Isherwood, *Diaries* (July 1941), 313.

125. Isherwood, *Diaries* (15 July 1944), 350.

126. He rejected Peggy Kiskadden's assertion that this was the cause. See Isherwood, *Lost Years; A Memoir 1945–1951* (London: Chatto and Windus, 2000), 45–46.

127. Isherwood, *Lost Years*, 227.

128. Bucknell, Isherwood, *Diaries*, xxxvii.

129. Hynes, *The Auden Generation*, 240.

130. Christopher Isherwood, *The Memorial* (London: 1973), 205.

131. Isherwood, *Christopher and His Kind*, 39.

132. Isherwood, *Christopher and His Kind*, 76.

133. Isherwood, *Christopher and His Kind*, 239.

134. See Mendelson's explanation of the play in *Early Auden*, 248–55.

135. Isherwood, *Diaries* (10 July 1940), 102.

136. Isherwood, *Kathleen and Frank*, 361.

137. Sudhir Kakar, *The Inner World* (New Delhi: 1996). (From the composite edition, *The Indian Psyche*.), 112.

138. Personal interview with Swami Chidananda, Rishikesh, 12 November 1999.

139. Personal interview with Ashis Nandy, Calcutta, 6 October 1999.

140. Kakar, *The Inner World*, 80.

141. Personal interview with Swami Shantananda, the Vasitha Guha ashram, 11 November 1999.

142. Susan Bayly, writing about tribal societies, states: "their hills and forests commanded respect as the domains of blood-taking deities whose powers of *sakti* or activated divine energy empower both kings and gods to contend with unclean or 'demonic' forces which continually menace the dharmic world." *Caste, Society and Politics in India from the Eighteenth Century to the Modern Age* (Cambridge: Cambridge University Press, 1999), 45.

143. See Jeffrey Kripal, *Kali's Child: The Mystical and the Erotic in the Life and Teaching of Ramakrishna* (Chicago: The University of Chicago Press, 1995). I have drawn here on his observations of the Kali cult.

144. e.g., Andrew Harvey, *The Return of the Mother* (Berkeley: Frog Limited, 1995); Andrew Harvey, *The Direct Path: Creating a Journey to the Divine Using the World's Mystical Traditions* (London: Rider, 2000).

145. Sivananda, *Life Divine*, 41–42.

146. See Kumar Pal, "Yoga and Psycho-analysis," in Swami Atmaramananda and Dr. S. Sivaramkrishna, eds., *Art, Culture and Spirituality: a Prabuddha Bhata Centenary Perspective* (1896–1896) (Calcutta: Avaita Ashrama, 1997), 130, 137.

147. Dr Jacques Albert Cuttat, "The Spiritual Encounter of East and West," in Atmaramananda and Sivaramkrishna, eds., *Art, Culture and Spirituality*, 283–318.

148. Adam Phillips argues somewhat along these lines in his review of Lost Worlds in *London Review of Books* (16 November 2000).

~

Epilogue

To conclude this text two objectives are in mind, one, to adopt a more comparativist approach toward these three characters in their search for the divine and, secondly, to see if its explanatory approach can in any way be refined or expanded.

Drawing Comparisons

In terms of social background there were broad similarities. All three were upper middle class, though Isherwood had some pretensions to minor landed gentry. Carpenter's father retired as a naval captain, then turned city magistrate. His mother came from a ship-building family. Forster's father had been an architect. His father's family descended from the eminently socially respectable Clapham sect but his mother's had been more lower middle class—her father a drawing master—and she had been driven by that class's notorious search for social respectability. Isherwood's father had been an army officer, his mother from a family owning a wine-business. The young Isherwood's prospects of owning Marple Hall had been dashed by his Uncle Henry's late marriage.

In terms of familial relationships there were significant differences. Only Carpenter of the three was to enjoy a long-term relationship with a father. Both Forster and Isherwood lost their fathers young, Forster hardly yet born, Isherwood whilst at his prep school. But it made no difference in terms of a revolt against authority. Possibly vis-à-vis the conventions he was up against

Carpenter's proved the deepest rebellion of the three, Forster's the mildest, Isherwood's the most histrionic. But maternal relationships were the more dynamic and for reasons this text has tried to demonstrate this was to prove critical in their capacity for the mystical experience. However emotionally distant his mother had proved to be, Carpenter had been able to come to terms without any sense of conflict with the maternal. But it was to be a constant battle for both Forster and Isherwood, Forster, as ever, adopting a line of least resistance, keeping the conflict more under control for all its grinding away within, Isherwood, going through various rather melodramatic moves to come to terms with an equally dominant mother figure.

If, again, broadly analogous there were significant differences in their educational backgrounds. All three went to independent or public schools and onto Oxbridge. Both Carpenter at Brighton College and Forster at Tonbridge were day boys, but Isherwood a boarder at Rugby. Did this delay sexual experience for both Carpenter and Forster so that actual sexual fulfillment became such an issue for the two whereas for Isherwood here was a barrier overcome a great deal earlier? All three went to Cambridge but with very differing outcomes. Carpenter's was a success story and he went onto become a fellow of Trinity Hall. If he subsequently rebelled against Oxbridge privilege he never lost contact with Cambridge, one means of keeping in touch with his close friend, Lowes Dickinson. Forster's intellect was not quite tough enough to make it as an academic but King's College was always to be something of a spiritual home. Isherwood simply threw away his chances and deliberately failed his first year examinations. All three had been co-opted into the establishment. Why did they rebel?

The beginnings of that rebellion lay in a rejection of a Christian upbringing. Carpenter's was to be the deepest engagement with Christianity. Without it would seem any strong vocation he had drifted, as so many younger sons did in the Victorian era, into the Anglican clergy, in tandem with his college clerical fellowship. Seemingly he had almost as easily slipped out of orders, though George Bernard Shaw always typed him as the priest, but his later writings suggest that, to the contrary, his was to be a lifetime debate with the tenets of the Christian faith. Christianity he came to see, drawing on anthropology and comparative religion, as but another nature cult and Christ as a mythological figure. In Hindu Vedantism he acquired a new religious outlook. Forster's break from Christianity was altogether easier, no doubt facilitated by the revolt undertaken by Carpenter's generation, by Lesley Stephen, T. H. Huxley and their like. In his second year at Cambridge such Christian beliefs as he held just melted away. Even so, Forster was rebelling against a powerful evangelical background of the Clapham sect and, in part, he dealt with this by taking up just that aspect of religion where it was at its weakest, its attitude to mysticism. Forster was never to share in that ironic regard for religion of Bloomsbury. He was predisposed to be receptive toward Indian religions. Isherwood retained an adolescent hostility to all aspects of organized religion, above all to his mother's conventional Anglicanism, right through his twenties and thirties. He pronounced himself an atheist. But Auden had very perceptively seen that Isherwood's hostility hid its opposite, a very strong religious need. Isherwood, however, could only return to religion were it to be dressed in new clothes—any Christian associations remained anathema—and in the end the only way back lay through a new belief system of Hinduism.

Crucial in this religious reorientation had been the role of friends and gurus. They have to be differentiated. Carpenter's was to be the most drawn out involvement with Hinduism. As early as the 1870s he was wrestling, however imperfectly, with Vedantism. One catalyst was his friendship with the Sri Lankan Tamil, Ponnanbalam Arunachalam, a privileged member of the island's anglicized elite, a student at Cambridge at the same time as Carpenter, a friendship which did much to ignite Carpenter's interest in the subcontinent. It was Arunachalam who sent him a copy in 1881 of the *Bhagavad gita*, to exercise such an extraordinary influence over his prose poem *Towards Democracy*. Again, Arunachalam was to be the crucial catalyst in leading Carpenter toward Hindu mysticism through his invitation in 1890 to come out to Sri Lanka to meet his own guru, to become Carpenter's, Ramaswamy or Ilakkanam the Grammarian.

But friendship was even more critical in leading Forster toward the subcontinent and its religions. It is impossible to imagine Forster taking the interest that he did without his hopeless love affair with Masood, grandson of the great Indian Muslim reformer, Syed Ahmed Khan. Forster was his tutor for his Oxford entrance examinations and the friendship took off from there. Masood in time was to enjoy a not unsuccessful career in education, at Hyderabad and Baroda. Forster followed Masood out to India in 1912, the first of his three visits. But for all the sympathy Forster felt for Indian Islam, and quite probably he was more on its wavelength than he was for Hinduism, it was Hinduism that taxed his imagination the more. Here again friendship was the cause, with his two Maharajahs, of Chhatarpur and Dewas, both ardent devotees of the Krishna cult. Forster was fond of and intrigued by the eccentric Maharajah of Chhatarpur, in his turn a disciple of Carpenter, but Forster's deeper regard and friendship was to be for the Maharajah of Dewas. He returned to India in 1921 to be his personal secretary. And it was then that he was himself drawn into the whole cult of Krishna and its mysticism.

In terms of friendships Auden certainly accentuated Isherwood's turning toward religion but Auden himself, as a devout Anglo-Catholic, would have nothing to do with Hinduism. Here Isherwood's friendship with Gerald Heard was to be the catalyst. But the categories of friend and guru become confused. For Isherwood Heard was also a quasi-guru. Isherwood seems to have enjoyed no Indian friendships in the manner of Carpenter and Forster, though there was one massive exception, and his visits to India were even more fleeting than theirs. He did not really take to India at all. The exception was his guru, the Ramakrishna monk, Swami Prabhavananda, whom he also contrived to turn into a friend.

For both Carpenter and Isherwood gurus were far more the inspiration for their turning to Indian mysticism. If we go along with that taxonomy of the guru-disciple relationship so magisterially mapped out by Rawlinson, taken together with the more specific exploration undertaken by Feuerstein of the trickster teacher,[1] then Carpenter can be seen as torn between two very different kinds of gurus. Walt Whitman, so much his own voice, prone to whimsicality and swings of mood, falls into the category of the hot unstructured, a holy fool and trickster figure. As guru, he offered an entirely personal relationship. But Ramasawamy, so much the traditionalist, an expositor of Siddhantism, for all the flamboyance of his own guru, the ship builder turned naked holy man, Tilleneithan, was calm incarnate and offered, instead, a cool structured relationship. He came out of the same spiritual background as the later Ramana Maharshi, one of modern India's most exceptional spiritual counselors, and his impact on Carpenter was to be considerable. But he did not become a conventional disciple for all Arunachalam's expecting that Carpenter would return to undergo further spiritual training. In many ways Carpenter tried to impose something of Ramaswamy's more conventional guru mold onto Whitman. But some watered-down version of Whitman proved to be the stronger influence.

By 1939 Isherwood was spiritually rock bottom. The received version of Isherwood still tends to be of the rather decadent figure of the 1930s, the Herr Issyvoo or Christopher of the Berlin stories, immortalized in John van Druten's *I am a Camera* and the film *Cabaret*. What happened next is far less well known. He and Auden had left for America in 1939, both already high profile writers, but whereas Auden's career was to flourish in New York, Isherwood, in search of some form of spiritual salvation, felt compelled to escape to the west coast. The presence of Aldous Huxley, Gerald Heard, and Krishnamurthi had already put the west coast on the map as a hunting ground for gurus. There was indeed an embarrassment of choices. But in the end he ruled out Heard as a guru, being too close in age and too similar in background—

Isherwood needed the frisson of difference—and when Heard introduced him to Swami Prabhavananda, head of the Vedanta Center in Hollywood, he opened up a wholly new phase in Isherwood's life. In fact the crucial meeting was the second and private one, the mercurial Heard absent, on 4 August 1940. On 8 November 1940 he was initiated as a trainee or probationer monk. There followed a period of great uncertainty with Isherwood still torn between Heard, a gifted spiritual counselor, his own Quaker pacifism—all the while he was threatened with conscription—and the pull of the Vedanta Center and it was not till 6 February 1943 that Prabhavananda prevailed and Isherwood entered the Vedanta Center full-time. He was to stay there till 25 August 1945.

In Swami Prabhavananda, Isherwood acquired a guru in a direct line of descent via Swami Brahmananda from Ramakrishna himself. Admittedly Isherwood rather took the alleged continuing presence in Prabhavananda's life of his own guru, Brahmananda, on trust, but he could not help but be aware of this lineal descent from an avatar. Abbots or mahants of Ramakrishna mission centers abroad tended to be prima donnas and Prabhavananda could be jealous of any rivalry, either from outsiders like Gerald Heard or insiders like Swami Ashaktananda. But he was, for all that, a delightful, amusing, personality though Isherwood was always aware of another side to him, that almost frightening capacity to withdraw into spiritual meditation. All this might hint at a rather hot relationship but in fact Isherwood was exposed to the classic cool structured Vedantist guru-disciple relationship. It was a two-way exchange as Prabhavananda had serious need of Isherwood's literary skills as a translator. How far Isherwood proceeded in this vocation is hard to read but he claimed some small glimmerings of self-transcendence or non-duality. In the end he was unable to sustain the self-denial that a monastic vocation demanded and he left the Center. But the impact of Vedantism proved lasting. He and Prabhavananda never ceased to be friends. It has been argued, however, that Isherwood's continuing dependence on him as guru worked against his own spiritual enlightenment. As forewarned by Prabhavananda, Ramakrishna hounded him to the end and at the time of his death he was sent on his way accompanied by rather loud Hindu chanting.

Carpenter was exceptional in being the only one of the three to having pretensions to guru status.

Forster's was a different mode of entry into Indian mysticism. There was no guru. He did not practice yoga. He undertook some reading into Vedantism though much of what passed as commentary on Hindu mysticism was probably refracted through his reading of neo-Platonism. Still, he did undertake a careful reading of the *Bhagavad gita*. His way in to Hinduism came as a consequence of his befriending his two Maharajahs, Chhatarpur and De-was. Forster clearly read around the Krishna cult but it was the alchemy of his imagination working on his direct experience of the cult in action that explains his exceptional empathy for Krishna mysticism. If the approach adopted here has had to be somewhat counterfactual, there was good reason why Forster should have responded so creatively to the homoerotic implications of the cult as well as to the humanism of the Maharashtrian poet-saint, Tukaram. But here one could add a rider. There was always, of course, a powerful guru-disciple relationship implicit in the worship of Krishna-Krishna, indeed, was all demanding in his love and this was a hot unstructured relationship—and Forster seemingly succumbed to the demands of a love based on absence, brought about by Krishna's desertion of the gopis, inducing that longing for a lost lover, Forster himself reflecting on the impossibility of his love for Masood and missing his Egyptian friend. Mohamed el Adl.

What factors predisposed or limited their search for the divine?

At the center of this discussion has to be their sexuality. All three were up against intolerable constraints on their freedom of expression and faced an intolerant homophobia. In consequence they sought in other cultures a means of coming to terms with their inner nature. But they had likewise to work through internalized guilt and this was certainly one factor that warred against transcendence. So much of the mystical experience hinges on an openness, an absence of conflict within. Did Hinduism, either its Vedantism or the Krishna cult, speak to their needs? Carpenter was the best adjusted of the three, the least guilt-ridden, and this enabled him to read into Hinduism an assurance that it sacramentalized sex. Not that he could in all honesty claim that his Indian guru sanctioned his own permissive attitude toward sexuality. The subject of homosexuality had not even been raised in their conversations. Here he had to fall back on Whitman.

For Forster the Indian experience was to be transformative. So inexperienced, so little street-wise, though Egypt had been a breakthrough of sorts, by 1921, the year of his second visit to India, Forster still had a long way to go before he acquired any self-tolerance. In Dewas, through a very Forsterian muddle, he had to be open about himself in entirely new ways with the Maharajah. There was that astonishing arrangement of a licensed relationship with the court barber. It was a personal liberation that could then expand into a different kind of religious liberation. Through a combination of the bacchanalian and the mystical aspects of the Krishna cult. Forster came emotionally of age.

Quite clearly Isherwood's embarking on the monastic path would have been halted at its very beginning had his guru in any way held his homosexuality against him but Prabhavananda, in a very laid-back Hindu manner, had expressed his tolerance of homosexuality. He simply suggested that Isherwood adopt Krishna as a love object. Yet any real success in his monastic vocation lay in sexual constraint. Prabhavananda himself stood for a quite austere moral code or *dharma*. Such permissiveness as was shown at the time proved insufficient to free Isherwood from his internalized guilt and the way to the Atman remained blocked. It was to be a positively Dostoyevskyean period of indulgence—through sin comes salvation—that paved the way to a greater self-acceptance and opened up a greater access to the mystical.

Another potential hurdle lay in attitudes toward the maternal and the feminine. This has a special resonance for Hinduism, a belief system so intensely feminine, with that powerful role of *sakti* attributed to its goddesses. The question has been raised throughout the text if in-depth Freudian terms, with the anaclitic relationship of child to mother, if the very possibility of the mystical does not lie in crossing the threshold of the maternal incest taboo. Again Carpenter emerges as psychologically the best equipped of the three to address maternal love. If one of his leading female disciples, Kate Salt, came to doubt his real understanding of women, he certainly did enjoy strong female friendships and believed that the homosexual could play a vital intermediary role between the sexes. But both Forster and Isherwood were seriously shackled by antagonistic relationships with their mothers and in Isherwood's case rather more than in Forster's one can detect a real mysogynism that would certainly have been a barrier in the way of a Vedantist self-transcendence. Even so, both felt that the problematic of their mothers had been a major dynamic factor in their writing.

The most searching question about this encounter with Hinduism has to be, in what ways were their lives enhanced, just how liberating was its outcome? It is somewhat difficult to disentangle Whitman's influence from that of Vedantism in the light of Carpenter's rather disingenuous attempt to draw them together. It was probably Whitman's example that led Carpenter to throw up his privileged Cambridge way of life and look for comradeship with the northern working class, but a mixture of Thoreau and Vedantism that inspired him drastically to reduce his needs in a proto-Gandhian way in those experiments in market gardening at Bradway and Millthorpe and to engage with a kind of arcadian socialism. But his Indian guru, however predisposed Carpenter was already in these directions, certainly seems to have encouraged a change of direction. On his return from the subcontinent he was in time to alter his domestic arrangements, with George Merill moving in as housekeeper and live-in lover, to adopt a far more aggressive apologetics of sexual reform and to be far more driven toward a mystical experience.

Richard Bucke saw him as one of a small band of the illumined. If Carpenter in his mystical quest has been overshadowed by such contemporaries as Henri Bergson and Rudolf Steiner he was in many ways their pioneer. He was distinctive in seeing in the third sex some special access to the divine. His elaborate exposition of the evolution of consciousness in many ways ran parallel in their expression to Aurobindo's working out his ideas on the divinised body and the supramental.

Forster always seemed the least likely of the three to undergo any kind of sea-change through the Indian experience. Was he not too much the humanist, too strong a believer in the ego, ever to be likely to surrender to a faith system which sought self-transcendence? Alternatively, could it be argued that India proved a negative experience, one which overwhelmed him and led him to abandon the role of the creative writer? Should we read Mrs. Moore's breakdown into Forster himself? But, of course, Forster did not stop writing. There were biographies and family studies, of Lowes Dickinson and Marianne Thornton, his great aunt. There was another key text on the Indian experience, *The Hill of Devi*. He wrote a libretto for an opera, *Billy Budd*. If there was no new novel, there was an immense body of work in terms of radio talks, reviews, essays, even some creative short stories. Just as importantly, so much more of his life was to be put into his loves and friendships and he was in time to settle down into a kind of marriage with Bob Buckingham. Clearly he had moved on. In many ways, given his underlying rationalist skepticism, he had acted out of character through his extraordinary imaginative engagement with the Krishna cult, but that is all the more suggestive of just how forceful the experience had proved to be.

Rather less has been anticipated in the text to date on the long-term impact on Isherwood of his war-time experience as a monk. Clearly its immediate outcome seems to have been that period of frantic rebellion recorded in his *Lost Years*. One of Isherwood's reasons for turning to Vedantism had been a writer's block as a novelist, and here there was progress. There was that interesting joint venture with Aldous Huxley *Jacob's Hands* (1944), a rather moving account of how a holy fool could transform the spoiled lives of the American rich. Then came *Prater Violet* (1946), a novella in honor of an earlier guru, the film director, Berthold Viertel. This text is not intended as a literary study but the question has to be raised, to what extent did Vedantism inform his fiction? It clearly did so in the best of his novellas, *A Single Man* (1964), a day in the life of a West Coast professor mourning the death of his lover, with his very individuality falling apart but somehow subsumed into a wider consciousness. Here was Isherwood's adaptation of Ramakrishna's famous image of the salt-doll dissolved in the ocean. In *A Meeting by the River* (1967) Isherwood acts out in fiction that vocation he had failed as a monk, with one of the characters, after experiencing some horrible last-minute doubts that he might be acting out of some spiritual vainglory, takes *sannyas* at Belur, HQ of the Ramakrishna Mission. Maybe the clarity of Isherwood's fiction stands up well in comparison with the far greater intellectual pretensions of Huxley's mystical novels, though only *My Guru and His Disciple* matches the power of Huxley's study of the mystic in politics, *Grey Eminence* (1941). However, both were eclipsed by the sheer weight of the writings of Hermann Hesse, above all by *The Glass Bead Game* (1946).

But Isherwood's most significant further link with the Ramakrishna Mission and Vedantism was his biography of the Mission's founder, *Ramakrishna and His Disciples* (1965). It was in the proverbial sense a labor of love. He undertook it as a way of expressing gratitude to his guru. He had to bear with every chapter being vetted by Belur, an intolerable burden on a creative writer. Jeffrey Kripal believes Isherwood would have agreed with his own controversial account of Ramakrishna's sexuality.[2] But one can be selective in the way one uses Isherwood's comments in *My Guru and His Disciple*. After reflecting on the possibilities of Ramakrishna's experiencing homoerotic desires Isherwood finally states: "I couldn't honestly claim him as a homosexual, even a sublimated one, much as I would have liked to be able to do so."[3] Much of this controversy rages around the hidden meanings of the original Bengali text and only those who are linguists are in a position to judge between Kripal's account and the rejoinder by Swami Atmanjnanananda.[4] Looking at Isherwood's text through Kripal's eyes one can see something suggestive about the relationship between Mathur and Ramakrishna. Mathur had warmed to him as a youth, had provided him with female clothes, had believed Ramakrishna to be a woman when dressed in female clothes, and oscillated in his regard for Ramakrishna, sometimes seeing him as "his revered spiritual father, sometimes as an innocent irresponsible young boy."[5] If Tota Puri, the Naked One, became devoted to Ramakrishna there is nothing in Isherwood's text to suggest that the relationship was other than that between a guru and his disciple. And Isherwood describes Ramakrishna's love for his young disciples in terms of a motherly love. Within the canon of the Krishna story he became Yashoda, Krishna's foster-mother: "such a relationship is mysterious beyond our comprehension."[6] It is, of course, hard to deny the homoerotic implications of the way Ramakrishna worshipped Krishna as Radha in the *madhava bhava* or sweet mood. But Isherwood, in the end, sees Ramakrishna as transgender: "it was perhaps because the sense of sex-identity was so faint in him that he was easily able to assume the character of either sex."[7] Isherwood comes down on the side of seeing Ramakishna as wholly innocent and naïve,

as the holy fool. This was how he put it in an interview with Carolyn Heilbron: "actually, Ramakrishna was completely simple and guileless. He told
people whatever came into his mind like a child. If he had ever been troubled
by homosexual desires, if that had ever been a problem, he'd simply have told
every body about them . . . He was completely without any hang-ups, talking
about sex-roles, because his thoughts transcended physical love-making."[8] But
the point to be extracted from this debate is Kripal's conviction that the roots
of the mystical lie in the homoerotic.

A Correspondence

Another way of making comparisons between Forster and Isherwood is to
look at their wartime correspondence when Isherwood was struggling with
his religious vocation and Forster, as a good friend, was trying to be both supportive but honest. It demonstrates well their variance in the search for the
divine. Owing to the vagaries of the transatlantic post the letters are not always sequential.[9]

We pick up the correspondence with a letter from Forster to Isherwood 11
November 1941. "I got off a letter to Gerald (Heard) about a fortnight ago.
It was partly about praying. People over here are rather silly and shy about
prayer. Anyhow I find it easy to condemn them when they condemn it. I believe prayer is much more like going to bed with someone than is generally
supposed. Hence the shyness. Hence the great advantage or disadvantage
which may ensue." Isherwood's reply came from Haverford, Pennsylvania
where he was looking after Jewish refugees. "Mere pity is useless here," he
wrote. "True charity is the intense alertness which Gerald so often writes
about. Nothing less is any good." Then taking up Forster's observation, "I
agree with you about prayer. It is like going to bed: just as 'getting religion'
(that horrible expression) is like falling in love. And prayer in its turn has
various consequences, like consummation. After leading this kind of life or
intermittently trying to—for about a year and a half—there isn't anything
much I can say about it without embarrassment except that 'it pays' in better balance, better integration, greater contentment and much more important an increasing appetite for it and commitment to it. Anyhow with all my
backslippings, it's still a lot more satisfactory than physical marriage ever
was—not that the one excludes the other. If the right person comes along,
that could be more wonderful than ever. At present there is nobody and I'm
quite fairly content to have it that way."

At this point Forster had to undergo the tormenting prospect of losing his
friend Bob Buckingham to the airforce, prayer became in earnest, but there

was to be the almighty relief of his failing the medical: he went blind at 25,000 feet. Isherwood, 21 June 1943, sympathized: "Gosh that must have been awful to you about Bob. Thank heavens he finally didn't go. I wish I were a real Yoga and could utter authoritative prophecies that he will die at the age of 101 in bed." By now Isherwood had entered the Vedanta Center. "I know quite well that this is a pleasant period with a time limit to it, during which I have to prepare some steel cables which won't snap when strained. I honestly believe that I now believe in 'God' (can't explain what I mean by God) and that I rely on Him and will turn to him when things get tough. But of course I have no way of being sure of this or of what help I'd receive in say a crisis like yours; or of whether this belief of mine mightn't go away just as mysteriously as it came. If you can fall out of love you can fall out of faith (but can you fall out of love?) or anyhow William James says so." At that stage Prabhavananda was away in India. "I do the ritual worship most days which is probably familiar to you: the flowers and brass bowls and incense and candles. And the Sanskrit mantrams. I think of you very often while I am doing it—especially because everything Indian suggests you to me—and sometimes I talk to the Lord about you. Sometimes you and Bob are sniggering in the background because of the wrap I'm wearing and the flowers on the top of my head. 'Look at Chris in drag.' And I can see you at lunch with us; you and Swami warming to each other and you enjoying the curry which is good."

Forster responded 23 November: "I understand your ritual and drag easily. The universe is very odd and we don't recognize this enough. I do not understand your feeling that god will help you—i.e. I don't ever feel that I shall ever be thus helped myself. When I was so upset about Bob's being taken from me I seemed to get through it all alone—just behaving as any Englishman should, then breaking down and then behaving as a human being." Forster went on to express doubt that he would ever grasp any future accounts from Isherwood of trusting in God. Isherwood took up the cudgels: in his reply 27 November: "About God helping us. 'Helping' is a misleading word perhaps. Let's say for example that there is something inside you which is larger than your personality, and which has some kind of access to what is outside you, just as the smallest inlet of the sea anywhere has access to all the oceans, call it what you like. You half sarcastically acknowledged its existence when you burnt those stories in order to get on with The Passage to India (of course that could be written off to innate Puritanism but I think that's superficial). Well this genius lives in you all the time and it is not merely literary. Literature is only a function of it."

By now into Vedantist territory he elaborated: "Communicating with it consists in realizing that you *are* it—or rather *that it is you*—the only 'you' there is; because Morgan Forster is only real in a temporary sense, like a cloud or storm. While you are communicating with your 'genius' (and here Isherwood was in fact referring to the *Atman*) you lose all sense of being an individual Morgan Forster and so you lose all Morgan's fears, doubts, desires etc etc. You are just as much Bob (Buckingam) or Joe (Ackerley) or William (Plomer) as you are Morgan—because they too have inlets to the ocean and you are this ocean. And that helps. In fact it is the only thing in life which does help." He went on to describe the difficulties he was having with the translation of the *gita*. But then he came back to the letter with a postscript: "Reading through what I've written about God etc I feel bored. It is badly put. Full of religious clichés. And as I always feel: how impossible to say these things *directly*, much less write them. If I saw you maybe I could convey something which was nearer the actuality—while I was talking about the weather, or the poetry of Blunden or Prague. After all, what can you tell me in so many words about Bob? You can talk around it. But I get nothing of what you feel."

But Forster had his own ideas on why he destroyed his erotic short stories and did not take kindly to doubts about his personal autonomy. In a reply of 10 February 1944 he stated: "that sacrifice still seems to me right, still inexplicable, for I wasn't and am not ashamed of them. I will try to connect it to 'God.'" In a letter of 20 February he responded to the Vedantism: "Yes, I am aware of something of myself at times which isn't myself. I don't like to call it God nor do I think it wisely so called for the reason that the word 'God' has kept such bad company and hypnotizes its users in wrong directions. I even queried your saying it was infinitely greater than yourself; different yes but one hasn't the apparatus for measuring size."

Thereafter the correspondence became chattier with Isherwood discussing his translations, raising the possibility of a life of Vivekananda, mentioning his just finishing "a very priggish sounding article on the gita and War" (29 July 1944) and Forster expressing a wish to read the translation and later stating that he liked it "very much indeed, far better than Mrs Besant's" (18 December 1944).

And there we must leave this rather surprising correspondence between an erstwhile atheist and a liberal humanist. Carpenter would have endorsed Isherwood's Vedantist thoughts if in a more poetic and abstract way.

Expanding the Paradigms

All three writers had to endure a conflict between the demands of the flesh and their search for mystical transcendence. They were caught up in a dualism Freud came to characterize as one between Eros and Thanatos. In seeking a resolution of their conflict in the Indian spiritual tradition they may well have tilted the outcome heavily in favor of Thanatos. Jeffrey Masson has a devastating account of Indian spirituality as peculiarly susceptible to a form of masochism, of a wish, as he puts it, "to detach ourselves from other people, and then to exalt that detachment into a philosophical principle of sublime proportions." He elaborates: "I believe this retreat from the emotions, this dread of human feeling, is one of the fundamental disguised themes of almost all Indian writing and stands in need of both exploration and, finally, explanation." Fascinatingly, in analyzing tantrism he sees the immobilization of breath as camouflaging a fear of dying, immobilizing semen "as a barely disguised derivation of castration fears:" "this urgent desire for stillness may well derive from early fears of sexual excitement."[10] So was the quest for Nirvana essentially a flight from sexuality?

But Norman Brown opens up the possibility of a major qualification. At one stage he concedes that Freud's late dualism gave way to an all-encompassing death instinct, with the Nirvana principle as one and the same as the pleasure principle, though this may have been the only tolerable way out of the self-destructive sado-masochistic component of the psyche. As Norman Brown puts it: "thus interpreted, psychoanalysis reaffirms ageless religious aspirations."[11] But the corrective lay in recognizing two forms of mysticism, the Apollonian or sublimation mysticism and the Dionysiac or body mysticism. In the Dionysian "there is the possibility of human perfectibility and the hope of finding a way out of the human neurosis into that health that animals enjoy but not man." This "magical" body is one and the same as the "subtle" or "spiritual" body of oriental mysticism. Here there is convergence with "the polymorphously perverse body of childhood" of the Freudian canon, "the hermaphroditic body."[12] So is there a possibility of a reconciliation of spirit and flesh, one that Aurobindo so profoundly explored in his concept of the divinised body, Carpenter worked toward as he sought to reconcile the conflicting messages from his two gurus, Whitman and Ramaswamy, Forster intuited in the Krishna cult, and Isherwood looked at in a more repressed and conservative way in his account of yoga?

Another way into exploring this tension between sexuality and mysticism, between body and spirit, is by exploring the competing paradigms of carnival, so brilliantly explored by Mikhail Bakhtin[13] and of myth, Mircea Eliade[14] their persuasive expositor.

It might seem perverse to draw carnival as a paradigm into the debate, it being so much at one extreme of the body-spirit spectrum. Carnival's is a frank acceptance of the body in all its earthiness, a delight in all the orifices, in those ways humans connect. But it can tie in with India, the so-called *Indian Wonders*, a ghoulish account of the exotic and strange in India being one of the texts that profoundly influenced the medieval sense of the grotesque. And in carnival there is a clear convergence with the Krishna cult. Carnival is about play: to quote Bakhtin, "in reality, it is life itself, but shaped according to a certain pattern of play. During carnival time life is subject only to its laws, that is the laws of its own freedom."[15] Here there are clear connections with the subversive content of Indian folk culture. Forster, already fascinated by the pagan god Pan, picked up on this bacchanalian content to the Krishna cult. Carnival was also profoundly at odds with a bourgeois "individualized" sense of the body: it subscribed to "the collective ancestral body of all the people," "the people who are continually growing and renewed."[16] All this would have gelled with Carpenter's hostility to self-consciousness and his belief in man's wholeness in pre-civilization cultures. Maybe both Carpenter and Forster would always have favored the classic and Renaissance ideal of the finished and self-contained body over carnival's delight in the grotesque, in man's "ever unfinished and ever creating body," its dwelling on the phallus, the buttocks, the belly, but I am far from sure of this, and certainly Isherwood in *Down There on a Visit* (1962), if it all leaves rather an ugly taste in the mouth, was well able to describe grotesque bodily behavior. But then carnival can also share in the mystical. The grotesque body is seen by Bakhtin as "cosmic and universal"; "it contains the signs of the zodiac. It reflects the cosmic hierarchy. This body can merge with various natural phenomena, with mountains, rivers, seas, islands and continents. It can fill the entire universe."[17] All this was certainly true of the Krishna story.

Carnival simply will not go away. It keeps breaking through into a repressed middle-class culture. Stallybrass and White portray how it is incorporated as "the other": "the carnival, the circus, the gypsy, the lumpenproletariat play a symbolic role in bourgeois culture out of all proportion to their actual social importance."[18] "It encoded all that which the proper bourgeois must strive *not to be* in order to preserve a stable and 'correct' sense of self."[19] Here was Nietzche's concept of the return of the repressed reenacted: "the *disjecta membra* of the grotesque body of carnival found curious lodgments throughout the whole social order of late nineteenth and early twentieth century Europe."[20] But this incorporation had two contradictory functions, both to shore up a middle class sense of difference and superiority but also one of hybridization, a way of appropriating its subversiveness, its becoming enmeshed "in an inclusive, heterogeneous, dangerously unstable zone." "What starts as a *simple* repulsion or rejection of symbolic matter foreign to the self inaugurates a process of introjection and negation which is always *complex* in its effects."[21] The bourgeoisie needed Bohemia. Intuitively, one can see how all three writers, given their outsider status as homosexuals, would delight in the transgressive, be drawn to any inversion of the established order, but at the same time they were all products of that middle class order and found themselves also drawn, if not toward any affirmation of bourgeois values, then toward some new version of integration, be it socially shaped in Carpenter's quasi-socialist outlook, or more individually in Forster's and Isherwood's. And here lies the paradox: "transgression becomes a kind of reverse counter-sublimation . . . the bourgeoisie is perpetually rediscovering the carnivalesque as a radical source of transcendence."[22]

But the dialectic between carnival and mysticism only partially comes from within the carnival paradigm itself. It needed the input of the mythical.

Modern secular society has analyzed myth out of existence. Eliade's is largely a contrast between modern secular cultures and non-western religions. In large part in his analysis this is to do with a different sense of Time. As Eliade puts it: "it is only in modern societies that man feels himself to be the prisoner of his daily work, in which he can never escape from time."[23] The cult of history has usurped a sense of primordial or Great Time. Myth, in contrast, looks outside Time. In eastern religions, Hinduism, Buddhism, Taoism, the quest is rather to escape Time. Yoga leads the way. The assumption is of an easy access to the gods. Oriental religions really believe in their myths. In Carpenterish language Eliade points to the ease with which the shaman also can engage with the divine. In Vedantism the divide between substance, *prakrit,* and spirit, *purusha,* can be bridged. The great mother goddesses have the power to do so. Tantrism is here especially selected: it awakens the powers of the *kundalani*: he writes of the cosmic energy that is asleep in one's own body, of "an audacious act of interiorisation." Intriguingly, there is here a cross-over with the carnivalesque, for Eliade sees a positive value in the orgiastic: "the orgy is a symbolic re-entry into chaos, into the primordial and undifferentiated state." It gets back in touch with that original wholeness from which life and the cosmos originally sprang.[24]

Eliade makes a devastating contrast between those non-western cultures which have no trouble engaging with Myth and modern secular which do. Here, greatly contrasting attitudes to death come into play. Whereas those cultures who are indifferent to Time and with little sense of History have no trouble in embracing death—it is simply a rite of passage to another existence—in modern secular cultures all human existence is subject to History and hence faces the anguish of death. As Eliade bleakly puts it: "Anguish before Nothingness and death seems to be a specifically modern phenomenon." Vedantism argues, to the contrary, that this is only the death of "your illusions and your ignorance." Cleverly, Eliade anticipates the skeptical response of modern secular man: "you are asking me then to give up my authentic existence, and to take refuge in an abstraction, in pure Being, in the *atman*; I am to sacrifice my dignity as a creator of history in order to live an a-historic, inauthentic existence, empty of human content. Well, I prefer to put up with my anxiety: at least, it cannot deprive me of a certain human grandeur, that of becoming conscious of, and accepting, the human condition." But Eliade then replies from an Indian perspective: "we are beginning to realize that, perhaps more than any other civilization, that of India loves and reverences Life, and enjoys it at every level." "For Indian thought Maya is a divine creation, a cosmic *play* of which the end and aim is human existence, as well as deliverance from that experience." Hinduism can also calmly contemplate the end of the world, confident that it will be followed by the birth of another.[25]

All this permits a claim for a larger vision in the outlook of Carpenter, Forster, and Isherwood. If their's was a highly personalized endeavor to reconcile the sexual and the mystical, quite clearly there were serious limitations on how far they were prepared to sacrifice the pleasures of the flesh. Arguably sexuality took precedence over mysticism. But they were tantalized by the possibilities of transcendence, be it through Vedantism or the mysticism of the Krishna cult. They reached beyond their merely personal struggle. They saw the desperate need to come up with an alternative to modern man's pessimistic and nihilistic sense that beyond death lay nothingness. All three, though with varying conviction and ephemerality, were at some stage in thrall to a countermyth, that beyond death lay another experience, an alertness to a spiritualized version of Nietzche's concept of the eternal recurrence.

Notes

1. Only by sitting in on a course taught by my colleague, Leon Schlamm, did I get to know of a range of additional materials on the guru-disciple relationship, A. Rawlinson's magisterial, *The Book of Enlightened Masters: Western Teachers in Eastern Traditions* (Chicago: Open Court, 1997) and G. Feuerstein's, *Holy Madness: The Shock Tactics and Radical Teachings of Crazy-Wise Adepts, Holy Fools and Rascal Gurus* (New York: 1991), among the most important.

2. See Kripal's introduction to his second edition of *Kali's Child* (Chicago: The University of Chicago Press, 1998).

3. C. Isherwood, *My Guru and his Disciple* (London: Methuen, 1980), 249.

4. Swami Atmanjnanananda, "Scandals, cover-ups and other imagined occurrences in the life of Ramakrsna: An examination of Jeffrey Kripal's *Kali's Child*," *International Journal of Hindu Studies* 1 (2 August 1997): 401–20.

5. C. Isherwood, *Ramakrishna and His Disciples* (London: Methuen, 1965), 129.

6. Isherwood, *Ramakrishna and His Disciples*, 179.

7. Isherwood, *Ramakrishna and His Disciples*, 113.

8. Carolyn Heilbron, "Christopher Isherwood: An Interview," *Twentieth Century Literature* 22 (October 1976): 254.

9. This is drawn from the Forster Archives, King's College. Forster Correspondence to Isherwood, 1932–1962 and E.M.F. Correspondence, Christopher Isherwood, xviii. Forster's letters of 14 December 1943 and 28 February 1944 to Isherwood are published in Mary Lago and P. N. Furbank, eds., *Selected Letters of E. M. Forster Vol Two 1921–1970* (London: 1985), 204–7.

10. J. Moussaeff Masson, *The Oceanic Feeling; the Origins of Religious Sentiment in Ancient India* (Dordrecht: D. Reidel, 1980), 1–11. There is much further of interest on Ramakrishna, homosexuality and the oceanic, not to mention Buddha and depression.

11. Norman Brown, *Life Against Death: The Psychoanalytic Meaning of History* (Middleton, Connecticut: Routledge and Kegan Paul, 1959), 90.

12. Brown, *Life Against Death*, 310–13.

13. Mikhail Bakhtin, *Rabelais and His World*, trans. by Helene Iswolksy (Bloomington: 1984). And for a critical exploration of Bakhtin's account of carnival and its ongoing influence on modern culture see Peter Stallybrass and Allen White, *The Politics and Poetics of Transgression: a Critique of Bakhtin* (Ithaca, New York: Cornell University Press, 1986).

14. Mircea Eliade, *Myths, Dreams and Mysteries: The Encounter Between Contemporary Faiths and Archaic Realities*, trans. Philip Mairet (London: Harvill Press, 1960).

15. Bakhtin, *Rabelais and His World*, 7.

16. Bakhtin, *Rabelais and His World*, 19–21.

17. Bakhtin, *Rabelais and His World*, 318.

18. Stallybrass and White, *The Politics and Poetics of Transgression*, 20.

19. Stallybrass and White, *The Politics and Poetics of Transgression*, 178.

20. Stallybrass and White, *The Politics and Poetics of Transgression*, 180.

21. Stallybrass and White, *The Politics and Poetics of Transgression*, 193.

22. Stallybrass and White, *The Politics and Poetics of Transgression*, 200–01.

23. Eliade, *Myths, Dreams and Mysteries*, 37.

24. Eliade, *Myths, Dreams and Mysteries*, 186.

25. Eliade, *Myths, Dreams and Mysteries*, 234–45.

APPENDIX

~

Extracts from a Diary of the Visit to India 1999

I see these as field notes for the text. Any materials in the diary which bear on my inquiry into Vedantism, into the Krishna cult and into attitudes within India toward homosexuality have been selected. In its account of my experiences with swamis and inquiries into Vedantism and yoga it makes obvious links with Carpenter's and Isherwood's inquiries into the same. The account of Krishna and the Braj pilgrimage connects with Forster's own attempt to grapple with the Krishna legend. I have left in a certain amount of local color.

Calcutta, Vedantism, and the Durga Myth

28 September

A pretty grotty flight out. A smooth run to Heathrow—I drove—Brian K. threatening to let my house in my absence to Kossovan refugees. I arrived at the airport well before check-in time and got my aisle seat, only later to discover it was the row behind two very demanding babies—the noise throughout the flight was to be pretty unbearable. It did not help that the mother felt the cabin staff had failed to come to her aid and that her cause was then taken up by a fearful lady nearby—chaos reigned. I enjoyed watching Zeferelli's *Tea with Mussolini* which for all its overtones of anti-fascism and the holocaust was rather picaresque. Then I just plugged into Indian film music to blot out the hubbub. It dawned on me that Vedantism was India's leading strategy for coping with just such intolerable social demands.

But we arrived and then the adventure began. It took an age for my luggage to arrive on the carousel. A young representative from Magic India Tours was there to greet me but then abandoned me to the driver. So, through streets hung with election flags and heavily policed, past Salt Lake City and Science City, with buses coming full tilt at us on our side of the dual carriageway, to the Ramakrishna Mission Institute of Culture. Initially, it looked a little less gleaming than usual but, no doubt, the rains take the shine off everything. Calcutta has been experiencing post-monsoon late rains and the city is widely flooded. Water is pumped up and just flows along the roads. I'm, as requested, on the top floor.

29 September

I slept pretty well but it will take time for the effects of the lost night to wear off. Hari, the scout, woke me early and I had a series of knocks on the door—paper-man, dhobi man, sweeper—so I got the message and got up for breakfast.

Then a small miracle—Binoy Chaudhuri phoned. I think Reception had made contact with him. Certainly he had not received my letter. So I was able to get hold of Ranjit's new number and have a chat with him. Bits of the jigsaw falling into place. Then off to meet the new Secretary, Swami Prabhananda, though in the company of an Indian business man from Washington, here for the Durga puja. The new Mahant is quite different from Swami Lokeswarananda—he was avuncular and forgetful, a comfortable and large man—his successor is sharp, wiry and outgoing. Then I found myself in the library and soon with volumes in front of me—despite my fatigue. The Mission has gone to quite some trouble to track down books on my interests. Well, this will not be archival research but I will be keeping up the momentum of my present reading.

A longish sleep after lunch. No one famous staying at the Mission at the moment. I've taken to a social scientist from Stoke, a mature student, David Trelawny, working on the wetlands of Bengal.

Then a lecture by Prabhananda on Vivekananda's ideas on education. A very clear one, with much defining of terms. But Professor Das Gupta's concluding remarks—that none of us in any real way have been educated and maybe anyway our families really educated us—made more impact.

30 September

A day when central Calcutta passed before me yet again. Ranjit came, but without a driver, so the whole day became rather an expensive taxi drive. We couldn't find the ANZ Grindlay's bank I normally use. We went back to his flat. One telephone call established that my lawyer friend, Jatin Ghosh has died. Odd that they'd not written to tell me. I now fear for my trade unionist friend, Jatindra Biswas. I may have to open up a new front. Clearly Sujon is around but he's made no attempt to contact me. So off to the American Express office. Then to a government office. Ranjit has inherited a security firm from his father. He's kept it on, to continue providing employment for some hundred workers. We were there to sort out some business problem. So considerable is the respect for his father he is comparatively unharrassed over its affairs. Anyway, whatever the nature of the problem, it was promptly dispatched. All information is still kept in old-fashioned files, in danger of falling apart—were they to computerize, no doubt hundreds of filing clerks would be out of a job. But how do they know where to find anything? Then to the Tollygunge Club where, after being shunted from one office to another, I ended up signing in the Visitors Book. So I'm now a member and can use their handsome pool and sauna.

2 October
In fact Gandhi's birthday and a public holiday.

One of those tiresome Indian bureaucratic situations. I behaved badly and refused to go and get my passport photo taken for a borrower's card from the library. The library Swami politely stood his ground—I'd already lost my temper at the bookshop reception and he delegated someone to take me across the road to a small studio. Matter resolved.

I worked hard on the Friday on the journal *Vedanta and the West*—much Heard, Prabavananda, and Isherwood material. I have contrived to continue where I left off. In the evening a talk on the Hollywood Center by its present Assistant Minister, but rather rhetorical. Then Swami Ashaktananda spoke and here was a much tougher intelligence. He I must meet. Susan Walters, an American woman staying permanently in the Mission—she contributes to the Bulletin with articles on western mysticism—told me there had been some unpleasantness between him and Prabhavananda. The latter became jealous of the following he was acquiring at the Center and he was forced to leave prematurely. In the evening David Trelawny gave us a guitar recital.

But Saturday was a fulfilling day. Down Gariahat Road to Dolly's Teahouse where I was to meet Martin's friend, the delightful Dolly Roy. This promises well. Then to a barber's for a haircut and a facial massage. Good. Then off to the Tollygunge for a swim—I almost had the pool to myself—and for a massage by the exuberant Mr Chatterjee. Anxious to point out to me that he was a Brahmin. When I asked him how many children he had he had to think very hard before he said five. Then to Ranjit and Papiya for dinner, via his sister's house—and a good meal, though, in old-fashioned colonial style, they insisted that I eat first on my own. Young Krishna, their son, was very noisy. I was able to make several further telephone contacts.

Ranjit began to tell me a little about Durga. The triune Indian gods had been faced by a revolt from the Demon Buffalo king. He had been told that no man would slay him and this had encouraged his tyrannical ambition. But the gods produced Durga who was to slay him.

In another incarnation she had been Sati who, when her father had failed to invite her to a feast, had thrown herself onto a fire (or was it that her father had failed to attend her feast?). Anyway, her body was dragged out and then severed into fifty-two parts—each to become the site of a Kali temple.

It seems that each local urban district has its own Durga committee, together with its own annual festival committee and they run the show. I seem to be mapping out a good Durga festival. As Kaku Bose, another of Martin's (Gilbert's) friends, suggested, if my studies are interrupted through library closure, at least I'll be witness to a major cultural event and hence be learning about Indian religions.

Is part of my fascination with India to do with its apparently breaking so many rules? The sheer anarchism of the place? Does this gratify my own rebellious feelings about my own "establishment?"

3 October
Today India completed its elections—well, there's still some parts of the Christian NE to vote. Although warned against going out to have a look David Trelawny and I went and inspected the nearest polling booth. More policemen—who were inquisitive about us and friendly and insisted they were guaranteeing a free election—visible than voters. David and I came to the conclusion that shopping for Durga was more important to the Calcuttans than their franchise.

In the evening to Binoy's and Tripti's for supper. I asked several people in the immediate vicinity if they knew where the Sivanath Sastri Bhavan was—I'd lost my bearings in the dark. I drew a complete blank. But I don't feel today was any sort of a turning point in India's recent history.

4–5 October
A good day in the library on the Monday.

I'm getting into Paul Brunton's *The Quest for Secret India*, lightweight but readable. Then a lecture by the Mission's one and only swami in Moscow. Clearly Russian university students have some appetite for Vedantism, if more for Sanskrit. There was a moment when I thought him to say the Mission was under attack from the Theosophical Society. But he meant, as he later explained to me, that Christian students studying Theosophy attack the teachings of other non-Christian faiths. Clearly, Russian laws are hostile to any attempts at conversion. Still, the swami is regularly invited to give talks at the Indian Embassy in St. Petersburg and at like meetings in Moscow. Russians, he now sees, as lazy and work-shy. Clearly a dose of Vedantism would be good for them. But Russia he finds—maybe because of its snow—a good deal cleaner than India with its dust.

And then over dinner I recognized first my book *Religions in Conflict* and then Ashis Nandy—its potential reviewer—here on a visit to interview two Bengalis—one a famous environmentalist, or rather his son and the film director, Mrinal Sen, still alive. We seemed to spend our time discussing the disadvantages of staying in five star hotels.

6 October

So I had my conversation with Ashis Nandy.

This is an analysis of it rather than a descriptive narrative.

He corrects the idea of the dominantly feminine in Indian culture. He emphasizes, instead, the androgynous. Indians would not understand a specific choice of homosexuality.

There is more to be made of the Hindu pantheon. The lives of the gods may be projections of the human. Here there is a correspondence with Hellenism and paganism.

He made the fascinating point that often those who responded to Hinduism were Irish and maybe Catholic e.g., Sister Nivedita. Celtism has affinities with Hinduism. Catholicism itself can veer into Hinduism and both have a strong "maternal" element. In terms of the feminine one must distinguish between the maternal and the conjugal. The maternal he sees as on the decline. The conjugal offers a greater prospect of gender equality.

But why should Europeans respond to this faith?

If there is ambivalence over the feminine (let alone the androgynous) then some, of course, will reject it—think of James Mill, Kipling, all that attempt to denigrate Indian effeminacy (androgyny?). As long as there is ambivalence and a failure of self-acceptance, then the response to Indian religions may itself remain ambivalent. Clearly the discourse on androgyny in Indian culture, even when Europeans are subject to the mistaken hope that it will lead onto homosexuality e.g. Forster in his relationship with Masood, does act as a release. The European homosexual will feel freer, more liberated in the Indian context.

But you come back to the interaction of their relationships with their mothers and the maternal in Indian culture. Maybe here there is also ambivalence. But maybe also here is a "mythical" arena where they can work out some emotional relationship with the feminine. Or will there always be a final barrier?

What of incest?

Maternal—good and bad breast—Klein-Durga, Kali, etc.

On another tack, he wondered if we have really the evidence to decide on Ramakrishna. Maybe this is again androgyny and Kripal has it wrong. Certainly Ramakrishna cross-dressed.

He related the story of the nobel prizewinning Indian mathematician, Ramanujan and Professor Hardy—Hardy responded to his androgyny and Ramanujan flourished in that response but that is all there was to it.

There is little written evidence on homosexuality—some on lesbianism.

But there is some folk literature on homosexuality.

He was keen on the idea of the 'absurd' in this whole debate on Indian spirituality. Think of Madame Blavatsky. Do all cultures have this absurd element?

He has looked at some of these questions in his book *Alternative Sciences*.

I felt we were on a wavelength.

Ashis does see androgyny in western culture. Christ was androgynous. This was still there on through to the third/fourth C. But this has been obscured. He feels androgyny is there somehow in the Trinity cf the Triune figure in Hinduism.

Otherwise my day taken up by my lecture at the Rabindra Bharati University. A long car journey and another exposure to this ungainly city. Once again through streets flooded by late rains. The bypass is not the most interesting of journeys and I missed seeing all those great bhadralok houses. On the whole northern Calcutta struck me as more depressed than the south. I am even beginning to feel quite defensive of Gol Park and Gariahat Road.

Rabindra Bharati on a day such as this—it teemed down as we arrived—can seem a pretty derelict place. The large lecture hall incongruously had ceiling lights, candelabra I guess, which might have graced a ballroom. This was a repeat of my Calgary lecture. I suspect it was too complicated for this audience. I took to the slightly built but immensely good-humored Dr. Jahar Sen, ex-professor of the University of Calcutta, Ranjit's former teacher, who acted as my interpreter. From being a historian of China and the United States he's taken to compiling information on the Gandhian movement. Pratup Chandra Chandra, who arrived long after my talk, gave a lecture on

Gandhi's attitude to technology. He was a minister—was it Education or Culture?—in the Desai Janata government and one of 'the great five' in Bengal politics, Shankar Roy and Surat Bose amongst the others. A frail man of eighty but still shouldering burdens. I liked two of Ranjit's colleagues—Raj Sekhar Basu, a pleasant affable fellow, presently completing a thesis on untouchables in South India. He has reviewed books of mine in *Gandhi Marg*. Then there was Professor Kimadri Bannerjee. He's investigating how Sikhs assimilate with other Indians in their diaspora. Indeed, I espied some Sikhs on our return, physically three times the size of Bengali.

Then back to Ranjit's to celebrate his fortieth birthday. His two sisters present. Young Krishna as much of a handful as ever. Oddly, for so crowded a day, I was none too fatigued.

7 October

Stuck at it in the library. Huxley is so much more readable than Heard. I came across a play by Girish Chandra Ghosh, *Vilwa Mangal*. One can see why Isherwood should have been so attracted to Ghosh.

Over supper at the Mission a guest was announced and it was Sujon (Chandra) I'd almost reconciled myself to our not meeting. I had some mixed feelings at his reappearance. He probes and, true to form, there was to be a long discussion about Kripal's book. But this had its value.

8 October

I set aside ten minutes to talk to Professor R. Das Gupta and stayed for two hours. An Oxford man. In fact, though by then he was a mature student, we almost overlapped—he left in 1956. He was under Neville Coghill at Exeter though Helen Gardiner supervised his doctorate on Milton. I've reported the gist of our conversation elsewhere. He clearly enjoyed an opportunity such as I provided for a chat. I doubt if many share his field of reference. He clearly finds the role of guru imposed on him at the Mission burdensome and winsomely he observed, he'd like his own. He became quite confessional. It's interesting that he's a dualist—here he's under the auspices of a commitedly Vedantist Mission but he's not one himself. Clearly the intellectual doubt remains. But, judging from his pieces in the press, he's a strong moralist. I liked the discreet way he referred to Isherwood's "weaknesses." He wanted to know more of my family and clearly felt I was young looking for my age (indeed, India has given me a strange sense that I am getting younger!). He's physically very frail but mentally wide-awake. He reminded me of CR (Rajagopalachari) and this clearly pleased him. He had greatly admired CR, thought there was no one to equal him at the time and it was India's huge loss that he did not become President in 1950.

In the evening a "song" by a young choir that belongs to the mission and quite well done, if overlong. It was all about the Durga story. We were chilled by the air-conditioning in the Vivekananda Hall.

Some very likeable people have joined us at the Mission. There's a talented violinist learning to play the Indian violin. This is Michael. He's in his early fifties, wiry, lean, full of receptivity. A New York Jew. He gave me a tape of my favorite oboeist. He has a teacher here. He and David's recital was a surprisingly successful blend of two very contrasting personalities.

There's a Susan (surname unknown) who actually met Swami Prabhavananda at the age of fourteen—she'd strayed into the grounds of the Trabuco monastery. He was very benign. Gave her some books. It was the turning point in her life. Her family knew Rosalind Rajagopaul, so she was on the inside of that whole extraordinary Krishnamurti story.

Santiniketan

9 October

Got to Howrah station almost too early—an easy journey there. So onto the Santiniketan Express at 9:55. At one point the a/c was not working and I feared I'd be stifled, but a clever fellow knew how to turn it on. So into a pleasing green rice-field landscape, studded with orange and yellow washed houses and villages. I guess the high point was just short of Porbur South— the sight of a head swimming in a natural pond, then a gleaming broad-shouldered back and then this handsome fellow stood up and waded out—a truly excellent physique together with a roguish face.

Ajit Neogy waiting for me at the station. He's aged since our meeting in 1995 at the Aurobindo archives. But as I became reacquainted I realized how much nicer a man he be—less evasive. So to the Tata-built guest house, Ratti Kuti. Well appointed. Rather smart marbled surround. Simple but clean rooms. It should be fine here. Then at 3:30 Ajit called and we walked to his flat and I began to get a short history of the place.

Originally Debendranath came here to meditate and erected the Brahmo Mandir. This is important as it means some festivals, such as the Durga, are not celebrated here, deemed idolatrous (which I guess it is). Then in 1901 Rabindranath started his school. Brought boys out from Calcutta. Remember all this was then forest land, inhospitable and hardly the place to send your sons. Really it took the Nobel prize in 1913 to put the school on the map. Up to 150 students plus after that. The university started in 1921 but as a center for advanced study and clearly Ajit feels Tagore's vision of a research-based university was the right idea. But there was a period of weak administration after Tagore's death from 1941 to 1951 under his son, Rathindranath and, after that, the Center took it over. Nehru would have preferred the perpetuation of Tagore's approach but it was not to be—ineluctably it became like any other university, if a Central one.

A neighbor in the Agriculture department then called and we went over Tagore's and Pearson's experiments in agronomy. I'll see Sriniketan tomorrow.

Ajit told me something of his own life's history. Born in Chandernagore, hence his interest in French history. He hopes to move on from his interest in Pondicherry to Chandernagore. (Was I kind enough about his book in my review?) He taught in a Calcutta college. He came here in 1971. He still regrets not taking up a French scholarship, with the possibility of an academic career in France. He's had a distinguished administrative career here—head of department and Dean. He grows on me.

There is to be the celebration here of another festival, one dedicated to the welfare of parents. This takes the form of a kind of boot-fare in the central space of the campus, with wonderful old University buildings all around. Much bustle and excitement, the students here for the last day of semester. Rather bric-a-brac home-made products on sale. One of the historians spoke to us in this melée—a specialist in the history of ideas.

Somehow we raised the view that the "spiritual" does not pay enough attention to death. All religions, including Vedantism, are ways of weakening the fear of death. Is enough made of this fear?

The most attractive building is Debendranath's mandir, all made out of colored glass and lit throughout the night. The whole site reminds me of Adyar. Ajit feels the university has seen better days.

So back to my guest house and dinner.

10 October

An attack of cramp in the night. The leg was to remain stiffish all day.

After breakfast Ajit called and so to a meeting with the historians. Only a few were there. I tried out a few lines of enquiry. On the self—are western and eastern or rather Vedantist versions compatible? Someone from Ancient History (there are twelve teachers in Ancient, twelve in Modern) took up the running, but came at it from another direction—the west had impregnated the east—the impact of Alexander the Great—the Gandhara School. So from an early stage the east could recognize the west. But this still leaves open the question, from whence within the traditional culture came this susceptibility to western influence?

Otherwise, I asked if indeed Tagore shaped their syllabus—clearly its scope is fairly international. I rather liked the lady historian from Shillong, working on the Irish influence on the nationalist movement—she'd been taught by Irish nuns.

So to Sriniketan by car and series of visits to offices and research centers. This is, of course, far more Tagore's brainchild. It seems this whole wing of the university is attuned to the needs of the neighboring villages—in fact, it's all a large laboratory. I saw work on the making of organic soil—earth worms used to create a rich manure. (They are then taken out and survive when the manured soil is taken to the village.) There is something of a commitment to organic farming. In another office they have soil samples from many farms and can tell the farmer how best to fertilize his soil. Farmers on small plots of half to one and a half hectares are listening, but no co-operatives here. There are fish farmers and here there are co-operatives. Again, work is going on to improve the soil base of the pools, at the moment too porous. There are fish tanks. Farmers sell their surplus to middlemen, though always at a loss. The fat cats are in Calcutta. I began to conjure up a picture of whole swathes of university-trained agricultural officers, dispersed all over India, sitting on panchayats, giving free advice. Maybe here is a clue as to how India will feed its burgeoning population.

So back to Ajit's for lunch, prepared by his maidservant of some fifteen years standing. Fish, of course.

After a rest, back on the trail but rather too late in the day. Time only for a short visit to the museum. First a chat to its director, Professor Swapan Majumdar. He talked a little about the response of Indian intellectuals to Forster's writing—A Passage to India has been well translated into Bengali. The verdict is mixed. I tried to argue a case that through the creative imagination Forster transcended the conceptual limitations of his grasp of Indian religions. It seems, according to Majumdar, Isherwood might have taken his idea for A Meeting by the River from a sixteenth century text, translated with the title Meeting of Two Cultures-Hinduism and Islam, a translation by Obedullah-al-Obeidir of Mazma-ul-Bahrain-Darasukoh. He also felt something of Ram Mohan Roy's tract on monotheism might have influenced Isherwood. But is there any evidence for this?

What a look Tagore had. He comes across as such a studied, iconic figure.

After the museum a quick look at Tagore's homes, though only from the outside. The largest was a kind of miniaturized version of an 18th century stately home. There were three or four other homes, one of them made of mud, its sculptures blackened with tar as preservative. Needless to say, Gandhi stayed in this one. Tagore moved from one to another.

Then along the road to the School of Painting and Fine Art. This is filled with strong sculptures and highly ornately decorated buildings. But the great joy was our waylaying a baul, on his bicycle and on his way home to his village five miles away, and persuading him to stop and give us a recital. So Ajit and I sat at his feet as he sang a song all about social inequalities but how all are equal in the eyes of God. Maybe Das Gupta is right and that in Bengali songs we learn the true religious culture of Bengal. The singing was eerily beautiful but not quite satirical. His two instruments, both made from gourds, were a tabla—the drum made from a goatskin—and a single stringed instrument. Our singer was one Shyam Govinda Das. A small, lively compact face—one foot but a stump. Wearing a saffron shirt and I guess a colored dhoti. Well, one of my ambitions in coming to Santiniketan—Abode of Peace—was to hear a Baul sing.

Back round the rest of the central campus. Only saw the China and Hindi Bhavans from the outside, but impressive frescoes by one of the Tagores in the China. Chou En Lai came here in 1952.

And so back to Ajit's for another cup of tea, in the darkness of his veranda. I guess he's someone who has sacrificed his life to his work. Sees himself as a disciplinarian. Accepted all the social regulations at Pondicherry. But has friends, both Indian and European. Has taken to both France and Italy. I wondered with a photo of Aurobindo and the Mother on display if he was a follower—but not so it seems. He does not see himself as widely versed in this spirituality. He has the bleak view that everything has changed for the worse.

Another very good meal at the guest house, where I am now the only guest.

11 October

I went back to the Kala Bhavan to take some more photos. A few students present, painting or weaving. I also visited the Music Bhavan, with its attractive open stage, but all was shut down.

Then Ajit took me back to see the Hindi and China Bhavans. The frescoes inside the former pretty impressive—scenes of urban life, of Benares maybe—one of a rather plump sage in a cave. But who was the tall character at the center of one of the larger frescoes? Those in the China Bhavan were often merely decorative. These by a Thakur, just before Tagore's death.

Then the second great treat of the visit, a chance to see some of Tagore's paintings. The curator, a charming and scholarly fellow, Susobhan Adhikary, was my guide. He's written a very learned looking tome in Bengali on the possible sources of Tagore's paintings—German woodcuts, Jawlensky, Emil

Nolde, African and Oceanic masks, Modigliani. I felt all this was plausible. Tagore did visit many galleries during his visits to Europe in the 1920s. And he also read art journals. Odd that his painting all began with his doodling. It was Victoria Ocampo who persuaded him to become a painter. So, in his seventies, a new career began. The paintings began in black and white, rather cubist in style. They are hugely atmospheric. If one could point to influences, much however seems to be dredged from the unconscious. No doubt psychoanalysts could have a fieldday with all those circles of snakes and that crocodile's head filled with teeth. Much no doubt was drawn from his love of nature. Trees, rivers at sunset and dawn, all must have been drawn from the landscape of East Bengal he loved so dearly and from Santiniketan. One painting clearly showed the influence of Klee and this private showing of his work brought back memories of my like visit to the Klee museum in Bern. You come away from Tagore with a sense of how studied a person he be. Self-consciousness but with intense self-awareness. Self-exploration. But surely no one better looked the part. He was immensely photogenic.

So I ended my brief visit to the Abode of Peace. An uneventful return journey in which I finished reading Brunton. An uneven book, but here an relatively untested Englishman experiences and describes samadhi. Remarkable. I must read some more of his writing.

An easy journey back to the Mission as all taxis and buses are on strike in protest at the hike in diesel fuel prices.

Return to Calcutta and the Durga Festival

Then in the evening a talk with Saugata Roy, ex-Lok Sabha MP and MLA—I believe he is still the latter. I'd assumed he and Martin were friends of long standing. In fact they'd met on a train during Martin's visit last year. He came round to the Mission to discuss the elections. He incidentally teaches physics at undergraduate level at a woman's college as well. He emphasized the rise of the BJP and the decline of Congress. Vajpayee goes back to 1957, a laid-back character—doesn't work hard. Leaves the grind to others. Provides the flourishes. Older than Advani-Advani calls him Athali-Vajpayee replies with Advani. Advani dominated in the 1980s but saw the wisdom of giving way to Vajpayee's moderate appeal. But Advani is closer to the RSS. Interesting on George Fernandes. A Catholic Keralan with a Lodia socialist background. But fell out with Laloo Yadav. Now he's a workaholic, at it eighteen hours a day. He's become the BJP's arch fixer and Vajpayee is quite happy to use him. Then he turned to Mamata Bannerjee (I learnt later why she featured so strongly in his thoughts). She felt marginalized by Congress, though

Sonia Gandhi tried to woo her back. She's basically an anti-Marxist. Otherwise not very intellectual and without a policy. But many in West Bengal feel squeezed out by the Marxist establishment and have turned to her. There's nothing new about the Marxists losing in Calcutta. Then we looked at other parts of the National Democratic Alliance. The DMK simply ally with the BJP to keep Jayalalithaa at bay. Little really separates the DMK and AIDMK, though Karunanidhi is more the Dravidian. Can this motley alliance stay together? Although the Congress is in decline it will survive. It is after all still more of an all-India party than the BJP. It's big mistake was to weaken its commitment to secularism and hence lose the Muslim vote. And the Dalits have moved towards the BSP. Indira Gandhi above all but also Rajiv played havoc with the Congress machine, determined to frustrate any political rival. The party is badly organized. And Sonia, who does possess charisma and did turn the fortunes of the party, clearly made mistakes in these all-India elections. But he resisted my parallel between the decline of Congress and the Liberal party. Congress is like the Labor party—it will fight another day.

12 October

The day I met Mohammed Ibrahim's family and friends. (Ibrahim is a friend I met in Manchester.) Uma Roy came to the Mission on foot and we walked back to her flat on the corner of Lansdowne Road. They live on the eighth floor. Present were her sister, and two other "sisters," cousins really. Her sister could speak some English but the others were very quiet. Uma's husband, Tapan is an architect who followed his boss to Southampton in 1958. They met Ibrahim in 1962. It seems Ibrahim left Calcutta even before partition in 1946 and was to spend sixteen years in Karachi training as an accountant. I wonder why he converted to Islam? He kept it a secret from his family. Uma was interesting on her acquiring a guru—some ten years ago she became a formal disciple in the ceremony of *diksha*. She goes to see the lady once a month. In the flat there is a small shrine room—all the major gods feature. She'll give them gifts morning and evening, meditate there through yoga for a while, have a walk. She's a sweet-tempered lady with a rich vein of humor. I feel they are my best Calcutta family to date.

13 October

A day when I bucked the system and got the library to loan me a reserved book. But it took a direct appeal to the Secretary to do so.

A longish time at the Club—a forty-five minute swim, a sauna. And then with Martin's friend, Kaku Bose to the Bengal Club. I'd been taken there in 1991 by Debesh Das but I could not recognize it. It must have had a major face-lift. Much Kingfisher beer and a wonderful Chinese meal. I really enjoyed myself. Kaku and I discussed spirituality. His father was a Professor of English and maybe he was himself destined for an academic career but, in fact, it was to be in business. He pressed on me the limits of rationality. Clearly he's a devotee of Sir Isaiah (Berlin). He holds back from the Vedantist position. Likes the role of logic and reason. And I find myself concurring. I've been driven to the limit in accepting the possibility of Vedantism. Has all my life to date really been so wrong-headed? Can I really accept such an alternative? Is it wholly misguided?

But I do have this odd feeling my life has been one massive detour from its true purpose. Maybe when studying medieval monasticism as an undergraduate it was on the right path. Possibly Miss Davidson's (my psychotherapist's) dissuading me from reading William James's *The Varieties of Religious Experience* was another major step away from my true path. Have I ever since been circling round but never closing in on a kind of monastic, spiritual path?

15–16 October
What a catalyst this visit is proving to be in sorting out this debate on Vedantism. Does it all boil down to a definition of the self, to the meaning of existence? Intriguingly, we do have two analogous highly complex metahistories of the self, the Freudian and the Vedantic, but whereas Freud leads to some accommodation with the ego, strengthening it against the destructive forces of id and superego, the Vedantic requires us to slough off the ego for the sake of the Atman.

Why should we do so? Clearly, through the circumstances of our upbringing, the role models of our parents, peer group pressure, just living, we all emerge by adolescence with some kind of personality. In the Vedantist canon almost certainly this is one ensnared by *maya*—we have to shed this self if we are to find a higher self within. This is by a process of negation. All would agree with the Eriksonian account that we reach a crisis. It is of course just possible that one is born an illumined soul and there be rare individuals who attain the Atman without any need for negation.

Maybe we will never satisfactorily answer the question, what does this higher self look like, let alone, can this be?, but we can ask the question, why should anyone seek to slough off this personality, this maya-ensnared ego for the Atman? The question can just as reasonably be asked of Indian intellectuals as of western. Shils was, of course, half-way there in that contentious essay on Indian intellectuals and their limited sense of the ego/self, but whereas his approach was to argue that this led to a diminished sense of the ego, he would have been wiser to be more culturally neutral and just see this as a juggling of alternative definitions of the self. Why, indeed, should a western emphasis on the ego be a more acceptable role model?

For the western intellectuals, for the generation that interests me, there may be quite specific factors making this Vedantic ideal attractive. But in any cross-cultural situation the dynamic is just as much some debate going on within one's own culture as any genuine search for the meaning of another. Think of the eighteenth century and the way the *philosophes* used other cultures to attack their own. Why should this group, Huxley, Heard, Isherwood in particular, have sought to negate themselves? Maybe it was just part of a wider phenomenon. The civilizational breakdown of the Great War. The nihilistic atmosphere of the 1920s. All this opened up feelings of loathing and despair and a pursuit of some alternative persona. Vedantism would wrap itself around this situation very nicely. But the old ego ideals of imperialism and of upper-middle class Britain had not gone away and the requirement to match up to these standards—for this is the meaning of Isherwood's endless circling around the idea of the Test—was another huge demand which some intellectuals would be all too happy to jettison, even if the alternative might, in its moral requirements, ironically prove to be even more demanding. And then there is the sexual—the imperatives of mature sexuality, of heterosexuality, to some quite intolerable, and here we have another cause to try to begin again. And so much of this debate starts with the question, why should one reject one version of the self?

Of course this is what makes Forster relevant. In the end he simply couldn't see the wisdom of this strategy of negation. His chosen path was self-tolerance, Forster's brand of humanism.

16 October

This was a crowded day. A car came from Narendrapur but we got hopelessly stuck on the road heading south. It took us an hour. But Ashaktananda—he directs the place—was there and wearing one of those endearing saffron colored woolen hats. Ours was to be a good conversation, though I sensed he was not used to this probing of the psychological. Given a chance, he'd fall back on anecdotal evidence. I rather stopped his narrating his own career in Calcutta. I have to say, for a monastic movement committed to Vedantism, these monks seem to me a very self-centered lot. He himself is not that well. Has had a pacemaker inserted. And has had some gall stones removed.

Here is a man who was in touch with the Hollywood Vedanta center and who knew all the people I'm interested in. Clearly, as with Das Gupta, his favorite amongst them was Isherwood, though he was disaffected by his homosexuality. I think his really useful insight is his belief that Isherwood remained a dualist. It takes a special kind of mind, he insisted, to pursue non-dualism. He gave me an excellent lunch. He lives in an elegant house with a beautiful garden. Monks can live well. He recently received the Albert Schweitzer prize for his work at Narendrapur.

In the early afternoon my guide, Asifur Rahman, came to take me on a Durga puja tour. A plumpish, pop-eyed but mercifully clear English speaking fellow and so, just a little surprisingly, I had a Muslim to explain this Hindu festival to me. Michael Braudy, the violinist, joined us. He turned out to be even more neurotic than myself and an incessant chatterbox but I like him. I couldn't begin to name all the pandals we saw. We began in the southern part of the city and then, through ever denser traffic, drove to the northern. This was distinctive for its lights. Most of C R Das Avenue lit up. There were subtle differences between the images in the pandals and I took to them. I can see this is no fierce Durga. The demon king was of an athletic build but had the face of a Sylvester Stallone. In some ways the pandals themselves were the more remarkable—making wonderful use of natural objects, shells, maize, corn. The labor their construction must have entailed. It was the Notting Hill carnival writ large over the whole city. Asifur suggested there were as many as 2000 pandals but a thousand is probably nearer the mark. And the labor of the potters making all these images is incredible. They congregate in a part of north Calcutta. It felt more like a carnival than a religious festival though many entered the pandals in a spirit of devotion.

Later David Trelawny and I looked at some local pandals. In one we heard drummers and the beaters of other instruments. It was great fun and a wonderful commentary on local enthusiasms. And energies.

Pandal-hopping. It seems the more pandals you visit the more merit you acquire. One odd detail—to the left hand side of all the assembled images was a sapling in a bridal cloth—some kind of fertility symbol. The greenery of the tree kept peeping out. All the pandal displays had this feature.

Another feature. Within the mandalas there are paintings—in long curved spaces—of the great classics.

Why doesn't Siva visit as well? Well, that's because he's meditating in the Himalayas. In fact in eastern India the image of Siva is of a prowler in the cremation grounds. But remember Durga is not unique to Bengal. She's worshipped under other names throughout India.

The images are made from clay dredged from the Ganges (I guess the Hooghly) dried and then painted, bedecked and ornamented. Each local committee, and the whole city is divided into these, will commission images from its chosen artist. That is why artists will always indicate in the pandals that the work is theirs, an advertisement for next year's custom. By the Wednesday all images will be returned to the Gangetic slime—the whole image with all its dressings will be immersed in the river. But, later, dredgers will fish out the clothing and jewellery and the bamboo frames on which the images are constructed and these will be burnt.

17 October

Another round of pandals with Ranjit and family. I was to see the ones that dense crowds and the impossibility of parking had made inaccessible. And these were in fact the best—in College Square and Mehemet Ali Square, in that order. Calcutta's finest craftsman had done the former. A pandal behind the Oberoi had quite different images—Durga in all her nine incarnations. Ranjit rather muddied the waters by stating that this was not the real Durga festival-that comes in the spring. This is, in fact, a false prayer to the gods, for they are asleep at this time of the year and are only active in the other half. Also, this whole myth can coalesce with that of Ram. And in one of the pandals Siva was visible. So generalizations do not hold. It's all very intricate.

How very talkative these Bengalis be. From the decibel level of conversation you'd suppose something of moment was being discussed—but even trivial issues lead everyone to talk at the same time.

In light rain, off to Uma's and Tapan's for a puja meal. This is all very much part of the festival. Many communities, often those in the same block of flats, form their own special festival committees to organize communal meals and entertainments. Their sons from London and Delhi were there, Rathul and Uppal. Rathul rather threw me when I discovered that he owns a flat in Mayfair and a house in Cambridge. I asked him how on earth he could afford them—the answer, hard work.

The entertainment took the form of dancing in front of the images, the while carrying burning coconut coil in small urns. More and more were to join in, of all ages. But the one eye-catching fellow was the Manager of the block of flats, who pirouetted with his flaming braziers in quite some ecstasy and I began to imagine Ramakrishna dancing before Kali in the temple.

A light meal followed.

And then torrential rain. A taxi stopped but exploited my plight by demanding a huge fare. This is the cyclone that has edged away from Calcutta but has still brought the heaviest rain so far.

18 October

A water logged Mission confronted me at 5:30. This was the hour I expected my lift for Belur. Still no sign of anyone by 6:00, but then I saw two saffron-robed monks across the quadrangle, waded over and learnt that no driver had shown up—the journey postponed till 7:00. In fact we set off in a Toyota landrover at 7:15. This seemed impervious to the floods, though later its water pump was to go. So I got to Belur after all.

On arrival I caught up with the guest master, Swami Premayananda— some other monks were flirting with him, pinching his neck, etc—was directed to the guest-house for a second breakfast—I found it rather seedy looking—then back to the Math office. By sheer coincidence also present was a Dr Chitandra Shome (from Assam) and his wife. He's a GP from Warrington and knows well Dr Sarkar and his wife. They have been giving me introductions to their friends in Calcutta. Here was another of those weird conjunctions that make me feel I'm supposed to be here. So he kept me company and gave me some insight into the proceedings. To the temple. The first service was the Sunday puja. Very quiet at first. Prasad being devoted to Durga. Just two monks chanting. The whole event had been launched by conches blowing, with a kind of plaintive upward turn at the end. Meanwhile monks were fanning the goddess with huge fans. And so for almost an hour it proceeded, with more monks joining in the chanting. A multi-layered candelabra was lit up and waved in front of the goddess. Then, suddenly, all hell broke loose—heavy drumming, cymbals clashed, virtual shouting from the monks, with the audience responding. For some five minutes this cacophony prevailed. Flowers were then distributed, later collected and also donated to the goddess. Holy water was sprinkled on the congregation. I noticed one lean, bony-faced European/American amongst the white-robed brahmacharis. Not a friendly face. Later on in the day when we passed he stared straight through me.

Then it was announced the Kumari puja would be held outdoors. So we all swirled outside. Initially I and Dr. Shome took up a poor position but were, after much protestation by me, directed to a better vantage point. I'd none too high an expectation of the Kumari puja. Kumari means pre-pubertal. So the girl chosen has to be a pre-menstruating virgin. All a little Ruskinesque. The monks gathered round the steps and parapet. Then she appeared, a winsome doll-like little thing, though she was to keep up a good front throughout. She was then worshipped, one priest muttering prayers in front of her. Another multi-layered candelabra was lit, this one though inside a glass container. Floral wreaths were laid on her. At this point the crowd expressed their loud approval—well, more a kind of ululation. All this went on for an hour as well. Then it was all over. I broke away and almost missed seeing the virgin child carried shoulder high along the parapet. I went back inside the temple where people still awaited the sprinkling of water. Throughout the temple ceremonies the life-size model of Ramakrishna glowed in the far end of the building. The temple itself is a mix of Hindu, Christian, and Buddhist motifs—Dr. Shome thought Islamic as well but I couldn't see them. I was by then glad to take a breather by the Ganges. Indeed, the whole event, what with its early start, had taken its toll on me and I just went back to the guesthouse for a rest. The lunch served turned out to be the same as being doled out as prasad to the large crowd that had continued to flow in all morning.

I fear it all left me with a feeling of mild alienation. I can see why for some this ritual is off-putting and hard to stomach. It's interesting therefore that Isherwood did come to terms with it, partly at Prabhavananda's insistence, himself a reluctant convert to it. There was another European present, of thicker build, much more of an Isherwood character. He seemed relaxed. I was too embarrassed to catch his eye and anyway I am sure I was an unwelcome presence. Well, I had at least reminded myself of Belur and seen the guesthouse, quite central to the conversations in Isherwood's novel (A Meeting by the River).

Somehow we got back, with several stops to top up the radiator, once outside the Raj Bhavan. I was whacked. And still the rain pours down.

19 October

Conjunctivitis—I realized what it was, so didn't panic. Took myself off after breakfast to a nearby medical clinic, AMRI. Highly efficient. Straightaway a doctor saw me. Gave me good advice, wrote a prescription—within half an hour I was on my way back with my anti-biotic eye-drops.

Dropped in on the Chaudhuris nearby. In the end this became a good conversation about Indian radicalism. Where did Vivekananda get his "socialist" vision from? Tripti thought this a Christian socialist one. But Binoy, more convincingly, believed Vivekananda was simply reacting to what he saw all about him. He was outraged by Indian poverty and its customs. One possible ideological input was Caitanya's. But there is something almost Nietszchean about Vivekananda's radicalism.

This led onto a wider discussion of the Indian left. Where did the Marxists get their impetus from? Again, empiricism seems the answer. Theirs was a commitment to a working class struggle. Only subsequently did this become articulated through Marxism. One key figure was M. N. Roy, though he was to break away from his own movement, one of little impact, of Radical Humanism. Mysteriously he was assassinated. Now the Marxist mystique has faded. We speculated that now no party has any vision of social change. The BJP is just dredging up Gandhi and Nehru—no creative response to the present here. I wondered if these new popular-based parties—BSP, SP—might aggregate to form a force for change. Binoy cannot see them ever lending their support to violence. He does not see the Indian establishment ever having, for example, to call in the Indian Army to maintain the peace.

I like Binoy. He's much indebted to yoga. It's given him both the physical and mental strength to do his work. Early on he was supported by the Ramakrishna Mission at Narendrapur. Lokeswarananda was always very friendly, despite his leftism. No pressure was ever put on him to join the Mission. His class-mate was Prabhananda—then studying psychology. At the time a lively fellow and no indication he was to become a monk. Binoy sees the thrust of the Mission towards social and charitable activity, though a minority pursue the contemplative life. I am beginning to see how the Mission has fallen short of the vision of both Ramakrishna and Vivekananda, I guess inevitable in any institutionalized movement.

20 October
Pinkeye has spread to the other eye. All very tiresome.

I had a good chat to an American, Bernard Cicerone. A quiet self-sufficient fellow. Works in the computer side of a university. Dabbles in art-dealing on the side. But for two years he had embarked on a training as a Ramakrishna monk.

Ranjit almost but didn't let me down and we set off to see the immersion of the goddess. Passed trucks en route carrying images of the household gods. A few were being carried on poles. Here was real devotion. So to the Judge's ghat. They were still feeding the goddess and her friends, placing sweets, etc, in her mouth. This is a farewell to a beloved daughter. The mother, however, is not supposed to see her daughter once she's left, so, in some ways, the actual immersion was to be a cursory affair. But quite a business off-loading the images from the lorries and man-handling them down the steps. There they turn her around three times clockwise, apparently auspicious. Then, with the image face upwards she's tipped into the Hooghly. One saw images floating downstream the breadth of the river. They are partly made of straw and it takes time for them to sink. From the back they looked rather crude constructions, bamboo poles providing their frame. Finally it became clear to me the distinction between traditional images, which are all on the same frame, and the others, which are separately constructed. Bernard, who accompanied us, felt the occasion was both sad and joyous. The crowd was reasonably well behaved, for there was congestion, some considerable excitement, shouting, much physical demands. At a later stage, when the much larger images of the pandals are immersed, I can see it could all get completely out of hand. We got back to the Mission with once again the threat of rain.

24 October

No diary entry from Wednesday last till this Monday. A kind of inertia has set in, with some detachment from Calcutta. I've stayed in my room and read most of the time. I've kept putting off a second visit to Belur with either my conjunctivitis or my ever-worsening back as the excuse.

On the Sunday a Dr. Maitra came to see me, from the Woodlands trust, and here was professional care on a high scale. In fact he came to me from seeing Ranganathananda. I'm to have a course of physiotherapy.

Then Sujon reappeared and we got back onto our old wavelength. He told me of the rather distressing circumstances of the last few years which have left him holed up in a bachelor penthouse flat. None of this he brings to his monk at Belur. But then he is not his guru. This was another person, now dead, who initiated him not so long ago into his mantra. Someone he did not particularly like, disapproving of his cross-dressing—but all this was his sister's doing. When pressed, it becomes clear Sujon would not assail his monk with any of his personal problems, he just goes to talk for the sake of being in his presence. And maybe this is much what the guru relationship is about. You might just as readily talk about politics. The same spiritual benefits will result.

Much conversation on the subject of Ramakrishna. Later on in the evening Sujon reported a lady friend admitting to the most uninhibited intimacies between the young male child and his female relatives. Have we here the real origin of the mother cult in Bengal, so much stronger than elsewhere and so much part of Ramakrishna's own story? All this is beyond what Sudhir Kakar has to say.

David Trelawny is a man of conflict. Clearly in the past he's been deeply troubled. It seems his own meditation can take him over the brink. We are always advised to take care and here is one example of why.

Supper at Ranjit's. I had missed, through talking to Sujon, his Lakshmi puja. I noticed en route some of the Durga pandals double up for Lakshmi. More images for immersion in the Hooghly. His relatives all seem to be in corporate finance.

Sujon has made a number of political observations. It seems that the fate of the Congress in Bengal hinged on the strategy of Saugata Roy. Earlier he had kept close to Mamata Bannerjeee. But when she felt sleighted by the AICC and went her separate way Saugata decided to move away from her. Mamata went on to found the Trinamul Congress, to displace the Congress as the leading rival to the Marxists. At best she is a populist. The future of politics in West Bengal seems bleak.

But Sujon's readiness to see a threat in the higher demographic growth of the Muslims was disturbing and unacceptable. The Marxists it seems have turned a blind eye to illegal immigrants—the Muslims from Bangladesh are a useful votebank. Surely the answer has to be an improvement in their living standards and this will bring their growth rate down. Nehru got this right ages ago.

26 October

My physio-treatment under the caring eye of the young Sebroto Debnath proceeds apace. Mainly by ultra-sound treatment and by a twice daily regime of exercises. I've also now acquired a sacrolumbar belt. It should all be setting me to rights but the stiffness and discomfort remain.

An interview with Professor Prasad Bose fell through—he's broken a toe—but his son showed me round the Mission's museum. A rather impressive collection. I'm woefully ignorant of the Bengali school. Some wonderful contemporary folk art from the villages on show at the moment.

Das Gupta, if late for our second meeting, did not let me down and in many ways this was my best conversation to date. He's rather a subversive fellow. He's a dualist and no monist. He sees the serious limitations of the guru-disciple relationship—it robs the individual of initiative. He doesn't see Ramakrishna primarily as an avatar—thinks of him as rationalist and humanist. And he doubts if the Ramakrishna Mission can today produce a monk with the intellectual gifts to expound Vedantism in a modern idiom. A loveable man, of phenomenally wide reading—Schopenhauer, Sartre, etc.,—but one who wears his learning with wit and humility. He was a little sad on this occasion as he reflected on the death only last week of a younger sister.

29 October

Kaku invited me home for a meal. He lives in a stylish penthouse flat with his sister and brother-in-law. I could not have had a more English meal—well, Chinese soup, but then fish mornay followed by roast beef (succulent), ice-cream and apple pie. I indulged in it all. Here's another family where a talented son has chosen to live abroad. What a brain-drain India must be experiencing. He's an academic turned investment adviser, with a large house in Dulwich to show for it.

All evening we were threatened by another cyclone but it veered away and struck Orissa once again. (But this was the appalling super-cyclone. Little did we know the threat we were under.)

I think I have done all the reading I'm going to do here this time round. It still stretches away in all directions. And only now am I beginning to find the best books. Well, this is a long-term project.

30 October

A Ramakrishna day. Arranged by the Roys. Ibrahim's sister, Aparna Gupta present, plus that very quiet lady, Chitra Sen, and their son's wife's mother, a lively lady, Madhuri Sen Gupta. Two cars and an earlyish start. The first stop the potters quarters in north Calcutta, Kumer Tuli, where the artists make all the images. This time it was Kali's turn. So, up and down the street, clay images in the making of Kali in full stride, cheekily with her tongue out (nothing voracious here)—one craft shop had got as far as fashioning her necklace of skulls and her cleaving sword. Siva was rather odd—invariably very plump—Sujon felt he looked pregnant—often he had rather a Hellenic looking face.

Next stop was the Mother's house. Here we were really off the beaten track. I can see in my mind's eye a slightly built blind man, sidling along the street, begging rather charmingly, but being quietly moved along. A metal girded house. On the first floor was a room where her particular devotee, Swami Shraddananda, lived. And then her room, simple but filled with fruits for prasad. There was a particularly striking photo of Sarada Devi with Sister Nivedita—I suddenly recognized Sarada as a handsome even beautiful woman.

Last night Sujon and I had had a go at defining the eternal feminine in Hinduism. There was a false start with a Belgian Jesuit I'd met at K. P. Ghosh's house (he's Mrs Sarkar's brother). He proved to be a very retiring fellow. He's spent forty years as a schoolteacher in Bengal. He now teaches at St. Xavier's. A slight self-effacing man, though tough enough to drive round Calcutta on a motorbike. He simply wouldn't respond to my questions about the feminine, despite my drawing attention to the strong correspondence between the Marian cult and the mother figure in Hinduism. His interests turned out to be narrowly comparative religion. Our conversation in the end gravitated to a discussion of the BJP and we agreed that its primary interest is in power and a strong state—in fact a very western agenda.

But not even Sujon was really to respond to the question. His initial response was simply to question if Ramakrishna had indeed been under the sway of Kali. And he had had to wield the sword of discrimination to cut out her distracting image and grasp unitive knowledge. But, obviously, he was under her sway.

Do we need a Kali image for all those fears we have of our ambivalent mother figures, of the good and bad breast? Are European intellectuals, likewise, burdened and do they respond in a like way? And is their capacity to respond to this image the test of whether they can get inside Hinduism? Somehow here Sarada Devi emasculated sexuality as a mother figure. Not to overlook the pedophilia of the kumari puja.

Still, I liked Mother's house.

Then on to Kossipore and this was a moving experience. A handsome house, set back in a pleasing garden, adjacent to a small lake with a rare white lotus blossoming and another pinkish flower whose name I've already forgotten. Downstairs there were rooms with, in one, portraits of the household disciples and, in another, the monastic. Upstairs was the room where he died. It was in this house he'd passed on his powers to Niren. In the garden Girish had recognized him as an avatar. Here was a house and garden with sacred memories.

Then on to Baranagore. This has been absorbed into a school. The former math is well preserved—a long rectangular room—noticeable for Vivekananda's moral instructions published all around the walls. There was a shrine to Ramakrishna but, of course, he never came here. Remember that the disciples spent nearly ten years here. A very simple abode compared to Belur and, of course, they were broke at the time.

And so onto Dakshineswar. Absolutely no divide from the town now—it has been swallowed up. And with this being a Sunday it was a busy day—impossible with these crowds to sense anything of its former spirituality. But I was able to remind myself of its layout. There was that small figure of Krishna that had had its arm broken when dropped. Across to the debating chamber. Here Ramakrishna had his debates on ideas with visitors. Across to the Office—more photographs, including the one of the fleshy Tota Puri—great dugs. A pretty brutal lover, if Kripal is correct. And a glance at the Siva temples. Long queues for the Kali temple but I cheated and sneaked up the exit stairway and had a good look at the Kali image. Not really a bloodthirsty image. But black and red. Siva lay north/south under her body. And this one was not pregnant.

Then back through dense traffic till we broke away through side streets—on the return we passed Balaram's house, just across the road from Girish's—his is still kept in the middle of C R Das Avenue—till we arrived at a good Bengali restaurant for a late lunch. Simple but tasty food. This in Elliot Road.

So a good exposure to the Ramakrishna narrative.

In the evening, together with Susan Walters, to a flute recital at the Calcutta School of Music. One Alain Dabancourt. Best his performance of French music by Fauré and Poulenc. But a fine performance throughout, well accompanied by Jehmie Gazdar.

1 November

Nearing the end of the Calcutta visit.

Accompanied by Sujon, and it was a hard place to find, to the Center for Social Studies in Lake Terrace. I cannot say I recalled its acting head, in Partha

Chatterjee's absence, Saugata Mukherjee—we had apparently been colleagues at the JNU—but he was urbane and friendly. The Center is about to move out of its cramped quarters to a new site out of town. The idea was to have a work-in progress seminar to whoever might like to attend—and some six or seven did so. Obviously, the precise nature of my project was vague to them but its conceptual framework was of interest. One Gautam Bhadre let fly a volley of concern at how to define tradition. He recited numerous conflicting models of tradition. Spirituality, likewise, was not seen as a single phenomenon—it varies from section to section of society, from class to class. Likewise, and I found this more pertinent, there are numerous definitions of the self. I'll have to be careful with my methodology. Quite a profitable encounter.

Then over to Ranjit's and back to Park Street. This is clearly the place to eat. To a goodish if dowdy looking Chinese restaurant. Then the problematic of whether to buy an expensive replacement camera or a cheapie—in the end I went for the latter.

Then to American Express. On the return the traffic got worse and worse. The Fiat car broke down and had to be pushed. I was considerably the worse for wear by the time I returned to the Mission.

In the evening another terrible journey out to Martin's friends, John and Andrea Beenjes. In fact, one Karen collected me and I was rather rude to her en route. But they turned out to be a nice couple. He got a calling from Jesus and has since devoted his life to good causes—an orphanage in Bucharest, now a school in rural Bengal. Someone came to their Calcutta house to mend the telephone and told them of the needs of the village school. So it began. They go out several times a week, though fund-raising takes up much of their time. Their children gave me a song and dance performance—the same they do in hotels at Christmas and that's how they met Martin. I was a little thrown by his piety—at the end there was a prayer and blessing on my future journeys and no doubt I need this. The back is improving but far from better.

2 November
My last day in Calcutta. A day of farewells. Uma Roy came round bearing a small attractive present. She I have come to love. Kaku came. He has been a good friend. Sujon came round. I am glad we have met again. The back had a horrible twinge whilst talking to him and Susan Walters. It's all going to be touch and go.

3–4 November
Further farewells. Ranjit came to say goodbye, bringing the gift of a nice saffron colored shirt. Sujon couldn't make a final visit. Down with a cold.

Farewell to Prabhananda. A lively and likeable man but we failed to open up a conversation. So c/o of the Travel Bureau to Howrah.

A shoeshine boy at the station took great trouble in buffing up my sandals. On being offered twenty rupees, he returned ten. I had paid over the odds. An honest lad who should, but clearly won't, go far.

I was lucky in my travel companions. I was to be with two railway officials. One was a Chief Operations Manager, J. K. Mitra. I could not quite place the look of him till I realized how like in appearance he was to Faradh. (A Parsee psychotherapist friend in London.) The son of a judge: he now wondered if a legal career might not have been the greater challenge. But he passed out 132 in the IAS examination for his year. The other, Bradley Passal, was Assamese and a deputy Chief Security Commissioner. And clearly his rank counted. At our first stop, Ansifol, a wonderfully portly policeman entered the carriage and filled it with gestures of crisp deference. The advantage of his being Assamese was that they did not have Bengali in common as a language and they had to speak English. So here was a conversation from which I could not be excluded. The railway policeman was also a Christian, a Presbyterian, from Shillong. It has been dubbed the Scotland of India, though for its scenery rather than its faith.

We enjoyed a marvelous wide-ranging conversation. Much on the railway system itself. Interesting that it remains an All-India subject and is still divided into zones which straddle states. Also on railway security. There is some attempt by the center to claw back from states the devolved role of law and order. Bradley had not wanted to join the railway police but it was all that was on offer. I felt our conversation took its most urgent turn when we discussed the consequences of positive discrimination—quite clearly this is seen as prejudicial to morale. Career civil servants find themselves at a permanent disadvantage from reserved appointees when it comes to promotion. This saps initiative. Clearly they favored a meritocratic system. They were curious about England, about Blairism in particular. They wondered if English politicians swapped parties in the way Indians do—Mitra clearly rather ashamed of this practice, though I noticed they were well briefed on the murky complexities of the politics of Bihar. Reasonable meals served and a comfortable journey though this is an expensive service.

My first sight in the early morning was of a refinery—its jet of flame giving it away. A landscape quite crudely cultivated and curiously empty.

No one to greet me at Delhi station. So I allowed the porters to take me to an exit. Still no sign of Magic India so I allowed a plump Punjabi taxi driver to sweep me away and was appropriately hugely overcharged. But I got to the Delhi Gymkana Club. And am now ensconced in very comfortable quarters. After some initial muddle, began to get through to friends on the phone. This could be a pleasant four days in the capital.

5 November

And, indeed, today was a triumph. I wasn't initially too struck on having a lady guide to Delhi, one Dolly, but she proved engaging enough, but took to my driver, Vikram, a substantially built hillman from north of Rishikesh, a former truck driver and just bubbling over with bonhomie and animal spirits. If this was something of a whistle stop tour of the city I was reminded of its great buildings that I'd almost forgotten—the Jami Masjid, the Red Fort, the Purana Quila, and, later in the day, the Qutab Minar. In fact this was the most surprising—a tranquil setting for some highly wrought stone work and that great phallic tower. Dolly persuaded me to visit the Kashmir emporium—two more carpets purchased, setting me back £600. But I only buy in these circumstances and they were pleasing. Vikram and I tracked down Mahendra Kumar in the Gandhi Peace Foundation—he's a dry old stick and so soft-spoken I could hardly hear him. Then to the offices of OUP and a meeting, after many years of correspondence, with the startlingly attractive Bela Mallik and the pleasant Sikha Ghosh—I owe much to their support. I collected the paperback edition of *Religions in Conflict*, nicely done. It was pleasant to hear myself described as one of OUP's better authors—I do sell.

The day went on. In the evening Nazir Bhatt came to see me and discuss my itinerary. Clearly they are going to a lot of trouble on my behalf.

Then out in the evening to visit Muzaffur Alam and family at the JNU. Under pressure he did confess real anxieties about the fate of the Muslim minority, though he began by asserting that Muslims should have an absolutely free hand—why shouldn't they be free to vote for the liberal right? But this still seems a dangerous tactic to me.

6 November

I had Sudhir Kakar's address from Bela so we took pot luck and we were to be lucky. He was in his consulting room and ready for a conversation. I set out the parameters of my project. Our first theme was homosexuality itself. The great taboo in India is anal penetration—it makes the subject unmentionable. And this is what people understand by homosexuality. All other forms of sexuality fall outside the category, leaving a wide scope for powerful expressions of male friendship. In Hindi films the male hero will invariably give up his girl friend in favor of his best friend. But this remains culturally ambiguous. If androgyny is a norm men still have mixed feelings about acknowledging their feminine side. Gandhi did so. But to do so is in no way to admit to homosexual feelings. Admission of homosexuality by a son or daughter would be absolute disaster for a family—no one would marry into such a family. There are enormously strong incentives to keep silent about it. You'd really have to hate your family to "come out." There is homoeroticism but it is undefined. Are we back in an era, I'm wondering, in India before any modern gay movement? There are of course the *hijiras* but this is a narrow and extreme safety valve for such sexuality. Some homosexual practices would be accepted at the hands of the low caste e.g. the barber, from whence come the masseurs. This is seen as no more than physical release and hardly constitutes any acknowledgement of homosexuality. You certainly wouldn't enter into any form of relationship with members of such castes.

So foreign homosexuals would find themselves very confused by what they encounter. They could easily misconstrue the signs of friendship. Seeking working class friends would be fairly incomprehensible and frowned on.

We switched to the inner link between sexuality and spirituality. Kakar quite clear that the view that semen can be stored and passed to the brain is central to Indian attitudes. Chastity is a strong imperative for anyone on a spiritual quest. He made the astonishing comment on the guru-disciple relationship, that what a disciple would most like from his guru is some of his semen (by sucking). Given that even the dirt washed from the feet of a guru is sacred, how much more valuable would a drop of semen be? The guru-disciple relationship is of reasonably recent vintage—eighth to tenth centuries. Did it reflect a greater need for moral support at a time when Hinduism was on the defensive?

And what of the feminine? Clearly there is a deep fear of the voracious female, a reflection of the castration complex. Maybe you have to go to inordinate lengths to compensate for this. Would not a foreigner likewise, particularly a homosexual, not also come up against this fear? It seems a foreign homosexual would find much to fear in this religious tradition.

The question of the ego/self. Kakar was quite clear that one could not safely embark on a Vedantist quest if one was not psychologically very well adjusted. But many do so, just because they are fractured, and hence get ill. These become his patients. I wondered if the Vedanta concept of the Self entails some extension of the existing ego or entails a hiatus. Kakar came squarely down on the side of hiatus. But he was at a loss to explain why one might in the first place embark on this pursuit. He'd never himself do so. And, clearly, he is much mystified by aspects of this spirituality.

He's currently writing a novel about Ramakrishna. He has already written one about the author of the Kama Sutra. Only fiction permits one to address those very questions that Kripal came a cropper over. He's in contact with him. Clearly Sudhir is one Indian mind which can get round my project.

But am I not really writing about myself and the answers lie within?

Kakar reported an extraordinary conversation with the Dalai Lama. The Dalai Lama believes that the existence of a higher ego is proven by the way some dead bodies continue to show some signs of life some time after death. If a scientific explanation could be found for this, then, the Dalai Lama concedes, that the claims of the Buddha would be destroyed.

I was running very late and missed meeting Siddiqui and Bhattacharya at Harbans's house—all former JNU colleagues—but he accepted my excuse. I enjoyed talking to Harbans. We discussed his new journal *The Medieval History Journal*. We talked of his expectations of his new role as Rector, in particular setting up two new Institutes, one for Law and Governance, one for Advanced Studies. He feels India has failed to absorb those norms that make for good governance. Government she may have but not the back-up from those internalized restraints that make for governance. Frankly, his belief that they prevail in the west is rather starry-eyed.

Then to Panikkar's for lunch and another long conversation. KN is clearly highly hostile to the way religion is institutionalized. In his version of secularism he'd want a complete separation of religion and institutions. He's not opposed to religion as such or to spirituality, but he kept angling for a definition of spirituality. His own was nice—what is best in human beings—a humanist version. But I think all this is out of his response to the rise of the BJP and Hindu fundamentalism. He's completely unconvinced by the idea of the BJP and Vajpayee as moderate. He's sure the RSS pull the strings. He was fascinating in showing how the RSS spreads its tentacles through cultural organizations. It might be something as simple as a Temple restoration committee. Of course, almost inevitably, these cultural committees play into its hands. Can one imagine any Hindu front organization which did not? The whole culture tends in their direction. And beyond the cultural influence will lie the political. His own brother has become a staunch BJP supporter though this has not stopped them being friends. Could people, he wondered, be religious in such a way that a true secularism prevails? His is an embattled position and I may not here do it justice.

I think he sees the very concept of 'spirituality' itself as the key difficulty in my project. What did he mean by seeing Ashis Nandy as an anti-modern?

Enjoyed a diwali feast in the club but was rather on my own.

7 November

Diwali—and the barrage intensified throughout the day. I doubt if I'll get any sleep tonight.

A day at the club. A long swim in the morning. Chatted to my neighbors, Harbans Singh and his lively wife. They have a spastic son. Pleasant people, clearly successful. We share the same number in our streets. Clearly we were destined to meet.

The handsome head porter, in fact in the security wing of the club, came to have his photo taken. Krishna Yadav. A wonderful swagger and vanity to the man. He's from Shantanapur. His father runs a shop. His younger brother also works in the club. Married with four sons. Aged forty-two.

And then Gowher Rizvi came to collect me for a fashionable Delhi supper party, in honor of Roger Owen, an old friend from St. Antony's. I spoke about Indian spirituality to a Professor of English, Melanie—I've forgotten her surname. She was interesting on the way Japanese novelists see nothing but Indian spirituality. She wonders just how stereotyped all this is and whether it's an equivalent to medieval Christianity and bound to go away in time. Also present a very nice Iranian, running some Asia-Africa legal organization, an intergovernmental one. Mushirul Hasan present. And R Kumar, the former Director of the Teen Murti Library. He felt India was really dictated by its rites of passage—social mores really explains the survival of this spirituality. Intellectually, India is wide open to ideas. A pleasant evening but conducted against an ever-increasing barrage of sound. It rather diminished the appeal of all those guttering lights.

Amongst the Swamis: Rishikesh and Hardwar

8 November
Awoken at 5:45 and collected at 6:15. To be my last look at Vikram—looking slightly Japanese with a neckerchief tied around his head. Sentimentality got the better of me and I gave him £20 towards the costs of his sister's wedding. Money maybe I should have given to the Orissa fund.

So safely onto the Hardwar train. My next door neighbor turned out to be a South Indian lady, married to a Maharashtrian, living in Poona. She had some good ideas on where I should holiday in India, Kasauli near Naini Tal, Aleppey and Cochin in Kerala.

What did I make of Hardwar? Rather an ugly town. It seems most of it was put up in the last 50 years. Hard to find anything spiritual here. Those I'd assumed to be saddhus on the bridge approaching the bathing ghats turned out to be beggars. But there were also quite inscrutable gnarled old saddhus also begging. No temple of any distinction was visible.

Here the Ganges runs fast and cold and it takes some courage to have a dip, but this clearly was the main activity. And the sight of male flesh caught my eye as much as anything. The ghats are subject to an organizing committee. But how on earth this enclosed space hosts the kumbh mela is inconceivable. Yes, as Sujon alerted me, some bathers do cling to chains to prevent themselves from being swept away. Only once did I experience any spirituality—there was a frail elderly saddhu clutching an enormous volume of what I was told were Vedic hymns. He, at least, was on a spiritual path.

But some of the ashrams en route to Rishikesh were more spiritual. One had great statues to Hanuman and Siva, but rather a glossy place. But another, off the main track, the Ashram of the Seven Rishis, was quiet and had the feel of a religious site. It seems that seven rishis quarreled over their share of the Ganges and in consequence it was split into seven ways and this is indeed the case at Hardwar.

Through Rajaji park, filled with colorful yellow flowering trees, monkeys by the roadside. My hotel, the Ganga Kinare, (translates as On the Banks of the Ganges), nicely sited on a bend in the river, the town upstream and the hills at last visible. Eventually sorted out a room to my liking—top floor, quiet, with fine views across the river.

Well, by 5:30 we were off to the Sivananda ashram, that belonging to the Divine Life Society. A long way from the hotel and I suspect I am going to run up a big taxi bill. We climbed steeply up into the ashram itself. My first encounter was with a lively ebullient monk from Malaysia. There are many centers of the movement (It began there.). Clearly he wishes to stay on in Rishikesh for ever if he can extend his exit visa from Malaysia. Desultory chanting from the prayer room. This recitative chanting goes on most of the day.

Then I found myself in the company of Swami Dharmatmananda, the man who'd answered my letter to the society. But he was rather a sweet but deaf old man and it was clear this frail figure was not going to tell me much. But he pointed us in the right direction and this was to the Reception Office and to nearby Swami Pranavaswarupa Nandaji Maharaj. Rather a swarthy fellow, with good English. He fussed around thinking of people I might meet. Swami Chidananda is away in Delhi but it seems he will return during the time of my stay here.

Then we were joined by Swami Nirvikananda, a crop-haired rather handsome fellow, an engineer who had joined the Divine Life Society. So what was, I asked, the meaning of life? I'll give you an answer, he replied, but in a short speech. It was an answer based on asking the question, what is the length, breadth and height of life—the length was to be righteous, the breadth was to serve others, the height was to seek God. He fell back on parables and analogies. I couldn't quite follow these but these were ways of pointing out that things are not what they seem, that without experiencing these truths we cannot understand them—you cannot tell a person what sisterly love is like if they do not have a sister, what the taste of alcohol might be like if you have not tasted it yourself. Well, it wasn't a bad off the cuff speech. He felt it had been predestined that he should come into the room at the moment that I was present.

But I was more curious to know what the priorities of the Society were. Swami Pranavaswarupa put the emphasis on social work, in the way it takes destitutes off the street and gives them a decent death, on the care of lepers, of the outcastes of society. Social philanthropy comes across as more important than the study of philosophy or yoga, though this does occupy most of the time of the majority of the actual residents of the ashram. I could discern little connection between the philanthropy and the yoga. I really know nothing about the Society and its origins though from his photographs I thought the founder, Swami Shivananda, handsome in a Yul Brynnerish sort of way.

It's clear that the Divine Life Society is run on different lines to those of the Ramakrishna Mission. They see themselves as far less structured. It's a question of how the mood takes you. Swami Pranavaswarupa himself came here on a visit, with no thought of joining the Society but stayed on and has been here ever since. Clearly, they see the Ramakrishna Mission as being very self-consciously organized, with lots of specialized roles. Here you continually ring the changes. Swami Nirikananda in his time has worked in the library, the cash office, taught yoga and managed the electrical side of the ashram. Swami Pranavaswarupa sees this flexibility as the hallmark of the Society, though you were just doing what was most helpful to the community. Many of them are at the moment helping in Orissa. It's a little surprising though how dominant this social side is.

But, in all, this was a good start to my week in Rishikesh.

9 November

Awake at dawn—the chanting from the ashrams filling the air. The sun broke across the river and the light stole upstream to the town and the hills beyond.

This was to be a long day of ashrams and temples. First, back to the Sivananda ashram and a meeting with Swami Krishnanandaji. At first I just stood in the back of the room, several others present—he seemed to be reading out a letter. Every word was being recorded by a rather enigmatic western woman. Eventually he took me in and wanted to know why I was there. He's a short squat man, his legs miraculously tucked under him; he could have been a dwarf or a paraplegic. But a large friendly mobile face suggested a man of good humor and humility. I am tending to put the same kinds of questions to people; what is the purpose of it all, what is the self, do we need a guru, etc? But it's hard to record his conversation. It's increasingly clear that social work is given priority by the Society. It is so much more spontaneous a movement than the Ramakrishna Mission. Work has an almost Fourierist approach. But what you do, who you are, seem to be unimportant questions, though to Krishnananda they were. What matters is, are we serving the divine, are we realizing the divine? There was no point in asking who he once was, that past has ceased to have any significance for him. As it happened, he's another who had a chance meeting with Swami Sivananda and stayed on. His was a kind of reductionism—everything is harnessed to a quest for the divine. In some ways he was ambivalent about gurus—you need to move beyond this relationship. But clearly he takes his own role as writer seriously, for he gave me all his books or at least a good number of them. I doubt if I've recalled all he said.

Then Swastik, my new guide, and I crossed the bridge and proceeded to temples and ashrams on the other side. The main encounter was to be with the Parmath Niketan ashram. Swastik had taken me there to meet a doctor; Swastik's own approach to the spiritual life is rather skeptical and he's only impressed by doers, those who make a change in society—but the doctor was away in London. But we pressed on and were first met by a highly intelligent lady, Majaji Pratiba, new to the ashram. Quite young. I'd think she had an academic background, extremely clear-thinking, with immaculate English. My first question was again on the paradox of yoga centers being so involved in social work. But she was not non-plussed. Wasn't it a case of being in the right state of mental equilibrium to serve the world? And wasn't God in everything, animal and non-animal, and in serving society and nature do we not serve him? You do not choose your guru. You have to wait for one to appear. When the time comes, when you are ready for one, he will appear. Again, no problem with the self—there simply is a better non-self-regarding Self which grows stronger and stronger.

She was good on Krishna. He was born at the end of the golden age and is very much the God for the kali yuga. He's there to offer practical advice. Hence his all pervasiveness. Swastik put this a little differently. Krishna reached out at different levels to all of society. He met many needs. Both the apocalyptic moment in the Gita and his anomalous past.

Again, she must have said a great deal more. This ashram is peculiarly involved in raising literacy rates in the villages. Some 300 schools or was it more? They acquire practical skills but all are taught Sanskrit and the elements of Hinduism. The ashram is also concerned about the plight of the destitute. They have a hospital.

She thought the Prabhavananda/Isherwood translation of the Gita one of the best.

This long conversation deferred our meeting with the swami of the ashram, Swami Chidanand Saraswati. Here was a quite different personality to Swami Krishnanandaji. Elegantly dressed, wearing ornaments, sitting in a sheltered spot in the garden. Youngish. Long hair and bearded. Indeed, the very conventional image of the holy man. But, again, he was in no way arrogant. If I have an overall sense of what he said, it is his view that we extract what we need from those around us, books, people. The main thing is to pursue our own spiritual growth. But he listened to my view that a historian cannot just extract what he wants and has to see a subject in the round. You might do that, he said, and you will, but for him the essence might only be ten percent. You go for what you need.

He was good on gurus. They do not themselves chose to be such. They are chosen. There's no inherent reason why gurus should have disciples. He does not attract them. They come to him because of their needs.

He conceded there might be cultural barriers in the way of foreigners grasping the Indian spiritual tradition. But in principle this is simply one way to a universal absolute. All are equally well placed to realize it. He was clearly impressed by Jesus and saw him as one excellent way through to the divine. Again, there must have been more he said. I understood from Swastik that Swami Krishnanandaji is highly respected as a spiritual man by local people, and, indeed, there is a pleasing, almost childlike, innocence about him. This man, however, was your up-market guru, highly sophisticated. Not held in such high local esteem. I couldn't register a deep spirituality but nor could I see anything at all arrogant or hypocritical. In his own way a genuine person.

We had lunch in the ashram. Our lady joined us and spoke of the kinship between all forms of music. She tried to argue that it is what you discover in music that counts, be it classical, film, etc all are equally valid, but she rather agreed with me when I insisted that classical music was superior and that we should cultivate superior tastes. The rewards will be greater.

Then we walked along the ghats, heard some "gypsy" music—tribals from Rajasthan, plus a cobra, looking suitably spellbound. As expected, we were turned away from the Maharishi ashram—you have to come armed with a letter of introduction. We then explored a yoga ashram, attracting European visitors. I find I rather dread these intense automata-like Europeans. They never greet you. They seem wholly self-centered people and rather grim. Why don't Europeans greet one another in India? Is it that India is an escape from the self and hence we dread meeting ourselves in India? I wasn't sorry there was no one there to speak to.

So we crossed back across the bridge, back to the car and to the top end of Rishikesh to visit its temples. Here we had to cross a very narrow footbridge—though mopeds use it. Two temples dominate, belonging to the Kailashanand ashram. (Or were there two ashrams?) We went to the older of the two.

Every floor filled with figures of the gods. I tried to get Swastik to make more sense of these. Kali, he explained, in terms of the release of the kundalini, of shakti energy, which drives out the forces of the ego. Why, I asked, was there so much violence in Hinduism? It's because it initially spoke to a primitive age, one itself riven by warfare and violence. But he couldn't really get round the phenomenon of androgyny. All gods are images of aspects of ourselves. They are also symbolic. The whole temple, multi-storeyed, and more than a little vertiginous at the top, had a rather Tibetan feel to it. But no prayer wheels.

We then moved down to an older temple, though the priest we'd hoped to meet was away. There was an extraordinary American woman living in the temple, one Om Shanti. She has been living in India for twenty-two years. In India she feels herself to be freer than in Los Angeles. Indeed, India does liberate. But what endurance. Admittedly she lives in a highly evocative set-ting, but what an extraordinarily basic way of life.

It struck me most that almost everyone I'd spoken to saw the spiritual life as one trimmed to individual needs. There were no set rules. We each select our own path. Does this suggest, in fact, Indian spirituality reinforces indi-viduality?

The day was not over. Back to the Sivananda ashram to hear a swami from South India talk on self-knowledge. It was a complex way at looking at the story of Skaldi, Shiva's son and of his great battle with a demon. The demon took on numerous disguises to escape defeat but Skaldi saw through them all, eventually co-opting two of these disguises, peacock and cock, into himself. Somehow this was seen as the kind of development that goes with self-knowledge. We have to defeat both our karma and our mental weaknesses. Our fate goes before us, but we should not despair. Our karma is only com-mensurate with the scale of our faults. And mental limitations can be over-come. In some ways he implied, it is all very easy. God lies within. We have already arrived. It is just a matter of perception, of seeing that we can reach out to the divine by looking within. All this suggests a comparatively easy struggle and maybe here is a foil to my view of the sheer problematic of the transition from one self to another.

Afterwards there was wonderful singing. One of the monks had a strong gravelly voice, yet plaintive, which spoke direct to one's inner self—I sud-denly felt I could be a Hindu.

The service ended with the Homa fire service.

10 November

First of my stomach upsets—must have been the ashram meal. A ciproxin pill sealed me up by 9 am but I was a little under the weather all day. Shiva Balak, whom I'd met yesterday by the first bridge, and who promised to explain yoga to me, was at the hotel on time, so I had my lesson, but this little more than a summary of Patanjali. He gave me a mantra. I rejected the one for the sun in favor of Siva. Then he wrote down and sang his hymn to Ganga. He also read out a passage from Rajaji's Ramayana. For that he received 100 Rs, more than he deserved. Clearly this is the way he survives, importuning gullible Europeans. He looks far more than his fifty-two years and I guess his has been a harsh life.

The next expedition, to find Vandana Majaji, a European yoga specialist recommended by Swami Ranganathananda, was a failure. She lives in a wonderfully sited house beyond Rishikesh, upstream, in fact in the district of Shivand Nagar, but it was locked up and she is somewhere in the mountains.

So it was to be Swastik's choice that prevailed. I fretted at the length of the journey it entailed and I had no wish to return almost all the way to Hardwar, but eventually we arrived at our destination, Shantikunj. This a very Indian ashram. No sign of any Europeans. As we entered we passed two music classes in progress, for drums and for flutes, and so to the Reception office. There we found ourselves questioning Piyush Rastogi, born in Meerut but brought up in Madras, in charge of News features. Swastik had told me this was an ashram based on the lives of the rishis. Very much a householder community and if marriage is not an absolute prerequisite (later, and in seeming contradiction to all I had been told, I gathered single people can be members) the family is paramount. The order of priorities, however, seems to be the self, then the family, then the community. But everything derives from the Absolute and everything is undertaken in its name.

It seems the community is comprised of some 500 families, so called volunteers—you are not committed to stay, you can come and go—but, as with the Aurobindo ashram, it's a sort of lifetime commitment. And this community serves the needs of the visitors—maybe they are potential volunteers—visitors who come for a month. They are measured and assessed on arrival and on departure, hence permitting the measurement of how efficacious the various forms of treatment available are on their mental and physical well-being. The two basic ones appear to be the singing of the gayatri and meditation. I was only moderately impressed by Priyush, though he fended questions adequately and appeared to have a grasp of the whole.

But my next informant was in a quite different league, a ferociously tough-thinking doctor, a Bengali, Dr Datta. It was here that the whole ashram became so unusual and weird. There is a real attempt to turn the whole approach to yoga and related spiritual exercises into a kind of scientific laboratory. There are machines for measuring brain pulses, seen not as electricity as such but as brain electricity. And the brain is seen as merely a conduit; I suppose the energy is seen as coming from God. Ears, eyes, all our organs, they do not generate our senses—it all comes from some other source. There was an encephalogram. Another machine measures stress—a kind of lie detector, I guess. There were machines for measuring the blood. He was very comforting on diabetes. Certainly you can die of complications but if you keep the blood sugar levels normal, then there is no risk. Indeed, it's a good disease to have as it always leaves you with a healthy appetite. And there was an incredible apparatus just for finding out what is happening to one. But, quite seriously, they do monitor changes in perception and concentration that flow from reciting the gayatri and from meditation. Is all this science gone mad and is Dr. Datta some kind of crazed scientist?

The last machine was the weirdest. It was of a figure with the chakras showing and this you shouted at. This will again measure your voice and assess the connection between its strength and your powers of focus and concentration. It was all very odd but within its own definitions plausible. Datta himself had a very powerful voice, and I'd guess exceptional powers of concentration.

It had all begun with Datta showing me a recently completed Phd on spirituality, one adopting a comparative cultural approach. He cited the appalling fact that the Chinese extracted 5000 (or was it 50,000?), kidneys from prisoners for the American market. But he would not buy a polarization of materialism and spirituality. One goes with the other. A society with low material standards has low spiritual standards (and vice versa). But you can not measure emotion, truthfulness, compassion, etc. Dr. Datta sees the real key to religion through morality and ethics. Is this really what the ashram is about? Its role is to encourage a greater sense of moral and social responsibility. Is its role really essentially educational? How can society improve, etc?

Where do women and children fit in? Women can in the ashram assume similar roles to those of men. But the point was made that there are physical differences and that men would undertake the rougher and more demanding tasks. Children are educated up to the age of eight in the ashram but then go outside. Families get together in committees and exchange information, but it's more a case of reporting one's achievements than working out collective strategies.

The ashram also has a developed horticulture, contributing to all branches of medicine, but the dispensary was ayurvedic. There was a weird meditation center, with a kind of symbolic Himalayan landscape as its main feature. It seems that the sadhana of the founder of the ashram, Pandit Shriram Sharma Acharya, was largely spent in the Himalayas. I guess here is a kind of an answer to Koestler's skepticism.

11 November
Stomach back to normal. Off to the small Kunjapuri temple and this soon turned out to be an astonishing exposure to the lower Himalayas. I loved all those moral precepts placarded on the roadside—"the road is hilly, don't be silly;" "All haste administers badly." The plains fell away and we were climbing quite steeply through heavily forested hillside to some 6000 feet, much the same height as Mussoorie and Naini Tal. It was after we'd broken away from the road to see the temple that the amazing snow-clad range of the Himalayas capped the horizon and, from the temple itself, there was a considerable panorama. This was the Shivalik range, Bandar Paunch to the left, then Gangotre, Trishul, Kedarnath, Badrinath. Mussoorie visible to the west. This was a shakti temple, the only one of some 300 in India to have a Kshatriya priest. In fact, a female relative was in charge on the day. Swastik told me that all temples to goddesses are on hilltops. It gives them the gift of sight and they can act as watchtowers. Temples to Siva, on the other hand, are down in the valley. Further evidence of female dominance over the male. Hard to drag ourselves away from such tranquility, such utter calm. Incidentally, some 200 steps up to the temple.

But back down the hill, making an arrangement at the bottom to meet a swami in a Swiss yoga center (in fact postponed till tomorrow) then up through another remarkable landscape of the Ganges valley till we came to Vasitha Guha ashram. And what followed was yet another of those small miracles India always seems to lay on.

I had a picnic lunch. Then I was introduced to the swami in charge of the ashram but clearly his English was not strong and he passed me onto Swami Shantananda Puri Maharaj. He turned out to be a wholly engaging and intellectually able swami from Tanjore. He'd been drawn to the place by the reputation of the remarkable inhabitant of its nearby cave, one Param Poojya Sri Swami Purushottamandaji. He I'll have to find out more about. He was a disciple of Brahmananda but broke away from the Ramakrishna Mission to go his own way. Then I think they broke off relationships. He became Shantananda's guru. Shantananda had hoped himself to take sannyas and others were initiated but he was told by his guru that he still had too much of the householder in him and that he would have to wait. He was told to get married and have children. I asked him if he had strong parental feelings to which he replied the sexual were stronger. He'd had an administrative career and at one stage had been posted to Tanzania (What did he do?). But in the 1980s he felt he could renounce these ties and so he was finally initiated (he told me by whom but I've forgotten) but with instructions never to stay in any one ashram for more than four days. One place he recommended above all others is the Ramana Maharshi ashram. There he gives lectures. But he's a trustee of the Vasitha Guha ashram and this is really his home.

On my raising the subject of Indian spirituality he protested that there were too many books on the subject. Surely no more are needed. I said I was writing about the attitudes of foreigners to the tradition. I asked the usual question about different kinds of the self. He came at this by an elaborate commentary on consciousness. He pointed out that this is never referred to in the plural. His metaphor was about electricity. We are bulbs. The electricity passed into us. The other metaphor was about a conductor. Science has obviously shaped his understanding of Hinduism. This, incidentally, is, he claimed, wrongly so called. It's really Sanatan Dharma. But we are all receivers of this consciousness. Our old selves simply fall away. We may retain memories of our former selves but they have no emotional affect. Clearly, he does see the end of this process as a dissolution in the absolute, a return to zero. I put to him the Proustian theory of memory but he did not buy it. I expressed to him my sense of puzzlement that, on the one hand, you had the all embracing undifferentiated Brahma, on the other, such highly individualized characters as himself, yet still laying claim to some transcendental Self. The seeker is sought, was his reply. There is no paradox.

On the guru relationship he admitted this was crucial and intense but accepts it can become idolatrous and you should endeavor to become your own guru.

I asked him what he read but he saw books as irrelevant. It's a question of experience. The means are again irrelevant—any means of approaching the divine will do, any saint or prophet will do. The paths are manifold. But he was detached from all worldly involvement. The ashram does have a small free hospital.

And he has written books on Krishna and the *Bhagavad gita*.

He wants to be free of all organization. The moment you organize, you've fallen away from a spiritual path. He felt the Ramakrishna Mission has lost its way. The monks eat too well. They are missionaries. They have little time for the contemplative life. But Ranakrishna had been for him the beginning of his own sadhana.

On sexuality he had little difficulty in being frank. Some were lucky. It just faded away as an instinct, a matter of grace. But for most it never went away and was a problem. He didn't buy the usual argument about sublimation though quoted it.

On the feminine, he thought its influence was partly an obvious consequence of the way Indian boys were afraid of their fathers, a distant figure, often not at home, and they naturally turned to their mothers. They would grant their wishes. He also said, rather curiously, that praying to mother goddesses was one way of acquiring wealth. But when I pressed him on Durga and Kali he admitted there was a fear of female sexuality. It was different for householders who had overcome their fears but remained problematic for the monastic and celibate. He wasn't opposed to my idea of a ferocious female sexuality but saw it as a benefit, a fighting on our behalf. But he accepted, as females came together, India might begin to give more weight to father figures and the masculine.

He had a new angle on Krishna. Krishna means to draw, to attract. All this is probably in his little book. Swastik reminded me of his own explanation, that Krishna was himself so manifold, poet, dancer, intellectual, administrator, etc, he offered multiple identifications. He reaches out to so many different people.

One of his favorite metaphors is that of being a character in a play. We are all programmed. My meeting him was predetermined. But we still want to get out of the play and escape. His outlook struck me very much as a philosophy of withdrawal. No real interest in social activity. We shred the past and our former egos. We seek the zero, the eclipse.

I liked his skepticism about Freud. Because he and western psychologists dealt only with consciousness and unconsciousness but failed to relate these to the superconsciousness, they had let the genie out of the bottle but then had not known what to do with it.

The cave itself was a little alarming. The saint had lived in the first chamber. I guess here was also his sleeping and eating quarters. Beyond was another chamber, a small light indicating how deep it was. In time I could pick out its shape but it felt inhuman. Further into the rock, but with the access now blocked off, had been the area where asceticism had been practiced by saints I believe in the past. Anyway, the vibrations were felt to be so powerful but private that the saint had seen fit to wall up the aperture and leave these spirits to themselves.

In the evening back to the Divine Life Society, expecting to hear a lecture by a High court Judge on Spirituality. On arrival one devotee said she had no idea what the lecture was to be about but then serenely informed me that their guru had returned. And so it was—Swami Chidananda was present. He arrived unheralded, a slight quite tall man, wrapping his saffron robe around himself as he walked to his seat. (I was very touched that the community had remembered my back condition and, unsolicited, brought me a chair.) In some ways once again it was the singing that made the evening and the swami's own singing was pretty strong for a man in his eighties.

I struggled to grasp the meaning of his talk. It didn't help that I was once again dead tired. He began very soft spoken in Hindi, with occasional English interjections e.g., there was no church at the time of Christ, etc (I guess a reference to the distaste of the Society for organization). I could see why his long account of oceanography, of the exploration of the sea, from divers to the bathysphere—and he always spelt out unusual names—was a kind of metaphor for man's inability to plot the absolute on his own. We need divine assistance etc. But why did he go on at such length on the death camps, and I have to say, seemingly relishing the gruesome details of the showers etc? Was this some indirect way of talking about the Orissa tragedy? And, if so, this is clearly right. Its enormity needs to be addressed. He quoted the BBC's calculation that the death toll will be 100, 000. But then why the reference to Pakistan and the emergence of Bangladesh? He seemed to be saying that Zulfikar Ali Bhutto, who had hated India so much more than Jinnah, got his justified come-uppance when he was hung. He forgot things e.g., what language the Old Testament was written in. It was a rambling performance. I felt he was at his best as leader of the chanting. Here was, alas, no guru for me.

12 November

I should record the stories of my two travel companions in Rishikesh. Firstly, my driver, Rakat. A Kshatriya. Maybe being a driver is an appropriate role for a warrior. Rakat comes of military stock. His father had been a havildar in the Garhwal regiment. Rakat was then but a few months old. His father had died at sea en route to take up a post in the UN peacekeeping force in Korea in 1953. He might himself have joined the army to fight for the liberation of Bangladesh but he had an injury to his arm. He's married with five children. Slight of build but tough as they come.

Swastik comes from a local landholding family. His father is a senior veterinary surgeon. His great grandfather was an army captain under the raj; not many of those. His grandfather a colonel. So a good military background. So here he is, an army son, but yet to marry, yet to have a real career. He has an MA in Medieval Indian history. He runs both a restaurant and a training college for management. Clearly he's driven himself to find out about Indian spirituality but his is an emphasis on the practical, on results. I suspect he's quite enamored of the siddhic and occult. But he also wants social activism.

Sports a baseball cap and a beard. Aged thirty-two. A clever man but I feel he only goes for what fits his expectations—not an open-ended agenda.

I'm glad I persevered with visiting the Omkarananda ashram. This is the inspiration of Swami Omkarananda, an Andhra, whose main ashram is in Zurich. In 1965 the man I was meeting, a young Swiss, had met him in Zurich and adopted him as guru and he became Swami Vishveshwaranda and now runs this ashram in Rishikesh. Quite a tall, well preserved, half-moon spectacled man, benign in appearance. Capable of great verbal address. I'd come to ask him what problematic faced the European in coming to terms with the Indian spiritual tradition. He tended to answer in practical terms. This is a tradition open to anyone, though there is some difficulty for Europeans being accepted by Indians. The way of life in India and its culture he sees as superior to those of the west. Indians are basically kinder, feel more in their hearts, tend to want to please.

I couldn't really get him to face all those conundrums of the ego/self. He just didn't seem to see a problem here; the former self will just fall away. How to achieve this? Well, the paths are numerous. He was best in describing himself as a karma yogi. The virtue of being this is its intense and continual activity. You really do not have time to be preoccupied with yourself. You move towards desireless action.

He rated the guru-disciple relationship very highly. Clearly his guru was still crucial for him. But you grow into being a guru and master in your own turn. He was uncritical of the relationship.

He got better as my questions became more pointed. What about sexuality? This he saw as the key. The reproductive drive is the major source of your energy. If you divert it into sensuality then it will diminish your powers and cut you off from spirituality. If you invest it in subtle ways, if it is redirected, then you rejuvenate yourself and spirituality can be pursued. The ideal seeker is one who is unaware of gender—has transcended even an awareness of female sexuality.

I asked him about homosexuality. He saw it as a barrier but maybe no more serious than fornication or alcohol abuse. You would just have to grapple with it and overcome it. You had to reach beyond sexual appetite.

What of the feminine? Again he tended to see this in practical ways. He went on about the comparative status of women in India and the west. In the west women are looked on as but a housewife; in India she's revered as a goddess. He went along with arranged marriages. Again, in India the reproductive element in sexuality takes precedence over enjoyment. But this had not been my question, so I tried again. How does a response to the feminine affect a European response to Indian spirituality? And I must say I am beginning to see this question more clearly. There is a dread of female sexuality and both Indian and European would feel threatened. The Kali image is real. He felt he was somewhat on the outside of this question as he was not married. But if the Indian child is so smothered by maternal love how much more likely it is there would be this ambivalent mother goddess image. And for a homosexual the ambivalence would be even more acute.

I liked him. Yoga was seen as a major way of pursuing the divine. He believes karma yoga is the most positive form. Clearly he is himself totally fulfilled by an active life. The ashram runs several schools, a high school and a degree giving college in management studies. It is a yoga center. It also teaches music and dance.

And here another person became visible. This was Kumari Bharati Somashekhari. A tall, thin, rather fey German lady from Heidelberg. Fourteen years in the ashram. And now an Indian citizen. She teaches dance mainly. She was persuasive in seeing this as a spiritual activity, referring to the temple dancing tradition which led to the divine. The wide-ranging symbolism of it all e.g., pearls that adorn the hair, symbolize divine powers flowing from the brain.

This was an impressive ashram and might be one for me to attend. Nice flats along the way to stay.

Back to the Divine Life Society to collect some literature and to a yoga center run by the Swiss ashram. They were unfriendly at first but we were lucky—we met an ordained Buddhist monk from Canada, who went either under his Indian name, Kittipalo Bhikhu, or Thai, Phra Eddy (Hagan). He'd become interested in Theravada Buddhism in Canada and this took him variously to Burma, Thailand and eventually he discovered a sangha in Thailand conducted in English. After a five-year apprenticeship he was ordained. Clearly he's a specialist in meditation. He spends on average eight hours a day meditating, and just about anywhere—traveling, in restaurants. No two meditations are the same. He is also a yoga teacher. He showed us around the Iyengar yoga center where, in fact, we were. The gymnasium was just a little Sadean, with ropes everywhere. The photos of Iyengar himself in various yogic poses were pretty impressive. Wonderful strong legs. But this emphasis on the physical may, our Canadian stated, be less important than the moral. A clean mind will get you further than a fit body. Again and again you come up against this paradox of a Buddhist/Vedantist path which leads you to an impersonal absolute, yet all are, in fact, carving out for themselves a highly distinctive personal path. You'd think it would lead to sameness. How can a transcendence of the ego or self be compatible with this individualized path?

The Canadian thought a large part of the difficulty in grasping this paradox simply lies in language. Maybe the very concept "self" has so many resonances that to try to offset a lower and higher self doesn't really convey the right meaning. But he was clear that only practice can reveal the truth of all this.

I guess he was thirty or so, trim and fit. One of those polite and well-mannered Canadians. He sees no divergence for him in the future from this path. He's actually convinced it is the right one for him. Here is a rare non-Indian on the path who did not come across as too tough and too driven and was much more at ease with himself. Here the cross-cultural experience is working.

I should not have been so skeptical about Swami Chidananda. I was to enjoy a rich if at times predictable conversation with him. It was very different, sitting before him in the office of Guru Niwas, than seeing him on his throne in the prayer or samadhi room. Once he had settled down—and he is frail and this was all in slow motion—down to business and his saying; "I am at your disposal." And this he, indeed, was for an hour and a half and I was certainly to be the more fatigued by our conversation.

My first question: is there a paradox that a yoga center prioritizes social work? The explanation for this lies with the founder, Swami Sivananda. He was a doctor who went to work in the rubber plantations in Malaysia. It was his recognition of the impoverished lives of the workers that led him to question his own way of life and social conditions. It led to compassion for the poor and a new ideal of social service. But beyond this, serving man is serving God; there is no paradox.

Then I posed another paradox; that the quest for the Atman seemingly led all in one direction, yet everywhere I find completely distinctive personalities engaged in the quest. This prompted an attractive metaphor about those seeking to climb a mountain. They all approach by quite different routes, though their end is the same. There are as many different approaches as there are individuals. And this raised a very important possibility. In the transition from the lower to the higher self, you may well retain a strong sense of individualism. But he did backpedal a little—there were laid down only a number of paths.

So was there in fact hiatus or continuity? He emphasized the latter. You climb up step by step but, at a certain point, you take a bold leap onto the balcony above. At that point you discard the past. Even memory. He agreed memory is crucial to the ego and you hold onto to it till the very last but even this had to be surrendered if one is to obtain absorption in the divine.

So what was the role of the guru? Here another kind of analogy. What can you learn on your own? Who teaches you how to read and write? to make shoes? Cook? All skills have to be learnt. Why should it be any different for the spiritual life? But at a certain point the guru will take the initiative and set you free to work it out for yourself. If you come unstuck or run up against new problems you can return to the guru, or, if he has died, seek another.

I switched direction to the role of the feminine. He agreed it was omnipresent in Indian culture. Maybe Hobbes and Locke would put it down to nature, he reflected, India was a matriarchal society, etc. He also elaborated on the childhood dependence on the mother. The father was largely absent. But then he switched gear and found the answer in Indian philosophy: how to explain a self-sufficient static Absolute yet its movement? The self-sufficient Absolute is masculine. It is shakti or the female energy that gives it movement. At the heart of this spirituality is a being which is both male and female. So maybe, I asked, the accent on the role of androgyny in Indian culture is correct? He thought this might be true of Indian religions but not of philosophy. This was beyond gender.

This led onto sexuality. He was happy to fend the question. He's contributed an article to an issue of a journal entitled *What Is Enlightenment*, edited by Andrew Cohen. He conceded that the force that shapes the cosmos is one and the same as the sexual drive. It is a highly powerful drive and informs all activities. This led to his account of the four asramas. In the first the sexual drive has to be curtailed. This is the time for laying the foundations of life and these must be sound. Only after this brahmacharya phase of student life can one enjoy sexuality as a householder; then anything goes. Then comes the third stage of voluntary celibacy and then the final stage of withdrawal to the forest (is this correct?) But I said this was fine for the householder. What of the monk? Then he made a surprising statement. The ideal of monastic celibacy was only introduced by Vivekananda, influenced by catholic monasticism. In other Indian monastic traditions you may have to become celibate on joining the community but you can previously have enjoyed a married life. Vivekananda imposed high expectations on his monks and Chidananda conceded he may have made a mistake. I asked, what happens if a monk slips up? He would be asked if he wanted to leave the community to get married. But if he wanted to stay then he would be told this was no great lapse and he must take up the quest again. There is no concept of sin.

We chatted at the end about Krishnamurti whom he'd met. He'd also met Prabhavananda but I failed to follow this up (Well, the other monks were now anxious to call this long conversation to a close). And Huxley and Isherwood as well. Even more extraordinarily back in the 1930s he'd met Annie Besant in Madras.

He had a vivid description of Kali, of how she was born out of Durga, commissioned to slay the demon king. Her tongue—and he pushed his out vigorously—was to lap up any drop of his blood which would otherwise reproduce himself. So what was this all about? Your mother smacked you. There was a bad mother. But those who sought God would see in Kali their supporter, fending off all those threats, the demands of the ego, etc.

But if there is no sin, he could still see good moral conduct as the most important foundation for the spiritual life. There is this core conservatism in so much of Indian spirituality. He narrated many familiar aspects of Buddhism e.g. the eight fold path as well as of Hinduism. I can see that this is a missionary movement. They really want to put across the Hindu message.

Into Krishna Country

14 November

Mathura

Up very early, in fact too early—the Birth of Krishna morning service had reverted to its winter time. A phone call from my new guide, Mathuresh Chandra Bharadvaj, to say he was coming later than planned. But it was still dark as we set off for the Kesavo Deo temple. Here is one of India's fraught situations. The temple is cheek by jowl with Aurangzeb's mosque, one that cannibalized a temple and probably the one over Krishna's original birthplace. Hence the extensive military presence—some 400 soldiers on duty here. All this to fend off another Ayodhya. Indeed, seeing this mosque and imagining its destruction brought home the full enormity of that act. But the mosque is shut up and no Muslims worship here.

The morning *aarti* is less crowded than the evening but those who were attending it more than made up for this with their passion. There was one rather pleasing looking character, round-faced and quite fleshy, who shouted and shouted his adoration. One or two fell prostrate on the ground. There were three shrines at which prayers were held, the priests fanning the gods with a *chamma* or fly whisk or some other article, then flinging holy water at us. I guess the small shrine where Krishna was allegedly born—there's a kind of marble slab there of great antiquity—was the most historically significant, but the prayers in the main temple building, with subordinate shrines to Durga, Shiva, etc, were more sumptuous. Note there were sculptured heads of Vyasa and Caitanya on either side of the main shrine to Krishna. Well, I found it all rather powerful. Even the priests were dancing little jigs. Have I done *bhakti* justice?

Then on the road to Vrindaban, calling on the Ramakrishna Mission and its hospital en route. The Abbot was hard pressed to point out on a map where Ramakrishna had stayed but had a guess, and that was to be our first venue, the Ramakrishna Fauzvarkunj. This was just one of numerous such small temples, managed now by a rather decrepit, gap-toothed old monk. But here indeed was Ramakrishna's photograph. He'd stayed here for two weeks, not I think with Mathur but on his own. We were unable to trace the site of the hut where he lived with one of the widows but, as the Abbot had pointed out, tradition and authenticity are at loggerheads on this one.

Nearby was the temple of Nikhivan and here we picked up the Krishna story. It was here that Krishna and Radha sported amongst the brindavas or forest trees. This is still a large enclosed space filled with shrubs where monkeys live. I couldn't help feeling when it comes to the concept of "play" the monkeys are truest to the tradition. None, however, tried to pinch my camera or specs, though I kept them carefully out of sight. There was one small temple selling all kinds of make-up, keeping up the story of Radha decorating herself for her night with Krishna.

I rather forget the order in which we now proceeded. Nearby there was a trust building, the Bhajan ashram, set up to look after widows. Apparently, after the 1971 war, this was overrun by widows. We saw a haggle of them in one room, all making a show of prayer. We attended a small prayer meeting in one shrine. All the walls here and throughout the ashram covered with plaques from all over the world of, I guess, grateful customers.

Then we moved onto Vrindaban's most attractive temple, the Gobinda Dev, the divine Cowherd or Krishna. All in red sandstone and a genuinely attractive temple. It's clearly been recently restored by the Department of Archaeology.

Then we went to a small temple nearby, the Madan Mohan, and there we were to have our one encounter with a saddhu, a lovely old fellow, one Sri Madhan Das, apparently 118 years old. He came to the temple in the 1930s. In those early days there were some 130 saddhus, and I assume amongst these was his guru. Now there's but a handful. They survived on charity. His religious life was devotional, chanting to Krishna. No meditation. There was a small shrine to one of Caitanya's disciples and attending this has been one of his special responsibilities. Here was a quiet unassuming spirituality which I liked.

From the tranquility of Madan Mohan to the hectic overcrowded temple of Banke Bihari. This one grants your wishes and, unsurprisingly, is the most popular. Soldiers posted both inside and outside. I found all this rather alarming and decided to cut short the Vrindaban trip and head for Gobardhan.

We had also made an excursion to the Hare Krishna ISCON ashram, with its Krishna-Balaram temple. All this to honor their founder, Swami Pradhu-pada. There was a quite ridiculous museum of his artifacts, his final bar of soap, etc. There was another room devoted to his American trip, with huge blown up photos. I simply cannot take to the ISCON movement, though I am coming round to the Krishna legend.

Wonderful to journey through the countryside and we stopped on the way for a picnic. A village visible in the distance. The land roundabout parceled up into farms of varying size, a half to five acres or so. Ten acres are the max-imum permitted.

Not much to see in Gobardhan. Short of it we stopped to enjoy a beauti-ful Rajput building, the Kushum Sharvar, next to a tank, a "memorial" build-ing, built for meditation and in Krishna's honor. Gobardhan features strongly in the legend through the myth that he raised the whole village and its long plateau-like hill above his head to spare it the wrath of Indra and the flood she induced, out of anger that Krishna had refused to offer her gifts. In the town there was a large pleasing tank. Behind was a supposedly fine temple, also in red sandstone, but in fact falling into decay. My driver and guide then had lunch at my expense and I did some shopping. Bought a belt. Then we headed in through the countryside to Dig.

And this was the real surprise of the day. Here was the remarkable sum-mer palace of the Maharajah of Bharatpur. Quite stunning architecture and in a marvelous situation, overlooking one tank and close to another, the Rup Sagar lake. An engaging guide, an old retainer, I guess, showed us round the main palace building, with vast punkahs, a bed the size of a tennis court, or so it seemed, and a room set aside for chess. The guide, such a handsome old fellow, refused to let me take his photograph.

Other fine buildings were spread around a vast courtyard. I took most to the private secretary's palace, tucked away in a corner. We saw the rooftop reservoir from whence the water pressure worked the elaborate system of fountains, with each exit hole numbered to trace wherever blockages might occur. And, standing bold in the distance, the massive walls of the great fort of Dig, scene of Holkar's historic encounter with Lake in 1804. Quite awe-some, though sadly neglected. Inside it has just become a quarry.

On the way back we stopped off at a new temple in Gobardhan. On the way we saw quite a few pilgrims, barefoot, undertaking the pilgrimage round Gobardhan hill, some 20 kilometers. The whole Braj circuit is about 200 kilometers and would take a good month to do. The temple had numerous pictures of the Krishna story—I guess the one of Krishna holding aloft the village was the most intriguing. Note Balaram is an elder brother. It seems Lakshmai, Ram's younger brother, was told by his step-mother to bring Ram up well and he was reincarnated as an elder brother, the better to fulfill the same role for Krishna. Of course, one of Ramakrishna's best householder friends was called Balaram. One painting was of the child Krishna opening his mouth and, to one side above, was a cartoon, implying that the whole world was in his mouth. But it is all to do with pleasure, playing with men, dancing with the gopis. Then his uncle took him back to Mathura to slay the king Kamsa with his fist. Kamsa had a troupe of wrestlers on his side and Krishna and Balaram had to slay the lot. This prompted a discussion about wrestling, popular in this part of India. Mathuresh promised to take me to-morrow to a wrestling gym. On our return the car ran out of petrol but some diesel fuel was found in a village. So a crowded and informative day, arriving back at the hotel at 6:30 or so.

I couldn't really draw Mathuresh out on why Krishna is so popular. All he could say was that Krishna offers, over and above all the other gods, love.

15 November
Another day to be devoted to the Krishna trail.

It began with a real treat. It's clear that wrestling is a part of the Krishna story—Balaram was a fine wrestler—and Krishna flays Kamsa with a body blow. And this part of India, with all those sturdy Jats, is keen on wrestling. Mathuresh took me in the early morning to a local training center, the Bhooteswar Akhada (Lord Shiva Temple Wrestling Place). The wrestlers were just resting from their morning practice. Fine figures, possibly only in their twenties, but with mature physiques. Oddly, their guru, a former wrestler, now old, was a whisp of a man. One swarthy fellow, with much curly chest hair, stood out. When I asked them if they were married and only one, it seemed, was, and then I asked why not, one just smirked. I am pretty sure these wrestlers are for the present homosexual in their sexual acts.

But such delights could not last long, so back on the trail. Now we were going south east of Mathura. Our first stop, Baldev. This visit began with my being bitten by a bee. This rather frightened me. Mathuresh pulled out the sting and told me to drink plenty of water to prevent swelling. After ten minutes or so the pain subsided. But I was little inclined to like this Balaram temple. Clearly there is quite a cult around him. Behind the temple was the smelliest of tanks.

Then down to the river and the Brahman ghat. We were now downstream from Mathura. The river Jumna had divided but rejoined at this point. We went inside the Darshanand ashram to find it filled with pilgrims, on a month long Braj pilgrimage. They were just starting up their journey again, on a day's journey from Baldev to Mahevan. Some 2000 of them, from all over India. Mainly elderly, and mainly women. You walk barefoot to be in touch with the sacred soil trodden by Krishna, not to punish yourself.

One attractive Punjabi stopped for a conversation. From an early age of eighteen he's been a saddhu. At first his shopkeeping family had opposed his wishes, but, in the end, agreed. Even his mother was to join him on a pilgrimage. He's now in his forties. Very good looking fellow, with a nice smile. Why, I asked him, had he done it? Devotion. Clearly for him no other way of life is conceivable.

Then there was another treat. Sitting basking in the sun was a great heap of man. This a Brahmin saddhu, one Sri Ramanand, from these parts originally, though he's spent much time in Varanasi reading scriptures. But he's taken as his guru the leader of a nearby ashram, the Raman Reti ashram, and over time has made a commitment. He was appointed to this place to teach grammar to some ten to twelve youngsters. But they also receive a broader education in the ashram. He'd contracted polio in one leg at the age of eight and I guess had gone to some trouble to develop his upper body as compensation, and indeed, he has a huge chest, though when I got him to stand up, with the aid of crutches, so that I could take a photo, an equally large stomach was on display.

Then we took ourselves off to the Palace of Nanda at Mahaban and its palace of Nanda. Quite impressive, though I missed out on seeing the details in the temple to do with Krishna's infancy. There was an amazing picture of the baby Krishna sucking the poison out of the dying woman. What does that tell us?

Then onto the ashram where I had my picnic lunch. The pilgrims had spread out along the road, though some had got ahead of us. We found them caught up in an ecstatic dance and singing inside the ashram. Clearly the pilgrimage is all highly organized. They bring all their tents with them in lorries. They had set up camp in an adjacent field. Medical services, communications, all accompany them. My Punjabi reappeared.

In the ashram resides the guru who Mathuresh has also adopted. The last time they had met had been but brief, just to exchange greetings, but this was enough for him. The ashram has small cottages for some 200 permanent residents. It follows the Vaishnavite cult of the younger son of Guru Nanak, in the Vallabchariah lineage.

We spoke to one of the residents in these huts, an old saddhu of 83. He had turned sannyasin on his retirement from being a station-master, had left his wife and children behind. They don't know where he is. He's a Bengali and spoke good English. But he was not to be drawn out. Would not really explain why he had joined this sect, spoke only of Krishna as lord of the universe. He had a drawer full of homeopathic medicines and gave me one for my bee sting.

This looked like being the end of our journey but as we drove back to Mathura I realized we had bypassed Gokhul. So back on our tracks. Quickly I took to this small town on the river, on a manageable scale and peaceful. Some extraordinary buildings, like the telephone exchange, all decorated with Krishna/Radha motifs. I knew the town was the HQ of the Vallabchariah sect, but how to find them? Down at the steps to the river we found a small temple and they gave us two books by one Shyam Das. But when we arrived at what I'd taken to be the HQ it turned out to be another temple and anyway it was shut.

But it seemed Shyam Das was to be found. So back through the town and so into a courtyard where indeed his wife was to meet us and invite us up to their rooms. He later joined us. He is a typical rather overbearing large American but here's a man who has studied the Krishna cult for thirty years, collecting materials on it. He gave me yet another of his books. Clearly the Krishna cult is the other face of Hinduism. How contrasted it be with the Vedantic, Saivite tradition. He lamented the way the west has accepted but one version and not the other. Only ISCON has tried to redress the balance and they are a missionary movement. A true Krishna cult does not proselytize. I was also told that Vedantism has a larger meaning than just the followers of Sankara. The Krishna cult is clearly a life-affirming movement, one of joy in all the senses. All these experiences are but a window on God. It's a kind of seeking of darshan with nature. But if this is a kind of pantheism, for God is everywhere, it is not dualist. God and the world are one. But whereas Vedantism sees the world as maya, the Krishna movement sees the world as God. Yes, it is about suspended animation and there is a rich tradition of music and poetry. But it is sexually quite strict. It consciously rejected the left-handed Tantric path. The enjoyment of sex is only within marriage. It is not a hedonistic movement. So that underlying conservatism is here also. But these were useful insights.

Two other temples on our return journey, one to Chandravali, a goddess, in fact a kind of stone face, the temple never completed and nowadays a marketplace, and the Raval temple, birthplace of Radhaji, Radha's mother.

En route we'd stopped at the burning ghats. One body still being incinerated. And flames from the ghats to be visible during our hour on the river, by boat along the riverside of Mathura, picking our boat up at Yamuna ghat and going upstream to the Vishram ghat. There we stopped to visit the Dwarka Dhish temple, a busy one, set back from the ghats, with what looked like classical paintings of the Krishna story. This an old temple. Also on the riverside a sati tower and upstream a great fort. Was this Kamsa's palace? Now in part it houses the local branch of the RSS. Mathura's Lok sabha MP, unsurprisingly, is BJP. Mathuresh turns out to be apolitical and took all his family off to the temple on election day.

16–17 November

A bad start. Breakfast came late. I refused to pay for it. No sign of the taxi to take me to the station. So I behaved badly. However, belatedly Mr. Patnesh got organized and got me to the station and onto the train for Gwalior.

The landscape changed as we passed from UP to Madya Pradesh, the soil now reddish and no longer an endless plain but a broken landscape with small copses and, in the distance, lumpy hills. All went well on arrival at Gwalior and so to my luxury hotel, the Usha Kiran, former guesthouse of the royal palace and on loan from Scindia to the Welcome group. I'd forgotten how pleasurable such hotels can be.

I rested and then went out to the son et lumiére at the Fort and it soon became apparent here was a building to rival any I've ever seen. Far more romantic than the rather lush Taj Mahal. Wonderful enameled tiles. I enjoyed the way its history was presented. Clearly Gwalior was one of India's great music centers and from Man Singh in the fifteenth century onwards this flourished. Under Akbar there lived here one of the nine jewels of his crown, Tansen. I later saw his rather modest tomb.

Initially, on the following day, I was rather cross at the switching of guides as I'd been rather attracted to a Mr. Singh but it was his Muslim "brother" who took over, Vakal Ahmed, with a patch over one of his eyes. He'd fallen on a stick in a flower pot. But he has the reputation as Gwalior's best guide. He was brought up inside the Fort and had as young as ten embarked on his career as guide. His English was excellent but only as long as he remained on familiar ground. So it was back to the Fort and back to the Palace and from the outside it lived up to all my expectations. Inside, it felt a little claustrophobic going down to the swimming pool where the ranis had chosen to commit jaur, widow sacrifice other than on the funeral pyre. Their husband had died in battle, was it at Panipat?

Then we visited some rather splendid North Indian temples. Some handsome Sikhs were visiting. There was a brand new Sikh temple nearby, the real cause of their pilgrimage. There was also a South Indian style temple, for one of the early Rajput rulers had married a lady from the south and had indeed learnt how to become man and wife during a three day stay in a south Indian temple in the south, learning how to please one another. The old barracks—and the British had been as bad vandals of the Fort as the Moghuls—has been converted into Scindia's school, so prestigious that moneys are routinely spent to keep the great twelve mile circuit of walls in good repair, to protect India's élite.

But the real treat were the great Jain rock temple carvings, huge figures of the saints. The best were to come on the other side of the Fort and Vakal was wonderful in the way he scampered up inside one of these temples to get a worm's eye's view of its substantial private parts. How odd that the Jains, a microscopic minority, if a rich one, have left so many dominant monuments behind them. Carpets took up much of the day and much expenditure but Christmas presents purchased.

It was interesting to discover that one of the waiters, Narayan Singh (they are all Singhs as far as I can gather) had been on the Braj. He's done the circuit of Gobardhan hill with his wife and family. He'd gone onto Hardwar and done his dip, holding onto the chains. I cannot say I found out what all this meant to him.

I am really leaving behind now one set of enquiries and crossing into Forster country. The insights will be less interesting and more oblique. But maybe it will be more of a holiday and more hedonistic.

18 November
Today in Gwalior is the festival of waking up the gods. Gwalorians buy sticks of sugar and erect a kind of wigwam of them at home. Lights are placed in the middle. The gods go to sleep for several months (Ranjit's point) and during this time no real ritual can take place. The marriage season can only begin from this date.

Safely onto the train to Jhansi. A brief conversation on the platform with a highly traveled, clearly highly successful orthopedic doctor. He thought the BJP had been misrepresented and were not communal. All Indians were one happy family, etc. The landscape got more and more interesting, though the plains are still there, if between hills. But a desiccated landscape, more scrubland than forest.

So a tour of Jhansi. To its museum and its director, Mr Tiwari. Some good things here, Gupta period pieces. I liked the folk art gallery. Then to the Fort. This had suffered at the hands of history, but the Rani of Jhansi shines through as national heroine. She had jumped from the parapet here, her adopted son strapped to her back. The horse died but she made her ground to join Tatya Tope. Defeated, she went on to the final showdown at Gwalior. The only building of any beauty is her palace in the town, but sadly neglected. There were signs of fine painting in a kind of Indo-Moghul style, some figurative, some merely ornamental.

So I was glad to be heading off to Orccha. Not far to go. I abandoned plans for a swim at a new hotel. Instead, off to the village of Chandrapura through the teak forest. Here was entirely the right landscape for the Krishna Braj. The village itself wonderfully clean and well-kept. Carefully subsectioned according to caste, with fine decorative features over the doorways. Then off to an old hunting lodge of the British by a lake—a wonderful place for meditation—and then back to watch the sunset over the river and the memorial hall temples. In Wahib Qureshi I have another good Muslim guide. He's persuading me to give up the idea of going to Datia and instead to areas of Muslim influence.

In the evening I had a stroll in this deeply atmospheric small town, the great palace a daunting silhouette in the darkness. Much music in the background, this, I gather, the Hanuman festival. Well, I can listen to this tomorrow night. A good meal of fish curry and vegetable pulao at prices well below those of the Usha Kiran. For all its former glories, the Sheesh Mahal is rather a simple hotel, with frequent power cuts, though my room is spacious, with a wonderful bathroom and loo—a real throne—and spectacular views.

19 November
A stroke of luck, my visit coincides with the end of the month long Krishna festival, the Kartik festival (the name of the month in the Hindu calendar). Today's events were for women only. They come in from the surrounding villages, from up to 200 kms away, to take a bath in the sacred Betwah river—it runs into the Yumuna. Then they have to get by men posing as Krishna—possibly temple priests but could be laymen—who demand a kind of toll duty before they can proceed to the King Rama temple. They were gathered along the river and the ghats in their thousands. This was the last day of the festival so it was now or never they could make the journey. Some were clustered in circles, chanting over various gifts for Krishna. A wonderfully colorful sight, especially where they had stretched out their saris to dry. Husbands can be no part of this. Indeed, for a month they are denied intercourse. Families, dispersed among the villages, get together. It's a great time to gossip, all of which will get back to the village.

But also taking place, quite incidentally, was a gathering of the local brahmin elite, drawn from at least 100 ks away. This the 108 brahmins (I have still to find out the significance of this number), all seated around in their pandal, reading, in the course of the week, the *Bhagavad gita*. One of them, I'd have thought disconcertingly, was reading it aloud at the same time. Nearby in the evening was the venue for a performance—and here something straight out of Forster—of boys in drag, though some were well into their thirties, and on the whole entering with enthusiasm into their female impersonations, flouncing and prettifying really quite effectively. I heard them sing songs but there was no performance of the Ramayana that evening as promised, not enough spectators.

Otherwise a day of sightseeing. As background for the riverside festival are the great memorial temples or cenotaphs of the Bundela Rajputs. The name is a corruption of Vindya hills and this is also a reference to the Durga cult. There has been a strong local Bundelkand dynasty since the fifteenth century. One of their descendants had been a close ally of Jehangir and one of the two great palaces was erected in his honor. This palace had some remarkable paintings if in need of restoration, but this is happening. We went outside the town to a Tantric temple. Here a triangular shape enclosed a square and the sanctum sanctorum was at the center of the temple. Again, fine frescoes, some sixteenth, most nineteenth. In the late nineteenth century, Orccha had a strong local school of painting. We also went to see a Hanuman temple further out. Here is another means for avoiding marriage. As a devotee of Hanuman you can remain single. How much of the spiritual life is, I wonder, an escape from marriage and a safety valve for the homosexual?

In the afternoon we went even further beyond the town to see a Lakshmi temple. Was it a penis drooping down in one of the decorative features? These elaborate formal designs in the vihara are in imitation of jewellery. And the whole concept of the shape of the temple is, according to popular legend, modeled on the shape of the coconut. This is a peculiarly clean fruit to offer to the gods. Then to a lakeside with the ruins of a small castle, the Barwa Sagar, once the lodging home for the Resident, based at Jhansi, on tour, plans for it to be converted into a hotel.

And finally to a small ashram and temple complex, where we met the head of the order, a Swami Sankacharya, who itinerates between the four maths of Sankacharya. He only spoke Hindi but was happy to talk about how the ashram began and about the saddhu who had first found water here. The swami apparently owned to medical knowledge so I asked him what advice he had on my back. I was instructed to lie flat on my back and do various exercises, though some of these would have been against the physio's recommendations. Clearly, these swamis are just as likely to offer medical advice as any other information. According to Qureshi, the swami said only a good life would contribute to any cure for these problems. I rather took to this member of the saffron community.

The security guard at one of the palaces was a real killer—indeed, Qureshi says he belongs to the bandit caste—where does this virility come from in a minority of Indians? Again, that wonderful knowing look they give but what does it really signify?

20 November

A return after all to my original plan of visiting Datia and a neighboring Jain pilgrimage site. A good decision. Back through horrible Jhansi and back along the Gwalior road to Datia. It was at this distance that Lutyens saw the two great palaces of Datia and was so impressed he got off the train to visit them and returned for another visit. Their influence on the New Delhi buildings is transparent; the Rajput style cupola is simply transposed to the Raj Bhavan and elsewhere. Datia once belonged to Orccha but the son of its Maharajah had, whilst heir apparent, done Jehangir a great favor and it was at his request that the son had come into this separate fiefdom. He repaid the favor by building this palace in Jehangir's honor but he was never to visit and it was never to be occupied. Such was the wealth of feudal India. But the palace is still maintained, was even to be decorated with paintings; its ghosts had to be entertained.

But palaces apart, the huge success of the day was finding two of the Maharajah's sons at home in the Raj Mahal palace. Imagine dropping in on royalty in this way anywhere else? I met the elder brother first, Rajendra, rather a handsome fellow, a businessman in Nagpur and not really much interested in my questions. He tended to shrug off any question of a historical nature as a matter of the past and not really for consideration. So it was just as well the younger brother, Ghansyam Singh, had returned from electioneering, for he was very enthusiastic in replying. He's a Congress politician, has been an MLA and would like to be a Lok Sabha MP.

My most fruitful line of enquiry was to ask how the princes fitted into local life, past and present. I am, of course, particularly interested in their contribution to local religious life. The answer—quite a considerable amount. Recently there was a Krishna festival, the Gopalsthani, for Krishna the cowherd. All the local cattle, gaily festooned, leave the town for a neighboring temple—Krishna himself now carried in a cart, previously slung on poles in a palanquin. The Maharajah would be present, his appearance almost de rigeur. It soon became apparent Krishna worship is strong in the court. If the younger brother insisted no one had to worship any particular god—it was, as I put it, a cafeteria system—Krishna was almost the formal court faith. There was a Krishna temple attached to the wing of the palace and in the past there had been a Krishna shrine inside the palace. It seems just about anybody can take on priestly functions. Certainly the Maharajah might do so. This could be at the expense of other courtly functions—and this seems to have been the trouble with Dewas, religion took over from other crucial roles—but the court here has ties with Mathura and this son had, as it happened, been educated in Mathura.

Incidentally, they have no recollection of any festival in which the image of Krishna himself is immersed. Did Forster get it wrong or have I misread him?

I couldn't elicit much on their attitudes to the Maharajahs of Chhatarpur and Dewas but that, crucially, as Dewas was Mahratta there could be no intermarriage with Rajput Datia and Chhatarpur. As Datia and Chhatarpur were both Rajput there were family ties. It seems father-son conflicts equally plagued this family and the grandfather had been expelled from the state by the great-grandfather, or whichever it was. Both rulers, though, had decent periods of office, up to fifty years each. I guess they have come to terms with their loss of status and have just buckled down to making a living. Plans to convert this wing of the palace into a hotel; it has at least one substantial assembly room. Filled with stuffed animals and large often decayed portraits. Much faded glory here. But the family still have a sense of their public role as princes and are, it seems, still looked up to. Maybe they still have enough wealth not to be seen as embarking on politics to make money. The younger son was far more lively, more receptive—a vigorous fellow, of some intelligence and I suspect of considerable drive.

Next came the Jain pilgrim shrine at Sonagir. Surprisingly 15 percent of the Madya Pradesh population are Jain. Here is rather a spectacular site for a shrine, one that has accumulated since the 16th c. On a steep hillside and commanding at the top extensive views on all sides. Qureshi told me much about Jainism. Buddha had started out as a Jain but found it too difficult a religion. Note Jains do not believe in reincarnation. Hence these twenty-four Messengers or Tirthankars are just that—not reincarnated avatars. Mahavir the 24th and last. It was the Messengers who found the world such a warring place that they insisted on an absolute code of non-violence. This meant vegetarianism—and you can only eat vegetables grown above ground—and a business career, because this is an activity which poses no threat to life. Clearly asceticism is important. Just a little disappointingly all these exposed penises are witness to the fact that the Messengers have become indifferent to sex—the limp penis bears witness to this—other faiths have not had the courage to bear witness to this asexuality—so, alas, no humanist delight in the body on display. One shrine with a kind of switchback built into it, built in honor of their realized nature, their achieving moksha. White is the Jain color. White rice is the special offering to the Messengers. All the Messengers look alike, a kind of anonymity and so a sign of holiness, though each has a distinctive sign on his chest. One shrine at the bottom was all of glass and clearly no money is spared in these shrines. The Jains are an immensely wealthy community.

Our first visit in the morning had been to a Hindu temple and ashram, the Tombala, this another version of Parvati. It had been founded back in the 1920s by Shri 108 Anant Vibhusit Swamaji, a real podge of a man, with an enormous belly button. I couldn't quite grasp what was distinctive about his ideas. Chief Minister Digjivay Singh had raised a small fortune so that the temple could build a brand new tank, all constructed out of marble. As with most "live" temples, people in some number come to make obeisance, several well clad men, all humbling themselves before the gods. You do not have to look at all spiritual or ascetic to be a practicing Hindu.

Qureshi made the interesting comment that Indians are so surrounded by old buildings that they hardly notice them—they are much more excited by the new.

Another small ambiguity in the evening. I went to see the Ramayana performed at the Bhagavad Gita center. Less camp than the singing though as much slapstick as melodrama. A short, rather inebriated, character attached himself to me—I took him to be a peasant. Yet the extent of his English should have belied this. It turned out that he was a teacher in a Sanskrit college, a Brahmin, and attending the Gita reading. Three of us and I then walked down to the river. But all his questions were on the availability of European women. Would they sleep with him? Indian men were very tight, he boasted. Presumably a claim they were well endowed.

Into Forster Country

21 November

What can be said about homosexuality in India? I asked the excellent Qureshi what he made of same-sex relationships and sexuality generally. It seems heterosexuality is in the ascendant. Television has brought home to Indian women the possibilities of their sexual allure and more and more are trying it on. Indian men respond. One clue is the way when women are bathing in the river or tanks they play to their male audience, readier to expose themselves. Qureshi thought the percent of homosexual men in Bundelkhand would be less than 1 percent. He had no trouble in discussing such matters. The most likely homosexual acts would be between men over fifty/fifty-five and boys—their relationships with their wives get more and more impossible through lack of privacy as the family grows—wives anyway are increasingly caught up in the management of the home—it's then that these older men turn to younger boys. Older men and young boys naturally associate but this is dangerous. From the newspaper reports of criminal trials these men are getting five to seven year sentences. You'd never know who the 1 percent are. All this is very covert. It is bad morals and a social disgrace, though Qureshi thought Ashis Nandy's verdict was too extreme—it wouldn't spoil the marriage chances of other members of the family.

I asked about relationships with Europeans. It seems if Indians have lived alongside Europeans then they would not be shocked by such approaches. Those unfamiliar with Europeans would be more puzzled than put off—it would be outside their experience. The usual response of Indians is, what is there in it for me in the short and long run? The more knowing ones might expect as much as 1000 Rs. Europeans with their higher salaries can afford some of the consumer goods they want. But really, and this was more my idea, sheer curiosity would keep them in play. AIDS was a worry however.

I then asked him why anyone should choose to be a religious. And he incidentally thought homosexuality to be more likely amongst the religious. He thought it would be through not getting on with one's relatives, having few friends, etc. Social isolation would lead one to look for a guru and then to join a religious community.

Now we were closing in on the first of the Forster venues, Chhatarpur. The first familiar landmark was Nowgong. We stopped at a church, clearly the former cantonment church. A good Victorian one, c 1843, in good order outside but stripped and sad inside. Few memorials. One to George Francis Blowers of the Bombay Fusiliers and another to the soldiers of the North Staffs Regiment. All had died on duty, no deaths in the Mutiny or wars.

Further on we came to village of Mausanias, Forster's Mau, and so to the summer palace of the Maharajah. Though quite what was what was unclear. One section has become a Museum, the Dubela. Here I believe was the seat of government. Certainly one room was where the Maharajah held court. Over the throne a striking portrait of the founding father of the dynasty, Chaitanal, a forbidding forebear for Forster's HH. Beyond the choked up lake were two cenotaphs, one for the Maharajah, one for the Maharani, and the ruin of what I thought might have been a summer palace. But when did this fall into ruin and where did Forster and Ackerley stay? (In fact it became clear the Dubela museum had to be the former summer palace.)

We quizzed those working outside the Museum on their attitudes to the Maharajah. They'd respected him the more when he had been in government but, even so, still looked up to him. But this would be more true of ordinary folk, less true of the middle class. Yes, the Maharajah would be expected to attend some festivals, a key one being the Diwali, which he would attend. There was one Krishna festival, the Janmasthami, celebrating his birth, when they'd meet at the temple at midnight and say bhajans, but that seems to be all that happens. (Surely the Maharajah I was later to meet would be too frail to do any of these things?).

One temple up the hill to Gauri Devi.

On leaving, further up the road, we found another track that took us down to the head of the lake and to the other buildings. There, by the lakeside, a small temple to the founder of the dynasty and inside—we were ticked off by a youngster for going in—was a shrine room with his bed and beneath it his crown. In all a beautiful site. This would have been a tranquil and pleasing place to stay. I wonder if Forster with his reference to the image of meeting a king on the lake in the novel was not drawing on this royal shrine?

So we passed onto Chhatarpur itself and clearly this has grown out of all proportion to the town in Forster's and Ackerley's days. Qureshi tracked down the Hanuman temple. Adjacent a Sita Ram temple where two ghastly children were chanting 'sita ram' noisily. And just below was the guesthouse. This is now the Circuit House and the District Commissioner was expected that evening. Quite plain but spacious and cool inside. An impressive portico as entrance. We had a look at one of the bedrooms, filled with the rather grand heavy teak furniture, made in Chhatarpur. And so down into this ugly town to track down the old palace. This has seemingly been taken over by the government and leased out to schools, the Aurobindo Society, whatever. The former glories of the Raj Mahal still apparent but they've just thrown this handsome building away.

Then onto Khajuraho and to Clark's Bundela Hotel.

Qureshi has a bizarre explanation for Khajuraho. The society at the time in the tenth century were failing to reproduce. Society was divided according to clans and the marriage rate was low. These erotic temples were the ruler's attempt to get the population interested in sex. Qureshi claims to have discovered some even more erotic temples in the jungle south of Chanderi.

22 November

My rest day. Even so, after getting my money from the bank, across the street and a conversation with Mr. Gupta, Director of the archaeological museum. I tried him out on the temples. He showed me an extract from Richard Burton's Introduction to his translation of the Kama Sutra—the claim that the union of male and female is analogous to that with the divine. He himself recognizes that sexuality or kama is a key part of the Indian rites of passage. But he's not impressed by any religious explanation for Khajuraho. He felt it was to do with the shortage of women. This was a kind of medieval Indian rape of the Sabine women. It's more predatory sex than anything idealized.

In the evening I met up with Vikram Singh, grandson of the present Maharajah of Chhatarpur. A young man of twenty-nine, who had to step into the breach with the early death of his father at fifty from a heart attack. He was all set, after an elite education at Dehra Dun, for an airforce career. He had flown MIGs and parachuted from 30,000 feet. But at that height in the plane he had blacked out and plummeted to 20,000 before recovery, and that put paid to his career. His own response had been by sheer will power to climb up to 42,000 feet. But he has come to terms with it and now pursues a public, political career. He's already been nominated Chairman of the Local District Council (half the size of the Lok Sabha constituency) and is now standing for election as an independent and feels he is sure to beat his Congress and BJP rivals. But his real passion is hunting. At twenty he shot a rogue elephant. He described a close encounter with a sloth bear. Once he shot for excitement, now it's to provide for his dinner table. I must say for someone who will become Chairman of the Local Wild Life Society, he's very happy to slaughter animals. The family own 600 acres—the ex-maharajahs are not, he claimed, subject to land ceiling legislation (can this be true?), though Congress would like to cut him down to size. He's in politics to preserve his power. Very formally dressed and upright in his manner. Moustachioed and just a little bit of a caricature. But a quick intelligence and I think a serious man, certainly a strong willed one. I could kind of see in him his great-grandfather, the Maharajah Viswanath Singh, who's clearly been misrepresented. The Maharagah was a supporter of public works and a perfectly plausible ruler. Ackerley's campness has obscured this. Still, the shadow of Chaitanal must have hung heavy. But that ancestor does shine through in Vikram. Those lustrous eyes still burn with proverbial fire, the light of the hunter, of the pilot, of a man ready to take risks, etc. I still feel India was mistaken in stripping the princes of their powers. Had their mystique been preserved India would have been spared the deification of its corrupt political élite.

23 November
The rather plump but engaging Brijendra Singh was to be my guide round the western temples. A man who obviously enjoys his job and hopes to find

time, once his large family is off his hands, to read more. Clearly he's already widely read in Hinduism. Once he lived in a tribal area and tried to get the tribals closer to Hinduism but the priests there told him his best role was to talk to the tourists. There was rather a sad story of how he was able to repay his mother, struck down with cancer, through belonging to the same rare blood group, AB positive, and so able to give her an extension of life.

His attitude to the sexuality of the temples is a different one. His is a theory of an exemplary morality. Here was a society, to the contrary, too preoccupied with sex and at risk from debauchery. The three-tiered temple friezes shows how this moral campaign might work: on the first, carnality on display, on the second, how it is controlled—the tranquility that comes from moving to a higher plane—and then, on the third, how it is finally transcended and you discover the divine. Maybe. But some sets of friezes reveal ever higher levels of orgasmic sex. A man having sex upside down may symbolize tantric mastery. Clearly Tantrism and Brahmanism have mingled here. One of the Vishnu statues in the sanctum sanctorum was carved by a Tibetan tantric. Brijendra, however, pointed out that only a small percentage of the friezes describe the erotic; foreign tourists, in their shallow way, have got it all wrong. The sculptures represent everyday life, those very lifelike particularities of the apsaras, convincingly portrayed, caught in little acts of vanity and seductiveness. In the end this is the union of male and female and the transcendence of duality, the unitive experience. It has to be said if there are scenes of bestiality, there are no scenes of sodomy between male and female nor any homosexual or lesbian sex is portrayed. This has to be some sort of statement.

The silhouette of the temple is another symbol, with each phase of the temple from the entrance to the sikhara ever more steeply stepped. The sikhara itself symbolizes Mt Kailash, and the higher the more sacred. The temple is well ventilated and well lit from the inside, the coolness and light coming from side apertures in the walls. The whole has been constructed from yellow sandstone, quarried from nearby and simply pinioned together, no joining materials.

Once these were centers of learning—one could study here. Not exactly a university. The whole Chandela state was divided into three, the royal, the military, the priestly, and this was the priestly part. Once it was all on a far grander scale. Note the diamond mines nearby. Buddhism had influenced the exterior style of the temples; exterior features similar to stupas. But Buddhism collapsed around the eighth century. All the gods recognized here. But the Chandela empire itself collapsed. When in the nineteenth century new temples were added the old skills had vanished—there is a plain temple from that period with no friezes. But the site had been sufficiently off the center to escape the vandalism meted out elsewhere e.g., at Ujjain by the Moghuls. The British rediscovered them in the 1820s. It's possible much earlier expressions of tribal religion lie behind the temples. Clearly the Kannauj state was fashioned out of tribal society.

But then a disappointment. Vikram Singh did not keep his appointment. And hence I may not meet the present old and allegedly senile Maharajah of Chhatarpur. Brijendra Singh was quite revealing about him and his predecessors. Vishwanath Singh had lost his first wife early on, and they had no children. He had loved her. In her absence he turned to boys. Brijendra wondered at the reason for this attraction and I could only suggest a search for variety—very highly sophisticated people need a new stimulus. Clearly he was a cultured man viz the way he built up his library. Late in life he married for a second time and hence the present Maharajah. There was a regency under the Queen-mother. The present Maharajah ruled the state through till 1947. Did he then fall foul of bad advisers? Certainly much of the state was frittered away. Brijendra cannot forgive him for selling the library. I think the son who died of a heart attack at fifty, to the great distress of the eighteen year old Vikram, was the product of this early marriage. It seems Forster's Maharajah was actually a good ruler, founding colleges and hospitals. And maybe both Forster and Ackerley have given a distorted view of the man. But the present Maharajah might have met Forster (in fact here I am wrong) and was a close friend of the son of Forster's Maharajah of Dewas.

24 November

After all I was to have more joy of the royals. On the last day I went out to see the Rajgarh palace, the royal hunting lodge. I had to get a pass from a Mr Bhatia of the Oberoi hotel: Oberois have bought it to convert into a hotel. It must rank as one of India's most scenically sited buildings, surrounded by deeply forested hills on three sides, the plain on the other. This is the tiger inhabited Panna forest. It's a gem of a Rajput palace and not surprisingly it has been chosen as a backdrop for several films, Ivory's *The Deceivers* and a Hollywood/India production of the Kama Sutra. I'm lucky to have seen this Forster haunt before it is taken over by the hotel.

As all the road signs encouraged me to do so, I decided to keep going for Panna, through the Vindya ghats and the beautiful Panna forest, into deep countryside. In Panna itself "live" temples of some antiquity and one, the

Baldev/Balaram temple, could have been a seventeenth century cathedral, a classical austerity on the outside and curiously unadorned in the inside, just the Baldev shrine. Very odd. The Krishna temple, where I had a brief conversation with an albino, so easily mistaken for a European, as his friend suggested, is much used—a kind of market in trinkets going on. But alas through coming here, I later discovered, I'd missed a tour of the eastern and southern temples with the excellent Brijendra.

So the return trip to Jhansi. On the off-chance we broke off in Chhatarpur to visit Narayan bagh, the quarter where the present Maharajah lives. We found his home, rather run down but clearly a royal palace. All was very quiet and seemingly deserted. I announced my arrival rather tentatively and caught a glimpse of an elderly man, tidying himself up after his ablutions—could this be some elderly retainer? Outside was a car laid up—it couldn't have been driven in years. "I'm looking for the Maharajah of Chhatarpur." I declared. "I'm Bhowani Singh," he replied softly. As his name was unknown to me I still couldn't quite believe this was he—but eventually decided to give him the benefit of the doubt. And soon the grace, good manners and transparency of the man convinced me here was indeed a royal. Yes, he's elderly but in no way senile. He was rather sharp about his grandson. Clearly he sees him as a Walter Mitty with too many daydreams. He himself has learnt the better to live with the present. Clearly he was a late child of his father, but twelve when Vishwanath Singh died. Never close to his father, though he'd attend him at meal times and be given tid-bits. His mother had succeeded as President of the Council and ruled whilst he was a minor. I have the impression that she was always the real powerhouse. She founded the Maharajah school, for example. The house he presently lives in was built by her back in 1936. She died in 1964. But he also referred to a step-mother? Meanwhile he received an education in Indore. There he was under the watchful eye of Colonel Johnson-Cole, the Malcolm Darling equivalent in his life. There's a striking photograph of his clean-cut, well-chiseled face on the wall. He was not to succeed till 1940. He felt there was little that could be done—the knives were out for the princes, above all from Bengal and Gujerat. He was quite happy to go into retirement. If he had any regret in life it was that he had not practiced harder at cricket and polo—his cricket instructor had been an adjutant from Lahore who had also coached the Nawab of Pataudi. Clearly horses had played a big part in his life. But he had not met Forster. The photo of his father he clearly saw as the most valuable was the one with Theodore Morrison, principal of the Anglo-Oriental college. Here was really the introduction to Forster. He let me have a photo of his father being helped off his horse by an Englishman at Nowgong.

"Why'" I asked, "was his father so cultured a man?" It's clear his father was all too happy to pass from affairs of state to cultured conversation. The palace became the venue for religious debate. The Bishops of Calcutta and Nagpur were amongst its guests. His love of Krishna came from his study of the Gita and the Bhagavanam. There would be nightly performances of Krishna plays—it was a kind of evening puja. Afterwards he would go to bed. Bhowani Singh can recall seeing these performances from upstairs. He himself did not follow his father's love of Krishna and was a worshipper of Ram. His father was loyal to the Caitanya branch of the Krishna cult and had dealings with Mathura and the Krishna Braj.

His father would routinely visit Rajgarh every ten days or so. He'd go to the Summer palace less frequently and not stay long. The old palace was his main home.

Clearly Bhowani Singh welcomed the visit. At the end he wrote down his address on headed notepaper—it belonged to some conservation society of which he was, he somewhat pathetically told me, the President. A kind of shabby gentility and wistfulness about the whole visit. After taking several photos, departure for Jhansi.

25 November

The train journey to Ujjain wasn't too bad and I awoke to a spectacular dawn. The sky layered with gold and red, a great panoply of color. Somehow the sun itself seemed a little sheepish as it rose into splendor.

No one to meet me at Ujjain. Three porters took charge and we marched out of the station, I assumed to a taxi. But not so. As we marched further away from the taxis I wondered if I was being kidnapped. But no, my hotel, the Hotel Shipra was nearby. The porters delivered me there and then awaited their fee. It turned out later that the car en route to collect me from Bhopal had been delayed in a village; a truck had hit a cow.

.After this, to the ghats and here one of the four sites for the kumbh mela. In the distance a sculpture of a large pitcher or kumbh, reminding one of the story of the churning of the oceans and the great quarrel between the gods and the demons for the sacred nectar. Substantial ghats, and I could see how it could accommodate a quarter a million or so pilgrims. Buildings along the ghats attractive, especially Scindia's palace for spectators. Was it here Dewas would have gone to pay court to Scindia?

Then a magical moment. We stayed on for *aarthi*. As dusk stole up on us, so lamps were lit and to the accompaniment of three sets of cymbals, a large drum and the striking of a bell, the priest first swung an incense burner by the riverside and three other priests—I gathered part-timers, dressed in striking gold and red sashes, naked to the waist—did circles with lit candelabras, first facing the river, then turning right, then facing us, then turning back to the river. The lamps burned in the dark. But time was running out for my massage, so we didn't hear the mantras. A similar ceremony was being performed the other side of the river. But not many had turned up to witness this service. Some had occasionally burst into song. This was a powerful ceremony, more moving than anything I'd seen performed in any temple, except at Belur. All this was on the Ram ghat.

Rounded off this rather good day with another fish curry and vegetable pulao.

26 November

The Dewas day. Well, Forster had warned me that the countryside was flat and unrewarding and compared to that around Chhatarpur it was very dull indeed. Yet I gather it is fertile, with good vegetation. Acacia and mango trees break up the landscape. Quite soon we had arrived at an industrial town, all around smoke belching from modern factories, pharmaceuticals, etc. Really a rather ugly town. Only one street, the one leading down to the Old Palace, had any redeeming qualities. First, we met Bhoj Maharaj—the Major Pawer I'd been writing to. He lives in a house on the high road from Agra to Bombay, next, poor fellow, to some kind of warehouse, lorries piled up outside all day. He's the son of Forster's Maharajah by his mistress or second wife, Bai Saheba. So he inherited as step-mother the formidable Amazonian daughter of the Maharajah of Kohalpur, he himself a giant, a formidable wrestler, all six-foot, four-inches of him.

How did Tukoji Rao III stand a chance against such a family? He himself was adopted by his uncle, who had no natural family—the cenotaphs by the lake are to his adopted parents, though I think one was also to his natural father. His family hailed from Supa in the Deccan. He'd been taught at Daly College, Indore, and there had encountered his Sanskrit teacher who was to accompany him and Darling as tutor on the trip to Burma and was later, on Darling's advice, to be his dewan. I was to meet his son and grandson. It seems this tutor was the model for Godbole. His original house has now been turned into a school. It's something of a mystery where Tukoji acquired his culture and religious predispositions from. He came under the influence of the Maharashtrian saint, Tukaram, though Tukaram himself was a simple man and any religious input here was bhaktic. Tukoji's loyalties were to Caitanya, and the Bengal link with the Krishna cult signified by a large portrait in the Dewan son's house of a Bengali guru who in the 1960's had won over many disciples.

Bhoj Maharaj had been a late child and was only two at the time of his father's death in Pondicherry. He'd accompanied him there. Apparently the Aurobindo ashram had not accepted his request to visit—someone there must have turned Aurobindo against the self-exiled Maharajah—and when Aurobindo relented the Maharajah was too proud to accept. Later, Bhoj tried to see Aurobindo through his binoculars but failed. He accepts his father made a mistake. Bhoj held some military post whilst his brother was Maharajah. Later he went into education, holding a number of posts as a professor of English. He's an author, both on his father and has an unpublished manuscript on the theme of cosmology and man's emergence from outer space. On how to explain that "time" and "space" are essentially supra-conscious phenomena. This ought to make me doubt his credentials as a historian but he was to be an engaging guide throughout the day.

He shared Forster's distaste for the New Palace. Approached down a long driveway. I could see little objectionable to it. We saw the wing where Forster stayed. Next we went to the guest-house, close to the lake. I could see nothing particularly awful about the guest-house. It later became the private home of the Chief Surgeon in India, Sir John Roberts: alas, the garden that his wife had beautified has disappeared. I picked up a thorn in my ankle in her erstwhile garden. We walked over to the lake and saw the spot where in the novel Fielding and Aziz fell into the water and the small ghat nearby where Gokhul (not Krishna or Dolly as I now realize) is immersed. The water in the lake is clear—fresh water runs into it and the white lotuses were beautiful. Here was a kind of sacred place.

We followed the route taken by the gokul ashtami festival from the Old Palace through what then would have been slums, going by one route, returning by another. Clearly this was an immensely lavish affair, some £6,000 annually expended in Tukoji's day. He would personally finance many of the choirs and the musicians, mainly hired from Ujjain. Something like a 1000 people descended on the Old Palace, all of whom had to be housed and fed for twelve days. This rapidly added up. Senior figures at court had also to provide choirs, so some of the costs were shared. But all this a huge logistical demand.

The temple took up two floors of one wing of the Old Palace. It was from here that the four images, Tukaram, Dolly, Gokhul and one other were taken out and placed in a palanquin-Bhoj has a wonderful photograph of this taking place. It seems that the dewan was rather an austere man and did not approve of Tukoji's emotionalism, his dionysian dancing and said so: eventually he was to be pensioned off. The whole festival still takes place, though the outlandish costs have been severely pruned.

I climbed the Hill of Devi and visited Chaumanda's temple. There are in fact two caves, one with her image—she's a another version of Parvati and Durga. Rather a strange image I thought but I liked that of Siva in the smaller cave temple next door. Extraordinary that elephants could have climbed these steep steps. We looked at other temples on the hill, a Jain, another Vaishnavite one and a small Muslim shrine. It seems quite a busy place of worship. You get wonderful views of the lake from the hill but otherwise this is no romantic vantage point.

I guess I got a clearer sense of Forster's life in Dewas and some feel for the emotionally mercurial Maharajah. But the day was really Bhoj's. A rather shabbily dressed fellow, with a woolen cap askew on his head. Thin and very energetic and talkative. A nice sense of humor. I guess he is virtually alone in still being caught up in the story of Forster and his father. He learnt Tamil in Pondicherry. Started to learn French as well. A busy fussy fellow who kept saying "no" when he meant "yes" and our communication affected by his deafness. He entertained us—my guide as well—to a pleasant vegetarian lunch. A really likeable person. I can see, through him, why Forster would have found his father so engaging.

So back to Ujjain. A doctor removed the thorn free of charge.

27 November

I'm losing track of days. Saturday was a day when India struck back. If our departure from Ujjain not quite as early as planned, off along the road to Indore. This was pretty atrocious. Indore itself did little to redeem it, though the Holkar chattras were pleasing, covered in figures of what might have been Shivaji and Tilak. The Holkar palace now a shell, burnt down after the firebombing of the Sikh population in 1984, divine retribution for the Hindus. Indore itself just another vastly overextended Indian city. But once clear of Indore we began to see a more exciting landscape and soon we were cutting a passage through the Vindyas, commanding expansive views of deeply tree clad mountains. All this is tribal country and we saw a group of nomadic tribesmen making baskets. This another teak forest. One unusual tree or rather shrub, the flower tree. From its red leaf comes the powder for Holi. My back has suddenly become much better and it needed to be; these roads were the greatest test to date, though the Maruti car absorbed the shock pretty well.

And I'm increasingly grateful at having Israr as my driver. He knows these roads backwards. I belatedly discovered he's Muslim. Formerly a truck driver which took him all over India, his favorite cities being where he found the most attractive girls, Madras and Hyderabad. Still, he's now married and with three children and after that, "stop."

My guide, Ravendra Sristava, is rather a heavy going fellow. His brother is a professor of Journalism. He does not think the AIDS figures for India are accurate and doesn't believe truck drivers are responsible for its spread. India culture will ward off AIDS. I doubt this. It's the very conservatism of the culture that has bred such ignorance of the virus.

This was a day of landscapes. After transiting the Vindyas, down into a rich riverine area and then we crossed the sacred Narbadda. Quite wide at this point. A river I have been keen to experience. And so along the river to Omkarneshwar. So named as the island to which this small 2000 religious community adheres is in the shape of OM (but on this argument just about any island should be so named). There is a wonderful Holkar palace on the island, overlooking the ghats. Some other handsome looking dharamsalas or pilgrim rest-houses. Our journey was to the ancient temple, Shri Omkar Mandhata. Here was another jyoti lingam, but this a sad stump of a lingam compared to the majestic one in Ujjain. A reared cobra's head in the sanctum was more suggestive of Siva's power. Parts of the temple ninth/tenth centuries but badly vandalized, above all by Aurangzeb. In the temple we heard recorded chanting, which was quite powerful, but I'd been far more moved by the chanting of a Sikh priest in the gurdwara nearby, no doubt the presence of five bulky Sikhs had something to do with my preference. We didn't go on onto the island but had a pleasure boat trip on the river. The main festival here is the Sivaratri. If all on a minor scale, this was an attractive sacred site.

But time was against us and so we pressed on and here the roads just disappeared, hardly more than a track. We passed a cotton ginning warehouse. This is a cotton growing area, a sign of its prosperity. Also chillies, dal, bananas. Then a major delay.

One of the villages had been restricted to eight hours of electricity in any forty-eight and their patience had broken. They'd put up a barricade and no traffic could move. Without electricity they cannot work the tube wells, essential for their agriculture. I had a rather embarrassing discussion with them and I became briefly the center of attention. I noticed a small portrait of Gandhi on display, so this was a non-violent protest. One could hardly hold it against them. Significantly, though nothing had been done to restore the power, there was a strong police presence; the authorities tend to see such situations as firstly law and order ones.

Our delay was such that by the time we reached Maheshwar it was dark. Rani Ahilyabai's palace was shut so we could only see it from the outside. Wooden sculptures on display, one of a huge rider on a horse. This an eighteenth-century site. Below the palace was a large Mahratta temple, but we could in the dark only see its silhouette. But then we came on a complex of small temples, all lit with guttering butter oil lamps. One of the temples had another of those large candelabra, filled with lamps. All this greatly atmospheric and may be I got as much from Maheshwar by night as I'd have done by day. The Narmadda and the ghats were below the palace and the river was huge at this point.

And so, after alerting the guest-house at Mandu of our late arrival, a journey into another nightmare, third world roads, worse than anything I've ever seen, compounded by fleets of lorries coming down the other way. Further long delays, though Israr was agile in overtaking when he could. And then, great relief, the turning to Mandu and the road improved. Seemingly several outer walls to this fortified town—we passed through at least three gates— and so to the guesthouse. The same horrible yuppies who had disturbed my sleep in Ujjain were here. A tolerable meal cooked by the attractive Mr Thakkur, the former cook of the Shipra Hotel in Ujjain. So, once again, back into romantic India.

28 November

And romantic, indeed. Forster came here. I'll not describe all the pleasing buildings in Mandu. It's a little surprising that the Afghans both produced this fifteenth-century paradise and under Sher Shah laid the foundation of the Moghul Empire. The Afghan style is eclectic; Hindu motifs e.g., the half-opened lotus is incorporated into the Islamic style. The great tomb of Hoshang Shah was the inspiration for the Taj Mahal. I guess the classical quality of this building would have been the contemporary style; Islamic buildings always possess an austerity Hindu rarely possess. I was disappointed that the Narmadda was not visible from Rupmati's pavilion—the heat haze was too thick—but a spectacular view of the plains nevertheless. Forster claimed he could see the river. This was to be my goodbye to Ravindra, my guide, rather a tiresome communicator and at crucial moments I'd lose his English, but he was always determined to get his message across and he did so assiduously and well as we looked round the mosque area and the palaces.

But the unexpected treat of the day was meeting a Jain saddhu, being pushed about in a wheel-chair, though when I asked him if I could take his photograph, he stepped towards a nearby tree and sat down, raising his right hand in some kind of blessing. He looks older than his forty-eight years, but is fleshy and attractive. He has invited me to come and meet him in his ashram in the evening. One of the hotel staff suggested this has sexual implications. "A good-looking fellow like you, etc."

The whole day became a real delight. A lazy afternoon. Then at sunset back to the Rupmati—and for a while I had this vantage point of the Pavilion to myself—the ever more deeply etched landscape around and about was as striking as the westering sun. Here I am strongly reminded of Greece, both for its shrub-grown dry and arid landscape but also for the brilliance of its light. But the sun went down in grand style though the Narmadda remained out of sight.

Now came my visit to the Jain saint. He was at prayer when we reached his ashram, after several false journeys, at the end of a track and we waited outside for a while. But then we were ushered into his room. Lying on his bed. Rather a kindly face. This is Swami Ravindra Vijay Maharaj. This was always going to be a tricky encounter, with the language barrier, but initially with the help of one Madan and conversations on the phone with a Mr. Sharma Senior and then later with the arrival of his son, dispatched as an interpreter, Arvind Sharma, a lecturer turned bank official and a student of English literature, we made headway. Swami's first observations, rather disconcertingly, were a) that I had a bad temper and must learn to control it and b) that I had had three lady friends in my life, though not necessarily physical in character. All this he could read from my face and from my hands. He's struck up a partnership some two months ago with a swami from Poona, a Swami Uttam Maharaj, and it was through their combined mental forces that they could foresee my past and future. I told them something about myself, including the diabetes. After brooding for five minutes or so, they revealed I was in great distress in 1997, all will be well by 2001. My next book will be out by 2003 and by 2005 would be well known. I must be careful of June/July 2003 as I run the risk of a serious accident. I certainly must not fly then. But the risk could be fended off if each morning, after taking a bath, or, better still, a swim in the sea, I worship the sun for quarter an hour each day. I will return to India in 2001, 2003 and 2004, with the support of a trust. I was beginning to warm to these questions and answers. Would I, I asked, experience another great male friendship? I would have another lady friend who would help me with my work and this soon, and two male friends in the middle of next year. Would I find a guru? Yes, possibly as a result of the accident—he would be a younger man, thirty-five or so. So on the whole the omens are good. Clearly, forecasting the future is a major part of the power of these gurus. In a small collection of books in the ashram at least three were on Nostradamus.

The room began to fill up with those seeking darshan. There were several shopkeepers and one marvelously portly and virile fellow, a teacher of Hindi, though he looked like a peasant. As he had a small tuft at the back of his of his head I assumed he was a brahmin. But, in fact, he was a Rajput and this mistake caused much merriment. This was a Jagdish Thakur. I presumed they were all here likewise to air their questions and problems, but not so. They remained quiet. All they wanted was to be in the presence of the swami.

I pressed the swami on matters of value. Sexuality was one. It seems that until this is overcome nothing, in any spiritual sense, can happen. You had to learn to see all women as your mother, sister, daughter. He quoted Ramakrishna in this regard and clearly sees him as a great saint. We discussed Osho and the swami from Poona holds him in high regard. Osho thought sex was a major distraction and so only by going through the sexual experience, by putting this distraction aside, could you come out the other side and pursue the religious quest. The Jain swami thought that ordinary folk should worship God with form but that those on a higher plane could pursue God without form. He conceded that over time Jainism has borrowed aspects of other faiths and his own approach was ecumenical. He spent much time on the phone and in the end I had to leave whilst he was in the middle of a conversation. Quite an extraordinary evening—the 1999 analogue to my 1995 meeting with the trade unionists.

So back for another late supper and the inestimable Mr Thakkur standing by. We got talking in the kitchen. Politicians came up—he sees all politicians as corrupt though, alas, he votes BJP. I fear his English is not strong. He is of Nepalese stock though the family have settled for a long time in Gorakhpur, Eastern UP. Relatives have worked in the railways.

29 November

One more excursion, to a Moghul resort, overlooking a canyon. It's now a Siva temple. Monkeys squawking below. A better feel here of the shape of the gorge and seen even better on leaving Mandu. There really is only one access and it was a natural fort.

Israr gave me a breakdown of his salary and expenses on the return journey to Ujjain. 1500Rs a month salary. He pays out 350 on rent, 250 on school fees, (he has three children) a 700 monthly food bill. So 200 left for extras. A pretty desperate livelihood. He let me know how generous some Swiss tourists had been. I fear I shall not be so generous.

We had a glance at the fort at Dhar. But I was fatigued by now with sightseeing. Back by sunset to Ujjain.

30 November

Off early for the long journey to Bhopal and Sanchi.

Time for a second unheralded visit to Bhoj Maharaj in Dewas. This led to a surprisingly frank conversation. Apparently my taking photos of the two royal palaces had upset his nephew and he suggested I do not publish these. We got onto Forster the novelist. In his view all but *A Passage to India* are provincial in the manner of Jane Austen. Only in his last did he touch on universal themes, race, community. This novel will last. Then we got onto Forster and homosexuality and this he found easy to talk about. If Forster felt embarrassed about his homosexuality at Dewas it was a projection of his own sense of guilt. The court itself would not have felt put out. One of the senior nobles at court shared similar tastes. Bhoj was curious to know what role Forster played and thought in India he might have played the active role. Homosexuality had been widely practiced in royal courts, Moghul, Zamindari—the Sikhs were particularly keen on it. They all kept harems of boys. Boys had several advantages over women. They would not gossip; women had great skills in wheedling secrets out of rulers. And they did not bear children. This did not complicate the succession. Unlikely that strong affections would prevail between rulers and these boys; they were just for sexual amusement. But there could be relationships between those of similar age. These were usually between people of different social levels and were not disparaged. He made the surprising observation that same-sex friendships amongst Indian POW's and front line troops were very intense and more important than relationships with their wives. Clearly he himself has no sense of disapproval of homosexuality. He cited the example of one reprobate Maharajah who would point to his body and say; "this is mine—I do with it what I please." This was a very refreshing conversation.

Am beginning to wonder if Sudhir Kakar has got it wrong. Maybe he is reflecting middle class mores, one absorbing western prejudices. Maybe Victorian respectability is a catching disease.

After this, a long tedious drive to Bhopal. Here is India's largest mosque. And we passed by the Union Carbide factory. There was a powerful statue nearby to commemorate the dead. On the wall a slogan, "Hang Anderson." Out of the town we came across a weekly cattle market, goats, prize cattle, etc, a great bustle of activity and one or two striking looking men. All ready to be photographed. But this caught on in an unpleasant way. They brought some monkey faced monster to be photographed. I urged Israr to depart.

And so to Sanchi and the guest-house. I seemed to be the only person staying but later an MP (Madya Pradesh) film director arrived and a whole set of people turned up for a late meal. But straight onto the Udaigari caves. These were rather disappointing though the head of Vishnu in his avatar incarnation as a wild boar impressive. Then to the Heliodorus column where we witnessed one old man come to fulfill an evening puja. It was nearby an attractive village, all the cattle put to rest under the eaves of the houses.

1 December
Rather jaded in the morning.

By nine, off for a tour of Sanchi. Here I was in unknown cultural territory and maybe I should have done more homework. I later consulted the Director of the Archaeological Museum. At the same time the President of Kobe University came to his office, requesting permission to photograph the Ashoka pillar. So the atmosphere was a little edgy and the Director was initially too lazy to talk and tried to fob me off with a catalogue in English. But I persisted. Buddha's relics had originally been divided eight ways. Some of these found their way to Sanchi. Ashoka reassembled them and redistributed them to 80,000 sites. Stupas double up as mausoleums, shrines, places for votive offerings. Ashoka fell in love with a lady from Vidisha and it was to please her that he built Stupa No 1 and one of the monasteries; he left but she stayed on. There is little information on the size and recruitment of the monasteries. But they existed from third century BC to twelfth century AD. (We must know something?) Apparently, Chinese visitors to India made no mention of Sanchi.

It is a beautiful site. The shape of the stupas echoes the shape of the surrounding hills. The site is entirely at one with its environment. Surely this was a peaceful, meditative place. Buddhist art has a classical purity to it which compares well with the sweet Hindu style that was to succeed it. This was reflected in the sculptures of the Gupta buildings. There are really only two buildings of merit, Stupas 1 and 2. I need to know more to decode these—I simply don't know the Buddhist folklore. With Buddha himself symbolized as a lotus/bo tree/stupa some of the humanism of the stories is lost. But there was a plainness about them for all the exuberance of their content. Richly woven sculptures of animals and humans. On Stupa No 2, down the hill, a different format to the great gateways of No 1, with carvings direct onto the surrounding walls of the stupa. I of course took to all those pot-bellied dwarves. I cannot say I found the whole particularly religious and Romanesque sculpture here has the edge in terms of spirituality. This was just good narrative stuff. Maybe something of the Greek about it.

The nearby Maha Bodhi temple had strange wall paintings by a modern Sri Lankan painter, on Buddha's struggle with the flesh, the temptations of the daughters of the hag, Mara, given prominence. One picture of him fleeing the city in search of non-attachment. Then one of a great sleeping figure of Buddha as he achieves nirvana. But surely all this is to corrupt his message?

Just beginning to feel the pressure.

1–2 December

Israr and I set off for Bhopal in the late evening and after a visit to a new Birla temple in the city,—a temple to Lakshmi—full of admonitions from the *Bhagavad gita* about the pure life, onto to a heritage hotel and an excellent meal, served by another of those well-clad handsome waiters. He, however, is on an English language course and none too fluent, so my conversationalist was a Keralan Christian, but a little too unctuous for my taste. Then came the local Magic of India rep, a Mr. Gopal Das, friend of Maharajahs, and he took me to a wedding—of a rather antique looking couple, surely the last chance for both and looking rather sheepish by their thrones—and so onto the night train, the Radjhani express, for Chennai. Farewell to Israr and I did reward him pretty generously. I was tired, so happy to have a compartment to myself.

By dawn a new landscape—coconut trees, and, in fact, we are heading down the coast and by the eastern ghats, not inland via Hyderabad as I'd been mistakenly informed. What made the journey for me was a long chat with a chunky, elderly Chief Ticket Collector from Delhi, Om Prakash Channa. The family originally from Multan and he can still recall living there pre-1947—he's now fifty-eight or fifty-nine—his grandfather had left them a family home in Ambala—and his father from nothing had built up a sanitation business in Jaipur. But because Om Prakash has seen more eye to eye with his grandfather he and his father had fallen out and he had not taken on the family business. Instead, he's become a ticket collector and he's worked his way up to the top of a railway career and now has a monthly salary of 15, 000Rs (c £200). Married with three children, his two daughters married but his son, evidently a late child, still establishing himself in a computer software business. To look after his interests Om will stay in Delhi.

He himself worships Hanuman and when I told him, as a bachelor, I was the better devotee, he shook my hand. He has been on pilgrimage, if by bus, to Badrinath from Hardwar. He had a nice philosophy of life—not to be greedy. To be contented with how things are. I fear when I asked him if his wife wanted to stay on in Delhi he said he never consulted her; wives in India can only agree with their husbands. His is clearly a very traditional marriage.

He corrected me about Jains and their hairlessness. They only take hairs wholescale from their heads, not from the rest of their bodies. He explained the difference between the two Jain sects, September and December was the way to remember them, but I cannot recall how it goes—one is a naked sect.

Then he told me the extraordinary tale of how some naked nagas lock their foreskins and only unlock to urinate. Was he being a little forward in this conversation? He had a pleasing accent and it seems that accent is dependent on one's regional language; he's a Punjabi-speaking Hindu, and indeed his accent was identical to Bipan Chandra's. Well, I doubt if I'll ever meet him again.

Got cross at the station as the agent was late and then began to haggle over the payment for the porters, but eventually into our taxi and to the Theosophical Society and I was relieved to be here. I really am not drawn to staying in Chennai proper.

3–4 December
So to the tail end of the School of Wisdom. By one of those synchronicities that have marked the journey these were lectures on yoga, given by Professor T. R. Anantaraman, an Oxford D. Phil in chemistry. So his approach was all rather scientific, drawing analogies with the transformations of metals. It turns from solids to gas, but then changes its composition to alloys and so likewise is the process in yoga. He was interesting in making links between Patanjali and Gopi Krishna—and clearly discovering his book by chance in Higginbothams in Calcutta was another stroke of luck—his book commands great respect—he went to Germany and Richard Weizacker, brother of the President, was so impressed by him that he cancelled all his other interviews for the day to learn from him—but this again is to do with a scientific explanation for yoga. He also pointed out chance similarities in the ideas of Aurobindo and Teilhard de Chardin. Aurobindo has to be drawn into any discussion of the tradition of yoga. On the second and final day he gave a lucid account of the *Bhagavad gita* and yoga. I still have a problem with the role of the mind. How is the mind both brought under control and then somehow jettisoned? It seems and is contradictory.

In the evening, after a conversation with Professor Gopalkrishnan—obviously very relieved to see me—I should have kept in touch but he had not received my letter from England—I am to lecture on Saturday—and then Mr. Krishna, the local agent, came round to sort out the final stages of my journey. After tea with Paul, a Dutchman who works at the TS on and off, who seems a perfectly sensible man but then announced that he's an expert on the Mahatma Letters.

4 December
My talk to the Center for Contemporary Studies at the Bharatiya Vidya Bhavan. This was in Mylapore and in one of the more ancient quarters of the

city. From 4 to 6 there was a book launch and as almost all of this was in Tamil I felt rather excluded.

Gopalkrishnan saw my presence as a way of demonstrating that the Center has claims to be an international body. In fact my talk on Jinnah and the partition went down well and a Tamil translation is to be made and it is to be serialized in a local Tamil paper. Only one awkward question came up, on conversions: if Indian Muslims had fought for Pakistan, might not Indian Christians do the same? I pointed out there was no necessary link between faith and political nationalism but it is up to the majority not to drive minorities into a corner—only then they will start looking to their political defenses. The worst risk India runs is to the contrary the politicization of Hindus. This really will threaten secularism and then the whole system of pluralism is at risk.

A meal at Adyar Woodlands afterwards. I really ought to explore this local area. On my bike?

5 December

I am feeling tired.

But I did some useful bibliographical work on the computer terminals newly installed in the Adyar Research Library. On Krishna. Began to look through the card catalogue on yoga. The literature is endless.

Then Gopalakrishnan's driver, Poonaswamy, came to collect me and a rather harassed day ensued. First, after going round in small circles, to an Ayurvedic Health Center nearby. This looks promising if a trifle dear. After a major confusion between Ramakrishna Street and Radakrishnan Sarai to Sarvepalli, Gopal's house but all was locked up and all appeared to be asleep. But I raised someone and was encouraged to return later. So to the Madras Club for a good swim. Back to Gopal. He's very frail and visibly older. As usual he had little to say. I did all the talking. And then after my misunderstanding in which direction of the city Gopalakrishnan lived and realizing it was in quite the other direction to the TS, back on our tracks and a stop for another vegetarian meal.

6 December

A long conversation with Professor Anantharaman whose lectures had concluded the School of Wisdom. In fact these were the lectures he routinely gives at his Ashram Rishi, south of Delhi. He's a Tanjore Brahmin. His career has been as a scientist, as a metallurgist; for many years at the Benares Hindu University. It was an experience of social violence at a research center in Bihar that led him to look again at the great religious texts and to try to find out what had gone wrong. On one occasion, twelve young engineers had been murdered. He's always followed Vinoba Bhave and J. P. Narayan, so his credentials are excellent. He clearly feels at some stage India lost the race for science, technology and the industrial revolution and he seemed to be saying the rot set in with those movements of thought that led India away from this-worldly concerns; Buddhism. Jainism, Sankara, etc. By the eighteenth century the decline was marked. You can see why he would latch onto Aurobindo. One way he sought to demonstrate that India had in the past been in the forefront of applied science was by analyzing the iron composition of some of its ancient monuments. e.g. the Qutb Minar. This is high-grade iron.

In a way it was of a piece with this approach that he emphasized the normality of the yoga path. Indians go through various stages and it is up to each individual whether he pursues karma, artha or moksha. All are valid pursuits. He wanted to play down the ascetic dimension. He thinks the concept of brahmacharya been mistranslated as continence; it really means pursuing a dharmic path. (At least I think that's what he said.) So, in the end, he'll have little truck with those who want to accelerate the process and embark on moksha at an early stage. He himself was something of an ascetic when young but he came to love a German girl by whom he had two children. She died in a car accident and he has since married a much younger girl. So he's in no way averse to physical pleasures. But he did point to the Buddhist middle way; neither lust nor asceticism.

He's very much of the persuasion that yoga is a process in which there is continuity and not hiatus between the lower self and the higher. But you need a guru. Only a guru could guide you through the process. And you bring your temperament to the process, be it tamas, rajas or sattwa. He seemed again to be saying all are equally valid but I think his preference was always for sattwa.

You cannot escape this moral conservatism in Hinduism, the law of dharma. And even he seemed to be saying that at a certain point a process of transformation takes place—the lower self is transformed. He'd agree with Swami Chidananda that even memory goes. But he wants more emphasis on the role of *bhuti* or intellect. This is never lost, not even in Aurobindo's supramentalism. All this seems eminently sane.

7 December
The day I was once again interviewed by *The Hindu*, this time by Randor Guy. Last night our Nigerian at the TS, Mr. Eckekwa, my next door neighbor in Leadbeater, had excitedly informed me that he'd seen me on TV. The

launch of the Tamil book (not, alas, my lecture) was clearly quite an event.

I liked Randor. He's a media columnist. A film man. But he's also been working away at the transfer of power and today it was on the partition that the interview focused.

Tomorrow we'll look at my other interests.

8 December
I felt better by the time Randor came to continue the interview. We ranged over my other interests. (This interview was only to be published much later.)

9 December
The day I volunteered—well, really Dr. Sudhakar pressured me into it—to give another talk at the Loyola College. Three undergraduates came to collect me—one of them driving his own Maruti. Being mission educated all spoke impeccable English. I gave the same lecture but spoke ex tempore and it went well. Even on such an occasion as this there are a series of formal, introductory speeches, an opening prayer and, at the end, a singing of the national anthem. A young Spaniard taking a degree and I smirked at one another during this. One question I did find penetrating was whether, had the protests of 1946 been better policed, partition might have been avoided.

Afterwards we had rather a good lunch—I gather plantains are used as plates on special occasions such as this and weddings, etc—Sudhakar had picked up on my liking fish so this was provided. Jayasekaram joined us for lunch. Just a little grey on top now, but recovered from his heart operation and in goodish form. After lunch a very bright student joined us and plied me with all kinds of questions about the church. Clearly he's something of an anti-clerical. In this centenary year the college is organizing a seminar on Religion and Humanism. Yes, that is a forum I would have liked to address.

And Sudhakar had been trying to organize all week, but we'd failed to make telephone contact, a meeting with the granddaughter of C P Ramawami Aiyer. On the off chance we went round to the C P Ramaswami Aiyer Institute, with its attractive courtyard, but she had just left.

10 December
My sore throat is worsening. I suspect I caught it from Sundari's friend, Sarada.

I called on Sundari again and her musician friend from Stroud, Sridar, was there. A lively, rather self-centered fellow, a brahmin from Tanjore. I wonder how good a musician he is. His performances take him to Israel and America but he rarely performs in England or India. He feels that promoters in England only go for well-known performers from India. He feels the level of musical skills is in decline. People are driven by mere material factors and not by a love of music.

11 December

Now real fatigue has taken over. I visited the TS's doctor, medical services in India as efficient as ever. He gave me antibiotics for the cough and some cough mixture. I also learnt that the reason why Indians have to ration their rice intake for diabetes is simply because it forms so large a part of their normal diet.

Could hardly keep my eyes open in the library.

Christopher then took me to the Madras Club. The weather became overcast but I was too late anyway for a swim. The evening spent with Verghese, Randor Guy and Gopalakrishnan at the last's flat in the north of the city. The one thing I learnt was that the BJP won on a sympathy vote—Congress's sabotaging Vajpayee's government backfired on them. (But surely it did Mulayam Singh no harm?) Gopalakrishnan in a very round about way raised the question as to whether Hinduism was a religion at all. It lacks a bible, a church, etc.

Then an immensely long journey back to the TS, traversing the length of the city though I was spared Mount Road. To bed for the last time at the TS.

12–13 December

So the airport and my flight to Madurai. True to form the 10am IA's flight was delayed till 1pm.

The weather now rather grey. On arrival at Madurai I decided to head straight for Kodaikanal in the hope that I'd see something of the landscape en route as well as, with the cloud density, see a good sunset. And this I did, but it was dark before we began the climb, some forty kilometers or so. In the dark our headlights picked up slogans painted on the rock face, "Use Condoms, Avoid Aids." Why was this route chosen for such a campaign? My initial response to the Carlton Hotel was hostile but by then I was very tired and factious. I didn't want a buffet meal. I hated the western music being played in the restaurant. It rained heavily in the night. In the morning from my balcony there was the lake, shrouded in a dawn mist, though it soon began to clear. Even so, in a tour arranged by the hotel of Kodikainal and its environs, almost all the views looking down to the plains still obscured by mist.

I took myself off for a walk around the lake which was pleasant enough.

In the evening a weird folk dance performance. A troupe from Madurai, here to entertain a conference of astro-physicists. First a lady dancer smashed a coconut on a man's head, then another lady sliced bananas on his stomach with one held in his mouth, and another lady somehow sucked up two spherical fruits from his body. One way or another they had cut off his penis and swallowed his balls. All to a frenzied accompaniment of horns and drums.

14 December
The first of my long treks. The threat of a cyclone had gone away and the weather was nice enough. I recruited a stooped, myopic old fellow—he looked eighty and was indeed seventy—as my guide. This was Daniel. It took me time to work out that his slowness was the price of his myopia; in the forest he could hardly see the ground.

We did the eight ks to Pillar Rock and back, traversing five different kinds of forest on the way, eucalyptus and mimosa, (it had a white budding sweet smelling flower), pine, a mixed soft-wood (used for making matches) and one other. We saw unusual flowering shrubs, one called the bird flower, with a beautiful yellow flower, another the angel trumpet flower. It was wonderfully still in the forest. Some cattle on the loose. Women collecting firewood. Daniel related his life story. Once a wireless operator for the media in the Gulf. Then organizing tickets for travelers, with daily visits to Madurai, Trichy and even Hyderabad. No wonder he looked so ancient. His wife and family cannot take the cold and live in the plains. A good walk though a question mark still over the back.

15 December
On the trail once again, with Daniel looking frail and forlorn. The wretched cloud level still obscuring the view. This time to Dolphin's Nose, passing a vigorous waterfall en route and then a steep drop, another good eight kms, arriving at what I imagine is a perilous outcrop of rock and maybe, with my vertigo, it was just as well all was blanketed in mist. I began to feel more and more as if I was a lonely wanderer in one of those Caspar David Friedrich paintings. On return we talked to an almost blind coolie who lived in this remote area. We visited the La Salette church, Kodi's oldest catholic. And after circulating Coaker's walk—the sun had penetrated just enough to permit some distance views—a visit to Daniel's own church, St. Antony's. He's no longer a regular worshipper but does drop in for a silent prayer. Christianity means much to these Indian Christians. I wasn't too struck on Bryant's park.

Then my free Sikhara boat trip on the lake. I had hoped that Godwin Joseph, a senior dining room supervisor at the hotel, would join me, but he arrived too late. In his uniform, with his upright stance, he's a wonderfully martial figure. All this runs in the blood as he claims his father was a colonel in the war, later joining the railway service. This the usual profession for the Anglo-Indians. He was himself born in Pondicherry but just outside the frontier that would have made him a French citizen. Last evening we began by talking about the métique football team in Pondicherry; they fulfilled an analogous defense role to the gurkhas. All now draw French pensions. It seems he was reluctant to marry. He preferred meditation and doing good works. He's a genuinely devout Catholic. But his mother persuaded him to marry. But it was a late one for both and it looks as if they will remain childless. (In fact they now have a son.) Well, we took a second boat and crossed the lake to see where Sai Baba stays on his annual visit in the hot season.

16 December
Godwin took me to his church, though it was locked and we could only see it from the outside. A nicely sited church. Then back to his home. But two rooms and the roof is damp—it might explain his touch of arthritis, but quite a pleasant cottage. We visited the International School to see what they might have to let. Eventually I was taken to a number of cottages, one of which would suit me admirably.

In the afternoon, having betrayed poor Daniel, with Vijay Kumar as trek leader instead, for a walk. The first section was striking—a long walk up the escarpment—along a track laid down by the Jesuits linking the Convent of the Sacred Heart with another above the town. This, as we discovered at the top, has been deserted for several years. The wretched mist descended as we set forth. The rest of the walk weaved itself in and out of walks I had already done, though for all that, the long one through the forest was rewarding. Vijay raised the specter of stampeding bison which added an element of suspense. I crossed the golf course rather nervously.

After dinner I walked out to the nearby shops and there met a charming Tibetan who runs a restaurant. I think these Tibetan faces are just about the most attractive in the world. He's been in India since 1962 or so. Has a strong political sense. Was familiar with all these new films on Tibet. Is bringing up his children to learn Tibetan. A Tibetan friend is the P T instructor at the International school.

17 December
A long walk with Vijay through Gandur forest. For once the mist did not obscure the view. Mainly pine, both the drooping needlepine and the rounded pine. We walked back along the river Gandur, making a sortie to a wonder-

ful waterfall. Indications of the presence of bison and wild boar and fresh droppings of the sambur deer. Our taxi had endured a double puncture so back by local bus, playing intolerably loud music, though it survived the appalling road. I liked Vijay. He's a committed conservationist and an informed naturalist. We visited a conservation project for the forest. I hope he doesn't give up on his project of mapping all the tracks around Kodi.

18–19 December
The last two days had disturbing contrasts. The journey down to Madurai was spectacular, particularly overlooking the reservoir of the river Vagai. But the contrast between Kodi and Madurai brought home once more how uncontrolled and anonymous India's big cities have become. I'd remembered the Meenakshi temple as an open one. In fact it is completely wedged into the city and not very attractive. But some of the sculptures in the museum were striking, especially a bisexual Siva.

So back to Chennai, with no delays.

Up horribly early the next morning for my return flight. I had to pay, despite all my pleas, a huge excess baggage fee, £200. On arrival, VAT payments on the carpets. Ivy and Brian there to meet me. So I returned to an England, lightly clad with snow and distinctly cold. All was well with my cottage and garden. This time, a distinct feeling of relief to be back.

Bibliography

Primary Sources

Edward Carpenter Papers, Sheffield Archives
MSS 270 Somasundaram to Carpenter.
MSS 271 Arunachalam to Carpenter.
MSS 349 Charles Carpenter.
MSS 351 Carpenter to Charles Oates.
MSS 354 Carpenter to Kate Salt.
MSS 355 Kate Salt to Carpenter.
MSS 357 Havelock Ellis to Carpenter.
MSS 358 Edith Lees to Carpenter.
MSS 362 George Hukin to Carpenter.
MSS 363 George Merrill.
MSS 378 Maharajah of Chhatarpur to Carpenter.
MSS Carpenter Pamphlets.
MSS Carpenter C Per.
MSS Reel 35 Press Cuttings.
A Bibliography of Edward Carpenter, Sheffield City Archives 1949.
The Humanities Research Center, University of Texas, Austin.
Edward Carpenter Correspondence.
E. M. Forster Papers, King's College Archives, Cambridge.
EMF Vol 3/3 Indian Journal.
EMF Vol 4/4 Locked Diary.
EMF Vo6 Broadcast talks 1930–1943.
EMF Vo/8 20 The Poems of Kipling.

———. Vo/8 21 We Speak to India, Some Books.

———. Vo/8 21 Three Generations.

———. Vo 8/21 Romain Rolland.

———. Vo/8 22 Talk to Cambridge Humanists (1958).

EMF Typescripts Vol 8 22 Vol 1 Series II.

EMF iv/21–6 Tagore.

EMF vi/14–A The Last Moment of Life.

EMF vi/32 A Pater.

EMF xi/4 Colonel Leslie.

EMF xxix/3 Obituary of Maharaja Sir Tukoji Puar.

EMF Letters.

———. Ackerley, Isherwood 1932–1962, Mohammad el adl, Syed Ross Masood, Elizabeth Trevelyan.

EMF Corr in/i Eunuchs or Hijaris.

Primary Texts

Edward Carpenter

Carpenter, Edward. *Towards Democracy*. Manchester: John Heywood, 1883.

———. *England's Ideal*. Manchester: John Heywood, 1884.

———. *Civilization: Its Cause and Cure*. London: Swan Sonnenschein, 1889.

———. *From Adam's Peak to Elephanta: Sketches in Ceylon and India*. London: S. Sonnenschein and Co.; New York: MacMillan and Co., 1892.

———. *Love's Coming of Age*. Manchester: Labour Press, 1896.

———. *Homogenic Love*. Manchester: Labour Press Society, 1896.

———. *Iolaus*. London: Swan Sonnenschein [etc.], 1902.

———. *The Art of Creation*. London: George Allen, 1904.

———. *Days with Walt Whitman*. London: George Allen, 1906.

———. *The Intermediate Sex*. London: Swan Sonnenschein, 1908.

———. *Sketches from Life in Town and Country*. London: George Allen, 1908.

———. *The Drama of Love and Death*. London: George Allen and Company, 1912.

———. *Intermediate Types among Primitive Folk*. London: George Allen, 1914.

———. *My Days and Dreams*. London: Allen and Unwin, 1916.

———. *Pagan and Christian Creeds: Their Origin and Meaning*. London: Allen and Unwin, 1920.

———. *The Teaching of the Upanishads*. London: Allen and Unwin, 1920.

———. *Light from the East: being: Letters on gnaman, the divine knowledge by P Arunachalam*. London: Allen and Unwin, 1927.

E. M. Forster

Forster, E. M. *Maurice*. New York; London: W. W. Norton and Comp., 1913 but published in 1971.

——. *A Passage to India*. London: Edward Arnold and Co., 1924.

——. *Goldsworthy Lowes Dickinson*. London: Edward Arnold and Co., 1934.

——. *The Hill of Devi*. New York: Harcourt, Brace and Company, 1953.

——. *Two Cheers for Democracy*. London: Edward Arnold and Co., 1951.

——. *Marianne Thornton*. London: Edward Arnold, 1956.

——. *Albergo Empedocle and Other Writings*. New York: Liveright, 1971.

——. *The Life to Come and Other Stories*. New York: W.W. Norton, 1972.

——. *The Hill of Devi and Other Indian Writings* (The Abinger edn of E. M. Forster). London: Edward Arnold, 1982.

——. *Selected Letters of E. M. Forster 1879–1920*, Vol One, Mary Lago ed. London: Collins, 1983.

——. *Selected Letters of E. M. Forster 1879–1920*, Vol Two 1920–1970.

Christopher Isherwood

Isherwood, Christopher. *The Memorial: Portrait of a Family*. London: Hogarth Press, 1932.

Isherwood, Christopher, and W. H. Auden. *The Ascent of F6*. London: Faber and Faber, 1936.

Isherwood, Christopher. *Lions and Shadows*. London: L. and Virginia Woolf at the Hogarth Press, 1938.

Isherwood, Christopher and W. H. Auden. *Journey to a War*. London: Faber and Faber, 1939.

Isherwood, Christopher. *The Day at la Vierne* (Penguin New Writings No 14), 1942.

Isherwood, Christopher and Aldous Huxley. *Jacob's Hands* London: Bloomsbury, 1944 but published in 1998.

Isherwood, Christopher. "What Vedanta Means to Me." In *Vedanta and The West*, Vol 14. New York: Harper, 1951.

——. *Prater Violet*. London: Methuen and Co., 1946.

Isherwood, Christopher and Swami Prabhavananda, trans. *Crest-Jewel of Discrimination*. California: Vedanta Press, 1947.

——. *The Bhagavad Gita*. Hollywood: The Marcel Rodd Co., 1951.

——. *Patanjali Yoga Aphorisms*. New York: Harper, 1953.

Isherwood, Christopher. *The World in the Evening*. London: Methuen, 1954.

——. *Down There on a Visit*. London: Methuen and Co., 1962.

——. *An Approach to Vedanta*. Hollywood, Calif.: Vedanta Press, 1963.

——. *A Single Man*. New York: Simon and Schuster, 1964.

——. *Ramakrishna and His Disciples*. London: Methuen, 1965.

——. *Exhumations*. London: Methuen and Co., 1966.

——. *Kathleen and Frank*. London: Methuen, 1971.

——. *Christopher and His Kind*. New York: Farrar, Straus Giroux, 1976.

——. *My Guru and His Disciple*. London, Eyre Methuen, 1980.

——. *Diaries Volume One 1939–1960*. Edited by Katherine Bucknell. London: Methuen, 1996.

——. *Lost Years: A Memoir 1945–1952*. Edited by Katherine Bucknell. London: Chatto and Windus, 2000.

Robert W. Funk, *Christopher Isherwood: A Reference Guide*. Boston: Hall, 1979.

Interviews 1999

Ashis Nandy, Ramakrishna Mission Institute of Culture, Kolkata 6 October.

Professor Das Gupta, Ramakrishna Mission Institute of Culture, Kolkata 8 and 25 October.

Swami Ashaktananda, Narendrapur, 16 October.

Bernard Cicerone, Ramakrishna Mission Institute of Culture, Kolkata, 20 October.

Sudhir Kakar, New Delhi, 6 November.

Swami Krishnananda, Sivananda ashram, Rishikesh, 9 November.

Majaji Pratiba, Parmath Niketan ashram, Rishikesh, 9 November.

Swami Chidanand Saraswati, Parmeth Niketan ashram, Rishikesh, 9 November.

Dr. Datta, Shantikunj ashram, Hardwar 10 November.

Swami Shantananda Puri Maharaj, Vasitha Guha ashram, Rishikesh,, 11 November.

Swami Vishveshwarananda, Omkarananda ashram, Rishikesh, 12 November.

Swami Chidananda, President of the Divine Life Society, Sivananda ashram, Rishikesh, 12 November.

Sham Das, Gokhul, 15 November.

Rajendra and Ghansyam Singh, sons of the Maharajah of Datia, Raj Mahal palace, Datia, 20 November.

Vikram Singh, grandson of Forster's Maharajah of Chhatarpur, Khajuraho, 22 November.

Bhowani Singh, former Maharajah of Chhatarpur, Chhatarpur, 24 November.

Major Puar, Bhoj Maharaj, son of Forster's Maharajah of Dewas, Dewas, 26 and 30 November.

Professor Anantharanam, The Theosophical Society, Adyar, 6 December.

Unpublished Phd

Brown, Tony. *The Personal and Social Ideals of E. M. Forster and Edward Carpenter*. University of Wales, Bangor, 1982.

Secondary Sources

Acharya, Shriram Sharma. *My Life: Its Legacy and Message*. Hardwar: Yugtirth Shantikunj, 1998.

Ackerley, J. R. *Hindoo Holiday: An Indian Journal*. London: Chatto and Windus, 1932.

Anandaprana, Pravrajika, ed. *A Historical Record: from Conversations with Swami Prabhavananda*. Hollywood: nd.

Ananthanarayanan, N. *From Man to Godman. The Inspiring Life-story of Swami Sivananda* Erode: Private publication, 1970.

Anantharanam, T. R. *Ancient Yoga and Modern Science*. Delhi: Mushiram Manohar-lal Publishers, 1996.

Archer, W. G. *The Loves of Krishna: Krishna in Indian Painting and Poetry*. New York: Grove Press, nd.

Aronson, Theo. *Prince Eddy and the Homosexual Underworld*. London: John Murray, 1994.

Atmaramananda, Swami and Dr. S. Sivaramkrishna, eds. *Art, Culture and Spirituality: A Prabbuddha Bharata Centenary Perspective 1896–1996*. Mayavati: Avaita Ashrama, 1997.

Atulananda, Swami. *Atman Alone Abides*. Madras (Chennai): Sri Ramakrishna Math, 1978.

Bakhtin, Mikhail. *Rabelais and His World: the Scope of Carnival*, translated by Helene Iswolksy. Bloomington: 1984.

Bayly, Susan. *Caste, Society and Politics in India from the Eighteenth Century to the Modern Age*. Cambridge: Cambridge University Press, 1999.

Barua, Dilip Kumar. *Edward Carpenter 1844–1929 An Apostle of Freedom*. Burdwan: Burdwan: University of Burdwan, 1991.

Beaumann, Nicola. *Morgan: A Biography of E M Forster*. London: Sceptre, 1993.

Bhattacharyya, Haridas, ed. *The Cultural Heritage of India Vol III The Philosophies*. Kolkata: 1937 *Vol 1V The Religions*. Kolkata: The Ramakrishna Mission Institute of Culture, 1956.

Blodgett, Harold. *Walt Whitman in England*. New York: Russell and Russell, 1934, Reissued 1973.

Brown, Norman. *Life Against Death: The Psychoanalytical Meaning of History*. Middleton, Connecticut: London: Routledge and Kegan, Paul, 1959.

Brown, Tony, ed. *Edward Carpenter and Late Victorian Radicalism*. London: Cass, 1990.

Brunton, Paul. *In Search of Secret India*. London: B. I. Publications PVT Ltd, 1983, New Delhi: 1998.

Bucke, Richard. *Cosmic Consciousness: A Study of the Evolution of the Human Mind*. Philadelphia: Innes and Sons, 1901.

Calder-Marshall, Arthur. *Havelock Ellis*. London: Rupert Hart-Davis, 1959.

Campbell, John. *The Masks of the Gods Vol II Oriental Mythology*. London: Oxford University Press, 1962.

Ceadel, Martin. *Pacifism in Britain 1914–1945*. Oxford: Oxford University Press, 1980.

Chetanananda, Swami. *God Lived with Them: Life Stories of Sixteen Monastic Disciples of Sri Ramakrishna*, Mayavati: Advaita Ashrama, 1997.

Chitre, Dilip. *Says Tuka: Selected Poetry of Tukaram*. New Delhi; Harmondsworth: Penguin, 1991.

Clarke, J. J. *Oriental Enlightenment: the Encounter Between Asian and Western Thought.* London: Routledge, 1997.

Coates, J. B. *Ten Modern Prophets (7th edn).* London: F. Muller, 1944.

Cohen, S. S. *Guru Ramana.* Tiruvannamalai: Sri Ramanasraman, 1998.

Collingham, E. M. *Imperial Bodies: The Physical Experience of the Raj c 1800–1957.* Cambridge: Cambridge University Press, 2001.

Colmer, John. *E. M. Forster: The Personal Voice.* London: Routledge and Kegan Paul, 1975.

Copley, Antony. *Religions in Conflict: Ideology, Cultural Contact and Conversion in Late Colonial India.* New Delhi: Oxford University Press, 1997.

Copley, Antony, ed. *Gurus and Their Followers.* New Delhi: Oxford University Press, 2000.

Crawford, Alan. *C. R. Ashbee: Architect, Designer and Romantic Socialist.* New Haven and London: Yale University Press, 1985.

Crews, Frederick. *E. M. Forster: The Perils of Humanism.* Princeton: N.J.: Princeton University Press, 1962.

Cronin, Richard. *Imagining India.* Basingstoke: Macmillan, 1989.

Daley, Harry. *This Small Cloud: A Personal Memoir.* London: Weidenfeld and Nicolson, 1986.

Das, G. D. and John Beer, eds. *Centenary Essays. E. M Forster: A Human Exploration.* New York: New York University Press, 1979.

Das, Veena, ed.*The Word and the World: Fantasy, Symbol and Record.* New Delhi; London: Sage, 1986.

Dalmia, Vasudha and H. von Stietencron, eds. *Representing Hinduism: the Construction of Religious Traditions and National Identity.* New Delhi: Sage, 1995.

Davies, Tony and Nigel Wood, eds. *A Passage to India.* Buckingham: Open University Press, 1994.

Delany, Paul. *The Neo-Pagans: Friendship and Love in the Rupert Brooke Circle.* London: Macmillan, 1987.

Deleury, G. A. *The Cult of Vithoba.* Poona: Deccan College Postgraduate and Research Institute, 1960.

Delavenay, Emile. *D. H. Lawrence and Edward Carpenter: A Study of Edwardian Transition.* London: Heinemann, 1971.

Dewey, Clive. *Anglo-Indian Attitudes: The Mind of the Indian Civil Service.* London: The Hambledon Press, 1993.

Eliade, Mircea, translated by Philip Mairet, *Myths, Dreams and Mysteries: The Encounter Between Contemporary Faiths and Archaic Realities.* London: Harvill Press, 1960.

Ellis, Havelock. *The New Spirit.* London: George Bell and Sons, 1890.

———. *Sexual Inversion Vol II Studies in the Psychology of Sex.* Philadelphia: F. A. Davis and Co., 1922.

———. *My Life.* Kingswood: Heinemann, 1940.

Entwistle, A. W. *Braj: Centre of Krishna Pilgrimage.* Groningen: Forsten, 1987.

Feuerstein, G. *Holy Madness: The Shock Tactics and Radical Teachings of Crazy-Wise Adepts: Holy Fools and Rascal Gurus.* New York: 1991.

Finney, Brian. *Christopher Isherwood: A Critical Biography.* London: Faber, 1979.

First, Ruth and Ann Scott. *Olive Schreiner.* London: Deutsch, 1980.

Foucault, Michel. *The History of Sexuality: An Introduction.* London: Allen Lane, 1979.

Fourier, Charles. *Le Nouveau Monde Amoureux.* (1840) Reissued Geneva: Slatkine Reprints, 1979.

French, Harold. *The Swan's Wide Waters: Ramakrishna and Western Culture.* Port Washington; London: Kennikat Press, 1974.

Fryer, Jonathan. *Isherwood: A Biography of Christopher Isherwood.* London: New English Library, 1977.

Furbank, P. N. *E. M. Forster: A Life.* Oxford: Oxford University Press, 1977.

Gambhirananda Swami. *History of Ramakrishna Math and Ramakrishna Mission.* Mayavati: Avaita Ashrama, 1957.

Ganguly, Adwaita. *P India: Mystic, Complex and Real.* New Delhi: Motilal Banarsidass Publishers Private Limited, 1990.

Godman, David, ed. *Be As You Are: The Teachings of Sri Ramana Maharshi.* Calcutta: Penguin, 1992.

Gold, Ann Grodzins. *Fruitful Journeys: The Ways of Rajasthani Pilgrims.* Delhi: Oxford University Press, 1989.

Greig, Noel, ed. *Edward Carpenter: Selected Writings Vol 1.* London: G.M.P. Publishers Limited, 1984.

Grosskurth, Phyliss. *John Addington Symonds; A Biography.* London: Longmans, 1965.

———. *Havelock Ellis: A Biography.* London: Allen Lane, 1980.

———, ed. *The Memoirs of John Addington Symonds.* London: Hutchinson, 1984.

Haberman, David L. *Journey Through the Twelve Forests.* New York: Oxford University Press, 1994.

Harvey, Andrew. *The Return of the Mother.* Berkeley: Frog Limited, 1995.

———. *The Direct Path: Creating a Journey to the Divine Using the World's Mystical Traditions.* London: Rider, 2000.

Hawley, John Stratton. *At Play with Krishna: Pilgrimage Dramas from Brindavan.* Yale: Princeton University Press, 1972.

Hayne, Donald. *Batter My Heart.* London: Hutchinson, 1963.

Heard, Gerald. *Social Substance of Religion.* London: Allen and Unwin, 1931.

———. *Pain, Sex and Time.* New York; London: Harper and brothers, 1939.

———. *Man, the Master.* London: Faber and Faber, 1942.

———. *Training for the Life of the Spirit.* London: Cassell, 1944.

———. *Pamphlet Two.* London: Cassell, 1944.

Hibbert, Gerald K., ed. *The New Pacifism.* London: Allenson and Co., 1936.

Hynes, Samuel. *The Edwardian Turn of Mind.* Princeton: Princeton University Press, 1968.

———. *The Auden Generation: Literature and Politics in the 1930's.* London: Bodley Head, 1976.

Jackson, Carl T. *Vedanta for the West: The Ramakrishna Movement in the United States.* Bloomington and Indianapolis: Indiana University Press, 1994.

Jaffrey, Zia. *The Invisibles: A Tale of the Eunuchs of India.* London: Weidenfeld and Nicolson, 1997.

Jeffrey-Poulter, Stephen. *Peers, Queers and Commons.* London: Routledge, 1991.

Jnanendranatha Mitra, Baba. *Sri Krishna: A Critical Biography Based on Original Sources.* Bankipore: 1900.

Joshi, N. P. *Iconography of Balarama.* New Delhi: Abhinav Publications, 1979.

Kakar, Sudhir. *The Indian Psyche.* Oxford: Oxford University Press, 1996.

Kaplan, Justin. *Walt Whitman: A Life.* New York: Simon and Schuster, 1980.

Kaufmann, Walter. *Nietzche: Philosopher, Psychologist, Anti-Christ.* New York: Meridian Books, 1956.

Knowles, Dom David. *What is Mysticism? Prayer and Practice.* London: Sheed and Ward, 1966.

Koestler, Arthur. *The Lotus and the Robot.* London: Hutchinson, 1960.

Kripal, Jeffrey. *Kali's Child: The Mystical and the Erotic in the Teachings of Ramakrishna.* Chicago: The University of Chicago Press, 1995.

———. 2nd edition: 1998.

Krishna, Gopi. *Kundalini: The Secret of Yoga.* Indian edn: U.B.S. Publishers Distributors Ltd., 1992.

Krishnananda, Swami. *An Introduction to the Study of Yoga.* Delhi: The Divine Life Society, 1983.

———. *Self-realisation: Its Meaning and Method.* Tehri-Garwhal: The Divine Life Society, 1987.

Laplanche J. and J.-B. Pontalis. *The Language of Psychoanalysis.* London: Hogarth, 1973.

Ludowyk, E. F. C. *The Story of Ceylon.* London: Faber and Faber, 1962.

Mahood, Molly. *The Colonial Encounter: A Reading of Six Novels.* London: Rex Collings, 1977.

Mendelson, Edward. *Early Auden.* London: Faber, 1981.

Mason, Michael. *The Making of Victorian Sexuality.* Oxford: Oxford University Press, 1994.

Martland, Arthur. *E. M. Forster: Passion and Prose.* Swaffham: GMP, 1999.

Masson, Jeffrey. *The Oceanic Feeling: The Origins of Religious Sentiment in Ancient India.* Dordrecht; London: D. Reidel, 1980.

———. *My Father's Guru.* London: Harper Collins, 1993.

Morgan, Lewis H. *Ancient Society or Researches in the Line of Human Progress from Savagery through Barbarism to Civilisation* (1877). Reissued New York: Gordon Press, 1976.

Naipaul, V. S. *Half A Life.* London: Picador, 2001.

Nugel, Bernfried, ed. *Now More than Ever: Proceedings of the Aldous Huxley Centenary Symposium, Munster 1994.* Frankfurt: Peter Lang, 1994.

Page, Norman. *E. M. Forster's Posthumous Fiction.* Victoria B.C.: University of Victoria, 1977.

Paine, Jeffrey. *Father India: How Encounters with Ancient Culture Transformed the Modern West.* New York: Harper Collins, 1998.

Pawer, Bhojsinharao Tukojirao. *Aspects of a Passage to the Hill of Devi.* Kolhapur: Private publication, 1993.

Pemble, John. *The Mediterranean Passion: Victorians and Edwardians in the South.* Oxford: Oxford University Press, 1987.

Prabhavananda, Swami. *Vedic Religion and Philosophy.* Mylapore: Sri Ramakrishna Math, 1937.

Prabhavananda, Swami and Christopher Isherwood, trans. *Viveka-Chudamani (Crest Jewel of Discrimination).* California: Vedanta Press, 1947.

Prabhavananda, Swami. *The Eternal Companion: Life and Teachings of Swami Brahmananda.* Hollywood: Vedanta Press, nd.

———. *Vyasa's Srimad Bhagavatam (The Wisdom of God).* Trans. Mylapore: Sri Ramakrishna Math, 1947.

Prabhavananda, Swami and Frederick Manchester, trans. *The Upanishads.* New York: New American Library, 1957.

Prabhavananda, Swami. *The Spiritual Heritage of India.* London: G. Allen and Unwin, 1962.

———. *The Sermon on the Mount According to Vedantism.* London/Madras: Allen and Unwin, 1964.

Prabhavananda, Swami and Christopher Isherwood, trans. *How to Know God; The Yoga Aphorisms of Patanjali.* Hollywood: 1966; Mylapore: Sri Ramakrishna Math nd.

Prabhavananda, Swami. *Religion in Practice.* London: George Allen and Unwin, 1968.

———. *Yoga and Mysticism.* Hollywood: Vedanta Press, 1969.

Purushottamananda, Shri Swamiji. *Autobiography or The Story of the Divine Compassion.* Tehri Garwhal: Private publication, 1956.

Ranade, R. D. *Mysticism in India: the Poet-Saints of Maharashtra.* Albany: State University of New York Press, 1983.

Rawlinson, A. *The Book of Enlightened Masters: Western Teachers in Eastern Traditions.* Chicago: Open Court, 1997.

Redington, James D. *Vallabhacarya on the Love Games of Krsna.* Delhi: Motilal Banarsidass, 1983.

Reynolds, David S. *Walt Whitman's America: A Cultural Biography.* New York: Knopf, 1995.

Rowbotham, Sheila and Jeffrey Weeks. *Socialism and the New Life: The Personal and Sexual Politics of Edward Carpenter and Havelock Ellis.* London: Pluto Press, 1977.

Robinson, Paul. *The Modernisation of Sex.* London: Elek, 1976.

Rutnam, J. T. *Ponnambulam Arunachalam 1853–1924 Scholar and Statesman: A Brief Account of His Life and Career.* Colombo: Ponnambalam Arunachalam Centenary Committee, 1953.

Sahni, Chaman L. *Forster's A Passage to India: The Religious Dimension.* New Delhi: Arnold-Heinemann, 1981.

Salt, Henry. *Seventy Years Among the Savages*. London: George Allen and Unwin, 1921.

———. *Company I Have Kept*. London: George Allen and Unwin, 1930.

Sastri, K. A. Nilakanta. *History of South India*. London: Oxford University Press, 1955.

Seabrook, Jeremy. *Love in a Different Climate: Men Who Have Sex with Men in India*. New York: Verso, 1999.

Seth, Vikram. *A Suitable Boy*. London: Phoenix House, 1993.

Shah, Tahir. *Sorcerer's Apprentice*. London: Weidenfeld and Nicholson, 1998.

Singer, Milton, ed. *Myths, Rites and Attitudes*. Chicago: University of Chicago Press, 1966.

Sivananda, Swami. *Bliss Divine: A Book of Spiritual Essays on the Lofty Purpose of Human Life and the Means of Its Achievement* (4th edn). Delhi: The Divine Life Society, 1992.

Stallybrass, Peter and Allen White. *The Politics and Poetics of Transgression: A Critique of Bakhtin*. Ithaca, New York: Cornell University Press, 1986.

Storr, Anthony. *Feet of Clay: A Study of Gurus*. London: Harper Collins, 1996.

Suleri, Sarah. *The Rhetoric of English India: Forster's Imperial Erotic*. Chicago; London: University of Chicago Press, 1992.

Thompson, E. P. *William Morris: Romantic to Revolutionary*. London: Merlin Press, 1955.

Thoreau, H. D. *Walden*. First published 1854 New York: Random House, 1937.

Tsuzuki, Chushichi. *Edward Carpenter 1944–1929 Prophet of Human Fellowship*. Cambridge: Cambridge University Press, 1980.

Trudgill, Eric. *Madonnas and Magdalens*. London: Heinemann, 1976.

Tulpule, Shankar Gopal. *A History of Indian Literature: Classical Marathi Literature*. Wiesbaden: Harrassowitz, 1979.

Varenne, John. *Yoga and the Hindu Tradition*. Trans. Derek Coltman. Delhi: Motital Banarsidass, 1989.

Weeks, Jeffrey. *Coming Out: Homosexual Politics in Britain from the Nineteenth Century to the Present*. London: Quartet Books, 1977.

———. *Sex, Politics and Society: The Regulations of Sexuality Since 1800*. London: Longmans, 1981.

Welbon, Guy R. and Glenn E. Yosum. *Religious Festivals in South India and Sri Lanka*. New Delhi: Manohar, 1982.

Whitman, Walt. *Complete Poetry and Collected Prose*. New York: Literary Classics of the United States, 1982.

Wilson, A. Jeyaratnam. *Sri Lankan Tamil Nationalism: The Origins and Development in the 19th and 20th Centuries*. London: Hurst and Company, 2000.

Winsten, Stephen. *Salt and His Circle*. London: Hutchinson, 1951.

Yale, John. *A Yankee Among the Swamis*. London: Allen and Unwin, 1961.

Yogananda, Paramahansa. *Autobiography of a Yogi*. New York: Philosophical Library, 1946; Mumbai: Jaico Publishing House, 1998.

Articles

Amiya, Sister. "Vedanta in Southern California." *Vedanta and the West*. Vol 14, 1951.

Brown, Tony. "Figuring in History: The Reputation of Edward Carpenter. Annotated Secondary Bibliography." *English Literature in Transition*. Vol 32 No 1, 1989.

———. "Annotated Bibliography 11." *English Literature in Transition*. Vol 32 No 2, 1989.

Chase, Richard. "The Huxley-Heard Paradise." *Partisan Review*. Vol 10, March/April 1943.

Dewan, Janet. "The Barber, the Narrator and The Private Life of an Eastern King." *Indo-British Review*. Vol XXIII No 2.

Dhondy, Faroukh. "Talks to V S Naipaul." *Literary Review*. August 2001.

Gerschenowitz, Harry. "Two Lamarkians: Walt Whitman and Edward Carpenter." *Quarterly Review*. Summer 1984, Vol 2 (1).

Haynes, E. P. S. "The Taboo of the British Museum Library." *English Review*. December 1913.

Maguire, J. Robert, "Oscar Wilde and the Dreyfus Affair." *Victorian Studies*. Vol 41 No 1, Autumn 1997.

Neve, Michael. "Sexual Politics." *London Review of Books*. February 1981.

Pierson, Stanley. "Edward Carpenter: Prophet of a Socialist Millennium." *Victorian Studies*. 13, 1969–1970.

Phillips, Adam. "Lost World." *London Review of Books*. 16 November 2000.

Rahman, Tariq. "Edward Carpenter's *From Adam's Peak to Elephanta* as a Source for E M Forster's *A Passage to India*." *Forum of Modern Language Studies*. Vol XXII No 1, January 1986.

———. "Edward Carpenter and E M Forster." *Durham University Journal*. Vol XLVIII No 1, December 1986.

———. "The Alienated Prophet: The Relationship Between Edward Carpenter's Psyche and the Development of the Metaphysic." *Forum for Modern Language Studies*. Vol XXIII No 3, July 1987.

———. "The Literary Treatment of Indian Themes in the Works of Edward Carpenter." *Durham University Journal*. Vol 80, December 1987.

Rowbotham, Sheila. "In Search of Carpenter." *History Workshop*. No 3, Spring 1977.

Seabrook, Jeremy. "It's What You Do in Out South: Sexual Minorities in the Majority World." *New Internationalist*. 328, October 2000.

Yeo, Stephen. "A New Life: The Religion of Socialism in Britain 1883–1890." *History Workshop*. 4 Autumn 1977.

Index

~

About the Author

Antony Copley is an Honorary Reader, University of Kent. His teaching covered both Modern European and Afro-Asian history. He was a Visiting Professor at both the Sri Venkateswara University, Tirupati, and the University of Paris VIII. His publications include biographies of Rajagopalachari and Gandhi, studies of sexual morality in France, and religious conflict in nineteenth-century India. He has edited numerous editions on Indian studies and reviewed extensively. His current interests are in art, music, and spirituality in the twenty-first century.